D0742230

GAYLORD   PRINTED IN U.S.A.

PRODUCT INNOVATION, INTERACTIVE LEARNING AND ECONOMIC PERFORMANCE

RESEARCH ON TECHNOLOGICAL INNOVATION AND MANAGEMENT POLICY

RESEARCH ON TECHNOLOGICAL INNOVATION
AND MANAGEMENT POLICY   VOLUME 8

PRODUCT INNOVATION, INTERACTIVE LEARNING AND ECONOMIC PERFORMANCE

EDITED BY

JESPER LINDGAARD CHRISTENSEN

Department of Business Studies, Aalborg University, Denmark

and

BENGT-ÅKE LUNDVALL

*Department of Business Studies, Aalborg University, Denmark
and School of Economics and Management, Tsinghua
University, Beijing, China*

2004

ELSEVIER
JAI

Amsterdam – Boston – Heidelberg – London – New York – Oxford
Paris – San Diego – San Francisco – Singapore – Sydney – Tokyo

ELSEVIER B.V.
Radarweg 29
P.O. Box 211
1000 AE Amsterdam
The Netherlands

ELSEVIER Inc.
525 B Street, Suite 1900
San Diego
CA 92101-4495
USA

ELSEVIER Ltd
The Boulevard, Langford
Lane, Kidlington
Oxford OX5 1GB
UK

ELSEVIER Ltd
84 Theobalds Road
London
WC1X 8RR
UK

First edition 2004

British Library Cataloguing in Publication Data
A catalogue record is available from the British Library.

ISBN: 0-7623-1156-8
ISSN: 0737-1071 Series

⊗ The paper used in this publication meets the requirements of ANSI/NISO Z39.48-1992 (Permanence of Paper). Printed in The Netherlands.

Working together to grow libraries in developing countries

www.elsevier.com | www.bookaid.org | www.sabre.org

ELSEVIER   BOOK AID International   Sabre Foundation

CONTENTS

LIST OF CONTRIBUTORS

Jesper Lindgaard Christensen   Department of Business Studies, Aalborg University, Aalborg, Denmark

Ina Drejer   Department of Business Studies, Aalborg University, Aalborg, Denmark

Birte Holst Jørgensen   Systems Analysis Department, Risø National Laboratory, Roskilde

Alice Lam   School of Business and Management, Brunel University, West London, UK

Edward Lorenz   CNRS - University of Nice - Sophia Antipolis, Valbonne, France

Reinhard Lund   Department of Business Studies, Aalborg University, Aalborg, Denmark

Bengt-Åke Lundvall   Department of Business Studies, Aalborg University, Aalborg, Denmark and School of Economics and Management, Tsinghua University, Beijing, China

Jonathan Michie   Birmingham Business School, University of Birmingham, Birmingham, UK

Toke Reichstein   Tanaka Business School, Imperial College, London, UK

Mark Tomlinson   Department of Business Studies, Aalborg University, Aalborg, Denmark

Anker Lund Vinding   Department of Business Studies, Aalborg University, Aalborg, Denmark

Frank Wilkinson   University of Cambridge, Centre for Business Research, Cambridge, UK

INTRODUCTION: PRODUCT INNOVATION – ON WHY AND HOW IT MATTERS FOR FIRMS AND THE ECONOMY

Bengt-Åke Lundvall and Jesper Lindgaard Christensen

1. INTRODUCTION

The aim of this book is to contribute to the understanding of product innovation – how it takes place and how it affects the economy. Our analysis of product innovation links it to interactive learning and to the performance of firms. On the basis of unique data sets and detailed case studies we study the interconnections between these three elements from different angles. We believe that the book will prove helpful for managers, employees and policy makers as well as for all those in academia who wants to understand the role of product innovation in the economy.

Product innovation is a complex and multidimensional phenomenon and in order to capture this complexity we combine different theoretical perspectives, different levels of aggregation, and different methodological approaches. We apply economic, institutional, organizational and sociological perspectives and we combine quantitative studies with qualitative case studies. At the same time there is coherence across the different parts of the book reflecting a focus on product innovation, organizational change and industrial dynamics. The team that has produced the book has a long history of interdisciplinary collaboration. This is obviously the case for the Aalborg scholars but it is also true for the three

Product Innovation, Interactive Learning and Economic Performance
Research on Technological Innovation and Management Policy, Volume 8, 1–18
Copyright © 2004 by Elsevier Ltd.
All rights of reproduction in any form reserved
ISSN: 0737-1071/doi:10.1016/S0737-1071(04)08001-1

outstanding external scholars, Lam, Lorenz and Tomlinson, who have contributed to the book. The Aalborg researchers have been involved in long-term collaboration with them in several international research projects.

Important parts of the book are based on empirical material gathered in connection with the specific research project PIE – product innovation and economic performance in Denmark.[1] The project organized the gathering of different types of data sets on technical and organizational change in Danish firms. A major survey on innovation, organization and competence building that covered activities in 2007 responding firms for the period 1998–2000 was one source and to these data were linked register data on economic variables as well as the comprehensive labour market data base IDA. These data sets have been used to analyse what factors that promote product innovation and to analyse how innovation relates to economic performance (see Chapters 7, 11 and 14).

A different kind of data set was gathered through detailed consecutive interviews in firms and covering different specific product innovation projects. In each firm there were at least three consecutive interviews and in each firm several individuals involved in the product development process were interviewed. The major aim of this part of the project was to gain concrete and detailed insights regarding the role of knowledge and learning in the context of product innovation (see Chapters 4, 6 and 10).

2. PRODUCT INNOVATION AND THE PERFORMANCE OF THE FIRM AND THE WHOLE ECONOMY

Both at the level of the firm and at the level of the economy as a whole, product innovation is of major importance. For the economy as a whole, the introduction of new products is fundamental for economic growth. Process innovation without product innovation would sooner or later result in economic stagnation and in what has been called "technological unemployment." To avoid stagnation of demand, increasing income levels need to be sustained by the offering of new products and services.

Surveys addressed to firms show that, in high-income countries, the introduction of new products – not only modified ones – are events that take place frequently in most parts of the economy. For instance, over a period of 2–3 years, normally about half of all Danish private firms report at least one product innovation. The reason why firms introduce new products is that they want to attract demand and maintain their position in competition with other firms. In some sectors, such as information technology, frequent introduction of new products is absolutely necessary for the firm's survival while in other sectors, such as food industry, the rate of change in products may be slower. But also in sectors traditionally seen as low-tech due to their low level of R&D-intensity product innovation may be crucial to attract customers from competitors.

3. BUT PRODUCT INNOVATION IS ABSENT IN STANDARD ECONOMICS TEXT-BOOKS

Product innovations are thus important both for the survival of the single firm and for sustained economic growth. In spite of that, remarkably little is said about product innovation in standard textbooks in economics. Theoretical models of production, the so-called production functions, take into account technical progress when it results in more efficient processes of production but tend to neglect product innovations. One reason for this neglect is methodological and has to do with the predominance of quantitative models in economics (Lundvall, 1987).

There is a general ambition among economists to transform all aspects of reality into quantitative variables that can be manipulated within continuous mathematical models. This is one reason why, in general, innovation studies are not well developed in standard economics. There is little doubt that technological change, fundamentally, is a *qualitative phenomenon*. Discovery, invention, and innovation can even *be defined as* activities giving rise to new qualities, which did not exist before the act of discovering, inventing, or innovating.

In the real world, growing efficiency in production is, of course, a phenomenon inseparable from changes in product quality and the introduction of new products. New products stimulate aggregate demand and growth and it is the growth of real incomes, induced by growing productivity that stimulates the demand for new products (Pasinetti, 1981). This is reflected in the close statistical correlation between economic growth and structural change. It is impossible to understand the dynamics of industrial development, without taking into account that new products and new product qualities are introduced.

4. THE MANAGEMENT LITERATURE RECOGNIZES THE IMPORTANCE OF PRODUCT INNOVATION

The management literature gives much more attention to product innovation. It addresses the challenges of product innovation for management. It instructs managers to keep track of the process, to establish gateway meetings, to co-ordinate the efforts of different departments within the firm. As we will show, "to manage product innovation" is a very demanding task and one of the most efficient ways to do so is to establish a learning organization characterized by continuous horizontal communication. This reflects that product innovation processes mobilize knowledge and competence among many individuals belonging to different spheres of activity and the process is very much one of interaction between people and specifically about "interactive learning."

Related to the interaction between learning individuals is the interaction between organizations that results in inter-organizational learning. Long term relationships with other firms, knowledge institutions and consumers stimulate and shape product innovation activities in different ways. Firms that are customers signal new needs that may be addressed by new products. Firms that supply services, materials and equipments signal new technological opportunities that may be integrated in the new product. But it is not only by influencing the agenda for product innovation that external organizations play a role. During the development process there is often an on-going process of inter-organizational communication and co-operation and how well it works will be reflected in the market success of the new product.

5. INTERACTIVE LEARNING, MARKETS AND HIERARCHIES

Standard economics focuses too much on how markets separate one organization from another and has difficulties in explaining the frequency of long-term collaboration in dynamic sectors characterised by frequent product innovations. Industrial networks appear as anomalies as compared to the individual firm selling its services on an anonymous market. Transaction cost theory gives one explanation on why vertically separated units are brought together in hierarchies, but it has difficulties to explain the intermediate forms where firms remain legally independent but still get committed in long-term relationships. Here we will offer a different explanation of why network relationships and relational contracting are so frequent. We will argue that they are established *because they are the most effective institutional form when it comes to reaping benefits emanating from interactive learning*.

Such an explanation needs to take into account that interactive learning is deeply embedded in social life. The outcome of learning processes will depend on social relationships such as trust, authority and recognition. Therefore, the broader societal and socio-economic context needs to be taken into account when analysing the formation of network relationships. In this context the restrictive view of standard economics where everything is reduced to individual instrumental or strategic rationality is insufficient. To understand the dynamics of product innovation and the formation of network relationships it is necessary to broaden the perspective and to let insights from other disciplines than economics be integrated in the analysis.

6. PRODUCT INNOVATION AS A PROCESS OF COMMUNICATION IN AN ENVIRONMENT OF UNCERTAINTY

There are two characteristics of product innovation that makes it a process where social and economic elements are intertwined in a complex way. One is the fundamental uncertainty it involves. Uncertainty in connection with innovation is *fundamental* in the extreme sense that the very aim of the process is to come up with something unknown. While normally we define uncertainty as a situation where *the unknown may happen* innovation is a process where *we know that the unknown will happen*. We might define this as *radical fundamental uncertainty*. This is why it is a process where beliefs, intuition and creativity are as important, or more important, than calculation and optimisation.[2]

The second important characteristic is that it is a process where the outcome is highly dependent upon *interaction and communication* between people. Individual actors may try to realise their own intentions but they have to do so in a context where the resources they need to mobilize are shared with others and actually change in the very process of interaction. This is one reason why "methodological individualism" cannot be applied to processes where knowledge and learning are central (Arrow, 1994).

This combination of uncertainty and interaction makes product innovation a social phenomenon in two respects. First, social relationships are fundamental for commercial outcomes; the social institutions shape economic development. Second, the innovation process affects social relationships within firms and between individuals belonging to different organizations. Some of the learning that takes place is "relational learning" and this kind of learning affects how people and organizations relate to each other.

According to George Herbert Mead, the extension of markets has a civilising effect since the market is an institution where sellers have to take buyers seriously and regard them as "significant others." It is interesting to note that product innovation, much more than standard market operations, may be seen as a process where close interaction and understanding is required. The innovating producer needs to get an idea of user needs not served by existing products. This implies that in an economy where product innovation is a frequent phenomenon we would expect more closely knit social networks than in a static market economy where the focus is upon the exchange of commodities with given use value characteristics.

This implies that product innovation will flourish in contexts where there is a multitude of "strong and weak ties" among users and producers. Trust, common language, common routines are necessary prerequisites for a complex interaction with uncertain outcome. This is why short "social" or "cultural" distance may be a prerequisite for innovation. Sometimes there is also a need for short geographical distance making it possible for the interacting parties to meet face to face. These are some of the arguments behind the proposition that it is meaningful to analyse regional and national systems of innovation.

7. THE INNOVATION PRONE ECONOMY IS A MIXED ECONOMY

It follows that a market economy where product innovation is an important integrated process must be a "mixed market economy" rather than a "pure market economy." Markets are mixed – combining elements of markets with elements of trust, power and communication channels – and hierarchies are also mixed – combining elements of authority with elements of loyalty and commitment.

How people relate to each other and what categories of people that most easily relate to each other are crucial elements in what constitute the specificities of a society. In countries where the elite is trained in separate schools – France and England may be used as examples – we would expect a different pattern of communication and therefore a different mode of innovation than the one that we would find in Nordic countries with highly egalitarian education systems. If there is a strong tradition among experts to stick to what you know best and be sceptical to what other professions can offer (again France might be a case) that would give a different pattern of communication and a different mode of innovation than in a society where there are more fluid borders between professions.

It is evident from the above that human resources play a pivotal role in product innovation. Product innovation is based upon competences and it involves processes of interactive learning within as well as across organizational borders. Hitherto the literature on technological progress and innovation systems has tended to give too little attention to this aspect and given much more attention to research and development. However, in recent years the literature has caught up on this aspect. Innovation systems are increasingly seen as building upon the competencies embedded in people and organizations, and innovation studies increasingly give some attention to the education system and the labour market (Lundvall & Christensen, 2003). This book has the aim to move the analysis further ahead in this respect.

8. SOCIAL CAPITAL AND SMALL COUNTRIES

The sharing of a common language and the willingness to co-operate with parties with different interests are more or less easy to establish in different countries reflecting not only the education system but also how societies are stratified. To overcome uncertainty, to build trust and to establish a common language takes time and it may be seen in the light of accumulation and destruction of "social capital."

Small countries have developed dense social networks both at the national level and at the level of the single firm making adaptation more rapid and less costly. Nation wide networks, including representatives of workers and employers as well as policy makers, permit swift institutional reforms when external circumstances make it necessary. Combined with a reasonably high, rather evenly and widely diffused level of education these characteristics make it possible to be rapid in establishing new competences as these are required (Maskell et al., 1998). These "small country-advantages" may give an explanation of why many small countries, in spite of increasing returns to scale in knowledge production and use, are listed among the most competitive in the world in an era where knowledge is a key production factor.

The Danish economy may be of special interest as an illustration of this small country advantage since its formal knowledge base appears to be rather weak. Denmark is among the richest countries in the world. But Danish firms, with the exception of a few pharmaceutical firms, pursue relatively little R&D. Denmark is extreme among the small countries in actually increasing its specialisation in low technology products in the nineties. At the university level Denmark invests less money per student level than other OECD-countries when the income level is taken into account. On the other hand, Denmark is also extreme in the sense of social capital based on egalitarianism and small power distance. It is the country in the world with the most equal income distribution and with the highest rates of unionisation (Lundvall, 2002). These properties are important for understanding the context of the product innovations and interactive learning studied in most of this volume.

9. THE STRUCTURE OF THE BOOK

Our analysis of product innovation links it to interactive learning and economic performance. We tackle the interconnections between these elements from different angles. The first part is about how knowledge and learning relate to innovation – it introduces conceptual issues and alternative theoretical perspectives and models. The second part is about interactive learning in connection with product innovation. The third part considers how human resource management and industrial relations affect product innovation and learning. The fourth part explains how the organizational and inter-organizational context affects and shapes innovation processes. We pursue this aim by focusing upon the interaction between innovating firms and knowledge institutions. Finally, whereas we in several chapters discuss different kinds of performance in connection with product innovation we end up by relating product innovation to economic performance in a strict economic sense.

9.1. Perspectives on Learning

Chapter 2 by Lundvall gives an overview of how knowledge is treated in economic theory and makes an attempt to develop new concepts that makes the analysis of knowledge and learning more adequate and useful. It ends up by sketching the contours of a new type of economy – the learning economy – where the capacity to learn is crucial for the success of individual actors, organizations and regions. One central element in this chapter is the analysis of how learning and innovation are interrelated and it is argued that it is not possible to understand innovation processes without going deeper into the understanding of learning and knowledge.

In chapter 3 Alice Lam pursues this line of thought in an institutional context. She demonstrates that there are important connections between the formation of competences at the level of the individual, the structure of the labour market and the organizational framework within which learning and innovation takes place. A training system that fosters en elite isolated from workers will innovate differently than one where education is more broad-based. A labour market organized around professions will promote different kinds of learning than one where internal labour market in the firm is dominating. Lam uses national models (the U.S., U.K., Japan and Denmark) to illustrate her analysis. The chapter is an important contribution to a broader understanding of national innovation systems that gives adequate weight to the competence building as connected to education, labour markets and learning inside firms.

Chapter 4 by Reinhard Lund is one of three chapters in the book that draw upon a series of longitudinal case studies of specific product innovations in small and medium-sized Danish firms. In this chapter the focus is upon the use of knowledge in connection with the product innovation and upon the attempts to establish "knowledge management" to promote learning in connection with the innovations. Here the connection between innovation and learning as referred to in Chapter 2 are spelled out in a very concrete way. A point of departure is the analytical framework developed by Hargadon and Fanelli (2002) arguing that also seen from a management point it is extremely useful to keep track both of innovation and learning and to understand the linkages between the two. One interesting result in this chapter is that while only one of the five firms included in the study had an explicit knowledge management strategy all firms had elements of such a strategy that remained implicit. Normally people in the firms were not prepared to express themselves in terms of "knowledge" and "learning" but when probing it became clear that they have developed practices that aim at promoting the use of knowledge and learning.

9.2. Product Innovation and Interactive Learning

Chapter 5 by Lundvall and Vinding on product innovation and economic theory introduces the next section about product innovation and interactive learning. The chapter demonstrates that while product innovation is of major importance both for economic growth and for the competitiveness of firms it has been largely neglected in standard economic theory. It goes on to show that the real-world frequency and scale of product innovation cannot be explained neither by standard economics nor by transaction economics. It is shown that combining product innovation and interactive learning in the analysis of industrial organization leads to radically different conclusions than what would follow from an analysis based upon transaction economics. An important suggestion with major theoretical and practical implications is that "interactive learning" is a major element in promoting economic growth since it is one of the most important mechanisms that transform local knowledge into more generally accessible knowledge.

Chapter 6 is by Reinhard Lund and here the case studies referred to in Chapter 3 are used to identify and analyse *learning situations* in connection with the specific product innovation processes followed in the firms. The chapter illustrates at a concrete and detailed level the importance of interactive learning alluded to in Chapter 5 both within and across the organizational boarders of the firms. The interactive learning across divisions and with external parties was seen as becoming more important in all the firms. These changes were driven by the general understanding that earlier innovation strategies had been too dominated by technological concerns and engineering motivations and too little by market concerns and the over all business goals. The chapter reveals important trade-offs in connection with learning in the context of product innovation. One of the most important may be seen in the light of the speed-up that characterises the learning economy. The increased focus by top management on "speed to market" is reflected in developers feeling more restrained in their creativity and there is also a tendency that developers, production technicians and market people experience that there are too many unsolved problems with the first generation of the product. Interviews also imply that there is too little time for reflection and "secondary loop" learning.

Chapter 7 by Anker Lund Vinding analyses interactive learning within and across organizations on the basis of survey and register data using econometric techniques. The theoretical focus is on the absorptive capacity of firms giving equal weight to the internal competence (know-how and know-why) and the network relationships (know-who and seen as "social capital"). The analysis gives highly significant results that support what has been concluded in earlier chapters on the strong interconnection of innovation and learning – on the one hand the firms that have introduced "learning organizations" with dense internal interaction are much more innovation prone than the rest. On the other hand firms that establish "complete networks" -closer relationships vertically with users and suppliers as well as to knowledge institutions are much more likely to innovate than the average firm. An interesting result is that there is no positive correlation between the length of work experience of managers and innovation. This may be seen as an indication of the learning economy where competences tend to become obsolete at a high rate.

9.3. Industrial Relations, HRM and the Organization of Product Innovation

Chapter 8 by Edward Lorenz, Jonathan Michie and Frank Wilkinson compares two different innovation systems – the U.K. and France. The focus is on how far the use of high performance work practices can explain product innovation in the two countries. It is a pioneering study since earlier international comparative work, with few exceptions, have used other performance indicators than innovation. The method is first to pursue a factor analysis trying to locate clusters of firms that combine similar sets of practices and then to use these clusters as explanatory variables in relation to product innovation. A general result, in accordance with what was found in Chapter 7, is that the use of HRM-principles and instruments increases the innovative potential in the firms. It is also shown that there are complementarities between instruments that might make it difficult to get them implemented in an incremental fashion. An interesting result is that there are quite substantial and somewhat counter-intuitive differences that reflect institutional differences in the labour market between the patterns in respectively the U.K. and France. Firms in France have certain obligatory forms of representation of employees and that results in that the connection between such representation and innovation appears as not being significant for France but as being significant for the U.K.

Chapter 9 by Mark Tomlinson gives a useful complementary view of competence building in the U.K. labour market. He uses the Employment in Britain data set which has gathered information from almost 4000 employees and self-employed.

The focus is upon how far the employee felt strongly that he or she was learning new things in connection with the job. This variable is related to age, race and gender. It is also related to work practices that are connected to the Japanese model of learning organizations and to the inter- and intra-firm mobility between jobs. Again it is found that employees working in firms using HRM-practises learn more than the average. Also for the individual the performance of learning organizations is to prefer. One very interesting result that calls for international comparisons is the observation that while job shifts within firms promote individual learning this is not true for job shifts between firms. Finally, the observation that women learn less than men after all other factors such as sector and job position has been taken into account points to a kind of dynamic economic discrimination of women that is more serious than the one reflected in not getting equal pay. Again it would be most interesting to see if this reflects a nation specific pattern – the author mentions that he did not find any such pattern when studying countries in Eastern Europe.

Chapter 10 by Reinhard Lund is focused on innovation management and takes its empirical observations from eight specific product innovations in four medium-sized firms. It is interesting to note that in all the studied firms there seems to have developed a stronger consciousness among management about the importance of certain types of interaction in connection with innovation. This has been combined with a more systematic use of central management techniques such as regular stage-gate meetings and involvement of users as well as shop floor workers early on in the process. One interesting result is that there is always a dilemma when it comes to formalize and standardise procedures. On the one hand such standardisation may work as a checklist making certain that all necessary co-ordination actually takes place. On the other hand it may develop into routines that hamper the interest and creativity of participants. The chapter demonstrates that firms tend to adjust their procedures in these and other respects as new experiences are made. Innovation management involves learning by doing.

9.4. Interaction with Knowledge Institutions and Product Innovation

Chapter 11 by Anker Lund Vinding is focused on the interaction between firms and knowledge institutions in the context of product innovation. The chapter introduces a simple model combining the concept of "absorptive capacity" with the concept "strong ties" using the occurrence of academic employees and the strengthening of interaction with knowledge institutions as indicators. The econometric analysis demonstrates that the probability that firms introduce product innovations is the highest among those firms that combine strong absorptive capacity with strong ties. An important result is that the strongest correlation is found for small firms and firms that are not belonging to the science-based sectors. This indicates an opportunity for stimulating innovation by giving this kind of firm incentives to hire academic employees and to strengthen their collaboration with knowledge institutions. This is one reason why a one-sided focus on high technology and high technology sectors in innovation policy is detrimental to innovation.

Chapter 12 by Ina Drejer and Birte Holst Jørgensen differs in focus from most of the other chapters in studying the formation of new firms in connection with quite radical product innovations. This is an important complement to the focus on existing firms in other chapters. The chapter analyses two different cases – both within the broad field of sensor technology – and especially how the interaction between private and public actors evolve in different stages of the innovation process – using an extended version of the Rosenberg – Kline Chain link-model as organizing the presentation. One of the innovations (electronic pen) is defined as demand driven and the other one as technology driven (silicon microphone). The cases illustrate that public-private collaboration can be established and that collaboration supports interactive learning with benefits both for the firm and the public knowledge institutions. But it also demonstrates that there are some extra costs in building relationships from scratch as compared to already existing networks. Neither complete detailed and rigid contracts nor purely informal networking can stand alone and striking the right balance will typically require some "relational learning" among the parties involved. Especially in fields where there are high barriers to overcome before partners can join and where collaboration is crucial for exploitation of new technological opportunities public incentives have a role to play.

Chapter 13 by Jesper Lindgaard Christensen gives another complementary perspective on innovation and interactive learning. The focus is on the role of the national patenting office in Denmark – its internal learning and how it learns in interaction with Danish client firms. The chapter raises two policy relevant questions in this context. Does the organization of the patenting office promote learning internally and externally? Is there a rational for keeping a specific Danish patenting office or could the same functions be fulfilled by the EPO in Munich? The answer to the first question is ambivalent. The character of the knowledge flowing between departments within the Patenting Office may explain an internal organizational structure where the marketing department operates only with limited interaction with the main "production department" where patent applications are processed. A more interactive form was tried out but showed inexpedient even if it to some extent would promote and speed up learning internally. The result is in this sense an important complement to several other chapters pointing to the benefits of learning organizations: the practical implementation of such an organizational structure is limited by the specificties of the organization and the character of the knowledge exchanged. The answer to the second question is also mixed.

It is concluded that the Office takes on certain indirect services of importance for the national system of innovation – such as upgrading expertise among their employees in handling patents and then exporting them to private firms. Also, the Office is disseminating information on IPR, and has become the most central node in a national network of experts and practitioners on intellectual property rights. Regarding its primary function – to grant patents and trademarks – it seems as if the Office has a role as an entrance to the IPR-system for very small and weak players who cannot afford the services of a private agent and for very strong players who know how to get the best out of the patenting office. For firms between these extremes it is possible to use private patent agents and these could as well operate in direct interaction with the EPO.

9.5. Product Innovation and Economic Performance

Chapter 14 by Toke Reichstein analyses the relationships between the growth of firms and product innovation. He makes use of two data sets that are quite similar and include a combination of survey data and register data. The first data set covers 1003 firms 1994–1995 and the second covers 1678 firms 1998–1999. The chapter presents an econometric analysis where innovation is the dependent variable and growth in respectively employment and revenue are introduced together with a multitude of explanatory variables that have been shown to affect product innovation in Chapters 7 and 11. This procedure is chosen in order to avoid spurious correlation. The analysis ends up demonstrating that *there is a significant correlation between product innovation and growth in employment in both the periods studied.* The correlation between product innovation and revenue growth is significant for the first set of data but not for the second. An interesting observation made is that firms that engage in product innovation tend to be more reluctant to reduce the work force in situations with stagnating demand. The first period studied was part of a long period of stable economic growth while the other is one where growth stagnates.

10. CHALLENGES AHEAD

In this volume we have brought together different elements of a more complete understanding of product innovation and linked it to interactive learning and economic performance. Such a broader understanding raises new challenges for management, public policy and research. We conclude this introduction with some brief reflections on these challenges.

10.1. Challenges for Management

Within firms, learning for product innovation generally requires an interaction between the specialized divisions and functions in charge of respectively, sales, production and R&D. Sales departments will feed the firm's development process with information about user needs while the production department will contribute with practical information about what production costs for alternative designs of the new product. Development departments will keep track of and inform about new technological opportunities.

This is one reason why product innovation is very demanding for management in terms of organizing co-ordination and learning. It involves individuals from all parts of the organization in an interaction and co-operation over a period and at the same time it involves interaction and collaboration with external parties. Within the firm there is a need for individuals who work in different departments and functions and often belong to different "communities of practice" to understand each other and to communicate in a context of radical fundamental uncertainty.

In such situations it is problematic exclusively to trust incentive mechanisms related to pay or threat of job loss. And actually it might not be necessary. A context where a broader circle of employees get engaged in common search for solutions in the context of uncertainty may be felt to be "interesting" for those taking part. The most advanced managers are those who focus more on enhancing "the pleasure of learning" as incentive than on enhancing material incentives.

To manage innovation is also to manage conflicts in the organization. There is a need to establish some degree of trust between communities with different interests. The sales department and the production department will typically make attempts to impose their needs on the development department that also has its own agenda. Even so the collaboration between these different parties is often a prerequisite for the success of the product innovation.

A key problem is to establish communication vertically as well as horizontally. Here the language used in the communication is important. It can be formalized and codified giving a strong position to academically trained professionals or it can be informal and intuitive giving a strong position to "insiders" who have learnt the language in practice. And there might be parallel discourses that from time to time may get in dissonance with each other. To be aware of what languages that are used and to install "translation" at crucial steps in the innovation process is of key importance.

In the current context perhaps the most difficult daily challenge for management is *patience* in relation to the width and timing of innovation activities. To what degree can product innovations be narrowed down to operational adaptations to immediate market demands without undermining the long-term building of new capabilities? To what degree can the different stages of the innovation process be accelerated without losing control with the quality of the outcome, including the room for learning among the employees involved? A thorough innovation process that ends up with no need at all for debugging the innovation is normally not rational but on the other hand there are many examples of premature launching of innovations.

10.2. Challenges for Policy Makers

There are several more specific remarks in the chapters of this book on policy implications. What will be said here is brief and general. First, it is obvious from our analysis and many others that product innovation promotes economic growth and that product innovation promotes job creation in the economy as a whole. This implies that policy makers should reflect upon how they best can stimulate product innovation.

There are several generally accepted lines of action that find support in our analysis. Education and training is crucial. Basic research is important as well. Access to venture capital is important especially for stimulating radical innovations and start up firms. These are uncontroversial instruments but even those are not always used fully because there is an unwillingness to allocate the necessary resources.

We would like to add some remarks on instruments that are popular but that might not be very efficient seen in this dynamic perspective. The general assumption that it is always a good idea to make life as easy for private firms as possible is basically unsound. Low wages, low taxes, trade protectionism, undervalued currencies and a slack regulatory policies do not stimulate innovation. Rather they increase slack in existing firms and they guarantee the survival of firms with limited life expectancy. Neither is it clear why "entrepreneurship" in the elementary form of a high frequency of new firms would promote innovation. Most start-ups are based on old trivial technologies and their life expectancy is low. It is true that in some sectors technology based start up firms may be necessary to exploit new technological opportunities but this is a different issue than the general promotion of as many new small businesses as possible.

Third there are instruments that need to be taken seriously into account but appear to be controversial. These are instruments that can be seen as legitimate only if we assume that firms do not by themselves find the best way of doing things. This might be because they follow old routines and trajectories reflecting that they operate in a context of (radical) fundamental uncertainty or because they operate on the basis of compromises among different interests that make change difficult.

The reader of this book will find at least two types of examples where policy could make a positive difference. One is related to the hiring policy of small traditional firms and to the fact that such firms are reluctant to the hiring of employees with academic degrees. There is quite strong evidence that a change in behavior in this respect would have a major impact on the innovation activities in the firms as well as in the economy as a whole. The other refers to organizational forms. There is strong evidence indicating that a diffusion of good practice regarding networking, HRM, Industrial Relations and organizational flexibility would have a major impact first on innovation and second on economic growth in the whole economy.

One way to promote the diffusion of good practices is to make sure that the transformation pressure (competition) is strong. We have seen how firms that are exposed to intensified competition tend to be more active in introducing good practices. But from the point of the view of the whole economy this mechanism might be seen as working to slowly and as being too costly as compared to other more direct forms of intervention. Bringing together managers, employees, scholars and policy makers in co-ordinated discussions and actions aiming at finding the best ways to stimulate organizational up-grading could be a first step toward developing creative public-private programs aiming at promoting the diffusion of good organizational practice.[3]

10.3. Challenges for Theory and Research

One implication of the important role of social dimensions is that it is difficult to develop a *general theory* of innovation and interactive learning. The processes involved are highly context dependent and the best we can do is to develop models that bring to the fore differences in context as *different patterns*. We need to ground theory in case studies and comparative work and only on this basis is it possible to approach more general insights.

In order to understand how technical and organizational change affect economic growth it is necessary to establish a link between the macro-, meso- and the micro level of analysis. For instance our analysis demonstrates that more intensive competition – something that might emanate from macroeconomic change – has an impact both on efforts to innovate and on innovation outcomes. On the other hand, we can show that the job creation that results in employment growth at the macro level reflects a multitude of specific innovations and learning experiences at the level of the single firm and at the level of the single individual. A major challenge is to develop a theoretical understanding of how the transformation pressure experienced by firms is an aggregate outcome of actions and learning within and between those same firms (Lundvall & Nielsen, 1999).

In order to respond to this challenge we need to go even further into what role different types of knowledge and different forms of learning play in connection with product development. Such an approach is reflected in the present book. Some of the chapters deal with the innovation system as a whole, others look for sector specific patterns and still others analyze what is going on inside firms. But all of them try to be explicit in their attempts to understand the role of learning and knowledge in relation to innovation.

NOTES

1. This project was part of a large-scale Danish research project called LOK – Management, Organisation and Competence building. We thank The Social Science Research Council for financial support for this research.

2. We do recognize that the kind of innovations studied in the Danish surveys and case studies reported in this volume are incremental and sometimes have elements of imitation. Even in these cases surprises are bound to happen both on the side of technologies and the side of markets. Taking into account the capability of the agents to cope with change the uncertainty might be quite high also in such instances.

3. It might be worth noting that the two examples illustrate a counterintuitive pattern found in our analyses of product innovation in Danish firms. We find that the small low tech firms are the ones that have most to gain from strengthening their connection to academic knowledge while we find that organizational change bringing firms closer to the ideal of learning organisations have most benefits to offer for high technology and science based firms. The results are not incompatible with standard economics since we might put this in terms of decreasing returns. The explanation can be that high technology firms have already satiated their needs for access to academic knowledge while they often have problems with speeding up the learning in all activities outside research and development. In the small traditional firms the gains from speeding up organizational learning may be limited as long as they are weak in coping with formal and codified knowledge.

REFERENCES

Arrow, K. J. (1994, May). Methodological individualism and social knowledge. In: R. T. Ely (Ed.), *AEA Papers and Proceedings* (Vol. 84, No. 2).

Hargadon, A., & Fanelli, A. (2002). Action and possibility: Reconciling dual perspectives of knowledge organizations. *Organization Science, 13*, 290–302.

Lundvall, B. Å. (1987). Technological unemployment in a small open economy. In: R. Lund, P. Pedersen & J. Schmidt-Sorensen (Eds), *Studies in Unemployment*. Copenhagen: New Social Science Monographs, Institute of Organisation and Industrial Sociology.

Lundvall, B. Å. (2002). *Innovation, growth and social cohesion*. Cheltenham: Edward Elgar.

Lundvall, B. Å., & Christensen, J. L. (2003). Broadening the analysis of innovation systems – competition, organizational change and employment dynamics in the Danish system. In:

P. Conceicao, M. V. Heitor & B. Å. Lundvall (Eds), *Innovation, Competence Building, and Social Cohesion in Europe – Towards a Learning Society* (pp. 144–182). Elgar.

Lundvall, B. Å., & Nielsen, P. (1999). Competition and transformation in the learning economy – illustrated by the Danish case. *Revue d'Economie Industrielle, 88*, 67–90.

Maskell, P., Eskelinen, H., Hannibalsson, I., Malmberg, A., & Vatne, E. (1998). *Competitiveness, localised learning and regional development. Specialisation and prosperity in small open economies*. London: Routledge.

Pasinetti, L. (1981). *Structural change and economic growth*. Cambridge: Cambridge University Press.

PART I:
PERSPECTIVES ON
LEARNING

THE ECONOMICS OF KNOWLEDGE AND LEARNING

Bengt-Åke Lundvall

ABSTRACT

This chapter is about the production, diffusion and use of knowledge seen in an economic perspective. Fundamental distinctions between tacit and explicit knowledge and between know-how, know-why, know-what and know-who are related to distinctions between public/private and local/global knowledge. It is argued that the idea of the economy as being knowledge based is misleading and that we have moved into a learning economy where interactive learning is a key to economic performance of firms, regions and nations. This is one reason why a narrow economic perspective is insufficient. When it comes to understand industrial dynamics in the learning economy it is necessary to bring in other disciplines than economics in the analysis.

1. INTRODUCTION

This book is about product innovation, interactive learning and economic performance. A central theme is the understanding of learning and knowledge in connection with processes of technical and organizational change. In this chapter we present a conceptual framework to analyse knowledge and learning from an economic perspective. The starting point is the assumption that we are in a knowledge-based economy but we end up proposing that it is more adequate to

Product Innovation, Interactive Learning and Economic Performance
Research on Technological Innovation and Management Policy, Volume 8, 21–42
ISSN: 0737-1071/doi:10.1016/S0737-1071(04)08002-3

characterize the current era as "a learning economy." Crucial issues analysed here are distinctions between private/public, local/global and tacit/codified knowledge. While appearing "academic" at first sight these distinctions have important implications both for innovation policy and for the management of innovation and knowledge at the level of the firm.

It has become commonplace among policy-makers to refer to the current period as characterised by a knowledge based economy and increasingly it is emphasised that the most promising strategy for economic growth is one aiming at strengthening the knowledge base of the economy.[1] This discourse raises a number of unresolved analytical issues. What constitutes the knowledge base? At what level can we locate and define a knowledge base? What are the specificities of local and sector specific knowledge bases? How stable is the knowledge base? In order to approach an answer to these questions three different themes are introduced: first, basic concepts related to knowledge and learning; second, the contribution of economic analysis to the understanding of the production, mediation and use of knowledge; and third, new economic trends and the formation of a "learning economy."

2. A TERMINOLOGY OF KNOWLEDGE

2.1. Is Knowledge a Public or a Private Good?

Sidney Winter concluded his seminal paper on knowledge and management strategy by pointing out that there is "a paucity of language" and "a serious dearth of appropriate terminology and conceptual schemes" for analysing the role of knowledge in the economy (Winter, 1987). Since then, the number of relevant publications has grown immensely, but little headway has been made in terms of a terminology acceptable to all. There is little agreement on questions such as: What is the meaning of knowledge and knowledge production? What separations and distinctions between different kinds of knowledge are most useful for understanding the interaction between learning, knowledge and economic development?

Knowledge and information appear in economic models in two different contexts. The most fundamental assumption of standard microeconomics is that the economic system is based on *rational choices made by individual agents*. Thus, *how much and what kind of information* agents have about the world in which they operate and how powerful their *ability to process the information* are crucial issues.

The other major perspective is one in which knowledge is regarded as an *asset*. Here, knowledge may appear both as an input (competence) and output (innovation) in the production process. Under certain circumstances, it can be privately owned and/or bought and sold in the market as a commodity. The economics of knowledge is to a high degree about specifying the conditions for knowledge to appear as "a normal commodity," i.e. as something similar to a producible and reproducible tangible product.

In what follows, attention is on knowledge in this latter sense. In analysing knowledge as an asset, its properties in terms of transferability across time, space and people is central. This issue is at the core of two different strands of economic debate. One is the public/private dimension of knowledge and the role of government in knowledge production, the second is about the formation of industrial districts and the local character of knowledge.

Is knowledge a private or a public good? In economic theory, the properties that give a good the attribute of "public" are the following: (i) their benefits can be enjoyed by many users concurrently as well as sequentially without being diminished; and (ii) it is costly for the provider to exclude unauthorised users.

One reason for the interest in this issue is that it is crucial for defining the role of government in knowledge production. If knowledge is a public good that can be accessed by anyone, there is no incentive for rational private agents to invest in its production. If it is less costly to imitate than to produce new knowledge, the social rate of return would be higher than the private rate of return and, again, private agents would invest too little. Nelson's (1959) and Arrow's (1962b) classical contributions demonstrated that, in such situations, there is a basis for government policy either to subsidise or to take charge directly of the production of knowledge. Public funding of schools and universities, as well as of generic technologies, has been motivated by this kind of reasoning, which also brings to the fore the protection of knowledge, for instance by patent systems.

In a sense, this fundamental problem remains at the core of the economics of knowledge production. However, another strand of thought, that has roots far back in the history of economic theory, has become more strongly represented in the debate in the last decades. It is the question of how to share knowledge that is difficult to mediate. Marshall (1923) was concerned to explain the real-world phenomenon of *industrial district*: why is it that certain specialised industries are located in certain regions and why do they remain competitive for long historical periods. His principal explanation was that knowledge was localised in the region and rooted both in the local labour force and in local institutions and organizations. This perspective, with its focus on localised knowledge, has, in the light of the Silicon Valley-phenomenon, resurfaced strongly among industrial and regional economists over the last decades. Correspondingly, the management literature has seen a growing interest in the promotion of "knowledge sharing" within and between firms.

These two perspectives, while seemingly opposed in their contrasting emphasis on protection and sharing of knowledge, raise the same fundamental questions. Is knowledge public or private? Can it or can it not be transferred? Is the consent of the producer needed for the mediation to be successful or can knowledge be copied against the will of the producer? How difficult is it to transfer knowledge and what are the transfer mechanisms? Is it possible to change the form of knowledge so that it gets easier (more difficult) to mediate? How important is the broader socio-cultural context for the transferability of knowledge? One reason for the distinctions between different kinds of knowledge proposed below is that they help to sort out these questions.

Responding to these questions is also a way of specifying what constitutes the knowledge base of the economy. If knowledge were completely public it would be meaningful to speak of one common knowledge base for the whole economy and there would be a strong need for co-ordinating investments in knowledge production at the global level. If, conversely, knowledge were completely individual and private there would be no common knowledge base at all and investment in knowledge production could be left to the individuals themselves. As we shall see, reality is complex and most knowledge is neither completely public nor completely private. The knowledge base is fragmented and may best be illustrated as constituted by a number of semi-public "pools" to which access is shared regionally, professionally and through networking.

2.2. Four Different Kinds of Knowledge

Knowledge is here divided into four categories, which in fact have ancient roots (Lundvall & Johnson, 1994).[2]

- Know-what.
- Know-why.
- Know-how.
- Know-who.

Know-what refers to knowledge about "facts." How many people live in New York, what the ingredients in pancakes are, and when the battle of Waterloo took place are examples of this kind of knowledge. Here, knowledge is close to what is normally called information – it can be broken down into bits and communicated as data.

Know-why refers to knowledge about principles and laws of motion in nature, in the human mind and in society. This kind of knowledge has been extremely important for technological development in certain science-based areas, such as the chemical and electric/electronic industries. Access to this kind of knowledge will often make advances in technology more rapid and reduce the frequency of errors in procedures involving trial and error.

Know-how refers to skills – i.e. the ability to do something. It may be related to the skills of artisans and production workers, but, actually, it plays a key role in all important economic activities. The businessman judging the market prospects for a new product or the personnel manager selecting and training staff use their know-how. It would also be misleading to characterise know-how as practical rather than theoretical. One of the most interesting and profound analyses of the role and formation of know-how is actually about scientists' need for skill formation and personal knowledge (Polanyi, 1958, 1978). Even finding the solution to complex mathematical problems is based on intuition and on skills related to pattern recognition which are rooted in experience-based learning rather than on the mechanical carrying out of a series of distinct logical operations (Ziman, 1979, pp. 101–102).

Know-how is a kind of knowledge developed and kept within the borders of the individual firm or the single research team. As the complexity of the knowledge base increases, however, co-operation between organizations tends to develop. One of the most important reasons for industrial networks is the need for firms to be able to share and combine elements of know-how. Similar networks may, for the same reasons, be formed between research teams and laboratories.

This is one reason why *know-who* becomes increasingly important. The general trend towards a more composite knowledge base, with new products typically combining many technologies, each of which is rooted in several different scientific disciplines, makes access to many different sources of knowledge more essential (Pavitt, 1998). Know-who involves information about who knows what and who knows to do what. But it also involves the social ability to co-operate and communicate with different kinds of people and experts.

2.3. How Public or Private are the Four Kinds of Knowledge?

The public or private character of these kinds of knowledge differs in terms both of degree and form. Databases can bring together "know-what" in a more or less user-friendly form. Information technology extends enormously the information potentially at the disposal of individual agents, although the information still has to be found and what is relevant selected. The effectiveness of search machines developed in connection with the Internet is highly relevant in this context, as this helps to specify how accessible the data actually are. Even with the most recent advances in this area access to this kind of knowledge is still far from perfect (Shapiro & Varian, 1999). Even today, the most effective medium for obtaining pertinent facts may be through the "know-who" channel, i.e. contacting an outstanding expert in the field to obtain directions on where to look for a specific piece of information.

Scientific work aims at producing theoretical models of the *know-why* type, and some of this work is placed in the public domain. Academics have strong incentives to publish and make their results accessible. The Internet offers new possibilities for speedy electronic publishing. Open and public access is of course a misnomer, in that it often takes enormous investments in learning before the information has any meaning. Again know-who, directed towards academia, can help the amateur obtain a "translation" into something more comprehensible.

This is one strong motivation for companies' presence in academic environments and sometimes even engaging in basic research. Some big companies contribute to basic research and they tend to take over functions of "technical universities" (Eliasson, 1996). But at the same time, the close connections between academic science and the exploitation of new ideas by business in fields such as biotechnology tend to undermine the open exchange that has characterised academic knowledge production.

To gain access to scientific know-why, it is necessary, under all circumstances, to pursue R&D-activities and to invest in science. This is true for individuals and regions as well as for firms. There is much less completely free "spill-overs" available than assumed in standard economics – absorptive capacity will among other factors reflect historical investment in R&D (Cohen & Levinthal, 1990).

In fields characterised by intense technological competition, technical solutions are often ahead of academic know-why. Technology can solve problems or perform functions without a clear understanding of why it works. Here, knowledge is more know-how than know-why.

Know how is the kind of knowledge with the most limited public access and for which mediation is the most complex. The basic problem is the difficulty of separating the competence to act from the person or organization that acts. The outstanding expert – cook, violinist, manager – may write a book explaining how to do things, but what is done by the amateur on the basis of that explanation is, of course, less perfect than what the expert would produce. Attempts to use information technology to develop expert systems show that it is difficult and costly to transform expert skills into information that can be used by others. It has also been demonstrated that the transformation always involves changes in the content of the expert knowledge (Hatchuel & Weil, 1995). This is true of an individual's skills and competence, of professional skills and a team's competence.

Eliasson (1996) has illustrated the limits of using management information systems as a substitute for management skills by pointing out the strategic failures of IBM and other big ICT-firms. Know-how is never a completely public good and normally firms get access to it only by hiring experts or merging with companies with the knowledge they want.

Know who refers to a combination of information and social relationships. Telephone books that list professions as well as databases that list producers of certain goods and services are in the public domain and can, in principle, be accessed by anyone. In the economic sphere, however, it is extremely important to obtain quite specialised competencies and to find the most reliable experts, hence the enormous importance of good personal relationships with key persons one can trust. These social and personal relationships are by definition not public. They cannot be transferred and, more specifically, they cannot be bought or sold on the market. As pointed out by Arrow (1971), "you cannot buy trust and, if you could, it would have no value whatsoever."

On the other hand, the social context may support, to a greater or lesser degree, the formation of know-who knowledge while the cultural context determines the form it takes. When characterising national business systems, Whitley emphasises factors having to do with trust and the capacity to build extra-family collective loyalties (Whitley, 1996, p. 51). This is also an important aspect of the concept of social capital (Woolcock, 1998). In situations where technology is characterised by rapid change or where the knowledge base is not well documented, it is necessary to meet face-to-face from time to time in order first to define and then to solve problems.

2.4. Most Knowledge is Neither Strictly Public nor Strictly Private

It is clear from what precedes that very little knowledge is "perfectly public." Even information of the know-what type may be impossible to access for those not connected to the right telecommunications or social networks. Moreover, the current state of information technology still limits access for those who are connected. Scientific and other types of complex knowledge may be perfectly accessible, in principle, but for effective access the user must have invested in building absorptive capacity. Know-how is never fully transferable since how a person does things reflects that individual's personality (even organizations have a "personality" in this sense).

On the other hand, little economically useful knowledge is completely private in the long run. Tricks of the trade are shared within the profession. Know-how can be taught and learnt in interaction between the master and the apprentice. New technological knowledge may be costly to imitate but, when it is much more efficient than the old, there are several ways to obtain it. Even when the possessor of private knowledge does not want to share it with others there are ways to obtain it, such as reverse engineering which involves taking products apart to find out how to produce them. If necessary, private agents will engage in intelligence activities aimed at getting access to competitors' secrets.

Different parts of economic theory handle this mixed situation differently. Underlying much of the neo-classical theory of production and economic growth is the simplifying assumption that there is a global bank of blueprints from which anybody can get a copy to be used for starting up production. This ignores the fact that only skilled agents can use most accessible knowledge and that skills differ and are not easily transformed into blueprints.

The resource base theory of the firm takes the opposite view and assumes that the competence of the firm determines the directions in which it expands its activities (Penrose, 1959). It is the specificity of the knowledge base that determines the specific pattern of economic growth. Actually, however, this model implies an even more dynamic perspective characterised by continuous creation of new competencies within the firm and it points toward the need to develop "learning organizations." Otherwise, imitation and innovations in competing firms would, sooner or later erode the firm's competencies.

In real life firms will have to engage simultaneously in copying well-known routines from others, exploiting internal capabilities and engage in building new ones. This is what makes management a difficult art and why firms cannot be reduced to maximising algorithms; the way they are presented in standard textbooks based on neo-classical economics.

2.5. On Tacitness and Codification of Knowledge

There is currently a lively debate among economists about the role of tacitness in knowledge (Cowan, David & Foray, 2000; Johnson, Lorenz & Lundvall, 2002). The reason for the interest is, of course, that tacitness relates to the transferability and to the public character of knowledge. It has been assumed that the more knowledge is tacit, the more difficult it is to share it between people, firms and regions. Specifically, markets might fail and other mediation mechanisms would have to be given more attention.

Tacit knowledge is knowledge that has not been documented and made explicit by the one who uses and controls it. The fact that a certain piece of knowledge is tacit does not rule out the possibility of making it explicit if incentives to do so are strong enough. To make this clear, it is useful to distinguish between tacit knowledge that can be made explicit (tacit for lack of incentives) and knowledge that cannot be made explicit – tacit by nature (Cowan, David & Foray, 2000).

Knowledge about the state of the world can to a certain extent be made explicit. Know-what can be entered into databases and know-why can be made explicit in theorems. Skills embodied in persons and competencies embodied in organizations can only be documented to a much more limited degree. There are "natural" limits to how far it is possible to make "know-how" explicit; only approximations are possible. This is why outstanding experts whose activities are based on their unique know-how and firms whose activities are based on unique competencies and permanent innovation may earn extra rents for long periods.

An important issue in this context is how much effort should be made to "codify" knowledge. Only those with access to the code can access knowledge written down in a code. Two parties can share the knowledge or one party can sell the knowledge to another. Codified knowledge is potentially shared knowledge while non-codified knowledge remains individual, at least, until it can be learnt in direct interaction with the possessor. Sectors where the knowledge base is dominated by non-codified but potentially codifiable knowledge may be sectors where systematic progress towards more efficient practices is difficult. Economists have used education as a typical example of a production process characterised by tacit techniques (Murnane & Nelson, 1984). OECD (2000) presents a unique attempt to compare the production, diffusion and use of knowledge across some important sectors – health and education among them.

The debate on codification has been complicated by the fact that two different meanings of "codes" have been alluded to. Some are explicit and available in the form of textbooks, manuals, formulas and organizational diagrams. Other "codes" have developed spontaneously as a means of communication within or between organisations (Arrow, 1974). The latter are implicit and no individual in the organisation may be able to give a full description. The issue about to what extent such implicit codes can be transformed into explicit ones is an important one. It is well known that organizational diagrams and management information systems lose some of the complexity and richness that characterise real existing social systems. If these codes could be made explicit, they could be made available to external parties, and mediation of knowledge would become less difficult. Another reason for making implicit codes explicit could be that, in some instances, codification might make it easier to formulate and realise strategies of change.[3]

What has just been considered as important attributes of knowledge (public/private; codified/tacit) suggests that there may be marked differences among various sectors with regard to their knowledge base. Some science-based sectors base their activities mainly on codified knowledge while others operate and compete mainly on the basis of unstructured and experience-based implicit knowledge. But there are no pure cases. Even in the most strongly science-based sectors tacit knowledge will be a key element in their competitive position and conversely it is difficult to find firms in the OECD area that can avoid completely the need to codify. Accounting and reporting to tax authorities requires a minimum in this respect and the wide diffusion of computers both contributes to and reflects the trend among firms toward operating on the basis of codified knowledge (information).

3. AN ECONOMIC PERSPECTIVE ON THE PRODUCTION, MEDIATION AND USE OF KNOWLEDGE

3.1. What is Produced When Firms Produce Knowledge?

Most authors using the concept of knowledge creation and knowledge production refer to technological knowledge and to technical innovation as the output of the process (Antonelli, 1999; Nonaka & Takeuchi, 1995). In the new growth theory, the output of the R&D sector is viewed either as a blueprint for a new production process that is more efficient than the previous one; it is assumed that it can be protected by private property instruments such as patents; or as a production of new semi-manufactured goods that cannot easily be copied by competitors (Verspagen, 1992, pp. 29–30).

A striking characteristic of knowledge production resulting in innovation is the fact that knowledge, in terms of skills and competencies, is the most important input. In this sense, it recalls a "corn economy," in which corn and labour produce corn. But it differs from such an economy in one important respect. While the corn used to produce corn disappears in the process, *skills and competencies improve with use*. Important characteristics of knowledge reflect that its elements are not scarce in the traditional sense: the more skills and competencies are used, the more they develop. This points to knowledge production as a process of joint production, in which innovation is one kind of output and the learning and skill enhancement that takes place in the process is another.

3.2. Innovation as one Major Outcome of Knowledge Production

There are two reasons for regarding innovation as an interesting outcome of knowledge production. One is that innovation represents – by definition – something new and therefore adds to existing knowledge. The second is that innovation is – again by definition – knowledge that is in demand (Innovation is defined as an invention that has been introduced in the market and it thus represents knowledge that has proven its relevance for the market economy).

On the other hand, it is important to note that innovation, as Schumpeter emphasised, is part of a process of "creative destruction." An innovation may open up new markets and create the basis for new firms and jobs, but it will, at the same time, close down some old markets and some firms and jobs will disappear. This has a parallel in the impact on the stock of knowledge used in the market economy. Moral depreciation of intellectual capital is the other side of innovation. For instance, the know-how necessary to produce mechanical office equipment and the competencies of firms engaged in their production became obsolete when semi-conductors and computers were introduced.

There are important sectoral differences in knowledge production. Such differences are reflected in the character, the mode and the outcome of the innovation process. The taxonomy developed by Keith Pavitt (1984) represents an important effort to capture these differences systematically. By analysing 2000 important technical innovations in the United Kingdom, Pavitt defined four categories of firms and sectors. First, there are *supply-dominated* sectors (e.g. clothing, furniture), in which firms develop few important innovations on their own, but obtain some from other firms. Second, there are *scale-intensive* sectors (e.g. food, cement), which focus their innovation activities on developing more efficient process technology. Third, there are *specialised suppliers* (e.g. engineering, software, instruments), and these carry out frequent product innovations, often in collaboration with customers. Finally, there are *science-based producers* (e.g. chemical industry, biotechnology, electronics) that develop new products as well as processes in close collaboration with universities.

For long, knowledge production/innovation processes were considered largely as the province of the fourth category, and still there is a bias in this direction, often in combination with a linear view which assumes that new scientific results are the first step in the process, technological invention the second step, and the introduction of innovations as new processes or products the third. There is now a rich body of empirical and historical work that shows that this is the exception rather than the rule (Lundvall, 1988; Rothwell, 1977; von Hippel, 1988). Of all scientific advances, very few are immediately transformed into innovations and, *vice versa*, innovations very seldom reflect recent scientific breakthroughs. It is nonetheless true that knowledge production/innovation processes are facilitated by science in various ways, although normally it is old rather than new scientific results that support the innovation process. Kline and Rosenberg (1986) have reviewed the complex interaction between science and technology throughout the innovation process. Their model is presented and used by Ina Drejer and Birte Holst Jørgensen in Chapter 12 in this volume.

The recent models of innovation emphasise that knowledge production/innovation is an interactive process in which firms interact with customers, suppliers and knowledge institutions. Empirical analysis shows that firms seldom innovate alone.[4]

3.3. Competence as the Other Major Outcome of Knowledge Production

The change from a linear to an interactive view of innovation and knowledge production has also been a way to connect innovation and the further development of competence. As now understood, the innovation process may be described as a process of *interactive learning* in which those involved increase their competence while engaging in the innovation process.

In economics, there have been various approaches to competence building and learning. One important contribution is Arrow's analysis of "learning by doing" (Arrow, 1962a), in which he demonstrated that the efficiency of a production unit engaged in producing complex systems (aeroplane frames) grew with the number of units already produced and argued that this reflected experience-based learning.[5] Later, Rosenberg (1982) introduced "learning by using" to explain why efficiency in using complex systems increased over time (the users were airline companies introducing new models). The concept of "learning by interacting" points to how interaction between producers and users in innovation enhances the competence of both (Lundvall, 1985, 1988; Lundvall & Vinding, Chap. 5 this volume).

In most of the contributions mentioned above, learning is regarded as the unintended outcome of processes with a different aim than learning and increasing competence. Learning is seen as a side effect of processes of production, use, marketing, or innovation. An interesting new development, which refers to learning as an instrumental process, is the growing attention given to "learning organizations" (Senge, 1990). The basic idea is that the way an organization is structured and the routines followed will have a major effect on the rate of learning that takes place. The appropriate institutional structures may improve or speed up knowledge production in terms of competence building based on daily activities.

The move towards learning organizations is reflected in changes both in the firm's internal organization and in inter-firm relationships. Within firms, the accelerating rate of change makes multi-level hierarchies and strict borders between functions inefficient. It makes decentralisation of responsibility to lower-level employees and formation of multi-functional teams a necessity. This is reflected in the increasing demand for workers willing to learn and, at the same time, skilful, flexible, co-operative and willing to shoulder responsibility. Inter-firm relationships with suppliers, customers and competitors become more selective and more intense. "Know-who" becomes increasingly important in an economy that combines a complex knowledge base and a highly developed, rapidly changing specialisation.

Apart from these organizational changes, there is growing emphasis on making employees and teams of employees more aware of the fact that they are engaged in learning. It has been suggested that second-loop learning, i.e. a process in which the crucial element is that agents reflect on what has been learnt and on how to design the learning process, is more efficient than simply relying on the impact of experience (Argyris & Schön, 1978).

It is difficult to capture, empirically, competence building through learning than innovation. Competence is primarily revealed in practice and sometimes in no other way. This may become a problem as experience-based learning and competence become increasingly important for the competitiveness of workers, firms and regions. Tomlinson (1999) has made an interesting and original attempt to map sector differences in competence building through experience. Using U.K. labour market survey data, he shows that learning is more intensive and extensive in the top than in the bottom of organizations. His data also indicate that learning is more important in sectors characterised by frequent innovation. When it comes to the development of indicators this is the most difficult but perhaps also the most important area. In Chapter 9 Tomlinson uses the same data set to link organizational forms to individual learning among employees.

These measurement problems reflect the general state of economic analysis in this field. While economists have made substantial contributions to the economics of innovation, their contribution to understanding competence building is more modest. With scholars such as Christopher Freeman, Richard R. Nelson and Nathan Rosenberg as entrepreneurs and spiritual leaders, there has been a massive effort to understand the process of innovation in relation to economic theory (Dosi et al., 1988) and in an historical and empirical perspective, including the development of statistical indicators. There is no parallel for knowledge production as learning and competence building. On this aspect of knowledge production, sociologists, psychologists and anthropologists have more to offer economists in terms of systematic insights than *vice versa* (see for instance, Kolb, 1984).

3.4. Production of Knowledge as a Separate Activity or as a By-Product of Regular Routine Activities: A Differentiation Which is Becoming Blurred

It is useful to separate two different perspectives on the process of knowledge production which are not mutually exclusive but which can be found, in more or less pure form, in the literature on innovation systems and the information society. They are also reflected in attempts to measure the relative importance of knowledge in the economy and in theoretical models such as models of economic growth.

On the one hand, one might look for *a separate sector* in charge of producing new knowledge or handling and distributing information. Such a sector could involve universities, technical institutes and government S&T policies, as well as R&D functions in firms. Here, the production of knowledge would take place as a deliberate activity, outside the realm of production. On the other hand, one might regard the creation and diffusion of knowledge as rooted in and emanating from routine activities in economic life, such as learning by doing, by using and by interacting. Here, the production of knowledge would take place as a by-product of production, through learning by doing or learning by using.

Another important distinction already touched upon is between "off-line" and "on-line" learning activities. Above we referred to the growing focus on establishing learning organizations. Another related new trend is the emergence of a form of learning qualified as "experimental." This form of learning taking place "on line" (that is to say, during the process of producing the good or providing the service) involves experimenting during the production process. By doing so, one creates new options and variety. This form of learning is based on a strategy whereby experimentation allows for collecting data, on the basis of which the best strategy for future activities is chosen.

With the emergence of experimental learning and learning organizations, the feedback and reciprocal links that tie "on-line" learning process and in-house R&D together become crucial. One issue here is determining the extent to which the knowledge produced "by doing" is valued. It might be a problem that management rarely considers routine activities as activities that produce knowledge, although different national systems differ markedly in this respect. The establishment of feedback loops requires effective recognition, identification and valorisation of the knowledge produced through the learning process.

3.5. Mediation of Knowledge

While the production of knowledge is important for the overall dynamics of the global economy in the long run, the greatest economic impact comes from broadening the use of knowledge in the economy. This is reflected in public efforts to increase the diffusion of innovations as well as in training and education aimed at the formation of skills and competencies. How can different aspects of knowledge be mediated? The natural starting point for an economic analysis is to see under what conditions the market can mediate knowledge.

Some of the difficulties in mediating knowledge through the market have already been indicated. Tacit knowledge in the form of know-how or an implicit code or competence cannot be separated from the person or organization containing it. This is what von Hippel (1994) calls "sticky data." In this case, mediation may take the form of the purchase by the customer of the services of the person or the firm rather than the competence itself.

Carriers of such knowledge may have a problem demonstrating the quality of their competence to potential buyers and buyers may have a problem locating the best offers in terms of quality. Reference from key customers, which can be shown as evidence to potential customers, is one strategy used by firms operating in this kind of market.

This form of mediation and the problems it involves tend to take on growing economic importance. The increasing specialisation in the production of knowledge makes mediation more crucial for the system as a whole. This is reflected in the fact that knowledge-intensive business services, a sector directly engaged in the production and sale of knowledge, are among the most rapidly growing sectors in OECD countries. Consultancy firms, accountancy firms and financial firms have taken over the role of "strategic sector" historically played by the sector producing machinery summarising and generalising experiencing from local learning and delivering embodied and disembodied knowledge to a broad set of users. This is confirmed by econometric studies demonstrating a close correlation between the input of these kinds of services and productivity growth in user sectors (Tomlinson, 2001).

A second way to mediate this kind of knowledge is to engage in a process of interactive learning with the carrier of the knowledge. This may be a conscious choice, for example when an apprentice enters into a contract with a master, or it may be a side effect of co-operation between people and organizations to solve shared problems. A third way to obtain this kind of knowledge is to hire experts as employees or take over the organization controlling the knowledge.

Even when knowledge is explicit and can be separated from its carrier there are problems with using the market as a mediator, which Kenneth Arrow, in particular, has worked to define. One is for the customer to determine the value of the information before the transaction has taken place; a user wants to know something in advance about the knowledge, and the seller does not want to give information away for free. Another is the difficulty for the seller to restrict the use of the information once it has been sold and, *vice versa*, the difficulty for the buyer to restrict its further distribution by the seller.

Despite these difficulties, a large and growing amount of knowledge is the object of transactions in something that looks like a market (there is a buyer, a seller and a price). One reason why markets work is that formal and informal institutions – including legal protection in terms of patents, licenses and copyright – support transactions. Reputation mechanisms lower the risk for entering into contractual relationships. Another, even more fundamental, reason is that many markets for knowledge transactions are not pure but rather organised markets. Long-term relationships with elements of experience-based trust often play a major role in knowledge markets (Lundvall, 1985, 1988; Lundvall & Vinding, Chap. 5 this volume).

So far, the discussion has been limited to the mediation of what economists call disembodied knowledge. Substantial flows of knowledge are built into products. Scientific instruments and computers embody a great deal of knowledge, and users with sufficient competence can perform very advanced operations with this kind of equipment. Mediation of knowledge via embodied technology is sometimes combined with a transfer of disembodied knowledge. For example, suppliers of complex process equipment may offer training to the personnel of the customer organization.

Finally, knowledge can be mediated in several other informal ways. One way to overcome market limitations is for professionals belonging to separate and sometimes even competing organizations to exchange pieces of knowledge on a barter basis (Carter, 1989).

4. TOWARD THE LEARNING ECONOMY

Many indicators show that there has been a shift in economic development in the direction of a more important role for knowledge production and learning. This section looks at some of these changes and the issues they raise for the knowledge base.

Moses Abramowitz and Paul David (1996) have demonstrated that this century has been characterised by increasing knowledge intensity in the production system. The OECD's structural analysis of industrial development supports their conclusion. It has been shown that the sectors that use knowledge inputs such as R&D and skilled labour most intensively grow most rapidly. At the same time, the skill profile is on an upward trend in almost all sectors. In most OECD countries, in terms of employment and value added, the most rapidly growing sector is knowledge-intensive business services (OECD, 1998, pp. 48–55).

These observations have led more and more analysts to characterise the new economy as "knowledge-based," and there is in fact little doubt about a relative shift in the demand for labour towards more skilled workers (OECD, 1994). However, this perspective may underestimate the destructive aspects of innovation and change. In an alternative interpretation of the change in the composition of the labour force, Anne P. Carter (1994) pointed out that the main function of most non-production workers is to introduce or cope with change. The rising proportion of non-production workers may thus be taken as the expression both of the growing cost of change and of acceleration in the rate of change.

Acceleration in the rate of change implies that knowledge and skills are more exposed to rapid moral depreciation. Therefore, the increase in the stock of knowledge may be less dramatic than it appears. An alternative hypothesis is that we are moving into a "learning economy," where the success of individuals, firms, regions and countries will reflect, more than anything else, their ability to learn. The speeding up of change reflects the rapid diffusion of information technology, the widening of the global marketplace, with the inclusion of new strong competitors, and deregulation of and less stability in markets (Archibugi & Lundvall, 2001; Drucker, 1993; Lundvall & Johnson, 1994).

In this context, learning is defined as a process, the core of which is the acquisition of competence and skills that allow the learning individual to be more successful in reaching individual goals or those of his/her organization. It will also involve a change in context of meaning and purpose for the individual and affect his/her existing knowledge. This corresponds closely to what is commonly meant by learning and to what experts on learning, who are not economists, understand by the concept (Kolb, 1984). It is also the kind of learning most crucial to economic success. At the same time it differs from some definitions of learning in standard economic theory, where it is synonymous either with "information acquisition" or treated as a black box phenomenon assumed to be reflected in productivity growth.

5. CONCLUSION

It may be argued that, in a sense, all economic theory is about information and knowledge. Problems of co-ordination have been at the core of economic theory since Adam Smith. Individual agents make choices independently on the basis of information offered by the market. Important differences between economic models and theories reflect differences in the assumptions made about what agents know and about the degree to which they learn anything from what they do. This separates neo-classical economics from Austrian economics; the former takes fully informed agents as the reference, whereas the latter emphasises ignorance as the starting point for learning (von Hayek). It also separates those who assume hyper-rationality and rationality from those who assume limited rationality (Herbert A. Simon).

Modern economics is more than ever aware of the importance of knowledge and learning. New growth theory and new trade theory assume a strong link between the increase in the knowledge base and the rate of productivity growth. Austrian economists treat learning as a fundamental process in the analysis of market transactions. The last decades have witnessed an explosive growth in institutional economics and the economics of innovation. In these new fields, knowledge and learning play a pivotal role in economic development. New theories of the firm focus on building capabilities and competencies. The management literature has made the concept of "learning organizations" central for theoretical developments and especially for practitioners.

However, in almost all of these contributions, the understanding of knowledge and learning remains narrow. In theories that form the core of standard economics, it is assumed that rational agents make choices on the basis of a given amount of information. The only kind of learning allowed for is agents' access to new bodies of information. The most recent developments within standard economics are contradictory and ambivalent in this respect. On the one hand, new growth theory and new trade theory focus on the importance of investments in education and research. On the other hand, some of the most fashionable developments in macroeconomics assume rational expectations and general equilibrium frameworks, thus operating with even more extreme assumptions, leaving no room for learning by agents.

Recent developments outside standard economics have been less constrained in these respects. Research on the economics of institutional and technical change has resulted in many new insights. Institutional economics, evolutionary economics, socio-economic research, industrial dynamics and the economics of innovation have typically developed in close interaction with historical and empirical research programmes. This is why we know much more than before about how innovation takes place in different parts of the economy now than we did 20 years ago.

When it comes to the other aspect of knowledge production, i.e. competence building and learning, research is only now beginning to raise fundamental questions about who learns what and how learning takes place in the context of economic development. In this area, economists have a lot to learn from other disciplines and not least from education specialists who have developed a more systematic and empirically based understanding of learning (Kolb, 1984). This reflects the fact that when economists begin to focus on learning, they face issues for which their traditional toolbox is insufficient. Scholars in philosophy, psychology, education, anthropology and other disciplines have illuminated different aspects of these issues. The increasing division of labour in the production of knowledge – useful as it might have been for the rapid advance within special fields – has had as a major negative consequence the lack of a deep and systematic understanding of the complex process of knowledge creation and learning.

In most of this book we use a broad definition of economics as our reference platform but at the same time we try to broaden the perspective whenever an understanding of the real world phenomena requires it. One of the major conclusions is that it is not meaningful to pretend that economic performance can be explained without bringing into the analysis social relationships and organizational structures. The innovation literature has been instrumental in opening up the black box of technical change: now the time has come to open up the black box of social interaction through focus on how learning takes place in the real world.

NOTES

1. OECD has pursued several analytical activities along these lines (Foray & Lundvall, 1996; OECD, 1996). The Portuguese chairmanship for the EU Ministerial council for the first half of 2000 was pursued under the theme of "a Europe based on knowledge and innovation."

2. Knowledge has been at the centre of analytical interest from the very beginning of civilisation. Aristotle distinguished between: *Epistèmè*: knowledge that is universal and theoretical. *Technè*: knowledge that is instrumental, context specific and practise related. *Phronesis*: Knowledge that is normative, experience-based, context-specific and related to common sense: "practical wisdom." At least two of our categories have roots that go back to these three intellectual virtues. Know-why is similar to *epistèmè* and know-how to *technè*. But the correspondence is imperfect, since we will follow Polanyi and argue that scientific activities always involve a combination of know-how and know-why. Aristotle's third category, *phronesis*, which relates to the ethical dimension, will be reflected in what is to be said about the need for a social and ethical dimension in economic analysis and about the importance of trust in the context of learning.

3. For two different perspectives on the limits and the usefulness of codification see Cowan, David and Foray (2000) and Johnson, Lorenz and Lundvall (2001).

4. This is also the background for developing a systemic approach to knowledge production (Edquist, 1997; Freeman, 1987; Lundvall, 1992; Nelson, 1993). Innovation systems may be defined as regional or national, or as sector- or technology-specific. The common idea is that the specificities of knowledge production reflect unique combinations of technological specialisation and institutional structure. In national systems, the education and training system and the institutional set up of labour markets are among the most important factors explaining national patterns and modes of innovation (see also Chapter 3 by Alice Lam).

5. A more recent analysis of learning by doing focuses on how confronting new problems in the production process triggers searching and learning, which imply interaction between several parties as they seek solutions (von Hippel & Tyre, 1995). This kind of learning

is richly illustrated in the analysis of learning situations in Danish firms in Chapter 7 by Reinhard Lund.

REFERENCES

Abramowitz, M., & David, P. (1996). Technological change and the rise of intangible investments: The U.S. economy's growth path in the twentieth century. In: D. Foray & B. Å. Lundvall (Eds), *Employment and Growth in the Knowledge Based Economy*. Paris: OECD.

Antonelli, C. (1999). *The micro-dynamics of technological change*. London: Routledge.

Archibugi, D., & Lundvall, B. Å. (Eds) (2001). *The globalizing learning economy*. Guildford and King's Lynn: Oxford University Press.

Arrow, K. J. (1962a). The economic implications of learning by doing. *Review of Economic Studies, 29*(80).

Arrow, K. J. (1962b). Economic welfare and the allocation of resources for invention. In: R. R. Nelson (Ed.), *The Rate and Direction of Inventive Activity: Economic and Social Factors*. Princeton: Princeton University Press.

Arrow, K. J. (1971). Political and economic evaluation of social effects and externalities. In: M. Intrilligator (Ed.), *Frontiers of Quantitative Economics*. North Holland.

Arrow, K. J. (1974). *The limits of organisation*. New York: W. W. Norton & Co.

Carter, A. P. (1989). Know-how trading as economic exchange. *Research Policy, 18*(3).

Carter, A. P. (1994, August). Production workers, metainvestment and the pace of change. Paper prepared for the meetings of the International J. A. Schumpeter Society, Munster.

Cohen, W. M., & Levinthal, D. A. (1990). Absorptive capacity: A new perspective on learning and innovation. *Administrative Science Quarterly, 35*, 128–152.

Cowan, R., David, P. A., & Foray, D. (2000). The explicit economics of knowledge codification and tacitness. *Industrial and Corporate Change, 9*, 211–253.

Dosi, G., et al. (Eds) (1988). *Technology and economic theory*. London: Pinter Publishers.

Drucker, P. (1993). *The post-capitalist society*. Oxford: Butter Worth Heinemann.

Edquist, C. (Ed.) (1997). *Systems of innovation: Technologies, institutions and organizations*. London: Pinter Publishers.

Eliasson, G. (1996). *Firm objectives, controls and organization*. The Netherlands: Kluwer.

Foray, D., & Lundvall, B. Å. (1996). The knowledge-based economy: From the economics of knowledge to the learning economy. In: D. Foray & B. Å. Lundvall (Eds), *Employment and Growth in the Knowledge-based Economy*. Paris: OECD Documents.

Hatchuel, A., & Weil, B. (1995). *Experts in Organisations*. Berlin: Walter de Gruyter.

Johnson, B., Lorenz, E., & Lundvall, B. r i n g A . (2002). Why all this fuzz about codified and tacit knowledge? *Industrial and Corporate Change, 11*(2), 245–262.

Kline, S. J., & Rosenberg, N. (1986). An overview of innovation. In: R. Landau & N. Rosenberg (Eds), *The Positive Sum Game*. Washington, DC: National Academy Press.

Kolb, D. A. (1984). *Experiential learning*. Englewood Cliffs: Prentice Hall.

Lundvall, B. Å. (1985). *Product innovation and user-producer interaction*. Aalborg: Aalborg University Press.

Lundvall, B. Å. (1988). Innovation as an interactive process – from user-producer interaction to the national system of innovation. In: G. Dosi et al. (Eds), *Technical Change and Economic Theory*. London: Pinter Publishers.

Lundvall, B. Å. (Ed.) (1992). *National systems of innovation: Towards a theory of innovation and interactive learning*. London: Pinter Publishers.

Lundvall, B. r i n g A ., & Johnson, B. (1994, December). The learning economy. *Journal of Industry Studies*, *1*(2), 23–42.

Marshall, A. P. (1923). *Industry and trade*. London: MacMillan.

Murnane, R. J., & Nelson, R. R. (1984). Production and innovation when techniques are tacit. *Journal of Economic Behaviour and Organization*, *5*, 353–373.

Nelson, R. R. (1959). The simple economics of basic economic research. *Journal of Political Economy*, *67*, 323–348.

Nelson, R. R. (1993). *National innovation systems: A comparative analysis*. Oxford: Oxford University Press.

Nonaka, I., & Takeuchi, H. (1995). *The knowledge creating company*. Oxford: Oxford University Press.

OECD (1994). *The OECD jobs study*. Paris: OECD.

OECD (1996). *Transitions to learning economies and societies*. Paris: OECD.

OECD (1998). *Technology, productivity and job creation*. Paris: OECD.

OECD (2000). *Knowledge management in the learning society*. Paris: OECD.

Pavitt, K. (1984). Sectoral patterns of technical change: Towards a taxonomy. *Research Policy*, *13*, 343–373.

Pavitt, K. (1998). Technologies, products and organisation in the innovating firm: What Adam Smith tells us and Joseph Schumpeter doesn't. Paper presented at the DRUID 1998 Summer conference, Bornholm, June 9–11.

Penrose, E. (1959/1995). *The theory of the growth of the firm*. Oxford: Oxford University Press.

Polanyi, M. (1958/1978). *Personal knowledge*. London: Routledge & Kegan.

Rosenberg, N. (1982). *Inside the black box: Technology and economics*. Cambridge: Cambridge University Press.

Rothwell, R. (1977). The characteristics of successful innovators and technically progressive firms. *R&D Management*, *3*(7), 191–206.

Senge, P. (1990). *The fifth discipline: The art and practice of learning*. New York: Doubleday.

Shapiro, C., & Varian, H. R. (1999). *Information rules: A strategic guide to the network economy*. Boston: Harvard Business School Press.

Tomlinson, M. (1999). The learning economy and embodied knowledge flows in Great Britain. *Journal of Evolutionary Economics*, *9*(4), 431–451.

Tomlinson, M. (2001). A new role for business services in economic growth. In: D. Archibugi & B. Å. Lundvall (Eds), *The Globalizing Learning Economy*. Guildford and King's Lynn: Oxford University Press.

Verspagen, B. (1992). *Uneven growth between interdependent economies*. Maastricht: Faculty of economics and business administration.

von Hippel, E. (1988). *The sources of innovation*. New York and Oxford: Oxford University Press.

von Hippel, E. (1994). Sticky information and the locus of problem solving: Implications for innovation. *Management Science*, *40*, 429–439.

von Hippel, E., & Tyre, M. (1995). How learning by doing is done: Problem identification and novel process equipment. *Research Policy*, *24*(5).

Whitley, R. (1996). The social construction of economic actors: Institutions and types of firm in Europe and other market economies. In: R. Whitley (Ed.), *The Changing European Firm*. London: Routledge.

Winter, S. (1987). Knowledge and competence as strategic assets. In: D. Teece (Ed.), *The Competitive Challenge: Strategy for Industrial Innovation and Renewal*. Cambridge, MA: Ballinger Publishing Company.

Woolcock, M. (1998). Social capital and economic development: Toward a theoretical synthesis and policy framework. *Theory and Society, 2*(27), 151–207.

Ziman, J. (1979). *Reliable knowledge*. Cambridge: Cambridge University Press.

SOCIETAL INSTITUTIONS, LEARNING ORGANIZATIONS AND INNOVATION IN THE KNOWLEDGE ECONOMY

Alice Lam

ABSTRACT

This chapter seeks to explain how societal institutions, which may exist at the national or regional levels, shape the types of organizational learning predominating at the level of the firm. It focuses on education and training systems, and labour markets as key societal institutions shaping the micro-level processes of learning and knowledge creation within and between firms. The chapter argues that tacit knowledge, which is difficult to create and transfer in the absence of social interaction and labour mobility, constitutes a most important source of learning and sustainable competitive advantage in the knowledge economy. It looks at the cases of Japan, the high-technology clusters in the USA and U.K., and Denmark as illustrative examples.

1. INTRODUCTION

There is a considerable body of evidence pointing to country- or region- specific trajectories of innovation giving rise to and reproducing distinctive national or regional patterns of technological specialisation and industrial development (Patel & Pavitt, 1994). The national innovation systems (NIS) literature has sought to explain such variations by going beyond strictly technological explanations and to

Product Innovation, Interactive Learning and Economic Performance
Research on Technological Innovation and Management Policy, Volume 8, 43–67
ISSN: 0737-1071/doi:10.1016/S0737-1071(04)08003-5

link them to national institutional arrangements (Freeman, 1995; Lundvall, 1992; Nelson, 1993). Its main emphasis has however been on the science and technology systems, and the links between public R&D and corporate innovation activities. Although the NIS perspective acknowledges that the set of institutions influencing the technological capabilities of firms and nations extends far beyond those directly impinging on technological innovation, its analysis focuses on a rather narrow range of institutions. The "varieties of capitalism" theoretical perspective adopts a much broader view (Hall & Soskice, 2001; Hollingsworth & Boyer, 1997; Whitley, 1999, 2000). It links the innovation trajectories within the economy to the development of particular forms of organization and the orientation of national institutional frameworks. It argues that societies with different institutional arrangements develop and reproduce varied systems of economic organization with different economic, social and innovative capabilities in particular industries and sectors. They will, therefore, "specialise" in distinctive ways of structuring economic activities that privilege some sectors and discourage others. The "varieties of capitalism" perspective also gives attention to a much wider range of institutional factors, including the state agencies, the financial systems and, labour markets and training systems in shaping economic organization and the innovative capabilities of firms.

Both the NIS and "varieties of capitalism" literature emphasise the importance of macro-level societal institutions in shaping the innovative performance of firms and economies. However, neither approach has given adequate attention to how these are related to patterns of learning and knowledge accumulation at the micro-level. There is a missing link in the literature. This has hampered our understanding of the interdependencies between institutional environments and organizational forms and how they generate patterns of learning and innovation underpinning different types of technologies or industries. This chapter seeks to bridge the gap in the existing literature. It develops a typological framework linking the micro- and macro-level analysis to explain the links between learning patterns, organizational forms and societal institutions. The chapter focuses on the education and training system, and types of labour markets and careers as the key societal institutions shaping work organization and the knowledge base of the firm. Education and training shape the social constitution of "knowledge," and thus provide the basis of qualification, work status and job boundaries. As such, they influence the relative status and importance of different types of knowledge, and the nature of their interaction. The types of labour market determine the locus of learning, the incentives for developing different types of knowledge, and define the boundary and social framework within which individual learning interacts with collective learning. These institutional features interact with organizational structures and processes to generate different types of knowledge, patterns of learning and innovation. The econometric analysis comparing the U.K. and France in Chapter 8 by Lorenz, Michie and Wilkinson confirms that national institutions affect organizational structure.

This chapter argues that there are alternative models of learning and innovation in the knowledge economy. Because these models are socially embedded, they give rise to alternative patterns of "societal strategic advantage" in technological innovation and industrial specialisation. The chapter uses the examples of Japan, Denmark and the high-technology clusters in the U.S. and U.K. to illustrate the logic of institutionalised variation in patterns of learning and innovation. It argues, in line with the analysis in Chapter 2 by Lundvall, that tacit knowledge, which is difficult to create and transfer in the absence of social interaction and labour mobility, constitutes a most important source of learning and sustainable competitive advantage. Institutions that are able to imbue trust and social capital into firms and markets encourage interactive learning and are more likely to produce strong innovative capabilities.

2. KNOWLEDGE, LEARNING AND ORGANIZATIONAL EMBEDDEDNESS

The concept of embeddedness, as used by Granovetter (1985), refers to how behaviour and institutions are affected by networks of social relations. At the *cognitive level*, the notion of social embeddedness underlines the "tacit" nature of human knowledge and the dynamic relationship between individual and collective learning. At the *organizational level*, it focuses on how the organising principles of the firm shape the social structure of coordination, the behavioural routines and work roles of organizational members within which the knowledge of the firm is embedded. At the *societal level*, it draws attention to the way societal institutions shape organizational routines and coordination rules. The typology presented below seeks to integrate the different levels of analysis into a coherent framework, linking national specificities in the formation of skills and labour markets to micro-level processes of knowledge creation and learning within firms.

2.1. Knowledge Within the Firm: Characteristics and Types

The knowledge of the firm can be analysed along two dimensions: the epistemological and ontological (Nonaka & Takeuchi, 1995; Spender, 1996). The former concerns the modes of expression of knowledge, namely, Polanyi's distinction between explicit and tacit knowledge. The latter relates to the locus of knowledge that can reside at the individual or collective levels.

2.1.1. The Epistemological Dimension: Explicit vs. Tacit Knowledge

Human knowledge exists in different forms; it can be articulated explicitly or manifested implicitly (tacit). Polanyi (1962) argues that a large part of human knowledge is tacit. This is particularly true of operational skills and know-how acquired through practical experience. Knowledge of this type is action-oriented and has a personal quality that makes it difficult to formalise or communicate. Unlike explicit knowledge, which can be formulated, abstracted and transferred across time and space independently of the knowing subjects, the transfer of tacit knowledge requires close interaction and the build up of shared understanding and trust among them. The main methods for the acquisition and accumulation of these two knowledge forms also differ. Explicit knowledge can be generated through logical deduction and acquired by formal study. Tacit knowledge, in contrast, can be acquired only through practical experience in the relevant context, i.e. "learning-by-doing." Although it is possible to distinguish between explicit and tacit knowledge conceptually, they are not separate and discrete in practice. Nonaka and Takeuchi (1995) argue that new knowledge is generated through the dynamic interaction and combination of these two types. However, firms differ in their ability to foster such interaction, and the relative importance and status of the two types may also vary. More importantly, the creation of new knowledge in itself will necessarily involve the use and generation of tacit knowledge. Polanyi (1962, 1966) sees the origin of all human knowledge in individual intuition. The learning and innovative capability of an organization is thus critically dependent on its capacity to mobilise tacit knowledge and foster its interaction with explicit knowledge.

2.1.2. The Ontological Dimension: The Individual vs. Collective

Knowledge within the firm can reside at the level of the individual, or be shared among members of the organization. Individual knowledge is a repertoire of knowledge "owned" by the individual, which can be applied independently to specific types of tasks or problems. It is also transferable, moving with the person, giving rise to potential problems of retention and accumulation. In contrast, collective knowledge refers to the ways in which knowledge is distributed and shared among members of the organization. It is the accumulated knowledge of the organization stored in its rules, procedures, routines and shared norms, which guide the problem solving activities and patterns of interaction among its members. It can either be a "stock" of knowledge stored as hard data; or represent knowledge in a state of "flow" emerging from interaction.

Table 1. Knowledge Types.

	Individual	Collective
Explicit	Embrained knowledge	Encoded knowledge
Tacit	Embodied knowledge	Embedded Knowledge

2.1.3. Four Types of Knowledge

The explicit-tacit and individual-collective dimensions of knowledge give rise to four categories of knowledge: "embrained," "embodied," "encoded" and "embedded" knowledge (see also Blackler, 1995; Collins, 1993) (Table 1).

Embrained knowledge (individual and explicit) is dependent on the individual's conceptual skills and cognitive abilities. It is formal, abstract or theoretical knowledge. It is typically learnt through reading books and in formal education. Embrained knowledge enjoys a privileged social status within Western culture. The high occupational status of science compared with engineering reflects this.

Embodied knowledge (individual and tacit) is action oriented; it is the practical, individual types of knowledge on which Polanyi focused. It is learnt through experience and in training based on apprenticeship relations. Embodied knowledge is also context specific; it is "particular knowledge" which becomes relevant in light of the practical problem solving experience (Barley, 1996).

Encoded knowledge (collective and explicit) is shared within organizations through written rules and procedures, and formal information systems. It is formed in making explicit as much as possible of tacit knowledge. This is well illustrated by the principles of Scientific Management, which attempt to codify worker experiences and skills into objective scientific knowledge.

Embedded knowledge (collective and tacit) is built into routines, habits and norms that cannot easily be transformed into information systems. It is produced through social interaction among different members of the organization and supported by its shared cultural norms. Embedded knowledge is relation-specific and dispersed. It is an emergent form of knowledge capable of supporting complex patterns of interaction in the absence of written rules.

2.2. Knowledge Types and Organizational Forms

All organizations potentially contain a mixture of knowledge types, but their relative importance differs. Organizations may be dominated by one type of knowledge rather than another. To each of the knowledge forms there corresponds

Table 2.   Organizational Forms.

	Individual	Organization
Standardized work	Professional Bureaucracy (embrained knowledge)	Machine Bureaucracy (encoded knowledge)
Non-standardized work	Operating Adhocracy (embodied knowledge)	J-form Organization (embedded knowledge)

an ideal type organization. Drawing upon Mintzberg's (1979) classic typology of organizational forms and the work of Aoki (1988), and Nonaka and Takeuchi (1995) on the "Japanese model," we distinguish four ideal typical organizational forms, using two dimensions: the degree of standardisation of knowledge and work, and the dominant knowledge agent (individual or organization) (see Table 2). These different organizational configurations vary in their ability to mobilise tacit knowledge, resulting in different dynamics of learning and innovation.

2.2.1. Professional Bureaucracy and Embrained Knowledge
Professional bureaucracy (based upon individual and standardised knowledge) refers to a hierarchical complex organization where individual experts are highly specialised and where they operate within narrowly defined fields of knowledge. Such organizations may be especially efficient when the environment is stable and the need for high degree of professional precision is necessary to avoid big negative risks. However, its learning focus tends to be narrow and constrained within the boundary of formal specialist knowledge. Tacit knowledge is circumscribed and contained; it plays a limited role in a professional bureaucracy. Professional bureaucracies are not innovative and they will get into serious crisis when faced with radical change in the environment.

2.3. Machine Bureaucracy and Encoded Knowledge

Machine bureaucracy (with a knowledge base that is collective and standardised) refers to an organization where the dominating principles are specialisation, standardisation and control. This is an organizational form that is well suited for mass production in a stable environment. It may be said to be the ideal type of Fordist production where principles of Taylorist management are predominating. There is a clear dichotomy between the "execution" and "conception" of knowledge. The managers are the key agents responsible for translating individual knowledge into rules and procedures and for filtering information up and down the organizational hierarchy. A large part of tacit knowledge is naturally lost in the translation and aggregation process. It is a structure designed to deal with routine problems but is unable to cope with novelty or change.

2.3.1. Operating Adhocracy and Embodied Knowledge
Operating adhocracy (the knowledge base is individual and non-standardised) is a highly organic form of organization with little standardisation of knowledge or work process. It relies not only on the formal knowledge of its members, but draws its capability from the diverse know-how and practical problem solving skills embodied in the individual experts. It has a strong capacity for generating tacit knowledge through experimentation and interactive problem solving. Organizations engaged in providing non-standard, creative and problem solving services directly to the clients, such as professional partnerships, software engineering firms and management consultancies, are typical examples. In these organizations, formal professional knowledge may play only a limited role; a large part of the problem solving activities has very little to do with the application of narrow standardised expertise and more to do with the experience and capacity to adapt to new situations. Tacit knowledge is generated through interaction, trial-and-error and experimentation. It is a very flexible and innovative form of organization. The fluid structure and speed of change, however, creates problems in reproducing what has been learned into organizational memory. An operating adhocracy is also vulnerable to knowledge loss when individuals leave the organization.

2.3.2. J-Form Organization and Embedded Knowledge
The J-form organization (with a knowledge base that is collective and non-standardised) derives its capability from knowledge that is "embedded" in its operating routines, team relationships and shared culture. Its archetypal features are best illustrated by some of the big knowledge-intensive Japanese firms (Aoki, 1988; Nonaka, 1994; Nonaka & Takeuchi, 1995). It combines the stability and efficiency of a bureaucracy with the flexibility and team dynamics of an adhocracy. One fundamental characteristic is that it allows an organic, non-hierarchical team structure to operate in parallel with its formal hierarchical managerial structure. Shared values and organizational culture form the environment where interaction across functions and divisions take place in a systematic manner. This is an adaptive and innovative form of organization. It has a strong capacity to generate, diffuse and accumulate tacit knowledge continuously through "learning-by-doing" and interaction. It is good at generating incremental and continuous innovation. However, learning in the J-form organization is also potentially conservative. Its stable social structure and shared knowledge base may block radical innovation.

2.4. The Institutional Framework: National Systems of Competence Building and Innovation

Organizations are socially constituted and their knowledge configurations reflect this. The relative dominance of the different knowledge types, and the ability of an organization to harness tacit knowledge as a source of learning are powerfully influenced by the broader societal factors. Here, I focus on the education and training systems, and labour market organizations as key institutional features shaping the knowledge and learning pattern of firms. The implicit argument is that these institutional aspects and patterns of learning within firms are inter-dependent and they constitute a sub-system within the wider national innovation system. There is a process of mutual adaptation between knowledge types, organizations and institutions. Other national institutions such as the capital market also affect learning within firms but in a less direct way, and the process of mutual adaptation is less obvious.

2.4.1. Education and Training Systems: Narrow "Professional-Oriented" vs. Broad "Competence-Based"

On the education and training dimension, national systems can vary according to the relative importance they attach to different types of knowledge (e.g. formal academic knowledge vs. practical skills), the level of formal professional control over the nature and content of high-level expertise, and the distribution of competence among the entire workforce. A narrow "professional-oriented" system is characterised by the dominance of formal academic knowledge, a high degree of professional control over training programmes and an uneven two-tier distribution of competence: a well-developed higher education system for the professional elites while the majority of the workforce is poorly trained. Such a system gives rise to a narrow conception of knowledge, and the expertise acquired tends to be highly specialized and distant from problem-solving practices. For example, the system in the U.K. and USA can be described as narrow "professional-oriented." It displays a strong bias towards academic education and attaches little social status and economic credibility to practical skills, which acts as a disincentive for investment in this area. As a result, there is a widespread lack of formal intermediate skills and qualifications among the general workforce in these two countries (Buechtemann & Verdier, 1998). Such a system creates a bias in the use of human capital and labour market polarisation. It is associated with a bureaucratic form of work organization. The wide disparity in the educational backgrounds and skill levels between the different categories of the workforce generates knowledge discontinuities and social distance within firms. It reinforces the domination of formal knowledge over tacit skills.

In contrast, a broad "competence-based" education and training system recognises the value of both academic education and vocational training. It is characterised by a widespread and rigorous general and vocational education for a wide spectrum of the workforce. Such a system is more conducive to a decentralised mode of work organization. A more even distribution of competence among the workforce provides a better basis for interactive learning and the cultivation of tacit knowledge as a source of organizational capability. The cases of Germany, Japan and also Denmark are illustrative (Koike, 1995; Kristensen, 1996; Soskice, 1997). The systems in these countries accord relatively high social status to "practical experience," and recognise it as a source of competence and qualification. This encourages investment in vocational training, which has resulted in a good supply of intermediate skills. This enables firms to organise work in a more cooperative and decentralised manner, conducive to the transmission and mobilisation of tacit knowledge.

2.4.2. Labour Market and Careers: Occupational vs. Internal Labour Markets

Labour market organizations constitute another important dimension of national systems of competence building. They influence the knowledge base and learning capabilities of the firm in three main ways. First, these determine the extent to which expertise is developed outside or within the firm, and hence the relative importance of formal education and training institutions vis-a-vis employers in defining the knowledge base of the firm. Second, they determine career mobility and incentives for individual workers and the capability of the firm in acquiring and accumulating different types of knowledge. And third, they shape the individual's career and social identity and define the boundaries of learning. A broad distinction can be drawn between systems where career takes place through job shifts in an occupational labour market (OLM) and where the typical career is connected to a firm-based internal labour market (ILM). The former implies a higher degree of market control over skills and competence criteria and hence a stronger tendency towards formalisation and codification of knowledge across firms. In contrast, the latter allows a greater degree of individual firm control over the definition of expertise, leading to a lower level of standardisation of expertise around formal knowledge.

2.4.3. Occupational Labour Market (OLM)

An occupational labour market (OLM) offers a relatively high scope for job mobility. Knowledge and learning are embedded in an inter-firm career. Formal education and training play a much greater role in generating directly relevant occupational competence. The type of qualifications generated can be highly task-specific based on standardised, advanced "packaging" of knowledge and skills (e.g.

craft-oriented training or professional education). Alternatively, it can be a broad-based general education that can be adapted and applied across a wide variety of work settings and tasks. The former approach assumes that the task environment is relatively stable and the knowledge required can be codified and pre-packaged in initial training programmes. The latter, in contrast, rests on the notion that the task environment is uncertain and the knowledge required is fluid and emergent. It cannot be easily bundled into occupations or codified in advance, and hence requires a broad-based initial qualification to enable individuals to pursue a more varied and flexible approach to continuous learning.

In an OLM, knowledge and skills are owned by and embodied in the individuals; they are personal properties for career advancement. The transparency and transferability of the knowledge acquired is of paramount importance for inter-firm career mobility. Such career mobility relies on effective signals: dependable information about the type and quality of skills and knowledge that individuals have. This can be based either on public certification (institutional signals), or peer group recognition (information signals). The former approach works well provided that the knowledge and skills required can be easily identified and codified, i.e. bundled into specific occupations with a distinctive set of tasks or problems to which these skills and knowledge are applied (Tolbert, 1996). In situations where the tasks are highly fluid and unpredictable, and the knowledge used constitutes a large tacit component, institutional signals become insufficient and unreliable. This is because tacit skills cannot be easily codified; they can only be revealed through practice and work performance. Their transfer will have to rely heavily on social and professional networks based on shared industrial or occupational norms. In other words, the efficient transfer and accumulation of tacit knowledge in an OLM requires the support of a "containing social structure," for example, the formation of a community-based OLM based on localised firm networks and industry clusters (Saxenian, 1996). Social networks facilitate the "marketability" of cumulative personal tacit skills.

Learning within an OLM tends to be person-centred and market-oriented. It is rooted in the individual's professional and career strategy, and characterised by a greater degree of autonomy and latitude in the boundary and domains of learning (Bird, 1996). This can potentially enlarge the knowledge base of the firm and stimulate radical innovation. Moreover, firms operating in an OLM are able to reconstitute their knowledge base through hiring and firing. This allows them to respond flexibly to shifting market requirements and technological changes.

2.4.4. Internal Labour Market (ILM)
Internal labour markets are characterised by long-term stable employment with a single employer and career progression through a series of interconnected jobs

within a hierarchy. Knowledge and learning are embedded in an intra-firm career; a large part of the knowledge and work-related skills is generated through firm-specific on-the-job training (OJT). Formal knowledge acquired through education serves only as an entry qualification and provides the basis upon which work-related skills are built within the firm. The nature of the work organization and careers determines the quality and boundaries of learning through OJT. Where jobs are narrowly defined and careers are organised around hierarchies of jobs with tiered boundaries based on formal entry qualifications as in the case of a machine bureaucracy, OJT will tend to be narrow and job-specific. In contrast, an ILM can also be organised around broadly defined jobs and a continuous career hierarchy based on a common ranking system (e.g. the case of Japan). Progression to upper level positions is achieved, in this case, through accumulation of a wide range of skills and organizational experience. Formal knowledge plays only a limited role in defining competence criteria and entry to senior positions; the key emphasis is on the long-term accumulation of firm-specific skills and practical experience. OJT is broad-based and linked systemically with career progression. This increases the variety of experience and facilitates the generation of tacit knowledge. Job rotation also serves an important socialization function and helps to reduce social distance between different categories of the workforce. The close integration of OJT with career progression also gives individuals a strong incentive to accumulate knowledge through practical experience. The career hierarchy becomes a device for tacit knowledge creation and learning.

Learning within an ILM tends to be organizational-oriented and self-reinforcing. It evolves along the internal requirements of the firm, and is rooted in a firm-based career and organizational identity. The stability of personnel within an ILM facilitates the retention and accumulation of knowledge. Firms may display a strong capacity for incremental innovation and focus on developing a distinctive core competence.

2.5. Four Contrasting "Societal Models" of Competence Building and Innovation

The education and labour market dimensions are inextricably linked and there is an institutional logic defining their specific configurations. The interaction between these institutions gives rise to four contrasting "societal models" of competence building systems (see Table 3). The term "societal" requires some qualification. It is used in a broad sense to point out the effect of institutional environments on ways of organising knowledge and learning, rather than simply to emphasise

Table 3.   Societal Models of Competence Building Systems and Their
                                Innovative Potentials.

	Occupational Labour Market (OLM)	Internal Labour Market (ILM)
Narrow "professional-oriented" education and training	Professional model (professional bureaucracy, embrained knowledge) Narrow learning inhibits innovation	Bureaucratic model (machine bureaucracy, encoded knowledge) Slow learning, limited innovation
Broad "competence-based" education and training	Occupational community model (operating adhocracy, embodied knowledge) Dynamical learning, radical innovation	Organizational community model (J-form organization, embedded knowledge) Cumulative learning, incremental innovation

national distinctiveness. The institutional environment may exist at the national,
regional or sector levels.

The *professional model* refers to an economy where the education and training
is governed by professions and education institutions and where the typical career
is one of moving between different employers. It is one where practical experience
has a low status while codified and scientific knowledge is regarded as very
important. Broad segments of the population have insufficient training. In this
context there will be a predominance of hierarchical forms of organizations.
Learning will be narrow and take place mainly among those who have already
a strong formal education background. The professional model is most likely
to be found in Anglo-American countries where the norms of "professional
specialisation" and "elitism" remain deeply rooted.

The *bureaucratic model* is one where careers take place inside firms but where
hierarchies are stable and connected with formal training and access to codified
knowledge. It seeks to control and eliminate tacit knowledge and its capacity to
innovate is very limited. The bureaucratic model prevails in economies or firms
that seek to sustain competitive advantage through standardisation and price-based
competition.

The *occupational community model* is one where there is high inter-firm mobility
in the context of a region. Inter-firm mobility fosters social and professional
networks. Education and training institutions may be well connected with
professional networks and with firms in the region. Italian industrial districts and
Silicon Valley are examples of this kind of model. This kind of context is highly
flexible and promotes continuous innovation as well as radical innovation. The
occupational community is an institutional prerequisite for fostering and sustaining

the innovative capability of the "operating adhocracy." In a "boundaryless" open labour market, the operating adhocracy will be under pressure to bureaucratise because of the difficulties in accumulating and transferring tacit knowledge. The tacit knowledge creating capability of the operating adhocracy can only be sustained if it operates as a member of localised firm network. Such networks of social relationships provide the "social capital" and "information signals" needed to ensure the efficient transfer of tacit knowledge in an inter-firm career framework (Saxenian, 1996).

The *organizational community* model is characterised by a broad based egalitarian education system and with careers that take place inside the firm. Training takes place inside firms or in activities organised by the firm. This kind of context is well suited to promote permanent incremental innovation but it might be difficult to start up completely new activities in such an environment. It might be combined with financial systems that give priority to existing firms. Japan represents a typical example of this model.

Of course, what has been presented is a set of ideal types and in reality none of the categories are pure. The typology is a heuristic tool. It helps us to understand how institutionalised variation in learning and innovation may enable, or constrain firms to create different organizational forms and related innovation trajectories. It also suggests that there are alternative models for generating different types of innovation that may lead to societal strategic advantage in different industrial sectors.

3. LEARNING ORGANIZATIONS AND INNOVATION IN THE KNOWLEDGE ECONOMY

The emergence of the knowledge economy has led to a growing emphasis on the importance of learning and innovation as the key to economic success. One fundamental characteristic of the knowledge-based economy is the rapid pace of change and acceleration of knowledge creation. Although the use of information technology enhances the incentives and possibility to codify knowledge, the rapid pace of knowledge advancement has also created immense barriers to codification. The limit of codification is especially obvious in skills and knowledge transmission in labour markets. In the high-skills sector, knowledge is now moving too rapidly to be encoded and institutionalised into a stable set of occupations (Lam, 2001). Traditional institutional signals, for example, occupational qualifications have severe limits in providing dependable information about the quality and contents of skills. Codification is indeed too slow a process for the transmission of rapidly evolving knowledge. The high rate of change and growing complexity of knowledge required for innovation has reinforced the importance of tacit knowledge and collective learning in the knowledge economy.

The above analysis suggests that both the "organizational" and "occupational community" models are favourable to the creation and transmission of tacit knowledge. However, the different labour market structures generate some significant contrasts in their learning and innovation patterns. The occupational community model operates within a more open and fluid labour market which permits extensive hiring and firing, risk taking and the development of human resources in a "competency destroying" environment. In other words, it facilitates the diffusion of tacit knowledge within a broader boundary and varied contexts. It encourages experimentation and entrepreneurial behaviour and has the potential to achieve radical innovation. In contrast, the "organizational community" model derives its competitive strength from the cultivation of firm-specific core competence. It allows the accumulation of tacit knowledge within the boundary of the firm, and the continuous combination and recombination of firm-specific product and process technology with industry technology. Firms within the organizational community may develop a strong orientation to pursuing an incremental innovation strategy and do well in established technological fields. The strong emphasis on "competence preservation" within organizations, however, inhibits the creation of active labour markets, and thus making it difficult for firms to renew their knowledge base and compete successfully in rapidly developing new fields.

The sections that follow examine three concrete examples to illustrate the theoretical argument developed in this chapter. The divergent innovation trajectories pursued by Japanese and U.S. firms in the high-technology sectors give the most vivid illustration of the contrasts between the "organizational" and "occupational" community model of learning and innovation. The example of Denmark provides another interesting example of an innovation system with characteristics of the occupational community model that differs from the high-technology clusters discussed in the context of the Anglo-Saxon economies.

3.1. The Japanese "Organizational Community Model"

Michael Porter, in his book on the Competitive Advantage of Nations (1990), notes that Japan is a "study in contrasts" with some of the most internationally competitive industries found side by side with some of the most uncompetitive. Japan's institutional features and organizational capabilities have enabled firms to succeed in a range of industrial sectors through cumulative learning and incremental product and process innovation. Over the past three decades,

Japanese firms have gained international competitive advantage in those industries such as transport equipment, office machines, consumer electronics, electronic components for computing equipment and telecommunication hardware, to name a few of the most important ones (Kitschelt, 1991). The strength of Japan in these sectors stems from the capability of firms to develop highly flexible production systems through the close integration of shop-floor skills and experience, the tight linkages between R&D, production and marketing, and a unique innovation strategy based on continual modification and upgrading of existing components and products (Odargiri & Goto, 1996; Westney, 1993; Womack et al., 1990). In contrast, Japan finds it harder to excel in sectors that do not exclusively rely on incremental upgrading of system components (e.g. aerospace; supercomputers) and those in which fast-paced radical innovation are crucial for success (e.g. pharmaceuticals and biotechnology).

The Japanese competence building and innovation system exhibits some of the most quintessential features of the organizational community model. The economy is characterised by a high level of cooperation and organizational integration (Gerlach, 1992; Lazonick & West, 1998). This occurs through extensive long-term collaboration between firms in business groups and networks. Additionally, integration within large firms is particularly strong. Japanese social institutions and employment practices foster the close involvement of shop floor workers in the development of organizational capability. The successful state education system and large company driven networks equip the majority of workers with a high level of skills that employers respect and so can rely on them to contribute usefully to innovation activities. The internal labour market system is characterised not only by long-term attachment but also by well-organised training and job rotation schemes. These practices promote continuous skills formation through learning-by-doing and systematic career progression and, hence, a strong organizational capacity to accumulate knowledge and learn incrementally. Moreover, the approach to engineering skills formation fosters strong cross-functional teams and extensive human networks in product development (Lam, 1996, 1997). Japan has historically placed a high value on the importance of developing the practical skills of their engineers in the workplace. This is due, in part, to the fact that industrial development in Japan was historically based on imported technology, and Japanese engineers have played an important role in translating theoretical knowledge into concrete operational details for shop-floor workers (Morikawa, 1991). Japanese firms have always placed a strong emphasis on developing the on-site practical knowledge of their graduate engineers in order to facilitate knowledge transfer. Formal university education is less important than practical learning in the workplace. The university degree in Japan is far more general and broad-based than that in the U.S. or Britain. Young graduate engineers normally spend their initial years in a wide range of peripheral technical tasks and gradually accumulate their knowledge and expertise through assignment to a wider range of more complex tasks. The type of knowledge transmitted tends to be judgemental, informal and tacit.

The knowledge base of the Japanese firm is characterised by a high degree of tacitness and collective knowledge sharing. Japanese firms deliberately organise the process of product innovation in ways that take into account the importance of tacit knowledge and intensive interaction between skilled workers and engineers. The semi-autonomous project teams, comprising members from different functions, constitute one of the most important sources of learning and innovation in the Japanese firm (Nonaka & Takeuchi, 1995). The low social distance between engineers and production workers facilitates an interactive and overlapping approach to product development. The close linkage between R&D and production allows the early integration of downstream knowledge in product design and planning. Japanese firms, for example in the automobile and electronics industries, have been far more successful than their Western counterparts in incorporating manufacturing criteria into their design process (Clark & Funjimoto, 1991; Womack et al., 1990). This contributes to the quality advantage enjoyed by many Japanese firms, and a greater capacity for incremental product and process improvement. The Japanese organizational community approach to learning has allowed firms to thrive in "flexible mass production" characterised by constant variation and improvement of basically standardised products. The capacity of the organization to create new knowledge through synthesis and combination of the existing knowledge has enabled firms to gain competitive advantage in relatively "mature" technological fields characterised by rich possibilities of combinations and incremental improvements of existing components and products.

Conversely, organization-specific and path-dependent learning have constrained Japan's success in a number of leading-edge technological fields. Japan finds it harder to excel in sectors which do not exclusively rely on incremental upgrading of system components (e.g. aerospace; supercomputers) and those in which fast-paced radical innovation are crucial for success (e.g. pharmaceuticals and biotechnology). The human-network-based interaction and internal tacit knowledge transfer appear to be less effective in coordinating systems involving complex interactions among components. The insular nature of the Japanese human resource development system, and the absence of an active labour market for experienced scientific and managerial staff has constrained the boundary of explorative learning of firms. They also reduce the incentives for firms and individuals to engage in risky new projects. The organizational community model of learning limits the development of highly specialised scientific expertise, and makes it difficult to adopt radically new skills and knowledge needed for radical learning. The disappointing performance of Japanese firms in such fields as software and biotechnology (Anchordoguy, 2000; Henderson et al., 1999) during the 1990s may constitute evidence of the difficulties faced by Japanese firms in entering and innovating in rapidly developing new technological fields.

3.2. *Occupational Community Models: High-Technology Clusters in the U.S. and U.K.*

While the dominant institutions of the Anglo-Saxon economies have less capacity to foster the organization-oriented type of collective learning observed in Japanese firms, they have the potential to accommodate a more market-based and individually-driven form of collective learning and to compete successfully in the highest-skill sectors (Casper & Kettler, 2000; Finegold, 1999). Some of the world's most innovative and prosperous high-technology clusters can be found in the USA and also in the U.K. California's Silicon Valley and the high-technology clusters surrounding Cambridge in the U.K. are two of the most famous success stories. These high-technology clusters provide good examples that illustrate the processes of knowledge creation and dynamics of innovation underpinning the occupational community model of competence building. They also highlight the importance for the "adhocracy" of supportive local labour markets and other external institutions typically included in analyses of national, sectoral and regional innovation systems.

Silicon Valley has been an enormously successful and dynamic region characterised by rapid innovation and commercialisation in the fast growing technological fields. The core industries of the region include microelectronics, semiconductors, computer networking, both hardware and software, and more recently biotechnology. Firms operating in these industries undergo frequent reconfiguration and realignment in order to survive in a constantly changing environment marked by incessant innovation. The availability of a large pool of professional experts with known reputations in particular fields enables firms to quickly reconstitute their knowledge and skill base in the course of their innovative endeavours. The rapid creation of new start-up firms focusing on novel innovative projects, and the ease with which project-based firms are able to assemble and reassemble their teams of highly-skilled scientists and engineers to engage in new innovative activities are central to the technological and organizational dynamism of the region. The high rate of labour mobility and extensive hiring and firing creates a permissive environment for entrepreneurial start-ups and flexible reconfiguration of project teams and knowledge sources (Angels, 2000; Bahrami & Evans, 2000; Saxenian, 1996). Labour mobility within the context of a region plays a critical role in the generation of professional networks and facilities the rapid transmission of evolving new knowledge, a large part of which may be tacit. Such a regionally based occupational labour market provides a stable social context and shared industrial culture needed to ensure the efficient transfer of tacit knowledge in an inter-firm career framework. The shared context and industry-specific values within the regional community ensure that tacit knowledge will not be wasted when one changes employers, and this gives the individual a positive incentive to engage in tacit "know-how" learning (DeFillipi & Arthur, 1996). A regionally based labour market and networks of firms create a stable social structure to sustain collective learning and knowledge creation within and across firm boundaries. The creation of a wider social learning system amplifies the learning and innovative capability of the individual firms locating within the system.

The "Cambridge phenomenon" (Segal, Quince & Wicksteed, 1985, 2000) – a clustering of small, but successful high-technology firms around Cambridge University in the U.K. – has been likened to Silicon Valley. Many of the new companies in the area started as university spin-offs by the Cambridge graduates and academic staff. The process has been continuing since the 1960s and has led to the area being dubbed as "Silicon Fen." Similar to Silicon Valley, the success of the Cambridge cluster has been helped by having a world-class research university, a highly networked community, a dynamic labour market and an entrepreneurial business culture. In terms of activities, the development of a distinctive micro-cluster of dynamic SMEs in biotechnology and telecommunications has been particularly notable in recent years. It is argued that these, in part, reflect the national picture, but it may be especially rich in the Cambridge area (Segal, Quince & Wicksteed, 2000). The same is also true for software which has been a strong sector in the region since the mid-1980s and is, arguably, even more important today. Another important activity in the area is technology consultancy, a highly successful and distinctive feature of the Cambridge high-tech scene. Technology consultancies play a vital role in spinning-out a large number of new technology companies, many of which continue to maintain strong formal and informal links with their former consultancy employers. Both the spin-out process and the extensive involvement of these technology consultancies in the local network have contributed to the development of a risk-taking and entrepreneurial business culture in the region.

The Cambridge area is marked by the existence of a dynamic high-tech labour market that has grown rapidly and become spatially more extensive over the years. The success of the high-tech cluster has continued to work as a "pull" factor attracting many qualified scientists and engineers from outside to work in the area. The workforce in the area is highly skilled and is dominated by qualified scientists and engineers. The technology consultancies have played an especially important role in attracting experienced consultants and researchers from outside the area. The inflow and mobility of people have contributed to the diversity of the workforce and dynamism of the region. Empirical studies also suggest that there is an active process of inter-firm mobility in the region, involving the movement of entrepreneurs, consultants and researchers (Lam, 2000; Lawson et al., 1997; Segal, Quince & Wicksteed, 2000). This takes place primarily between consultancy and clients, and between a consultancy and its spin-outs. Labour mobility and the personal and professional networks formed as a result of shared experiences in the region are important factors contributing to knowledge transfer and a growing capacity of the region for technological innovation.

It is clear from these accounts that what underlies the innovative capability of the world's most dynamic technological regions is the processes of knowledge creation and collective learning sustained by a community-based social and professional network. Labour mobility plays a critical role in the generation of these networks and facilitates the transmission of rapidly evolving knowledge, a large part of which may be tacit. There is a strong link between tacit knowledge and regional competitive advantage (Lawson & Lorenz, 1999). The analysis also suggests that the processes of developing the capabilities of the individuals and organizational knowledge in the most dynamic technological sectors may be best served by an open labour market rooted in an occupational community. Finegold (1999) argues that in the turbulent, high-skill environments, the responsibility for skills formation and career development shifted from the firm to the individual and regional cluster itself. This is because for the engineers and scientists, who are the key drivers of knowledge creation in the region, company-based formal training is often not the main vehicle for learning. Instead, these people enter the labour market with a high level specialised qualification. They then continue to learn through project-based work and solving cutting-edge technical problems. Their wider personal and professional networks are another important source of learning. Inter-firm career mobility promotes learning and knowledge transfer. The willingness of the individuals to change firms, on which the collective learning process depends, is made possible by the guarantee of job opportunities elsewhere within the region.

3.3. Denmark as Another Example of an "Occupational Community Model"

Denmark represents another example of a national innovation and competence building system that displays many of the characteristic features of the occupational community model. And yet, the country has developed a pattern of industrial specialisation that deviates sharply from that of the high-tech large economies. Denmark is one of the smallest OECD countries with a population of just over five million. It has one of the highest levels of GDP per capita in the world. The country is especially successful in the production and export of low- or medium-technology goods. The main industries include meat, fish, diary products, wooden furniture and related machinery. Maskell et al. (1998) argue that the economic success of Denmark, and also of the other Nordic countries, demonstrate the possibilities for economies to generate a high level of prosperity while retaining a low-tech industrial specialisation. The main reason behind the competitive advantage of these small countries, according to the authors, lies in the capabilities of the social institutions to promote shared trust and interactive learning resulting in a set of "localised capabilities" which are tacit and difficult to imitate for outsiders.

Denmark is characterised as a "village economy" with a strong tradition for consensus-building deeply rooted in egalitarian values (Maskell et al., 1998). It is one of the most equitable societies in the world and rich in social capital. The business community has developed strong social networks and trade associations enabling intense interaction and information sharing between manufacturers and suppliers. Many Danish firms have also adopted a flexible form of organization with a strong emphasis on cross-functional collaboration (Lundvall & Christensen, 1999). Denmark has a well-developed state-funded vocational system resulting in a good supply of skilled workers. The flexible work system is highly dependent on the competence and contribution of these workers. These institutional features have enabled many small Danish manufacturers to develop a superior ability to create and accumulate knowledge internally and between firms through "learning-by-doing" and "learning-by-interacting." The success of the Danish furniture industry is a case in point (Maskell et al., 1998). The industry has attained the highest productivity in the EU. It has been able to maintain international competitiveness through product innovation rooted in a deep history of inter-firm relationships. The industry is dominated by strong networks of small firms engaged in frequent exchange of personnel, information and expertise. The industry is also strongly agglomerated which further enhances interactive learning and the development of localised capabilities. The success of the Danish furniture industry suggests that it is possible for a high-cost country to gain international competitiveness in a low-tech industry through continuous learning and innovation.

Danish firms are responsive to changes and have been able to combine technological changes with organizational innovation (Lund & Gjerding, 1996). Such responsive capacity is facilitated by an active labour market. It is suggested that inter-firm labour mobility in Denmark is as high, or possibly even higher than in the U.S. but by a more limited geographical spread (Lundvall & Christensen, 1999). The willingness of Danish workers to change jobs is buffered by a good social security net that reduces the costs and risks of job changes. Such social protection also contributes to the positive attitudes among the workers and trade unions to technical and organizational changes. In addition, Denmark has developed an extensive and highly regarded public system for continuous training for adults. All these institutional factors have made it possible to combine a fluid and open labour market with a high level of trust and cooperation that promote the development of learning organizations.

Although Denmark is especially successful in the relatively low- and medium-technology sectors, it also has some successful niche products in the high-technology sectors such as mobile telecommunications and pharmaceuticals. However, the dominant strategy has been to absorb and use technologies from abroad and the approach to innovation is incremental. This can be partly attributed to the fact that Denmark does not have a strong science base and the interaction between the private sector and universities is not well developed. Moreover, the majority of the academically trained workforce has historically opted for employment in the public sector. On the whole, the Danish system of innovation and competence building is geared towards competence-intensive low- and medium-tech sectors. It is less well developed for the large-scale science-based industries.

The Danish "occupational community model" of competence building generates a learning pattern that is more similar to that found in Japan rather than in the high technology clusters in the U.S. or U.K. The strong ability of Danish firms to learn collectively is rooted in the shared culture and "village like" institutions of a small country. Such pre-existing social solidarity has shaped the formal social and economic institutions leading to a high level of cooperation and trust in the society as a whole. The whole country can be considered as a region like the industrial districts in the larger economies.

However, an important characteristic feature of "village-like" institutions is the exclusion of outsiders, as in the case of the corporate community in Japan. The Danish labour market is not open to immigrant workers. This is in stark contrast to the high technology community in Silicon Valley that builds on an extremely open and diverse labour market with a truly international character. Cohen and Fields (1999, p. 126) describe the foreign workforce as "a vital transmission belt, diffusing technology and market knowledge, sometimes establishing offshore facilities that seed new districts and serve as connectors into the Valley." The Silicon Valley labour market is local but borderless. This, arguably, is one of the region's most valuable assets and the main source of dynamism. In contrast, the localised learning capability of Danish firms is embedded in a truly local labour market with less scope for radical renewal.

4. CONCLUSIONS

The analysis presented in this chapter illustrates the logic of institutionalised variation in patterns of learning and innovation. It also discusses how such variation may enable, or constrain regions or countries to create organizational forms needed for generating the types of innovation associated with different technologies or industrial sectors. The chapter argues that tacit knowledge, which is difficult to create and transfer in the absence of social interaction and labour mobility, constitutes a most important source of learning and sustainable competitive advantage in an increasingly globalised knowledge-based economy. Learning builds on trust and social capital. Institutions that are able to imbue these elements into firms and markets encourage interactive learning and are more likely to produce strong innovative capabilities. The learning capability of Japanese firms is rooted in strong organizational integration and employee commitment. Social capital is built on long-term obligational relationships within and between firms. In Denmark, the networked learning organizations are supported by a strong sense of communal trust and social solidarity that has become institutionalised in formal mechanisms for collective decision-making. In the Anglo-Saxon economies characterised by liberal market institutions and professional individualism, the creation of regional clusters appears to be critical for promoting collective learning rooted in professional and inter-firm innovation networks.

There are a variety of approaches to promoting learning and innovation. They appear to generate and reproduce distinctive regional or national patterns of technological specialisation. The Japanese "organizational community" model continues to orient major Japanese firms towards adopting high-quality incremental innovation strategies and sustaining competitiveness in mature technological fields. Japan may find it difficult to develop a "societal strategic advantage" (Biggart & Orru, 1997) in areas characterised by rapid and disruptive changes. The R&D globalisation strategies adopted by Japanese firms in the science-based sectors appear to have limited effect in altering the established learning patterns and innovative trajectories (Lam, 2003). In contrast to Japan, the Anglo-Saxon "occupational community" model can better accommodate a science-driven, entrepreneurial approach to innovation and perform well in sectors in which radical learning is important. A major underlying structural weakness of this model, however, is the marked segmentation between professional and production workers, and the bias of the competence building system in favour of the interests of high-technology firms (Angels, 2000). Denmark, on the other hand, has developed a specialisation pattern in low- and medium-technology sectors with a focus on an incremental innovation strategy. The Danish case also suggests that an innovation-driven redeployment of competencies can be organised more collectively by public agency action with emphasis on workforce vocational training and lifelong learning.

Societies with different institutional arrangements will continue to develop a variety of organizational forms and learning strategies that privilege some sectors and discourage others. Learning and innovation are strongly embedded in societal institutions. Societal comparative advantage therefore resides in the "strategic fit" (Sorge, 1991) between institutionalised patterns of organising and creating knowledge and the requirements arising from specific niches.

REFERENCES

Anchordoguy, M. (2000). Japan's software industry: A failure of institutions? *Research Policy, 29*, 391–408.

Angels, D. P. (2000). High-technology agglomeration and the labour market: The case of Silicon Valley. In: K. Martin (Ed.), *Understanding Silicon Valley: The Anatomy of an Entrepreneurial Region* (pp. 125–140). Stanford: Stanford University Press.

Aoki, M. (1988). *Information, incentives and bargaining in the Japanese economy.* Cambridge: Cambridge University Press.

Bahrami, H., & Evans, S. (2000). Flexible recycling and high-technology entrepreneurship In: K. Martin (Ed.), *Understanding Silicon Valley: The Anatomy of an Entrepreneurial Region* (pp. 166–189). Stanford: Stanford University Press.

Barley, S. R. (1996). Technicians in the workplace: Ethnographic evidence for bringing work into organization studies. *Administrative Science Quarterly, 41*(3), 404–441.

Biggart, N. W., & Orru, M. (1997). Societal strategic advantage: Institutional structure and path dependence in the automotive and electronics industries in East Asia. In: Ayse, Bugra, Usdiken & Behul (Eds), *State, Market and Organizational Form.* Berlin: Walter de Gruyter.

Bird, A. (1996). Careers as repositories of knowledge: Considerations for boundaryless careers. In: M. B. Arthur & D. M. Rousseau (Eds), *The Boundaryless Career: A New Employment Principle for a New Organizational Era* (pp. 150–168). New York: Oxford University Press.

Blackler, F. (1995). Knowledge, knowledge work and organizations: An overview and interpretation. *Organization Studies, 16*(6), 1021–1046.

Buechtemann, C. F., & Verdier, E. (1998). Education and training regimes: Macro-institutional evidence. *Revue d'economie politique, 108*(3), 29–320.

Casper, S., & Kettler, H. (2000). National institutional frameworks and the hybridization of entrepreneurial business models within the German and U.K. Biotechnology Sectors. DRUID Summer Conference, Aalborg.

Collins, H. M. (1993). The structure of knowledge. *Social Research, 60*(1), 95–116.

Clark, K. B., & Fujimoto, T. (1991). *Product development performance.* Boston: Harvard Business School Press.

Cohen, S. S., & Fields, G. (1999). Social capital and capital gains in Silicon Valley. *California Management Review, 41*(2), 108–130.

DeFillipi, R. J., & Arthur, M. B. (1996). Boundarlyess contexts and careers: A competency-based perspective. In: M. B. Arthur & D. M. Rousseau (Eds), *The Boundaryless Career: A New Employment Principle for a New Organizational Era* (pp. 116–131). New York: Oxford University Press.

Finegold, D. (1999). Creating self-sustaining high-skill ecosystems. *Oxford Review of Economic Policy, 15*(1), 60–81.

Freeman, C. (1995). The 'national system of innovation' in historical perspective. *Cambridge Journal of Economics, 19*, 5–24.

Gerlach, M. L. (1992). *Alliance Capitalism: The social organization of Japanese Business.* Berkeley: University of California Press.

Granovetter, M. (1985). Economic action and social structure: The problem of embeddedness. *American Journal of Sociology, 91*(3), 481–510.

Hall, P., & Soskice, D. (2001). *Varieties of capitalism: The institutional foundations of comparative advantage.* Oxford: Oxford University Press.

Henderson, R., Orsenigo, L., & Rosenberg, N. (1999). The pharmaceutical industry and the revolution in molecular biology: Interactions among scientific, institutional, and organisational change. In: D. C. Mowery & R. R. Nelson (Eds), *Sources of Industrial Leadership* (pp. 267–311). Cambridge: Cambridge University Press.

Hollingsworth, J. R., & Boyer, R. (Eds) (1997). *Contemporary capitalism: The embeddedness of institutions.* Cambridge: Cambridge University Press.

Kitschelt, H. (1991). Industrial governance structures, innovation strategies, and the case of Japan: Sectoral or cross-national comparative analysis? *International Organization, 45*(4), 454–493.

Kristensen, P. H. (1996). On the constitutions of economic actors in Denmark: Interacting skill containers and project coordinators. In: R. Whitley & P. H. Kristensen (Eds), *The Changing European Firm: Limits to Convergence.* London: Routledge.

Koike, K. (1995). *The economics of work in Japan.* Tokyo: LTCB International Library Foundation.

Lam, A. (1996). Engineers, management and work organization: A comparative analysis of engineers' work roles in British and Japanese electronics firms. *Journal of Management Studies, 33*(2), 183–212.

Lam, A. (1997). Embedded firms, embedded knowledge: Problems of collaboration and knowledge transfer in global cooperative ventures. *Organization Studies, 18*(6), 973–996.

Lam, A. (2000). Higher education and industrial innovation: A case study of TTP communications in Melbourne Science Park (Cambridge). TSER report for the European Commission.

Lam, A. (2001). Changing R&D organisation and innovation: Developing the new generation of R&D knowledge workers. In: *The Contribution of European Socio-Economic Research to the Benchmarking of RTD Policies in Europe.* DGV, Brussels: European Commission.

Lam, A. (2003). Organizational learning in multinationals: R&D networks of Japanese and U.S. MNEs in the U.K. *Journal of Management Studies, 40*(3), 674–703.

Lawson, C., & Lorenz, E. (1999). Collective learning, tacit knowledge and regional innovative capacity. *Regional Studies, 33*(4), 305–328.

Lawson, C., Moore, B., Keeble, D., Lawton Smith, H., & Wilkinson, F. (1997). Inter-firm links between regionally clustered high-technology SMEs: A comparison of Cambridge and Oxford innovation networks. Working Paper 65. Cambridge: Cambridge University.

Lazonick, W., & West, J. (1998). Organization integration and competitive advantage. In: G. Dosi, D. J. Teece & J. Chytry (Eds), *Technology, Organization and Competitiveness* (pp. 247–288). Oxford: Oxford University Press.

Lundvall, B. Å. (1992). *National systems of innovation: Towards a theory of innovation and interactive learning.* London: Pinter Publishers.

Lundvall, B. Å., & Christensen, J. L. (1999). Extending and deepening the analysis of innovation systems: With empirical illustrations from the DISKO-project. Paper for DRUID Conference on National Innovation Systems, Rebild.

Lund, R., & Gjerding, A. N. (1996). The flexible company: Innovation, work organisation and human resource management. DRUID Working Paper 96-17. Aalborg: Danish Research Unit for Industrial Dynamics.

Maskell, P., et al. (1998). *Competitiveness, localised learning and regional development: Specialisation and prosperity in small open economies.* London: Routledge.

Mintzberg, H. (1979). *The structure of organizations.* Englewood Cliffs, NJ: Prentice-Hall.

Morikawa, H. (1991). The education of engineers in modern Japan: An historical perspective. In: H. Gospel (Eds), *Industrial Training and Technological Innovation* (pp. 136–147). London: Routledge.

Nelson, R. (1993). National innovation systems: A comparative analysis. Oxford: Oxford University Press.

Nonaka, I. (1994). A dynamic theory of organizational knowledge creation. *Organization Science, 5,* 14–37.

Nonaka, I., & Takeuchi, H. (1995). *The knowledge creating company.* New York: Oxford University Press.

Odargiri, H., & Goto, A. (1996). *Technology and industrial development in Japan.* Oxford: Clarendon Press.

Patel, P., & Pavitt, K. (1994). Uneven and (divergent) technological accumulation among advanced countries: Evidence and a framework of explanation. *Industrial and Corporate Change, 3*(3), 759–787.

Polanyi, M. (1962). *Personal knowledge: Towards a post-critical philosophy.* New York: Harper Torchbooks.

Polanyi, M. (1966). *The tacit dimension.* New York: Anchor Day Books.

Porter, M. E. (1990). *The competitive advantage of nations.* London: MacMillan.

Saxenian, A. (1996). Beyond boundaries: Open labour markets and learning in the Silicon Valley. In: M. B. Arthur & D. M. Rousseau (Eds), *The Boundaryless Career: A New Employment Principle for a New Organizational Era* (pp. 23–29). New York: Oxford University Press.

Segal, Quince & Wicksteed. (1985). *The Cambridge phenomenon, the growth of high technology industry in a university town.* Cambridge: SQW.

Segal, Quince & Wicksteed. (2000). *The Cambridge phenomenon revisited.* Cambridge: SQW.

Sorge, A. (1991). Strategic fit and the societal effect: Interpreting cross-national comparisons of technology, organization and human resources. *Organization Studies, 12*(2), 161–190.

Soskice, D. (1997). German technology policy, innovation, and national institutional frameworks. *Industry and Innovation, 4,* 75–96.

Spender, J. C. (1996). Making knowledge the basis of a dynamic theory of the firm. *Strategic Management Journal, 17,* 45–62.

Tolbert, P. S. (1996). Occupations, organizations, and boundaryless careers. In: M. B. Arthur & D. M. Rousseau (Eds), *The Boundaryless Career: A New Employment Principle for a New Organizational Era* (pp. 331–349). New York: Oxford University Press.

Whitley, R. (1999). *Divergent capitalisms: The social structuring and change of business systems.* Oxford: Oxford University Press.

Whitley, R. (2000). The institutional structuring of innovation strategies: Business systems, firm types and patterns of technical change in different market economies. *Organization Studies, 21*(5), 855–886.

Westney, E. (1993). Country patterns in R&D Organization: The United States and Japan. In: B. Kogut (Ed.), *Country Competitiveness: Technology and the Organising of Work* (pp. 36–53). Oxford: Oxford University Press.

Womack, J. P., Jones, D. T., & Roos, D. (1990). *The machine that changed the world.* New York: Rawson.

THE MANAGED INTERACTION BETWEEN INNOVATION AND LEARNING AND A COMPLEMENTARY PERSPECTIVE

Reinhard Lund

ABSTRACT

This chapter treats the management's understanding of the potential of managing interaction between product innovation and learning. The chapter draws its empirical results from interviews with the management, project leaders, and other employees working on product innovations in five manufacturing firms visited three to four times during 2001–2002. It is shown that the managed interaction between innovation and learning is promoted by explicit strategic consideration and most strongly by a knowledge management strategy. Important positive and negative structural conditions are highlighted.

1. INTRODUCTION

Organizational studies of product development were for a long time concentrated upon how the innovation process ought to be carried out to get success followed up by other studies of how the process was actually carried out (Cooper, 1993; Van de Ven et al., 1999). It is a later interest how firms may use product

Product Innovation, Interactive Learning and Economic Performance
Research on Technological Innovation and Management Policy, Volume 8, 69–98
Copyright © 2004 by Elsevier Ltd.
ISSN: 0737-1071/doi:10.1016/S0737-1071(04)08004-7

development as an important base for learning to be used during ongoing and future innovations.

The Danish project on Product innovation, Interactive learning, and Economic performance (PIE) (www.business.auc.dk/pie) aims at analysing elements which can enhance the understanding of how firms accumulate competence in connection with innovation processes and at the same time determine which factors are decisive for the success of product innovation. The study's focus upon *interactive learning* means that the PIE research interest centres around management's approach to the interaction within the firm as well as between the firm and its external partners.

A specific dimension of this interactive learning concerns the *managed* interaction between knowledge for innovation and learning from innovation as a management strategy. This chapter treats factors, which have been found to promote or hamper the management's efforts to activate innovative activities, accumulate learning from innovation, and determine measures promoting the managed interaction between innovation and learning. This interaction mirrors what March (1991) described as exploitation and exploration, respectively as was clear from Chapter 2 by Lundvall, knowledge has since long been recognised as crucial to innovation, and interactive learning is key in many innovation processes (as is argued in more detail in the next chapter by Lundvall & Vinding). Whereas most innovation studies see knowledge as a precondition for innovation, the focus in this chapter is on the knowledge generated by means of the innovation process, and on how such knowledge can be actively accumulated and stimulated. In this way, the chapter relates to the knowledge management literature. In Chapter 6, it is discussed how such learning may be organised and what are the roles of key actors in this. Hargadon and Fanelli (2002) have confronted innovation and learning by acknowledging their *complementarity*[1] and have discussed the importance of combining the innovation perspective and the learning perspective. Therefore, the results of the PIE-project can also be understood within such a complementary perspective and compared with the main conclusions of the Hargadon and Fanelli study.

2. INTERACTIVE LEARNING AND THE IDEA OF COMPLEMENTARITY BETWEEN MODELS OF INNOVATION AND MODELS OF LEARNING

2.1. The PIE-Study of Interactive Learning in Connection with Innovation

The data for this study comprise both data from a quantitative study and data from a qualitative study of innovation and learning. The qualitative study investigated product innovation in 11 small and middle sized (100–400) firms of which five form the empirial basis for this chapter. The five firms comprise two machinery firms one of which delivered its machines to the food industry (F) and the other to metal and transport (B), one metal firm (E), one firm producing for the graphical trade (H) and one electronics firm (D). Four of the firms had small development divisions with only eight to 10 persons, whereas the graphical firm employed around 40. In each of the firms, people from top management, persons responsible for major functions, project leaders and in a couple of the firms also technicians and a few workers were interviewed. The interviewing took place January 2000–December 2001 according to a longitudinal design and comprised three to four visits by the researchers. In each of the firms two development projects were followed in more detail besides investigating the firms' product innovation activities in general. All in all, the visits to the five firms implied that 29 persons were interviewed one or more times for about an hour, which resulted in 49 interviews.

A reservation as to the data and the related analysis has to be made. The investigated innovations refer to major changes of product features, which place them in between radical innovations and mere trivialities. Priority has been given to understanding the management's thinking as expressed during interviews (focussed upon business activities and social, technical and commercial behaviour related to product innovation) without trying to explore in depth how the interviewees constructed their world or were driven by more or less unconscious motives. Furthermore, it is not problematised how knowledge transfer may raise many intricate questions regarding common understanding, knowledge capacity etc. The aim has been to highlight the benefits and traps connected to an organized cycle of activating knowledge for innovation and drawing knowledge from innovation.

2.2. Hargadon's and Fanelli's Study Based on the Complementarity Perspective

Hargadon and Fanelli (2002, p. 291) juxtapose the innovation and organizational learning literatures. They contain two different theoretical perspectives on learning respectively based upon empirical knowledge of action as found in blueprints, products and processes and tacit knowledge of possibilities represented by the beliefs and values of organizational participants based upon their experiences. Their knowledge concept points to the same important knowledge dimensions as Christensen (2003) who distinguish between knowledge of perception and knowledge of experience. Within these perspectives empirical knowledge can develop into latent knowledge by reflexive experience, and latent knowledge into empirical knowledge by "the application of knowledge latent in individuals to generate a physical or social artifact." They argue that studies using only one of these perspectives miss important understandings of knowledge. Focus upon innovation underplays how the necessary knowledge is created, and focus upon learning neglects how the accumulated knowledge may be used in new ways. To overcome these deficiencies of each of the approaches they point to the *principle of complementarity* as known from physics to acknowledge for the dual characteristics of knowledge in organizations. So, taking a complementarity approach leads them to study the interaction between learning and innovation. This complementary perspective is used in two case studies of product development consultants in the United States, which document the fruitfulness of combining the dual perspectives. Hargadon's and Fanelli's studies result in the following discussion and conclusion.

Their first conclusion is that the complementary perspective demonstrates the mutual dependence between the consultancies and their clients. The consultancies need the clients for generating possibilities i.e. the learning perspective, and the clients need the consultancies to activate a broader input of tacit knowledge i.e. the innovation perspective. This conclusion is explicitly seen in relation to the balance, which has to be maintained between the single-mindedness necessary for action and the diversity conducive for creativity.

The second conclusion concerns the interrelationship between individual and social knowledge. Hargadon and Fanelli state that the complementary perspective shows how individual action and its individual tacit knowledge by transformation to an artefact such as a new product becomes collective knowledge by social interactions between individuals. This aspect was also discussed in Chapter 2 by Lundvall.

The third conclusion points to the contribution of the complementary perspective based on its cycle between internal tacit knowledge and external empirical knowledge. Activation of internal knowledge can be fertilized by the surroundings, but drawing upon the environment demands some specific prior knowledge. The generation of new knowledge depends upon "the cyclic interaction between the two," between the "energy" that resides in latent knowledge and the "matter" of empirical knowledge" (Hargadon & Fanelli, 2002, p. 300).

Hargadon's and Fanelli's contribution can be crystallized by Fig. 1.

After this presentation of the Danish and U.S. studies I shall go through the following steps similar to the complementary perspective upon product development and learning. First it is seen how product innovation according to the PIE-study implies processes by which the management and the employees integrate diffused information and convert latent knowledge in a context of promoting factors and constraining barriers. Next it is presented how the Danish management and employees in some instances seem to use product innovations as a source of

Within firm:
Activation of (latent) knowledge >
> PRODUCT INNOVATION and EMPIRICAL KNOWLEDGE >
> Possibilities for learning – New (latent) knowledge >
> Activation of (latent) knowledge
> PRODUCT INNOVATION and EMPIRICAL KNOWLEDGE>
Conditioned by constraints and furthered by external relationships

Fig. 1. The Relationship Between Product Innovation and Knowledge.

learning and latent knowledge, but are constrained by certain barriers. Thereafter it is described to which extent the Danish management directly manages the interaction between innovation and learning. A number of quotations from the interviewing illustrate the analysis. These quotations are edited for the sake of briefness and clarification. The results in this section are systematized along major organizational dimensions of the interaction between innovation and learning. The article ends with conclusions concerning the Danish findings and a comparison with the results by Hargadon and Fanelli (2002).

3. FROM INFORMATION AND KNOWLEDGE TO PRODUCT INNOVATION

An analysis of the Danish cases shows the management's conscious occupation with activating information and knowledge from both external and internal sources for the benefit of product innovation. Similarly project leaders gathered information and knowledge from the external environment as well as information and knowledge from colleagues. In general, technicians and workers took active part in this process contributing with their experiences. The following analysis of the interviews demonstrates a number of initiatives taken by the actors, which strengthened the application of knowledge and enhanced the product development process, but barriers were also found. Firstly, the analysis focuses upon promoting factors related to the activation of external knowledge, internal formal structuring for the benefit of more information as well as the acknowledgement of informal relationships. Secondly, barriers are highlighted with regard to strategy, structures and processes.

3.1. Promoting Factors for the Activation of Knowledge

Regarding *external relations*, top directors, development managers and sales/marketing managers told the researcher that visits to potential customers, fairs and information from sales and servicing people gave information input for new product ideas. Other information could be collected from other firms which themselves contacted the visited firms when wanting some help (interview reference code D010209:3; E0041113:3-4&9). A specific method mentioned by a product manager was to discuss focussed ideas about new products with selected customers.

> Product manager: In connection with some selected customers and discussions with them . . . I say you have these things, . . . is there a basis for sale if we do it in this way. This is an example of our increased marketing focus (D3010209:6).

Regarding *internal structures and processes*, the management had introduced a stage-gate procedure (Cooper, 1993), which furthered the integration of explicit and tacit knowledge situated within the different functions. Concerning the gate's role a supply manager's explanation was as follows.

> Supply manager: You take a look at the product, and the product responsible men go through the product. You look at it from an aesthetic and a functional point of view. Find out whether something has to be changed. You behave nearly as a consumer. Production takes part and tells you how the product should look like to get smoothly through production. The idea is to be frank and find the weak spots before the consumers get the product (E2000510:6).

Behind this lies the understanding of product innovation as implying innovative behaviour from not only development but also sales and marketing, production and distribution. As stated by a development manager, the product innovation was more and more seen as a concern across the various functions.

> Product development manager: Product development is everything from the first ideas from the market to the interaction with production, test activities, sales, sending and how you control the logistics afterwards. These things we did not speculate about previously. Today they are defined in the project (D091812:6-7). A specific reason for integrating knowledge within the firm can be seen by the change in the concept of product. To the extent a product had to be closely serviced by service people after sales, the knowledge of service was of much importance for design (H011112:5).

In one of the visited firms, a manager included external partners in its efforts to activate information and knowledge for innovation.

> Technical director: We believe that integrated product development must go beyond the firm, so we include to a wide extent the main suppliers. We are not producing, we outsource, we are pure assembly (H0051614:2).

By setting up an integrated procedure for product development, other functions than design and technique got a clearer picture of when to deliver an input and take responsibility for specific tasks e.g. writing the user manual (D3010209:8).

Also by thinking about the functional responsibilities in connection with input to innovation, it was possible to improve this input. An engineering manager succeeded in changing his input.

> Development manager: The new engineering manager wanted to have an influence upon product development from the start.... He has some production ideas, which we can get integrated in the product development from the start. Before, development alone made the prototypes. He said he would be glad to join because then he got a basis for experiences (D4011030:1).

Concerning influence from the firm structure upon the activation of knowledge, it could be seen that the managers in the visited firms favoured a structure, which contributed to widespread communication and little hierarchy.

> Development manager: We use each other very broadly. I will say we use the total organization. We use our welding people, our production people (E0041113:3).

A product leader in another firm referred to his development group.

> Product leader: We have a forum where we can talk with each other and draw upon each other's expertise . . . we take a brainstorming around the table . . . (D32714:1).

Communication was linked to easy physical access to colleagues.

> Product leader: We help each other . . . We are sitting together physically, it does not take many minutes to get contact. In case of serious problems we have our project meetings . . . or if the professional expertise is found in other projects, we will talk to those people (B2010118:11).

Furthermore production input was strengthened by having the workers' participation at gate meetings.

> Development manager: We have recently involved the skilled workers in gate meetings . . . to get them involved at an earlier time (D4011030:2).

A production manager at the same firm developed this point.

> Production manager: We have learnt from experience, it is very new, we have had to acknowledge that we must include some of our skilled people in production for the sake of their influence upon test equipment and the like (D4011030:1).

In another firm a development manager expressed his recognition of the workers' participation in gate meetings and their creativity in the following way.

> Development manager: The production participates. We include all the links in the development process. We look at the design. We have had fantastic luck by having shop floor people at the meetings. The man who has done welding for 30 years, he knows how the product should look. They have contributed to a decrease in unit costs by putting knowledge from production into design. We have to recognize that we have production people who are able to think rather creatively (E0041113:6).

In connection with the integration of knowledge, the problem of timing was important for the actors' ability to make use of their knowledge as an input for the innovation process.

> Product leader: We have an integrated product development model which we use ... We try to incorporate people at meetings at an early stage so they can get more influence instead of getting an instruction when they have to work on the product at a later stage (D032714:5) ... some thoughts will always appear (across the functions, rl) and which have to be looked upon, or investigated, or tried out (D091814:2).

A production planner pointed to the lack of knowledge among developers concerning lay out. He argued for an early involvement of planning in the product development process.

> Production planner: We want to join the discussions as early as possible because we do not expect the developers to have experiences with production, but this is what we have, so we can see to it that the process goes on smoothly when it comes to production (E2001005:1).

Besides formal meetings, *informal relationships* had their importance for the activation of latent knowledge to be used for product innovation. Project leaders in a couple of visited firms pointed out that the actors showed different behaviours regarding the blending of formal and informal input.

> Project leader: You find much informal talk. For myself I go directly to the sales people and talk with them. It differs how you make it. I am not the person who calls upon many big meetings and the like. I prefer to take direct contact to the persons who I know can give the answers (D3010209:3).

In another firm the product leader similarly drew upon his informal network.

> Product leader: There are both formal and informal reviews. You have formal meetings, but in other cases when I have made a certain part of the new product I will go to the operator and ask him to do the part and afterwards talk with him about the problems (E2001005:11).

3.2. Barriers for the Activation of Knowledge

During the interviews a number of hindrances for the use of knowledge concerning innovation were mentioned by the managers, project leaders and other participants of the innovation processes. In some cases the managers would also point to measures, which could reduce the barriers.

Yet, the first barrier to be mentioned was part of the management's strategy and intended to be upheld. So, some acquired knowledge had to be ignored because its use for innovation would interfere with the product strategy or bring the firm into unwanted conflicts with competitors or suppliers.

Department manager C: The product committee evaluates the project ideas to see whether they are in keeping with the product strategy. If they are not in keeping with the product strategy, they have to be approved by the top management to get started (H0091913:2).

Even though cooperation with customers had certain advantages, it might also have disadvantages because the customer might get too much influence and reduce the creativity.

Department manager C: We have had bad experiences with the inclusion of a customer when working on a new concept. Because it may be subject to the customer's terms, and we forget what we really want to do . . . we might loose focus (H0091913:6).

When thinking upon which knowledge could be activated for a given new product innovation the firms had to take reactions from competitors into consideration including the observance of patents.

Project manager: At a certain point in the development process we recognized that a firm holds a number of patents in the area in which we worked. In principle it has to be investigated in phase C, but we recognized it at an earlier point in time. So we introduced some details in our design to evade the patents (H010226:4).

Internally there might be disagreements between managers regarding product innovation. Strategic disagreements were mentioned by a development manager.

Development manager: The strategic guidelines are being strongly developed now. We have had the problem that sales and development would disagree about how long it would take to develop new products, and the reason was disagreement about strategy (B2010118:17).

Both old habits and political barriers were mentioned in another firm. A manager stated at the same time how to evade the barrier in a specific case.

Department manager A: The project is sort of skunk work. The agreement with the director is that if internal resources cannot be found, I shall find external resources. The project is not going to become talked about all over the organization in this starting phase. Some may say that usually we do not work along the lines which the project suggests and there are a lot of political barriers because those who are more interested in getting something they can sell tomorrow, they cannot see the perspectives of this project (H0091910:7).

Another hindrance for activation of information and knowledge was found in the structuring of review meetings. Their number was not optimal. It was recommended to extend the number of meetings for various reasons.

Product manager: Properly we shall introduce some intervening meetings where we can do a little more . . . It is limited what you can discuss during one hour at a gate meeting with participants from production etc. . . . instead we may sketch something and visit somebody and get feedback (D4011030:10).

A negative experience also related to the number of gate meetings. There small number might give too much room for the developers to work without the guidance of their colleagues. In this case the developers could miss the relevant experiences and knowledge from their colleagues. A project leader expressed his problem in this way.

> Project leader: I may go on in one direction which is not optimal when other eyes take a look, other constructors, and therefore a gate meeting on smaller parts of the new product would be a good forum for discussion of various solutions (D4011030:4).

Time pressure was seen as a possible hindrance for satisfactory preparation of a project and of later periods of sound reflections.

> Development manager: Time pressure and unrealistic planning are the greatest hindrances for our department. When you have a time pressure in the creative phase of the project, the result will usually be poor (E0041113:10).

Some tacit knowledge would not get activated at the gate meetings because of lack of time or interest among those participants who had the knowledge.

> Development manager: Sometimes some people cancel their participation at gate meetings because they feel they do not have the time, also you see that it is not everybody who are equally interested (D4011030).

Similarly, the project leaders also felt that due to time pressure they would sometimes have to disregard the participation of certain actors and their experiences (D4011030:3).

In one of the visited firms the management had introduced a production strategy, which prescribed a certain degree of reuse during product innovation. This rule contributed to the restraint of the activation of knowledge for alternative solutions.

> Product developer: The director has been very rigid concerning reuse of components . . . now we have run our head against a brick wall . . . the result of reuse is a construction which is larger than accepted by the sales people . . . we have to change some things . . . we have to use more time for design now than if we had fewer restrictions (H010226:4).

To some extent the development function had created the problem itself because it had presented the project as low-cost due to much reuse of known components to get acceptance from the top management. In reality the project turned out to be rather complex and expensive (H010226:6).

In this section we presented a number of elements that management has drawn upon to mobilise information and knowledge for the benefit of innovation. Similarly a number of barriers has been unveiled. A summary of the results is given in Fig. 2.

Promoting factors.

Contacts with markets and specific customers.
Positive attitudes towards functional integration.
Stage – gate procedure.
Widespread communication and little hierarchy.
Workers' participation.
Informal relationships.

Barriers.

Restraints due to product and competitive strategy.
Excessive influence by customers.
Divergent opinions among the management.
Internal structure and processes.
Sub-optimal gate meetings.
Time pressure.
Lack of interest among (potential) participants of gate meetings.
Excessive reuse of components.

Fig. 2. Overview of Promoting Factors and Barriers for Actors' Activation of Knowledge for Product Innovation.

4. FROM PRODUCT INNOVATION AND MARKET RELATIONSHIPS TO KNOWLEDGE

The ultimate success criterion for product innovation is its success on the market resulting in better firm performance. So when launching a new product, top management followed up upon the reception of the product by the market. In this way learning about market reactions and reflections about how to improve market position stand at the fore of management's thoughts. The middle management and project developers would learn from technical and commercial experiences and accumulate ideas for future innovative work. At the same time the work on innovations resulted in social experiences about internal organizational and social relationships and the behaviour of external partners, which could be taken into consideration for the future planning of new product innovations. Yet, a number of hindrances prevented the optimal use of the potential learning possibilities attached to product innovation. Firstly, the organizational and social experiences are treated. Secondly, the technical and commercial parts of the product innovative activities are analysed concerning their content of learning and delivery of knowledge.

Thirdly the barriers for learning are exposed. These three types of hindrances are discussed in sequence below.

4.1. Organizational and Social Experiences from Innovation

The management and developers felt that the product development activities provided important lessons regarding organizational and social relationships.

The introduction of the principles of integrated product development according to a stage-gate plan was the result of previous experiences with unsatisfactory use of internal tacit knowledge and too long periods of working on the various products. In this connection the management also worked upon reducing the number of active projects. Such a reduction was still an issue during the PIE-team's visits in the firms (D4011030:2).

> Project manager: Some projects have suffered much because of the big project, especially the other longer-term projects. Every time the big project ran into problems, it took resources from the middle term projects, whereas the short-term projects were allowed to continue. These experiences have given us a picture, which says that you must be careful concerning larger projects, because one of them always gets priority and the others suffer (H011112:8).

By experience the development managers had also taken structural initiatives for example by tightening the procedures of the stage-gate plan.

> Development manager: When we find out that things might work smarter, I will change the template in a way which makes people remember what to do. In this way we make changes continuously (D4011030).

One of the firms had its first experiences with a cross-functional project group headed by an external facilitator. Some participants hoped that certain characteristics of the teamwork would not be repeated.

> Project leader: It is worth to repeat some sort of team work, but the frequency of meetings was too high, so we could not prepare ourselves properly. And maybe the members of the group were not the right one. In fact it was other people who carried through the project, and they ought to have been involved from the start (F3010312:7).

The management was aware of the necessity of having a stock of people who knew the products because of their accumulated tacit knowledge.

> Project leader: The way we run our development department means that it is important that we do not have too much turnover. We do not write down too many things so, it is important to have a stock of people who have been here for five or ten years. They can teach their experiences to the new men. That is necessary (F3010312:10).

The management also felt that to get such a core of people it had to support the creativeness and motivation of the project leaders who had a major responsibility for securing the success of the innovative process. On the other hand, the management had also learned from the innovative tasks that a balance had to be struck between giving weight to activating creativeness by lean control of the project leaders' innovative experiences and management's control of having the time schedule observed. One manager had the following personnel policy.

> Product development manager: The starting phase has got some slack so the developers have some months to find out for themselves by experiments etc. followed up by some milestones which define the time for carrying out the project's phases (D0091812:6).

A similar point has been made by Tidd, Bessant and Pavitt (2001 p. 55) who reminded management that the various conditions supporting creative behaviour had to be balanced "with the somewhat harsher realities involved elsewhere in the innovation process."

Project leaders learnt to pay more attention to the project instead of focussing upon their own professional abilities.

> Project developer: One important experience is that I have been better to carry out the project leader role and to get more focus upon the project rather than my profession. And I shall certainly continue to work at this task (H011112:15).

In relation to milestone meetings to be treated below, the climate was of importance as well as acceptance within the different functions of critical remarks from the meetings. A production manager touched upon this issue.

> Production manager: We have introduced the participation of skilled workers from production at gate meetings... It demands that the engineering department gets accustomed to the interference by these people who may criticise the department's solutions (D4011030:3).

External relationships gave the product leaders experiences with disagreements with suppliers for various reasons. It could be delivery dates, quality demands or the understanding of the content of the delivery as in the following extract from an interview with a product leader.

> Product leader: We had some economic problems with the supplier. If you have not made your cooperation agreement very clear and explicit problems will suddenly arise. In the middle of the project we had to renegotiate the agreement because we did not agree on the term programming (E2001005:4).

Such experiences regarding deliveries made the product leaders think about improvement of their negotiation skills and better ways of controlling the suppliers and the firm might stop deliveries (F3010312:7).

4.2. Technical and Commercial Experiences

The technical and commercial experiences from product innovation related both to feedback from the market and internal experiments and tests carried out by project developers, technicians and workers.

The innovative work on new products involved *learning concerning market reactions* and produced new ideas for product innovation. This input was presented by external actors as well as the firms' managers, project leaders, technicians, other employees including the operators working on the new products and the service people handling the customers' problems with the products.

Just after launching a new product the management's interest might focus upon the difference between estimated costs and actual prices and learn from it.

> Development manager: One or two times after launching the product there must be made a business evaluation. How much is sold and how are the cost prices. Of course you have to learn from this (B0020715:15).

Information on this subject might lead to a search for cutting costs, which could relate to the design, supplies, production and/or distribution.

> Product manager: Sometimes we have got a chock due to calculations of costs . . . but many time you may start up under time pressure, and the chosen components were not the most cheap and the supply was not optimal with regard to the volume . . . or the technical solution could have been better . . . in this case we have talked with those customers who were interested in the product to discuss changes (D3010209:14).

Another firm had tried to evade this kind of above mentioned chock by running a continuous estimation of costs and expected benefits of new products during product development and make economic computations after half a year, one year, two years and three years after the launching of the new product. This sort of information raised a number of questions.

> Department manager B: We try to make an analysis. What sort of learning have we had; was the product more costly; why could we not control the cost price; what shall we do now about the costs. But it also taught us that there are certain things which are more difficult to estimate (H0091911:6).

Another sort of experience related to the balance between technological depth versus rapid reaction to the market demands. A couple of the visited firms had previously carried out more or less long term product innovations driven by advanced technological features, but not long before the PIE researchers' first visit it was decided by the management to direct more interest towards the markets. The consequence was that the technical developers had to get a broader perspective on their work and become better acquainted with the market.

Development manager: I work on making developers to generalists instead of specialists (B0020715:13).

Another consequence was that the projects were reoriented towards minor projects, which could result in new products ready for sale at an early time.

Development manager: Some projects have run during four years because they have been extended and remade. We want to leave that practice. Instead we shall have one month for the preliminary investigation, three month for the business case and one year for production or for beginning to deliver the product (B010118:7).

Practical information regarding the function of the product would be registered by specific process people and service people. Their experiences would be forwarded to the developers and used for adjustments of the product relative to other consumers.

Product manager: Process people will follow the processes of the new product and share the information with the product developer and other people from development, but not too many people. Instead we focus upon such activities which means that we can sell the product to those applications for which it is convenient (F3010312:5).

During the process of design and prototype work the project leaders, technicians and workers accumulated knowledge from ongoing *experiments and tests and on-the-job learning.*

Project leader: Regarding tests, we have got competence within an area, and we can work from here, and it gives a product platform from which to continue with new products and earn money (H011112:15)

A technician could tell about how his experiences and communications with production and development regarding his work with tests resulted in a new organizational unit, which would take advantage of idea accumulation concerning test equipment.

Technician: I started in production and I made test equipment. I had got some experience about how it was used in production . . . when we tested I found some errors in new products . . . the production manager asked me to establish a new department for test equipment (D091814:8).

The importance of workers' input was related to experiences from joint experiments as well as their participation in gate meetings within the firms' standard procedure for integrated new product development.

Production manager: The skilled workers join in leaving their stamp on test equipment . . . they know a lot about the products, our engineers ask them often about various things because they can supply answers on practical issues (D4011030).

Technical experiences of importance for future innovative work included work with new materials and processes.

> Project leader: It is the first time I have to make something with plastic tools so, this has been learning for me . . . I have got an experience with plastic tools which I did not have before . . . so if I have to make it next time I know about it (D3010209:10).

The same project leader meant that his experience pointed towards the necessity of acquiring more knowledge about specific technical processes.

> Project leader: At one time or another the firm becomes so large that it has to go deeper to get more knowledge and consolidate it's know-how. It's about motors. I want to work in depth with these things (D3010209:11).

When the prototype was ready for production, the project leader had to make an instruction for those who should have the responsibility for training the production workers how to carry out their new tasks. In one of the visited firms, the technician had chosen to discuss the procedures with those who had the responsibility for instruction to get their suggestions and be sure of full understanding and accept.

> Product leader: I talk with those people in production. They read my proposal and can come up with their input. This is also a tactical question, because you evade the troubles when they start working since they have taken part in the decisions (D3010209:9).

We found that innovative work continuously added new ways of working. In this connection new ideas may result in feedback to the product developers.

> Technician: If they (production people) find out about something when starting production for the first time, then we will make the necessary changes, if we can see it is a good idea maybe also psychologically (D3010209:9).

Besides production workers also service people and external actors contributed new ideas.

> Product leader: Follow-up upon new products in their early market phase is the task of the developers. In case of deficiencies you will try to minimize the damage, and change the product the next time. The products are developing all the time due to sparring with service, the market, production and component suppliers. We have strengthened our cooperation with suppliers (B3010522:9).

4.3. Barriers for Learning

A general condition for learning was reflection. In this connection the firms had a problem because of the felt lack of time for such activities.

> Project manager: We did not have the optimal time for reflections. We only had the necessary time for continuing the development work. I should have preferred to set some question marks by some features of the rules for accumulation of knowledge. But we did not have the time (H011112:4).

The developers had some difficulties in getting experiences from the working of their new products when they were exported to far away markets.

> Product developer: We cannot travel too much. Instead you have to speak to the firm's sales man and get him to get the information about the working of the new product. But when you travel and see the problems with your own eyes and talk with the customer, it is a good thing. But it is impossible by all the tasks (F041414:9).

For developers to extract knowledge from work done by their collaborators, it was a hindrance for sound reflections if operators followed their own routines instead of keeping strictly to the prescribed work descriptions made by the developer. On the background of such an experience a product leader (D091814:4,7) told the researchers that he had learned the necessity of making a checklist and having a supervisor to overview the process to accumulate the right information as early as possible about experiences with the production of zero series.

Persons outside the small group of developers and their collaborators could only learn from the innovation experiences by taking contact to those involved.

> Product leader: All the knowledge I have gathered during this project is now placed by a few colleagues and my manager, and also the consultant who helped us. What I know, they will also know because of our discussions. Much information is found in blueprints, process diagrams, sales material etc. There will be no meetings for my discussion of these things (F3010312:5).

Learning from the innovation process was dependent upon market constraints. One of the firms sold equipment, which had to fit in with equipment sold by a big company, which controlled the market. So the visited firm had to confine its thinking to possibilities which were useful for solutions for such equipment (H010226:6).

Learning from the innovation process was conditioned by taking responsibility for the process. The point is that the actors had to see the process as having consequences, which depended upon their actions before they would take an active part in the innovation process. Besides the general economic consequences there were consequences for the activities of the various functions. An example with regard to an active participation in review meetings was given by a project manager. He reasoned about the work of the service people.

> Project manager: After a number of years people begin to see the advantages of reviews. The next is that they begin seeing that they have a responsibility at the review meeting because they will be kept responsible, so if the service people do not mention that they will have a problem with a solution, then they will have a problem later on. We have seen this a couple of times, and we have been rather rigid towards them when they are too late with their input, and this has had a positive influence (H010226:5).

This section has exposed how the management, project leaders and technicians felt they learnt from the innovation activities. They could mention both organizational

---

Organizational and social experiences.

From unsatisfactory use of tacit knowledge to procedures for integrated product innovation.
Expected advantage of fewer ongoing projects within a given period.
Improvements of stage-gate procedures.
Management's awareness of supporting creativeness and motivation.
Project leaders' priority to the project rather than their own professional abilities.
The importance of the climate at gate meetings.
Acceptance of critical remarks.
Learning concerning negotiations with suppliers.

Technical and commercial experiences.

Feedback from the market.
– Registration of prices versus costs.
– Balancing technological depth with market considerations.
Experiences from experiments and tests and on-the-job learning.
Dialogues about instructions for production and assembly.
Production workers' feedback to developers.

Barriers for learning.

Lack of optimal time for reflection.
Keeping to routines.
Dependence upon market constraints.
Actors' lack of responsibility.

Fig. 3.   Overview of Factors of Importance for Learning During Product Innovation.

and social experiences as well as technical and commercial ones. At the same time they could also give examples of hindrances for learning. An overview of the results is found in Fig. 3.

5. THE MANAGED INTERACTION BETWEEN INNOVATION AND LEARNING

The preceding sections have shown how management in the visited Danish firms regard learning for the benefit of product innovation and the constrains, they have registered. These innovative activities have resulted in new experiences serving learning and knowledge accumulation, again within certain restraints. Now we want to highlight to which extent the management *directly manages* the interaction between the activation of information and knowledge as the basis for product innovation and learning from the innovation activities which can also be seen as a *complementary perspective* upon product development and learning as highlighted by Hargadon and Fanelli (2002) by making room for the reciprocal interaction between innovation and learning. At the same time we shall be attentive to potential traps connected to a cyclic interaction between innovation and learning. As seen from a complementary perspective you have to choose between the perspectives at a given moment, but the argument is that within a given period there will be advantages from connecting both perspectives. In fact, this way of thinking and acting is the core of *knowledge management* directed towards managing knowledge and converting knowledge into increased organizational competence (Sanchez, 2001, p. 3). Only one of the visited firms (H) had an explicit knowledge management strategy and it was only two years old at the time of interviewing. Yet, we can also find traces of knowledge management as an emergent strategy (Mintzberg et al., 1998, p. 189) in the other firms. First the presentation is concentrated upon the knowledge management as practised by the management in firm (H). Afterwards we give an exposition of the less systematic managing of the interaction between innovation and learning in the other four firms. Finally the results of this section are systematized by selected organizational dimensions of the managed interaction between innovation and learning.

5.1. Knowledge Management in the Graphical Firm (H)

The following presentation of knowledge management in firm (H) is based on those traits, which the management itself pointed to as an expression of its knowledge management strategy which was part of its more general business strategy. The strategy of knowledge management was seen as an integrated part of the product work flow where the product innovation project resulted in a product/concept which went to the market/customers but also delivered input to knowledge management and from there to new products/concepts.

The major areas for knowledge management in firm (H) concerned accumulation of knowledge, the sharing of knowledge, the structuring of innovation activities and the inclusion of the different internal functions and external partners. In spite of management's great interest in knowledge management it had to acknowledge certain limitations concerning the implementation of the concept.

In firm (H) the technical director defined the concept by pointing to regular feedback from product innovation activities for the sake of knowledge accumulation and later use in innovation projects.

Technical director: Whether or not a new product has success or fiasco, there is some knowledge which we accumulate, we call it knowledge management, and that is a factor that has come to our attention within the last two years. It is key to our existence. It means we can supply the key knowledge to every project. Each of the big customers know that some knowledge drops to the next customer (H0051614:3).

A department manager expanded on the firm's attitude towards knowledge management and pointed to certain limitations.

Department manager B: What we mean by what I will call a knowledge based system, knowledge integration, that is that we should reach a state where products and processes developed by us can be found again, can be reused. We begin by getting control of the knowledge concerning our physical products that is drawings, objects, constructions, tests, results, and then there may exist minutes of meetings with customers, which we find of interest for the firm, so they can be traced. But we have also chosen to exclude something such as project management. We are looking for more hard core knowledge (H0091911:4).

The introduction of knowledge management was based upon a structural framework headed by a steering group and supported by integrated product development procedures. So new product development experiences went into other projects via a small steering group. In this way there was established an interaction between innovative activities, learning and competence building.

Project developer: There is a fantastic learning during such a product innovation. It is very intense and very fruitful ... There exists a small steering group which governs competence development. In our project we have a man who brings knowledge from us to the steering group. Their task is to coordinate the various projects regarding documentation and see to it that it goes on to other projects (H010226:11).

The transfer of knowledge from one product to the next and from one customer to the next was partly facilitated by the structuring of integrated product development implying external participation. So, the firm had a clear operational policy of combining product innovation with competence building in an interactive way.

Technical director: I prefer to pay the sub supplier for lending one of his engineers ... then I feel sure that he has optimized the construction exactly to fulfil the knowledge you must have about his firm's supply ... I prefer they join our group. Physical presence in the group gives a breath of fresh air for the projects and new competence. They see many solutions from a different angle (H0051614:2).

When explaining the course of product innovation and knowledge management as described by a flow chart, the technical director underlined that the firm accumulated knowledge by information technology across a broad spectrum of dimensions which served as basis for future products.

Technical director: The tools used during the project is found as a template and saved. It is not only drawings, test reports and such things, but also acquaintance with people, a key by which you can find one's way back to specific people and use their knowledge. When this block of knowledge management is crammed with knowledge you will see, from time to time, that a real hard core project appears (H0051614:4).

The firm (H) established rather large project groups divided into a core group and a periphery group. The core group members would sit together in the same room to maximize knowledge sharing by the support of physical nearness.

Technical director: It is our philosophy that physical presence is important. It means that the hardware man sits opposite the software man, who sits opposite the assembly man, who sits together with the project leader. They talk about the product. The synergy, which appears, rubs off onto the solution in the single product (H0051614:1-2).

It was quite clear that the firm (H) had high ambitions regarding knowledge and competence in connection with innovation, but the firm also had to recognize that it had to counteract hindrances. It was not an easy task to implement the plans and carry out the prescriptions regarding knowledge management.

One thing was to overcome obstacles in knowledge sharing as seen in poor proactive participation in department meetings (H0091911:7).

An important part of the knowledge management strategy of the firm consisted – as mentioned earlier – in interaction with external partners. The firm (H) had joined a project in late 1998 with some other firms, which was directed towards the accumulation of knowledge from ongoing projects using advanced information technology. Regarding this project it had taken much time to get it implemented and only a feeble start was under way during the research period. Another weakness had to do with the follow-up of plans.

Department manager C: I do not think we are good at learning. We are not so good to follow up upon our plans even though the project leaders may say otherwise . . . some of the project leaders arrange a meeting to follow up upon the project and we try to accumulate experiences to get some learning (H0091913:3-4).

The technology part of product innovation was difficult to control with regard to both resources, costs and time in the firm. Therefore a specific project was directed towards solving problems, which would show themselves in a number of future projects. In this way knowledge input to future products and problems, which had been found in output from previous projects were seen under the same angle (H0091910).

A manager called attention to the problem inherent in knowledge management when understood as accumulation of historical data for the use in future activities. The benefits to be harvested from this accumulation of knowledge was conditioned upon staying in the business, but as the firm was active in a market with great turbulence it had to be kept in mind that one day the accumulated knowledge could loose its importance. So, knowledge management had to be tied strongly to the general strategy of the firm (H010226:8).

Besides its attempts to counteract hindrances for knowledge management, the management had to consider its explicit strategy of reuse of components during new product development. In one of the projects, which was studied by the PIE-team, the management had recognized a dilemma.

> Project manager: The experience that we have had is that when you talk about product concept, it is important not to place too heavy constraints upon your work, that is logical . . . But during the product development we did not have this discussion on reuse and constraints. We had just said, of course, we have to have reuse (H011112:3).

Besides its brake on creativity, reuse might also mean more time for development because of difficulties in finding suitable solutions within the given prescriptions. To overcome this dilemma the management had loosened its prescriptions for reuse.

Another way of counteracting restraints on using the possibilities created by innovative work was to introduce some kind of skunk work, which did not have to be formally recognized by the top management. This activity was exposed above when treating customs and political barriers for the activation of knowledge (H0091910:7).

5.2. Managed Interaction Between Innovation and Learning – Fragments Found in Firms (B), (D), (E) and (F)

Looking at *the four visited firms* (B), (D), (E), (F), the complementary perspective upon innovation and knowledge was part of the management learning and so expression of an emerging strategy (Mintzberg et al., 1998). The background for a change towards an explicit interactive view was strategic considerations and bad experiences with the one-sided view caring for either activation of knowledge for innovation or learning from product innovation. Typically the sales function and development function had each behaved rather autonomously. In firm (B) the developers had seen too many possibilities for new products which were criticised by the sales people. The management had reacted by focussing more on activating latent knowledge across the firm. In firm (D) the new manager of development accepted the learning perspective by the developers and gave them some room for looking into possibilities for innovation but after a period they had to concentrate on activation of existing knowledge. In firm (E) the management had recognized that it had not always given the problems enough thought before starting a new project and asked the right customers. Therefore the firm had been eager to activate functional knowledge by the introduction of integrative new product development procedures. In firm (F) a change was initiated by the mother company. In a concrete case at the time of the PIE research the sales people meant that enough functional knowledge was at hand to innovate, but by intervention from the mother company the sales people together with development and production were forced to look for new possibilities by external contacts and headed by a foreign facilitator.

The management's initiatives towards getting benefits from an explicit acknowledgement of the potential contained in the interaction of tacit knowledge for product innovation and learning from innovation activities can be crystallized from explicit strategic considerations and more attention to external relationships as well as structural changes and specific processes.

Even though the management did not know exactly how they should systematize the interaction between the innovative processes and the accumulation of knowledge, the management might have strong views regarding the necessity of connecting innovation and knowledge as manifested in explicit strategic considerations. One reason was the priority to hold on learning which was a result of the firm's innovation for the benefit of continuous improvements of the products.

> Top director: Besides buying competences, we consciously make sure to possess certain types of knowledge. We have an overarching strategy, which says that we will know something about the processes of our machines. We want to be able to develop such a machine and having control of the process (B0020713:8).

A common tendency in the visited firms was more attention to the market. This appreciation of the market also meant that knowledge activated by work for advanced customers was seen strategically as a fertile source for learning with consequences for future product innovations.

> Development manager: Many times we get knowledge by our customer designed tasks. From them we get new knowledge, and so we can develop our technology (D091812:5).

Customer reactions served as input for the developers when a new product was in its running-in stage by the customer. Besides immediate help to the customer, the new information would serve as knowledge for future product innovations.

> Product leader: A customer had problems with the new product because it was combined with a new product from another firm. Theoretically I might have foreseen the situation. But it was OK for me to meet the problem by the customer instead of having gone through all possibilities on beforehand and used half a year more on the product. The customer got the necessary help. But I am quite sure I shall use this knowledge in future product developments including that my intelligent product shall go together with other intelligent products (E4091001:3-4).

The management's structural initiative in all the four firms to introduce an integrated new product development procedure meant that tacit knowledge was activated for product innovation and results during the product development stages documented at gate meetings. So interaction between an innovation perspective and a learning perspective was instituted. However, the supporting processes were not optimal for several reasons. The written documentation was held to a minimum only of interest for the product innovation in question. Also the transferral processes of importance for the activation of knowledge to innovation and tacit knowledge and more innovation depended upon the individual participants or the group established for a specific project, and no organizational unit had the explicit responsibility to manage the interaction between innovation and learning as seen in firm (H).

> Product leader: We have no database or any other thing in which we can accumulate these things (knowledge acquired during the product development, ed.) and draw upon later on. It is something which is found in the group as such (D32714:7).

This meant that when working on a new product, the product leader would have to ask around about experiences from earlier cases and find out whether relevant information was at hand. Besides he could acquaint himself with blueprints and test reports from earlier projects. A development manager pointed to advantages of this oral procedure.

> Development manager: The structuring of information from review meetings is very difficult. You must use extra time at points in time when you do not have very much time, but worse, it is my experience that there is little possibility for anyone finding the document when starting a new project . . . I think we learn by meetings with the project leader (B2010118:10).

In this connection, the management's efforts to strengthen the role of product development leader promoted the broad interaction of knowledge activation for innovation and learning from innovative activities. The reason was that the projects leaders got the responsibility for the total development process and had to acquaint themselves with processes across functions and not only keep to technical specialties.

The management acknowledged the learning process going on during product innovation and its importance as tacit knowledge during future product innovations. One dimension of this knowledge was directly promoted by the management who made room for workers' participation in giving input to product development activities and learning from such activities.

Another dimension was related to the developers' organizational and social experiences with customers.

> Development manager: What makes us get success is application knowledge . . . Those who are good at application, who knows what after four or five times having worked along similar lines . . . they can also control the customers, so technical knowledge is not enough (D4011030:3-4).

In the beginning of this section it was mentioned that the management in firm (D) paid attention to the motivation of developers for both thinking at activating knowledge and having an eye for the creative possibilities by innovative work. The idea was to give the product developer some leeway at the beginning of the process, but also to put some restraints on tendencies for the developers to go astray.

> Development manager: You have tasks which must be finished and preferably to a definite point in time. But at the same time the development phase has been loosened so much that the developers may have some months where they can work according to their own choosing (D00991812:6).

The interaction between product development and learning implied some choices. Some sorts of knowledge accumulation might be demotivating.

> Development manager: Technology projects can supply new knowledge, but you have a choice between establishing standards either for the construction of the product or for the tests of the product. By having standard tests the developers will learn from work with the construction until it satisfies the tests, whereas they will not be motivated to follow standard construction rules . . . it kills creativity (B0020715:10-11).

Another problem consisted in underestimating the necessity of renewal taking the market experiences from a product and tacit knowledge as sufficient. In one of the firms interference from the mother company stopped this possibility and made

---

Knowledge management in firm (H).

The concept and its meaning.
Structural setting.
Information technology.
Physical nearness.
Implementation problems.
Technology projects.
Restraints on benefits from knowledge management.
The dilemma of reuse.

Managed interaction between innovation and learning – fragments found in firms (B), (D), (E) and (F).

Strategic considerations.
Introduction of an integrated new product development procedure with documentation.
– Limitations concerning documentation and organizational setting.
The role of new product development leader.
 Acknowledgement of learning processes as seen in connection with innovation.
Recognition of limits to the use of connecting innovation and learning.

Fig. 4. Items Concerning the Managed Interaction Between Innovation and Learning.

room for a combination of tacit knowledge and new experiences from preparatory work on product innovation.

> Product developer: At first the plan for the new product built upon the conviction that we knew enough to construct it. Because of other tasks the work was postponed. When the project should start again, the mother company interfered, a group representing the diverse functions was formed and a consultant acting as a facilitator was brought in. Documents were investigated and interviews with customers took place. On this basis the group decided to make a genuinely new product (F041414:4).

The two sub-sections on firm (H) and the firms (B), (D), (E) and (F) have presented the management's more or less explicit and comprehensive recognition of the necessity of combining the innovation perspective and the learning perspective to get a full picture of innovation and learning instead of only working along one dimension at a time. Yet, it has also been shown how the management has to deal with problems, which were a part of the implementation of a dual perspective. An overview of the items referred to by the interviewees concerning the managed interaction between innovation and learning is given in Fig. 4.

Organizational dimension	Firm (H)	Firms (B), (D), (E), (F)
Management's strategy.	Knowledge management. The dilemma of reuse. Restraints on the benefits from Knowledge Management. Technology projects.	Fragments of strategic considerations pointing towards better connection between innovation and learning.
Structure.	Structural setting. Physical nearness. The role of new product development leader.	Integrated new product development procedure. The role of new product development leader.
Processes.	Innovation. Learning. IT processes. Implementation problems.	Innovation. Learning. Documentation. Participation. Motivation.
External relationships.	Markets and customers Suppliers' role.	Markets and customers.

Fig. 5. Main Organizational Dimensions of the Managed Interaction Between Innovation and Learning.

The items contained in Fig. 4 together with the analysis in this section on the managed interaction between innovation and learning can be summarized from an organizational point of view comprising the elements of actors' strategy, structure, processes and external relationships, cf. Fig. 5.

6. CONCLUSIONS

The interviews with the Danish managers show a number of important insights into the management's understanding of a *managed* interaction between product innovation and learning which at the same time means that they in practice used a *complementary* perspective. From an organizational point of view the management's handling of the managed interaction relates to strategy, structure, processes, and external relationships as shown in Fig. 5 above. The treatment of these dimensions gives also a background for a comparison with Hargadon's and Fannelli's three major conclusions referred to in the beginning of this presentation.

Among the visited Danish firms the graphical firm (H) had introduced a *knowledge management strategy* within the firm's overall management strategy. The management's concept and practice showed an explicit understanding of the importance of connecting work on innovations with a learning perspective. The strategic implications aimed at strong external relationships, an organizational set-up for the coordination of experiences from innovative activities with new projects, and processes strengthening internal and external relationships.

It is important to notice that the advantages of connecting an innovation perspective with a learning perspective do not accrue automatically. Firm (H) gave the example how an important *strategic choice* has to be made by the management working in turbulent markets. The choice concerned the degree to which reuse of components should be made during innovations because reuse of prior learning from previous innovations put a brake on creative activation of knowledge. The interviewed manager's point of view was that a knowledge management strategy had to be part of a comprehensive strategy, which looks beyond current products. In this connection could also have been mentioned the *dilemma* between the costs of information accumulation and the doubtful benefits of reuse in a turbulent environment. Other experiences showed that the strategists could have an advantage of paying attention to a broad network of actors.

Regarding *structure* the results showed that the firms had introduced principles of functional integration including gate meetings and documentation to promote the managed interaction between innovation and learning, but except for the firm (H) there existed disadvantages connected to this structuring from a learning point of view. The reason was that the documentation was closely related to test results besides serving as a memo for the next meeting, but told nothing about social experiences and only little from experiments, which went astray. According to the management it was necessary to take individual contact to participants in older projects when new projects were started because the documentation was not satisfactory.

The management's choice of a structural setting in firm (H) meant that individual innovative activities based on tacit knowledge via an organizational unit were transformed to social knowledge for the benefit of other projects. This specific combination of structure and processes gives further substance to Hargadon's and Fanelli's second conclusion on how the complementary perspective highlights what can be called organizational knowledge. This knowledge is *created* by the recursive interaction between latent and empirical knowledge taking the form of blueprints, databases and other artifacts of the organization.

In the Danish firm (H) the knowledge management strategy meant the creation of a combined innovation and learning cycle by instituting an integrated product development procedure supplemented by an organizational unit as referred to above. So this Danish case gives an explicit example of the suggestion by Hargadon and Fanelli concerning how to generate new knowledge by the complementary perspective.

The Danish management's choice of giving more cross-functional responsibility to project leaders can be seen as promoting the interaction of innovation and learning. The project leaders' role as generalists who must take interest in the total product innovation process from the design phase to the products' introduction on the market promotes a better understanding of the accumulation of knowledge for the benefit of future innovations. The weakness is that the learning is found at the individual level or within small groups.

Regarding *processes* mirroring the complementary perspective, product developers' organizational and social experiences were seen to be consciously recognized as accruing during product innovation and explicitly drawn upon in future activations of knowledge for innovation. In this connection the management acknowledged how workers' participation supported the managed interaction of input to product innovation activities and learning from such activities.

From one of the firms was given an example how the management paid attention to the motivation of developers for both thinking at activating knowledge and having an eye for the creative possibilities. The idea was to give the product developer some leeway at the beginning of the process, but also to put some restraints on tendencies for the developers to go astray. This observation is in accordance with Tidd, Bessant and Pavitt's (2001) who argue that the management should balance the support of creative behaviour "with the somewhat harsher realities involved elsewhere in the innovation process."

A major drawback for managed interaction processes was time pressure which was felt both during product innovation work and when going from one project to the next. Such pressure was seen as negative for reflection.

Intense *external relationships* were an important part of the firms strategy as mentioned above. The Danish study found firm (H) drawing upon external partners by integrating them in certain stages of the product innovation with the explicit opinion that external partners' "physical presence in the group gives a breath of fresh air for the projects and new competence. They see many solutions from a different angle" (H0051614:2). This statement shows a recognition of the interrelationship between innovation and learning expressed by the combination of a broader input from another firm and new competence in the visiting firm. Similar to the first conclusion by Hargadon and Fanelli it is seen from this Danish case that the suppliers and the visited firm draw mutual benefit from their interaction. The suppliers obtained an improved input for their deliveries and the firm created a new product suited to the components from the suppliers.

NOTE

1. "Complementarity principle, in physics, tenet that a complete knowledge of phenomena on atomic dimension requires a description of both wave and particle properties. The principle was announced in 1928 by the Danish physicist Niels Bohr. Depending on the experimental arrangement, the behaviour of such phenomena as light and electrons is sometimes wavelike and sometimes particle-like, i.e. such things have a wave-particle duality (q.v.). It is impossible to observe both the wave and particle aspects simultaneously. Together however, they present a fuller description than either of the two taken alone." *The New Encyclopædia Britannica*, *3*, 504, Chicago, 1990.

ACKNOWLEDGMENT

I am grateful for helpful suggestions by my colleague Jesper L. Christensen.

REFERENCES

Christensen, P. H. (2003). *Knowledge management – perspectives and pitfalls*. Copenhagen: Copenhagen Business School Press.

Cooper, R. G. (1993). *Winning at new products*. Reading, MA: Addison-Wesley.

Hargadon, A., & Fanelli, A. (2002). Action and possibility: Reconciling dual perspectives of knowledge organizations. *Organization Science*, *13*, 290–302.

March, J. G. (1991). Exploration and exploitation in organizational learning. *Organization Science, 2*, 71–87.

Mintzberg, H., Ahlstrand, B., & Lampel, J. (1998). *Strategy safari.* London: Prentice-Hall.

Sanchez, R. (Ed.) (2001). *Knowledge management and organizational competence.* Oxford: Oxford University Press.

The New Encyclopædia Britannica (1990). *The New Encyclopædia Britannica, 3*, 504. Chicago.

Tidd, J., Bessant, J., & Pavitt, K. (2001). *Managing innovation.* Chichester: Wiley.

Van de Ven, A. H., Polley, D. E., Garud, R., & Venkataraman, S. (1999). *The innovation journey.* Oxford: Oxford University Press.

PART II:
PRODUCT INNOVATION AND INTERACTIVE LEARNING

PRODUCT INNOVATION AND ECONOMIC THEORY – USER-PRODUCER INTERACTION IN THE LEARNING ECONOMY [*]

Bengt-Åke Lundvall and Anker Lund Vinding

ABSTRACT

In this chapter it is shown that, in spite of the fundamental importance for economic growth of product innovation, standard economic theory – neo-classical as well as transaction cost approaches to industrial organization – tends to neglect it. It is also shown that moving the focus to product innovation leads to very different conclusions on how alternative institutional set-ups affect economic performance. Institutional set ups assumed to optimise allocation and minimise transaction costs do not support innovation and growth. That is why producer goods where innovation is a regular phenomenon are transacted neither in pure markets nor in hierarchies. The omnipresence of "organized markets" reflects the need for users as well as producers to engage in on-going information exchange and interactive learning in connection with product innovation.

Trust cannot be bought – and if it could – it would have no value whatsoever.

Kenneth Arrow (1971)

---

[*] This chapter develops further some of the ideas first presented in Lundvall (1985).

Product Innovation, Interactive Learning and Economic Performance
Research on Technological Innovation and Management Policy, Volume 8, 101–128
Copyright © 2004 by Elsevier Ltd.
ISSN: 0737-1071/doi:10.1016/S0737-1071(04)08005-9

1. INTRODUCTION

Product innovations – defined as innovations addressing users not belonging to the innovating firm – are important when it comes to sustain competitive advantage. The business sector allocates more than half their R&D resources to product innovation. Innovation surveys demonstrate that more than half of all firms have introduced at least one product innovation over a three year-period. There are sector differences in this respect but there is little doubt that most firms see product innovation as a necessary element in their business strategies. Several of the chapters in this book will demonstrate that firms introducing product innovations, ceteris paribus, create more jobs than those that do not.

For the performance of the economy as a whole, product innovations – defined as new products addressing consumers – are of fundamental importance. If technical progress exclusively took the form of increased technical efficiency in producing a given bundle of goods the end result would be stagnation, de-qualification of the labour force and technological unemployment. The introduction of new and more attractive consumer products are at least as important as sales efforts when it comes to counteract stagnation. This is obviously true in a closed economy-context. In the open economy the dynamic specialisation toward high income-elasticity products addressing the world market is crucial for competitiveness and growth.

On this background it should be expected that product innovation was at the very centre of economic analysis but this is not the case. As pointed out by Carter (1986) production theory abstracts from it and as to be shown here, so does the theory on industrial organization. There are several reasons for this neglect. One reason is that economics avoids analytical fields where qualitative change is important. It has a strong bias in favour of quantitative analysis. Its tools are not well suited to clarify what is going on in connection with product innovation.

In this chapter we try to work out some of the implications for industrial organization that follows from focusing on product innovations addressing professional users. We demonstrate that what appears to be the most efficient way of organising the economy when the focus is upon allocation – the pure market – is highly inefficient when it comes to promote product innovation. We also show that some of the conclusions reached on the basis of transaction economics need to be revised, if not reversed, when the focus is upon product innovation (Lundvall, 1988).

One fundamental assumption leading us to these conclusions is that innovators benefit from having access to feedback from and interaction with a diverse set of users. Being locked in with just one gives a too narrow basis for interactive learning. More generally the differences in analytical results emanate from the focus on innovation (not allocation) and from the elementary idea that economic agents may become more competent through learning processes (not just making choices on the basis information and competence given once and for all). This hypothesis is supported by econometric analyses in this book that confirm that firms that succeed in building more complete networks are more innovative than the others (see for instance, Toke Reichstein, Chap. 14; Vinding, Chaps 7 & 11).

2. STANDARD ECONOMICS IS BEST SUITED TO ANALYZE CIRCULAR FLOW

The core of neoclassical economics is about allocation of scarce resources and its most conspicuous analytical result is the possible existence of a state of general equilibrium where resources have been allocated efficiently and where there are no incentives to rock the boat. In a context with no innovation and no learning this abstraction would be more legitimate than it is in the learning economy.

In an economy with little change – in what Schumpeter refers to as circular flow – cost-saving routines would be developed and it may be legitimate to assume that firms would focus on how to allocate resources in an optimal way. And in such a context (and with convex production and preference functions etc.) the whole economy may actually converge toward general equilibrium.

Here it is plausible that producers and users through adaptive behaviour and learning converge towards what the theory prescribes as rational behaviour – rational behaviour might be seen as an emergent property of consumers and producers.[1]

On the other hand it follows that the assumptions related to rational behaviour are less applicable in an economy where producers are assumed to engage in innovation and consumers are assumed to develop new needs and wants. Here uncertainty is ubiquituous and the actual limits for access to information and of human intelligence becomes a problem. In a world with innovation there is no reason to assume that instrumental rationality or even strategic rationality will become the dominating rule of behaviour. Creativity, discursive rationality and even human virtues such as solidarity, loyalty and trust may affect the economic climate.[2]

Taking the next logical step and bring in the potential for learning and competence building among producers and consumers explicitly into the analysis gives even stronger emphasis on the diversity among the economic agents. In such a world there will be different satisfactory ways of making choices and the fact that different agents make different choices even when confronted with the same constraints and opportunities might actually be fundamental for the viability and performance of the economy as a whole.

The analysis of innovation and especially of product innovations is important in itself because innovation is a major driver in the modern economy. But it is especially important as a testing ground for the validity of standard economic theory. It is dubious to present a theory that does not remain relevant in an economy with innovations as a general theory.

3. FIRMS HAVE COMPLEX GOALS AND NEED TO DEVELOP COMPLEX STRATEGIES

Much of our analysis of user-producer interaction will have firms at both sides of the dyads and it is useful to reflect on why firms do what they do. In standard economics the ojective of the firm is to maximise profit and the major function of firms in the economy is to react on price signals and to allocate and reallocate resources accordingly. Modern industrial organization economics see firms as a system of contracts defining rights and obligations but the focus remains the efficient allocation of given resources.

In the real world, firms are organizations with complex sets of objectives. While it is reasonable to assume that they are profit-seeking organizations the time horizon may differ and the same is true for the span of attention. Management may focus their attention on allocation but they may also take into account the need to have some flexibility in the use of resources in order to be able to cope with unforeseen change. But management may also consider how to make the firm grow given the resources commanded by the firm – firms may introduce new products and enter new markets. Finally managers may consider how to engage the organization in creating new resources and capabilities through learning and competence building. There is no way to say that a focus on allocation is *more rational* than a focus on innovation and learning. In some sectors it might be fatal not to focus on innovation and learning while it might be more legitimate in some other more slowly changing sectors.

In this chapter we make a radical shift in theoretical focus by moving our attention from allocation to innovation. We will analyse what kind of institutional set ups that promote innovation. The classical question of Adam Smith around which much of economic theory has been built may be formulated as "how can the shoe-maker know how many pairs of shoes to produce when he addresses anonymous customers via the market." We are going to address another puzzling question: "how can the maker of a specialized machine tool know in what directions to develop a new and more attractive version of the machine tool when he addresses anonymous customers via the market." The classical response to the first question is that the "invisible hand" solves the problem while the response to the second question is that there is a need for a "visible handshake."

In order to clarify the argument we will go into some detail regarding the basic assumptions on which the analysis is grounded. Most of these are empirically founded and reflect stylised facts emanating from modern innovation research. We will present some of the evidence in brief texts put in boxes in order not to break the logic of the analytical argument. Our criticism of transaction cost theory will refer to the original version presented in Williamson (1975). This is not because we are not aware of Williamson's more recent work but because this seminal work serves so well as a contrast to our own. Later versions have more nuance but they are also more complicated without adding much new to the core of the argument (see also Lundvall, 1992).

4. CONCEPTUALIZING PRODUCT INNOVATION

4.1. Innovation as a Cumulative Process

Innovations may be seen as distinct events, which can be dated in time. Empirical work trying to explain innovation has often taken its departure in a list of such dated events.

In this chapter we see single innovations as elements in a *cumulative process*. The outcome of this process may be incremental technical change or discrete leaps in technical opportunities. But, the process from which it emanates is always cumulative – even the most conspicuous single innovation has its roots in accumulated knowledge and experience. For instance, the cumulative learning history behind the most radical innovation of our time, the computer, goes back at least to Babbage and the 18th century. It also implies that innovation is path-dependent and that theories focusing on innovation have to be designed so that they recognize historical time.

4.2. Innovation as a Collision Between Technical Opportunity and User Needs

We shall regard single innovations as the result of *collisions between technical opportunity and user needs*. We acknowledge that single innovations might result from pure accidents, but we do not see this as the normal pattern. Innovation takes place when there are new developments either in terms of technological opportunities or in terms of new user needs and normally it is when the two sides meet that innovation takes place.

A more mundane way to put this is that the innovating unit needs access not only to information about technical opportunities, but also to information about user needs. We assume that while information about user needs may differ in terms of complexity and appropriability, some costs and efforts are always involved in obtaining the information. The assumption that information about user needs is not a public good is of central importance for the results presented in Box 1.

Box 1: The Dairy Machinery Firm and its access to lead users

In the context of a study of dairy processing in Denmark we found that one of the major global producers of dairy machinery – the Swedish multinational Alfa Laval – had located a unit in Denmark reporting a financial loss to the mother company year after year. When asked why the unit was not closed down management told us that "we are willingly paying that price for operating in close interaction with the most advanced users of dairy machinery in the world" (Lundvall et al., 1984).

4.3. The Separation of the User from the Innovating Unit

Our analysis relates to the interaction between units innovating and other distinct units, which are potential users of the innovations. This perspective is relevant only if the innovator and the user are separate units. In the extreme case when, for example, a scientist as an integrated part of his research project, develops new methods and scientific instruments in order to solve a problem, no informational problems will be involved.[3]

If we disregard such extreme cases, there will always be some degree of separation between the innovating unit and the user. It is obviously the case, when there is a vertical division of labour between different organizations. But it is also the case when different individuals or departments will have to interact and exchange information within an organization. In most of this chapter we treat the special case where users and producers are separated by a market.

Most of the analysis could as well have been applied to how different departments within a firm interact and communicate. The R&D department developing new process equipment will for instance need to engage in communication with the potential users in the production department. Building channels and codes of innovation inside the firm is far from cost-less (Arrow, 1974).

4.4. Innovation and Production

Relating technical opportunities to user needs involves a logical problem. There is an immense amount of potential user needs in the economy and all individuals and organizations could in principle be regarded as potential users of an innovation. Is it possible to define a set of users, ex ante, that is before the new product has been developed and procured by the users?

To overcome this difficulty, we assume that innovation activities take place in units engaged in production. We also assume that this production addresses a definite set of users and that innovations are oriented toward the needs of a subset within this set. The product might be tangible – such as a machine tool – or non-tangible – such as a software package or even a new chemical formula emanating from outsourced R&D activities.

What is important is that we see production as a routine process resulting in a regular flow of products from producers to users. Innovation, on the other hand, is a search and learning process characterized by less regularity in its outcome. Production and innovation are interdependent. Learning taking place in production and in the context of the regular flow of products, feed the innovation process. On the other hand, innovations will upset and reconfigure production and the regular flows.

This assumption linking innovation to production does not fit very well with once-for-all inventors – such as the university professor selling the outcome of a single invention to a commercial user. We do not see this as a major problem. Even in such cases certain routine activities addressed towards a specific set of users may be identified.

The fact that innovation activities are addressed toward a specific set of users does not exclude the possibility that the result of those activities – the product innovation – ends up addressing new categories of users whose needs were not taken into account when the innovation was developed. Actually, innovations often result in an extension of the set of users related to the innovating unit.

4.5. Consumers and Professional Users

The concept of needs is fuzzy. But the problem of defining needs in operational terms takes different forms depending upon the character of the user. The distinction between professional users and consumers proves to be fundamental. The goal function of the average consumer is broad and vague; it can only be defined in very general terms – utility maximization, satisfaction, happiness, etc. The professional users – users acting within the formal part of the economy – has more well defined goals for their activities. In the former category, it is dubious to ascribe needs to the user and to separate needs from wants. This is much less problematic, when the user is professional. If the goal function is properly defined, bottlenecks can be identified and new and better ways to produce goods and services might be conceived and developed. Under certain circumstances it might even be possible for an external observer to reveal and address needs that the user has not yet been able to put on to his explicit agenda.[4]

In this chapter we are concerned with user-producer relationships were the user is a professional. This limitation makes it possible to operate with a concept of needs that is reasonably clear. Still, we can include innovative activities with a major impact upon the over-all process of technical change and economic growth. Some revolutionary innovations – the automobile, television, etc. – have, however, developed at the interface between producers and consumers and those fall outside the analysis.[5]

In this context it is interesting to note that in certain areas the distinction between consumer and professional user is becoming less clear-cut. Consumers acting as amateurs involved in hobbies might display behaviour similar to professional users'. The user-clubs related to specific brands of home-computers and computer games is just one example demonstrating that the amateurs might be as advanced as professionals in terms of both use and innovativeness (Jeppesen, 2001; von Hippel, 2001) (Box 2).[6]

Box 2: How users of computer games contribute to product development
In a recent Ph.D. thesis Lars Bo Jeppesen has analysed the role of consumers in product development using computer games as the case. He shows how the interaction among the users – in chat rooms provided by the producer – helps producers to sort out who are the lead users and how the producer links up with lead users in their product development. He also demonstrates how producers give consumers access to tools making it more easy and attractive for users to contribute to the product development process (Jeppesen, 2004).

---

5. CONCEPTUALIZING INFORMATION EXCHANGE AND INTERACTIVE LEARNING

5.1. Information Exchange and Interactive Learning

In this chapter we make frequent use of concepts from information theory and more specifically from the economics of information as developed by Kenneth Arrow. We refer to information as flowing between units, passing through information channels and getting transformed into specific codes. We assume, that each unit has a memory consisting of accumulated information, as well as an agenda consisting of items that attract the attention of the unit.

But the use of "information" and "information exchange" as being at the core of the process is just a first (and not quite satisfactory) step in the analysis. These are handy concepts not too far away from a standard economics vocabulary. But in order to fully understand the dynamics of innovation and institutional change it is necessary to introduce a broader perspective where "competence" and "interactive learning" become the crucial concepts. In the last part of the chapter we indicate some of the consequences of such a shift in perspective.

5.2. Information Channels and Codes of Communication

In a dynamic perspective, the establishment of information channels and codes of communication may be regarded as investments and as outcomes of learning. It is time-consuming, as well as costly, to develop new channels of information and for participants to learn new codes.

Box 3: Complementary channels used in exchanging information between the collaboration partners

Different types of channels have different abilities to convey information and to contribute to the process of transforming explicit and tacit information into knowledge. The tacitness and complexity of knowledge, which to a large extent is present for more science-based firms, is illustrated in Vinding (2002) who examines the use of respectively employee, prototype and internet exchange as three different types of communication media. The analysis shows that the three media are complementary. It also shows that 31% of the firms in more science-based oriented sectors have used two/three media when exchanging information from its partners while the percentages where less than half for firms operating in low-technology sectors.

However, the high intensity of media used and hence information exchanged may also reflect a large distance in the relative absorptive capacity between the firm and its collaboration partner. A large distance may for instance occur when the type of knowledge delivered from a partner is atypical and in order to compensate for these differences several complementary media need to be used. The analysis shows that in 26% of the cases where firms have received technological competencies from customers, two or three media have been used while two or three media have only been used in 9% of the cases when the technological competencies are coming from suppliers. For firms receiving market-related competencies from customers two or three media have only been used in 17% of the cases. Thus, when the firm requests an atypical competence from its partner, it is more likely that different kinds of media, which complement each other, are used (Vinding, 2002).

The content of the memory changes as new information enters it – either as the result of internal experience, or as the result of information brought into the organization from external units. To this should be added forgetting – a process that might be important for the implementation of any innovation.

As new information is obtained, new items will enter the agenda of the organization and old ones might get excluded.

The *linkages* between a user and a producer refer to regular flows of tangible or non-tangible products from the producer to the user. Such linkages can be described by an extended input/output table where capital goods are treated not as final demand, but as intermediate goods.

The *channels of information* between user and producer refer to a flow of signals not embodied in the regular flow of products.[7] We assume that the network of linkages and the network of information channels overlap to a substantial degree. An important aspect of the innovation process is the exchange of disembodied information between the producer and the user via information channels. This is another way to state the close relation between innovation and production.

The *relationship* between user and producer refers to the combinations of linkages and channels of information (Box 3).

5.3. User-Producer Interaction and Learning by Interacting

The interaction between user and producer takes three different forms: Exchange of products, exchange of information and direct cooperation. In connection with these three forms of interaction learning by interacting takes place. Learning may take the form of participants becoming more able to communicate (learning know-who and learning the local code), better informed (learning know-what), better analysts (learning know-why) or more skilful in action (learning know-how).

Co-operation may be routine based collaboration – such as when a firm out-sources regular activities to another firm. But co-operation may also aim at problem solving in connection with the innovation process. Especially in the later type of co-operation learning by interacting may be crucial linking together and generalizing learning by doing and learning by using (see the last section of the chapter).

5.4. The Stability of Relationships

There are several factors reinforcing relationships once they have been established. The channels of communication and the code used within a given channel are costly to establish. As the channel and the code are used, the effectiveness of the exchange of information grows. Alternative channels and codes become relatively less attractive. Only when alternatives offer substantial returns will it be rational to change channels and codes. Even in such situations inertia will tend to prevail, especially when the old channels can be operated under satisfactory conditions. This general observation deriving from information theory is reinforced by the characteristics of technology and innovations. When the information relates to technology, the code will be complex and specific making the change of channels and codes extra expensive.

To this should be added that uncertainty is a uniquely important characteristic of innovative activities. If the outcomes of innovation processes were well defined in advance they would not be innovations. This implies that the relationships between users and producers need to be founded in norms and principles that extend outside economic rationality. Trust becomes important for the parties involved and as illustrated by the introductory quotation this is something that needs to be founded in non-economic logic. We define trust, as a shared norm applied in practice telling agents not to exploit fully new opportunities in a situation where the other party has become the victim of unforeseen calamities. It takes time to build trust and this is another reason why user-producer relationships tend to be durable and not easily dissolved (Box 4).[8]

Box 4: The importance of established relationships with users in the product development process
In an evaluation of the most important product development project within a two year period, customers with which the firm has collaborated before, were attributed as being of more importance for the specific product development project compared to new customers. Established relationships with customers were also attributed as being of more importance for the firms' ability to develop new products in the future compared to new customers (Kristensen & Vinding, 2001a).

5.5. Producer Dependence – How Innovating Producer Monitor Users

The product innovating producer has incentives to monitor what is going on within user units and it is not primarily a question of getting an isolated signal about a new need. What is required is continuous process of information gathering that might involve considerable costs and resources. First, the producer will monitor *process innovations* within the user units; if the process innovations are successful, the producer might try to appropriate them and present them to other users as a product innovation. Sometimes users will be willing and positively interested in sharing such information with producers (Harhoff et al., 2003).

Second, product innovations within user units will often imply changes in process technology. The producer has therefore, as well, an incentive to monitor the product innovations within user units. If a certain product innovation becomes successful, it might open up a new rapidly widening market for new process equipment. The automobile makers will typically have a network of suppliers of components and machinery who need to be mobilized when a new product is developed. For these suppliers having access to information about the product development in the automobile firms is of critical importance.

Third, technological bottlenecks and technological interdependencies in user units offer potential markets for the innovating producer. Such problems might be complex, and in some cases the producer must have direct access to specific information about the production process of the user in order to contribute to a solution. Visiting plants or being linked up to the production process through information technology may be necessary.

Fourth, users of complex and changing technologies will be involved in a process of learning-by-doing. Access to experience and know-how accumulated in this process will be crucial for the producer.[9]

But the producer also needs to monitor the competence of the user in a wider sense. When developing a specific innovation, the producer must take into account the competence and learning capacity of the users. Very advanced solutions that demand too much of the users would not be diffused.

Finally, when a production innovation has been developed and adopted by some users a more specific monitoring process takes place. In order to debug the innovation and make incremental adaptation of the original innovation the producer must monitor its use, the learning-by-using taking place and new bottlenecks, etc.

5.6. User Dependency – Users Monitoring Producers

On his part the user is engaged in a (more or less intensive) search for information about new technical opportunities that may result in better performance. He will have incentives to monitor innovative activities among producers and also to monitor the competence and reliability of different producers.

To be aware of a specific product innovation is only a first step. The user has to gather information making it possible to assess the potential impact upon his own performance, and the compatibility with the competence and learning capacity within his own user unit. When the product innovation is radical and at an early stage of diffusion, such information will be extremely difficult to obtain and a considerable amount of uncertainty will be involved. Hands on experience and face-to-face contacts may be necessary.

The user will experience specific bottlenecks in the regular production process. When developing new products, he will discover that the process technology used must be changed. To solve those problems he might involve an independent producer in the analysis and solution. In order to do that, he must know which user to approach. This gives him an incentive to monitor the competence of producers (Box 5).

Box 5: The importance of users in product development
With respect to nine different partners, both within and outside the value chain of the product, users were the most frequent partner. Not just in general terms but also with respect to being referred to as most important partner in the most important product development project within a two year periode (Kristensen & Vinding, 2001b).

---

6. DISCUSSION

6.1. Dilemmas in the Exchange of Information

In order to get an effective solution to his problems, the user must give the producer a certain minimum amount of information about his needs. The more free access the producer gets to such information, the greater the chance for a successful solution. If the user is competing with other users, it might be problematic to give a producer free access to information about his technology and his evolving needs. There is a risk that the producer might appropriate information and distribute it to other users.

The producer is interested in diffusing information to users about his competence and about his product innovations. If he is involved in competition, however, he will also be in a kind of dilemma. On the one hand, he needs to convince users about the superiority of his competence, reliability, and product innovations. This might demand an extensive disclosure of the product innovations involved. On the other hand, he does not want his competitors to get access to his technology.

How this dilemma is solved in concrete cases will reflect individual characteristics of the involved parties as well as the context in which they operate and communicate. When the parties are opportunistic and legal protection is weak the information exchange may be hampered. The fact that benefits can be drawn from building trust may change the parties as well as the context. Trust and co-operative behaviour may be learnt and the rationality of the parties may be transformed in the process.

6.2. The Need for Cooperation Between User and Producer

Certain new products can be ordered by catalogue or bought off-the-shelf by the user. This is the case for low-priced standard components. Other products – typically specialized and expensive capital goods – can only be adopted in a process of cooperation between the user and the producer.

Box 6: The mutual interaction between the producer and user illustrated by channels of communication

Kristensen and Vinding (2001b) show by analyzing the use of three different channels of communication – exchange of employees from the firm to the partner and vice versa, exchange of prototypes and electronic media that.

- Exchange of employees from the firm to the partner has a significant correlation with the exchange of prototypes, and no correlation with use of electronic channels.
- Exchange of employees from the partner to the firm shows the reverse picture. It has no correlation with the exchange of prototypes, but shows significant correlation with use of electronic channels.

This may reflect that exchange of employees can be complementary to use of other channels in two ways: (i) in the coding during the capture (Nonaka & Takeuchi, 1995); and (ii) in the decoding during the interpretation of exchanged information (Sivadas & Dwyer, 2000). As pointed out by Cowan and Foray (1997), some tacit knowledge is needed in order to understand codified knowledge.

The role of employees who work on the partner's premises when a prototype is exchanged may be to capture and bring home to the firm information produced during observation of the partner's use of the prototype. The role of employees from a partner working on the premises of the focal firm may be to provide tacit knowledge that complements codified information exchanged electronically (Kristensen & Vinding, 2001b).

The cooperation might take place in different steps. The user might present the producer with specific needs that the new product should fulfil. When the product innovation has been developed, the producer might install it and start it up in cooperation with the user. In this phase, the producer might offer training in the use of the new product. After the product has been adopted, the user might have a responsibility for updating the product as well as for its repair and service.

The extent of the cooperation might vary with the type of product innovation. But we shall assume that most important product innovations involve at least some elements of cooperation. This increases the dependence of the user. The user does not only procure a product with uncertain properties – he also becomes dependent upon the future behaviour of the producer. This reinforces the user in his efforts to monitor competence and reliability. The choice of a specific producer might be as decisive as the choice of a specific product innovation.

We, thus, find that the users and producers of product innovations are mutually interdependent in a complex way. We shall now discuss how different institutional frameworks connecting users to producers may influence such interdependence. To which degree can the market mechanism intermediate this interdependence (Box 6)?

7. PERFECT COMPETITION AND PRODUCT INNOVATIONS

7.1. Perfect Competition does not Promote Innovation

In the pure market case, where a great number of producers are competing and users are anonymous and numerous, agents will have access only to information in the form of price signals. It is not clear how the users get acquainted with new products in such a pure market. Let us assume than they can observe new products at the marketplace by inspection.

It should be obvious that perfect competition does not induce product innovations. The producer does not get any information about user needs not already served by the market (the fact that we operate with professional users exclude the possibility of introspection and own-use, as a substitute for such information). The user can only observe superficial characteristics of new products. The uncertainty in assessing the impact upon performance will be enormous if the product innovation is radical and complex. Perfect competition implies a weak innovative capability on the part of producers and a weak incentive to develop product innovations with complex properties. Such new products will typically diffuse very slowly or not diffuse at all.

Perfect competition does not, however, affect process innovations negatively to the same degree. Here, the information about user needs is available within the producing unit and the user can get full and immediate access to information about the properties of the new process.[10] The most important limitation to process innovations will be the small scale of the operation involved. There will be no external market for the new process, and the appropriation of benefits will be related exclusively to cost reductions within the producer unit. This will put strict and narrow limits upon the amount of resources allocated to innovative activities. Process innovations will mainly result from learning-by-doing and learning-by-using – that is, from activities that do not impose any extra costs upon the producer.[11]

We have reached the non-trivial result that a market form, assumed to be the only one guaranteeing optimal allocation of resources in a static framework, might be the one least suited to promote technical change and economic growth (see also Johnson & Lundvall, 1989). Only if we assume that producers have immediate access to information not only about revealed preferences, but also about needs and wants in relation to products that do not yet exist, can this problem be overcome. As far as we can see, even the most extreme adepts of rational expectations would be reluctant to go as far as that.

In markets close to the ideal of perfect competition, we should expect product innovations to be developed by accident rather than as a result of purposeful innovative activities. Trivial changes in product design might be easier to introduce than complex product innovations. Process innovations – mainly based upon learning – might take place in parallel within different producer units. But the small scale of operation would reduce the incentives to innovate. And the lack of a mechanism that generalized the results of local learning would indicate a slow growing economy as the outcome.

7.2. A New Perspective on Innovation and Competition

The literature on competition and innovation has not taken into account the importance of learning by interacting. Some of the standard literature in industrial economics treats innovation on line with sales efforts as a strategic action aiming at raising the barriers to entry on line with sales efforts. The debate started by Schumpeter and Galbraith on innovation and competition has often been illustrated by data linking R&D efforts to the size for firms and given rather equivocal results – typically very small and very big firms perform less well than firms of an intermediate size.

Our own research has given very clear results using a different kind of data. We have found that firms that report that they have become exposed to stronger competition are more innovative than those that do not report stronger competition.

Basically we see this result as confirming that firms are organizations with slack and that slack is reduced when competition becomes stronger. More specifically firms realize that they need to produce new things, do old things in a new way or enter new markets in order to survive. Therefore stronger competition has little to do with approaching perfect competition. The number of competitors might not change and the challenge may be coming from competitors that either introduce new products or enter new markets.

Do markets characterized by perfect competition exist in the real world? Do they influence technical change in the way predicted? In markets where professional users operate, it is not so easy to find examples. Markets for vegetables and fruit where numerous restaurant owners come and inspect the products of numerous producers, might be one example. Product innovations are not frequent in this area, and process innovations are mainly reflecting learning.

This fact reflects, however, also a combination of conservative users and natural limits to product innovation. The potential for product innovations – in terms of the rate of change in user needs and new technical opportunities – influences the form of the market. Perfect competition can survive only when this potential is small or absent. In the case mentioned above, a future application of biotechnology to product development might undermine the anonymous relationships between user and producer. To which extent this will be the case, will depend upon the willingness to adopt new products in restaurants.[12]

7.3. A Growing Potential for Product Innovation Undermines the Pure Market

Let us see why a growing potential for product development undermines perfect competition. In a static framework the major concern might be that the new product constitutes a (temporary if time is allowed to be taken into account) monopoly for the producer. More interesting are the dynamic effects that relate to user-producer interaction. If the growing potential reflects new technical opportunities increasing the chance to develop new products in the future, the producer can benefit from vertical integration with one or more user units. He will get access to information about the needs of the users and he will be able to monitor the application of the new technical opportunities to those needs. On this basis, he can develop products superior to those of competitors and he can extend his share of the market.

If the new potential reflects new user needs, a user can gain from vertical integration. By integrating a producer the user will get immediate access to the technical competence within the producer unit and he can gear it towards the new needs he experiences. If the user is involved in competition with other users, he will be able to reduce his costs and obtain a growing share of the market.

Vertical integration undermines perfect competition in three different ways. Directly, it diminishes the flow of goods transmitted by an anonymous market. Indirectly, it gives rise to concentration both on the producer and the user side of the market. If we assume that learning by producing and learning by using are important in relation to the new products involved, the process of concentration will be reinforced by learning by interacting linking the two to each other.

In the treatment of vertical integration by Williamson (1975) the main explanation for this phenomenon is transaction costs whenever small numbers are involved. We suggest that vertical integration motivated by information problems and learning benefits, will take place also when large numbers are present. Furthermore, Williamson argues that technological factors do not play any decisive role in determining vertical integration. We suggest that the forthcoming of new technical opportunities are critical in inducing vertical integration when large numbers are involved.[13]

Our conclusion is thus, that perfect competition forms an environment hostile to product innovations but also that a growing potential for product innovations will undermine perfect competition. In a world where product innovations are frequent and important we should not expect to find perfect competition. In a world characterized by perfect competition we should not expect to observe frequent and important product innovations.

7.4. Small Numbers and Product Innovations

Within the category of non-perfect competition several different constellations might occur.

(a) One producer might relate to one user, a few users, or to numerous users.
(b) A few producers might relate to one user, a few or numerous users.
(c) Finally, many producers might relate to one or a few users.

Thus, there are eight different constellations involving small numbers either on the producer or the user side of the market. We will not go into detail with each of those constellations. We will only present some general implications of small numbers in relation to product innovations. In doing so, we refer to the ideas developed by Williamson (1975) and we use elements of his conceptual framework as far as it applies to the problems treated. Thus, we certainly accept that the actors involved are characterized by bounded rationality and that the environment is characterized by uncertainty and complexity.

Regarding product innovations within such a framework gives interesting results. In earlier sections we specified the information needs of the producer and the user in relation to product innovations. If we take a closer look at the distribution of information in relation to those needs, we find that "information impactedness" is a general characteristic of these relationships. The producer has access to information about technical opportunities that the user does not have, and the user has access to information about user needs that the producer does not have.

We also find that uncertainty and complexity emanates *from the product itself* and not just from the context surrounding the transaction. The user has – especially in the early stage of diffusion – very limited possibilities to assess how the new product will affect his performance. He will also have difficulties in assessing the future services to be delivered by the producer. If the producer is opportunistic, there will be ample room for misleading and cheating the user. The producer might exaggerate his own competence and the capacity of the new product in order to attract users. He may promise to solve problems that he cannot solve, and he may promise to deliver a package of services, which he knows he cannot deliver.

The room for misinformation is more limited on behalf of the user. He cannot misinform the producer without risking that it affects the effectiveness of the solution. He can, of course, misinform the producer in relation to factors not directly related to his technical needs. He can overstate his own capability to develop a substitute for the product for example. Finally, the producer as well as the user might spill information to competitors of the respective counterpart. Or they might use information obtained to invade the market of the other party. It should be observed, that those specific problems, having their origin in the fact that a product innovation is involved, should be added to the general problems concerning an uncertain and complex environment.

Can a contract be written which eliminates the possibility of cheating in such a situation? It is obvious that expectations of opportunistic behaviour on behalf of the other party would normally result in haggling and in tremendous transaction costs when complex product innovations were involved. This has two important implications. If opportunistic behaviour prevailed, small-number markets would be as inefficient as perfect competition in promoting product innovation. We should expect that all, or almost all, complex innovations were process innovations – i.e. developed by presumptive user units. Secondly, this would reflect a movement towards vertical integration where users and producers become joined within the same organization. We should expect that most important innovations were located within vertically organized firms. Also, we should expect a correlation in the opposite direction. The greater the potential for product innovations the more the user-producer relationship should be mediated by a hierarchy rather than by a market.

8. A LEARNING BASED EXPLANATION OF VERTICAL INTEGRATION AND RELATIONAL CONTRACTING

8.1. The Actual Importance and Frequency of Product Innovations

The frequency and importance of product innovations vary across sectors and across firm size but on average the evidence shows that among manufacturing firms.

- A big proportion of firms actually introduce product innovations (more than 50% over a 3-year period).
- A big proportion of sales are constituted by new products (more than 15%).
- Firms allocate a substantial share of their total R&D expenditures to product innovations (more than 60%).

These stylized facts are in contrast to the analytical results obtained above. If the world was according to standard economics or transaction economics we would not expect product innovations to be important and frequent and we should not expect private firms to use resources to develop them. In order to dissolve this paradox we need to take into account not only the transaction costs but also the benefits from co-operation and interactive learning. And we also need to revise the assumption of opportunism as *general* norm of behaviour.

8.2. The Limits of Vertical Integration

The informational problems related to product innovations can, together with the benefits that can be reaped from interactive learning, explain why vertical integration might be ineffective under certain circumstances when small numbers are involved.

If there is only one user and several producers, the user will control the producers by playing one out against another. All the producers will compete with each other when it comes to understand and address the needs of the user. There is little room for cheating and misinformation and the incentives to integrate are weak.

If there is only one producer addressing several users, an integration of one of those users equates an invasion of the market of the other users. Other users will assume that it increases the producer's incentives to cheat and favour the integrated user. The rest of the users might, therefore, be expected to react – either by developing their own capability in the field controlled by the producer – or by stimulating the entrance of new producers. It is reasonable to assume that the remaining independent users will become more reluctant to inform the producer about their needs.

If there are several producers and several users, the vertical integration might take place either up-streams or down-streams. If a user integrates a producer, he will get access to the technical competence of the producer and uncertainty can be reduced. At the same time it is to be expected that the other users will restrict their procurements from and interaction with the integrated producer. They will be less prone to give him access to information about their own process technology. Also, they will fear that he delivers less efficient technology than he delivers to his own user, as well as that he will be transferring critical information to his own user. The producer will get his information input regarding user needs restricted to what can be attained within the new organization and this would gradually erode his technological competence. This means that the user – by integrating one producer – in the long run might get stuck with more limited technical opportunities than other users.

If a producer takes over a user unit, the same type of problems will occur. His access to the rest of the users will become limited because he has become a competitor.

If there in only one user and only one producer involved, vertical integration might be effective in overcoming contractual and informational problems. Here, other limits – such as bureaucracy and other disadvantages of big size – might be operating. And anti-trust regulations might be especially important in blocking this kind of giant-mergers.

Our conclusion is that markets characterized by small numbers, and by frequent and complex product innovations, will not easily be transformed into hierarchies. Vertical integration might have detrimental effects for the dynamic performance of users as well as producers by reducing market shares and flows of information to the producer level. Only in the limiting case where there is one user and one producer operating on the market, no such negative effects can be expected for the firms involved.

This is another way of stating that product innovations will be superior to process innovations. Firms engaging in product innovations draw upon a broader set of user experiences as input into the innovative process than firms engaging in process innovations. *Diversity is key to interactive learning and, for the economy as a whole, product innovation plays the important role of generalizing the local learning taking place among several users.* Process innovation will only use the experiences and needs of one single user and they will only use this local knowledge locally (within the firm).

Here we reach a conclusion opposite the one reached when we applied transaction cost analysis. While transaction cost analysis would point to an economy with little product innovation in areas where small numbers are involved we have pointed to mechanisms that counteract vertical integration. We also argue that innovations will be stimulated by a vertical division of labour between producers and user belonging to different organizations. How to resolve this apparent contradiction? We believe that part of the answer lies in a revision of the assumption on opportunism.

8.3. Opportunism and Interactive Learning

First there are elements of self-interest that limits the tendency to misinform and exploit the partner in weak situations. If a producer aims at supplying a specific set of users on a regular basis, it would be unwise to become known as an opportunistic cheater. Especially if we allow for information exchange among users, opportunistic behaviour will be less rewarding from the point of view of the producer. Such an information exchange will often take place between professional users. Professional users often have their own organizations, which have as one important function, to supply their members with such information.

Especially, when complex product innovations are exchanged the trustworthiness of the producer becomes a decisive competitive factor. The costs inflicted upon the user by an un-reliable producer will be considerable, and the user will often have to accept the word of the producer as the only guarantee for that the innovation will perform according to specifications. Producers regarded as trustworthy will attract users, while producers regarded as unreliable can present advanced technical solutions without attracting users. This will counteract any tendency toward cheating. An important aspect of a producer strategy will be to build a relationship characterized by mutual trust with users.

This will be reinforced by the fact that producers depend upon information about user needs as an input to their innovative activities. A producer who acts opportunistically risks to be excluded from access to such information. That would put him into a serious disadvantage in relation to markets where there is a big potential for product innovations. In such areas, we believe that codes of conduct are imposed upon users as well as producers. Such codes might be tacit and vague, but still they will make distinctions between what is acceptable and what is not. They will impose responsibility and restraint upon the producers, defining limits for what is serious misinformation. They will also define limits for spilling information to the competitors of the other party. Such codes of conduct will take on a life of their own and systematically reduce opportunism as the normal form of conduct.

Such codes of conduct may also get some of their strength in societal norms developed outside the economic sphere. One might ask why opportunism should be a dominating rule of behaviour in the economic sphere. Substantial resources are invested in bringing up children to be honest, responsible, and caring for others. It is not obvious why the result should be cynical individuals or collectives willing to compromise on what is true and right. The predominance of competition, rent- and profit-seeking in the business sector may stimulate the diffusion of opportunistic behaviour; but even in this sphere, countervailing forces reflecting the social embeddedness of the economy are at work. The most important have to do with the fact that agents have a lot to gain from interactive learning and with the fact that interactive learning cannot thrive without a minimum of trust.

8.4. The Organized Market and Product Innovations

In the organization failure framework (Williamson, 1975), a clear-cut distinction is made between the market and the organization. Also, the only alternative coordination mechanism within the organization is hierarchy. We shall question all those assumptions and distinctions.

We have put forward several arguments why in the context of product innovation relatively stable user-producer relationships will develop. Every single user will establish special and durable relations with a subset of all producers and vice versa. This makes it easier to establish mutual trust and effective exchange of information. This vertical semi-integration differs from full integration, in that it is a more flexible and easily reversed relationship than full vertical integration and its negative impact in terms of reducing the diversity of the flow of information is much more limited.

Such subsets of user-producer relationships might involve elements of hierarchy. The user might dominate the innovative activities within producer units that are formally independent and vice versa. We do not, however, believe that all user-producer relationships can be described exclusively in terms of hierarchy. If mutual trust and responsibility were totally absent, such hierarchies would be difficult to operate for the dominant part.

We shall propose that the predominance of product innovations can only be explained by the fact that *most markets are organized markets*. The clear-cut distinction between market and organization might be a useful analytical tool, but it does not reflect reality. We shall also propose, that the element of organization entering the market cannot be reduced to a dimension of hierarchy. Hierarchical relationships are combined with elements of cooperation and mutual trust.[14]

The idea that there are only two ways to co-ordinate economic activities – either through markets or through hierarchies – reflects a very pessimistic and individualist view of human societies. Teams have been recognized as analytical units in the more recent literature on economic organization but there is still a long way to go to explain the frequency of people doing things together without having private economic incentives to bring them to co-ordinate their activities. The idea that individuals may value belonging and contributing to a community for its own sake has yet to be taken up by standard economics.[15]

9. CONCLUSIONS

In this chapter we have changed the analytical perspective of standard economics by moving the attention from allocation and co-ordination in a static context to innovation and learning in a dynamic context. This has led to conclusions regarding the importance and frequency of product innovation much more in accordance with the observed patterns than what we found when applying transaction cost analysis.

We have reached two conclusions regarding the validity of central assumptions of the original version of the Williamsonian analytical scheme. The first is that organized markets are strongly correlated with the occurrence of product innovation and that the distinction between pure markets and hierarchies is misleading. Williamson has taken account of the frequency of relational contracting in his more recent work but his lack of interest in innovation and learning makes this analysis incomplete. The second correction is that opportunism should not be assumed to be a general rule of behaviour in the business sector. The combination of mutual gains from co-operation and non-economic influences may be strong enough to keep opportunism at a level where incomplete agreements may work also in the absence of hostage taking and similar dirty tricks.

One important implication of our analysis is that learning by interacting in organised markets is a very fundamental form of learning in the economic system. Learning by doing and learning by using are local and if standing alone may take the form of process innovations that remain in-house. Learning by interacting, resulting in product innovations, brings together insights from diverse users and combine them in the new products that are then distributed as widely as possible by the producer. This is why learning by interacting and product innovation are fundamental in the learning economy. The major reason why, as argued by Adam Smith, there is a strong link between an extended division of labour and economic growth is not that it results in a better allocation of resources or local scale economies. It is rather the dynamic process where many local learning processes gets fused and transformed into product innovations.

This might be seen as bringing important lessons for industrial policy and innovation policy. To fight opportunism and to make it easy for users to establish informal collaboration with innovating producers are ways to stimulate learning and growth. Another hypothesis that can be raised is that vertical integration may have a stronger negative impact on dynamic efficiency than horizontal integration. The transaction costs saved may be lost in foregone benefits from interactive learning. This is especially the case in a rapidly changing world where the knowledge base is complex. In the learning economy attempts to gather too many stages of the production process into one organization may slow down innovation and learning.

NOTES

1. This kind of reasoning is not very different from the one presented by Milton Friedman in defence of profit maxismising assumption – over time firms that do not attempt to/succeed in maximising profits will have lower survival rates than those who do so and therefore the whole population of firms will be more and more densely populated by profit maximisers.

2. This implies that "culture," including national culture may affect innovation processes and economic transactions within and across national borders (Lundvall, 1993).

3. Separation and proximity in space – geographical as well as cultural – between user and producers is critical when it comes to explain regional and national systems of innovation (Lundvall, 1999).

4. This difference between consumers and professional users is also reflected in their respective expected behavior in relation to innovations. The professional user is expected to be active in his search for new ways to solve his problems. He is also expected to adapt his behavior and qualifications when new technical opportunities come forward. This might include formal training as well as learning-by-using. The role played by the consumer, on the other hand, is expected to be passive. He/she does not engage in systematic search for new products and he/she is not prone to adopt products, which involve extensive training and changes in behavior – at least not without having been exposed to major sales efforts from suppliers. Professional users are more apt to use "voice" when it comes to express needs while the typical consumer will be more prone to use "exit."

These differences in behavior are reinforced by the way producers address the respective category of users. Producers of consumer goods use market research to uncover the needs of the consumers and advertising both to make new products known to consumers and to influence their needs. They will also, ceteris paribus, tend to be conservative in their product innovations, in order to limit the change imposed on user behavior from the new product. Product innovations in this area might be radical in terms of the technology built into the product. In terms of the interface between user and product, however, they will tend to be incremental.

5. This point was made by Kenneth Arrow in discussions at Stanford University 1984 about the original draft paper (see Lundvall, 1985).

6. Other categories of consumers that seem to become as focused as professional users belong to "communities of practise" enjoying technically demanding hobbies – Harley Davidson bikers, surfers, skate-boarders and mountain climbers fall into mind.

7. This distinction does not always apply. An interesting exception is "the flying prototype" where the innovation is physically embodied in a product that is sent to the user

for him/her to respond to. Here the major role of the physical object is to carry information between the two parties (Kristensen, 1992).

8. The specific set of user-producer relationships and their stability tend to channel the innovative process in certain directions; but hamper it in other directions. The interaction between innovation and user-producer relationships is far from harmonious. The actual pattern of user-producer relationships does not easily adapt to radical change in needs and technological opportunities. Periods of slow-down in economic growth may reflect a mismatch between the pattern of relationships and radically new technological opportunities (Lundvall, 1991).

9. Converting this knowledge into new products is one fundamental way of generalizing local knowledge obtained by learning by doing and learning by using. This is why learning by interacting in connection with product innovation is of fundamental importance for the over all economic dynamics and growth in the learning economy.

10. As shown by Reinhard Lund in Chap. 4 in this volume there are important information problems to overcome across divisions within firms in connection with product innovation. Actually, our conceptual discussion on building codes and channels and information has been inspired by Arrow (1974) who analyses intra-organizational communication.

11. It is interesting to relate this result to the fact that product innovations are neglected within neoclassical theory. This is quite logical since the basic models operate on the basis of an assumption about perfect competition that leaves little room for product innovation.

12. The basic idea in this section, that pure markets are dynamically inefficient, has been developed further in a broader discussion of the limits of the pure market economy (see Johnson & Lundvall, 1989).

13. In Williamson (1975), there is a chapter on market structure in relation to technical and organizational innovation. It is, however characteristic that the part of it relating to technical innovation almost exclusively refers to scale economies and to how big firms perform compared to small firms. The exchange of information between user and producer relating to innovative activities is not taken into account. This might explain why Williamson concludes that his analysis.

> Makes it evident that it is transactions rather than technology that underlie the interesting issues of microeconomic organizations.

A user-producer perspective leads to radically different conclusions. The interaction between users and producers is a process related to technical progress and it has a strong impact upon microeconomic organization.

14. Our arguments against the transaction cost approach are akin to and compatible with the analysis of vertical integration developed by G. B. Richardson before Williamson (1975) introduced the transaction cost perspective in his seminar book. Richardson recognized the importance of hybrid forms of market and organization and built an explanation of vertical integration based upon the idea that firms will gather "similar" activities in house and establish durable network relationships to those suppliers that produce key inputs by processes that are not similar to the core activities of the firm (Richardson, 1972).

15. While organized markets may be seen as a necessary precondition for product innovation they may also be seen as lock-in mechanisms. Especially in periods of radical technological change this may be a major problem and result in a generalized productivity slow-down (Lundvall, 1991).

REFERENCES

Arrow, K. J. (1971). Political and economic evaluation of social effects and externalities. In: M. Intrilligator (Ed.), *Frontiers of Quantitative Economics*. North Holland.

Arrow, K. J. (1974). *The limits of organization*. New York.

Carter, A. P. (1986). Diffusion from an input-output perspective. Papers Presented at the Conference on Innovation Diffusion. Venice: Ca' Dolfin Dorsoduro.

Cowan, R., & Foray, D. (1997). The economics of codification and the diffusion of knowledge. *Industrial and Corporate Change, 6*.

Harhoff, D., Henkel, J., & von Hippel, E. (2003). Profiting from voluntary information spillovers: How users benefit by freely revealing their innovations. *Research Policy, 32*, 1753–1769.

Jeppesen, L. B. (2001). Making consumer knowledge available and useful. Working Paper. Copenhagen Business School.

Jeppesen, L. B. (2004). *Organizing consumer innovation*. Ph.D. Thesis. København: Samfundslitteratur.

Johnson, B., & Lundvall, B. Å. (1989). The limits of the pure market economy. In: J. Bohlin et al. (Eds), *Samhällsvetenskap, Ekonomi, Historia, Festskrift til Lars Herlitz* (pp. 85–106). Göteborg: Daidalos.

Kristensen, P. S. (1992). Flying prototypes: Production departments' direct interaction with external customers. *International Journal of Operations and Production Management, 12*, 197–212.

Kristensen, P. S., & Vinding, A. L. (2001a). Important collaboration partners in product development. In: B. Bellon, A. Plunket & C. Voisin (Eds), *The Dynamics of Inter-firm Cooperation: A Diversity of Theories and Empirical Approaches*. Edward Elgar.

Kristensen, P. S., & Vinding, A. L. (2001b). Exchange of employees, prototypes and use of electronic media in product development collaboration: Results from a Danish study. In: *Innovative Networks*. Paris: OECD.

Lundvall, B. Å. (1985). *Product innovation and user-producer interaction*. Aalborg: Aalborg University Press.

Lundvall, B. Å. (1988). Innovation as an interactive process – from user-producer interaction to the national system of innovation. In: G. Dosi et al. (Eds), *Technical Change and Economic Theory*. London: Pinter Publishers.

Lundvall, B. Å. (1991). Innovation, the organised market and the productivity slow-down. In: *OECD, Technology and Productivity, The Challenge for Economic Policy* (pp. 447–458). Paris: OECD.

Lundvall, B. Å. (1992). Explaining inter-firm cooperation and innovation – limits of the transaction cost approach. In: G. Grabher (Eds), *The Embedded Firm: On the Socioeconomics of Industrial Networks*. London: Routledge.

Lundvall, B. Å. (1993). User-producer relationships, national systems of innovation and internationalisation. In: D. Foray & C. Freeman (Eds), *Technology and the Wealth of Nations*. London: Pinter Publishers.

Lundvall, B. Å. (1999). Spatial division of labour and interactive learning. *Revue d'Économie Régionale et Urbaine, 3*, 469–488.

Lundvall, B. Å., Olesen, N. M., & Aaen, I. (1984). Det Landbrugsindustrielle Kompleks. Serie om industriel udvikling nr. 28. Aalborg Universitetsforlag.

Nonaka, I., & Takeuchi, H. (1995). *The knowledge-creating company*. New York: Oxford University Press.

Richardson, G. B. (1972). The organisation of industry. *The Economic Journal*, 882–896.

Sivadas, E., & Dwyer, F. (2000). An examination of organizational factors influencing new product success in internal and alliance-based processes. *Journal of Marketing, 64,* 31–49.

Vinding, A. L. (2002). *Interorganisational diffusion and transformation of knowledge in the process of product innovation.* Unpublished Ph.D. Thesis, IKE group/DRUID. Department of Business Studies, Aalborg University.

von Hippel, E. (2001, July). Innovation by user communities: Learning from open source software. *Sloan Management Review.*

Williamson, O. E. (1975). *Markets and hierarchies: Analysis and antitrust implications.* MacMillan.

THE ORGANIZATION OF ACTORS' LEARNING IN CONNECTION WITH NEW PRODUCT DEVELOPMENT

Reinhard Lund

ABSTRACT

This chapter extracts a broad range of learning situations *in connection with product innovation. The data comprise interviews with the management and employees in five Danish manufacturing firms visited during 2000–2001. Among important* learning situations *and* factors promoting learning *have been found the firms' contacts with customers, project leaders' cross functional coordinating activities, and cooperation with suppliers and knowledge institutions. The* restraints *upon learning comprise* inter alia *strategic patterns, tight time planning, old routines and communication difficulties, changing of roles, ad hoc decisions on training and education and some times among employees lack of motivation. Some policy perspectives are outlined.*

1. INTRODUCTION

Danish, national survey data for both 1995–1997 and 1998–2000 have shown that half the private firms report that they have undergone important organizational changes during these periods. The objectives for these changes have represented two main routes i.e. daily effectiveness and longer term renewal of products and quality, knowledge, and organizational cooperation and coordination. Furthermore

Product Innovation, Interactive Learning and Economic Performance
Research on Technological Innovation and Management Policy, Volume 8, 129–153
Copyright © 2004 by Elsevier Ltd.
ISSN: 0737-1071/doi:10.1016/S0737-1071(04)08006-0

analysis of the survey data has shown that product innovation is positively connected with internal and external coordination of activities (Nielsen & Lundvall, 2003). In this chapter I shall concentrate on the learning aspects of these activities using the qualitative part of the PIE project.

There is a rich literature exploring research on learning and knowledge in relation to organization and management (Sanchez, 2001; von Krogh et al., 1998; Weick & Westley, 1996). Instead of using such results for hypothesis testing I shall choose a "grounded" approach (Locke, 2001), which starts from the information supplied by managers and employees in a few small and middle sized Danish firms. Here the actors involved in product development were asked by repeated interviewing about their way of working and indirectly were questioned about promoting factors and barriers of learning and knowledge connected to product innovation. From this has been extracted important *learning situations* which will be put in perspective by comparisons with other research before conclusions are drawn. So the main focus of this chapter is upon situations of learning as planned and/or experienced by people working on new products. Compared to Chap. 4 the emphasis is more on organizational issues and human resources rather than knowledge management.

2. DATA COLLECTION

The qualitative part of the PIE project comprised eleven small and middle-sized firms. This chapter focuses upon information from five firms, which were visited three or four times during the period January 2000–December 2001. The five firms comprise two machine firms one of which delivered its machines to the food industry and the other to metal and transport, one metal firm, one firm producing for the graphical trade and one electronic firm. Within each of these firms a couple of specific product developments were investigated besides the gathering of general information on the firms' product innovation activities. Interviews were carried out with 29 persons coming from top management, the functions of development, sales and marketing, and logistics including production. All in all 49 interviews took place during the period as some central actors were interviewed at each of the three or four visits.

3. LEARNING SITUATIONS IN CONNECTION WITH NEW PRODUCT DEVELOPMENT

The product innovation activities build upon actors' theoretical and practical understanding. At the same time new product development implies the actors' acquisition of new experiences and related understanding which by definition means learning and so also a contribution to the actors' knowledge. When interviewing the managers and employees involved in new product development they did not refer explicitly to concepts such as knowledge and learning, but the researchers raised the question during the interviewing and got some reactions. Mostly the actors referred to such information and communication, which solved problems and raised new issues relevant for their work on new product development. Problem solving is one important way of learning, so, a good deal of the following description and analysis of the actors' product development activities is focussed upon what the actors had to say about their search for information in the context of problem solving. Other learning situations stemmed from formal teaching and informal discussions and sparring with colleagues and external partners about task related questions. An overview of the following analysis of learning situations as regard promoting factors is given in Table 1.

Table 1. An Overview of the Learning Situations and Related Promoting Factors.

Learning Situation	Promoting Factors
Contacts with customers and the product market.	Interaction with customers and other people related to the product market. Field tests.
The product committee.	Product strategy directed towards new product ideas. Work on business case.
Experiments and tests.	Trial-and-error activities.
On-the-job learning.	Project leaders characterized by sociability and oriented towards the whole new product development task. Project leaders promoting communication and consultation.
Gate meetings.	Drawing upon knowledge distributed among functional departments and supervisory as well as non-supervisory personnel.
Contacts with suppliers and knowledge institutions.	The developers sparring with external actors. Building and drawing upon personal relationship.
Formal training and education.	Educational plans. The actors' interest in supplementary courses.

The presentation of the interviews is arranged around some major steps of new product development which were in use in the investigated firms and mirrored suggestions well known in the literature on product development (Cooper, 1993). One part of the talk was concentrated around the *idea* for a new product. A second part concerned the development of the product and the related *coordination* of functional contributions. A third part it was directed towards the extent of *support from outside the visited firm*. For the sake of a clear presentation *barriers* for learning is gathered in a specific section, which follows the above mentioned three parts. At the end of the chapter we discuss the results regarding the connections between learning and new product development with specific emphasis on factors related to promotion and hindrances for learning. This discussion also relates the findings to other research.

4. IDEAS FOR PRODUCT DEVELOPMENT

The start of new product development was often a nebulous affair according to the managers who took the decisions regarding new products. Nevertheless the external input was stressed by all the managers. To give an example.

> We get incredibly much information from sales people, from service people, from customers, yes you know, I was just about to say from all the world. It's such things you listen to. And from this you make up a picture (B1).

The CEOs and managers of sales and development also made their own visits to (potential) customers and fairs and gathered their own information. The great interest in learning from the market and customers must to some extent be seen as a reaction to the greater weight previously given to ideas founded upon internal technical explorations. This change in strategic outlook showed itself most clearly by the recommendations from the technical managers given to their developing people. The developers were asked to direct more attention to the market and the customers. In one of the machine firms another sign was the splitting up of larger technical oriented projects in smaller customer oriented projects.

One thing was information, another was to develop an idea based on a picture – as mentioned by our manager above – of relevant traits of the competitive situation. Or to use the language of learning: How to learn from the information and understand the situation. Before an idea was transformed into a project a top level committee would decide upon a proposal, which outlined the business which could be expected from a product based upon the idea. The proposal would be prepared by the development department after contact with sales and other relevant people. Both the committee and the way the expected business was investigated pointed to the weight the firms gave to draw upon knowledge found across the functions of the firms. One of the managers of development explained the procedure and its motivation in the following way:

> We have established a new scrutiny or construction method. It is based upon the experience that from time to time we do not think carefully before we start. . . . So I have made a new method . . . where we simply take all possible functions into account. Let it be purchase, quality, sales, service, construction of course, and production . . . and then I have asked, I think it is about 400 questions. All those things which can interrupt the process when it starts, we try to collect them before we start from a proposal (E1).

The principles of the new method mentioned by this manager of development was also in use in the other visited firms. This fact could be attributed to the choice made more or less recently of the investigated firms to introduce a product development procedure termed Integrated Product Development or the Stage-Gate New Product Process, which the top managers knew directly or indirectly from Robert G. Cooper, the father of this procedure (Cooper, 1993). The procedure implied the formalization of a business case, and a stepwise continuation of the work on the new product through construction, testing, and production to launch and parallel activities on supplies, marketing and sales, and production layout evaluated by gate meetings between the stages. In this way learning and the use of available knowledge situated in different functions and among external partners came to the fore.

The survey part of the PIE project showed that 89% of the firms which carried out product development arranged formal meetings during the process (Christensen et al., 2005).[1]

But one thing was the intention of integrating knowledge and learning, quite another was really to secure the learning and the use of available knowledge. This will be illustrated from the case studies by concentrating upon the work of the project leaders, the experience from gate meetings and the contacts with external partners.

5. PROJECT LEADERS

For the purpose of integrating knowledge from the various functions, the management selected project leaders whom they expected to understand the importance of drawing upon and activating the knowledge situated throughout the firm. The managers pointed to those people who they called generalists.

> Project leaders are much more generalists than specialists. And the specialist can be as clever as a constructor can be and burn 100% for the project, but has no intention of becoming included in other phases of the project . . . there has to be a little touch of marketing man hidden somewhere

in him. There needs to be an understanding of production. There has to be a little of everything
in such a project (H1).

The interviews with the project leaders confirmed that they had this broader
understanding of their development task. One of those leaders pointed to the
difference between the old way of development and the new one in which the
departments had to learn from each other e.g. development and sales department.

The idea concerning . . . the developer to get involved early, that is also to secure that sales
is included all the time, . . . that demands more dynamics on the part of the development
department. It also demands that sales begin to get an understanding for what is actually
happening during the development phase. Why can't we do what they think we can . . . it
demands more of everybody, but it also means that at the end when production takes place,
there is no doubt that what we get is something which we have agreed upon (B4).

From the interviewing it could be seen that the task of the project leader concerning
construction and the related experiments and tests depended upon trial-and-error
learning. Again, this learning depended upon coordination of activities and the
use of distributed knowledge and cross functional learning. Here the project
leader based his work on such social processes as communication, sociability,
consultation, and negotiations combined with more or less conflict.

Besides electronic communication much mutual learning took place by
communication face-to-face. So was the case when developers carried through
design experiments together with a colleague with another form of advanced
training and/or workers with practical experience. Here mutual inspiration was
observed in several projects. Sometimes the communication was informal as when
a developer would go to the workshop and have a talk with the worker about
materials and work processes. In other cases a formal setup and measurements
were used, but again discussed between a developer and one or more partners
and during the design process commented upon by sales people. It was a
specific lesson according to one developer that it was necessary to write down
what happened along the process. If you did not, you could not reconstruct
the process and really learn what had actually occurred and explain your
results.

From the survey part of the PIE project it was seen that within 79% of the firms
that carried out product development, a written documentation was prepared at the
end of the process (Christensen et al., 2005).

The importance of interactive learning made project leaders' *sociability* i.e.
being friendly and ready to converse, important for successful development
processes. For instance they would start meetings by small talk, and be ready
to listen to suggestions from their surroundings. This was also confirmed by
their collaborators in the development department and in production. One of the

developers told the PIE researchers that this sort of sociability behaviour was learned by experience from less satisfactory gate meetings.

To some extent the project leaders promoted learning for themselves and their partners by using a *consultative* approach. As an example from the cases, it can be mentioned that the sales people were very satisfied with the developer at the metal factory because they found that he had "really" consulted marketing and sales at the beginning of his development task. But the sales' informant could also tell that such behaviour was not always seen. Nevertheless it seemed to marketing and sales at this firm that the time worked toward more such consultation between development and sales.

In the electronics firm an interview with the worker who assembled the product which was investigated told the researchers that she had got all the necessary information from the developer who had taught her the new task. But she had also been active herself in pointing out difficulties in the assembly process and in this way contributed to necessary changes in design. In this case the learning would spread to other workers through their autonomous groups because the assembly workers taught each other the work processes when a new product was introduced. The initiation would come from the assembly worker who had worked together with the developer on the construction of the prototype.

Part of the developers' learning showed itself as joint decision making when knowledge coming from actors in different functions was involved. Such decisions might imply some *negotiations* and contained the potential for conflicts. As said by a product leader.

We can't deliver a custom made solution from the prototype shop and introduce it directly in production (E1).

A problem concerning work processes could for instance imply a choice between welding or bending based on some trials. Another problem would be the layout. At this stage *negotiations* between product developer and product technical people became of importance as well as relationships with product responsible managers and production and/or assembly workers. These situations meant learning occurrences for the developers in relation to production layout and production processes. The solving of layout problems was primarily the task of production technicians. But developers had to think of the consequences for layout when making blueprints. In this connection talks between developers and layout people had become more common – as expressed by both the production manager and the developer in the metal factory – by which the developers had learnt more about the organization of work activities and would take this knowledge into consideration. Nevertheless in some instances the developer would evade negotiations and possible conflicts by letting the production people take the decision themselves instead of having trouble with the groups regarding their work loads and other interests which would be of importance for their decision.

In this section we have given examples of project leaders who with positive results based their work on social processes such as communication, sociability and consultation. Such traits are central to human resource management. The qualitative results are in line with the results based on PIE survey data cf. Vinding's analysis in Chap. 7 showing that firms that apply HRM practices to a high extent are in a better position to innovate.

6. THE GATE MEETINGS AND THE SCRUTINY PROCESSES

The stage-gate model in use in the five firms implied a number of gate meetings, which showed themselves as important for learning and the coordination of knowledge. One of the managers of development pointed to the joining of experiences in the following way.

> It's a routine that a scrutiny must take place at the end of a stage when we are finished. And you have to call across functions . . . we have production included . . . we have had incredible luck by having people from the floor. He who has been welding during 30 years, he knows how the product should look like. We have reduced our cost prices considerably since we started to look into that part where we try to draw production knowledge into development (E1).

In the beginning of product development it was typically sales and development who participated in a gate meeting. Later on by the development of the new product these people were joined by those who had taken part in the previous stage of the development and those who got to be active in the following stage. So, before zero-series and full production technicians and other production people from both supervisor level and workers would take part. Generally, recently the shop floor was included to a higher extent than previously and workers' creativity was underlined. In all the firms inputs from these various functions were seen as an important way to secure technical integration but also improved understanding of the necessity of cooperation. The differences between the inputs from the different functions were explained by a sales manager in the following way: Sales would look upon the aesthetic and functional side of the product and look upon the product just like a consumer. Production looked upon how easy the new product was to produce, and logistics look into the buying situation. Not every scrutiny was a success. Some conditions had to be taken into consideration as will be explained below in Section 8 on restraints on learning.

7. EXTERNAL CONTACTS FOR SUPPORT

The PIE survey data shows that 80–90%. of the Danish product developing firms to a high or to some extent have developed a closer contact with customers and suppliers whereas only between one fourth and one third have done so with consultants and research institutions (Table 2).

The investigated firms disclosed a number of external contacts from which they learnt, which kind of products they should focus upon and how to carry through some parts of new product development. In the words of one of the developers.

> The products are continuously developed as a consequence of the developers' sparring with service, the market, production and component suppliers (B3).

And speaking about the lack of certain competences, a top manager pointed to the following sources.

> From where do we get this knowledge? It can be AUC (Aalborg university). It can be DTU (Technical university of Denmark, Copenhagen). It can be some other external actors. And it need not only be technology (B1).

By drawing upon external knowledge the firms got that extra competence which was of importance for their total competence regarding new product development. In the following is illustrated learning from customers, suppliers and knowledge institutions. The learning situations comprise discussions and sparring as well as joint experiments.

Learning from *customers* was important for the firms to be able to develop successful products. In this connection the informants stressed that customers of the same product did not all demand the same. Their opinion on for instance design or quality would differ. So, the input from customers and about customers had to be used selectively both by developers and production people. Learning from customers specifically oriented towards the new products occurred both in the beginning of new product development, during development and at the end of

Table 2.   Product Developing Firms and Their External Contacts.

Firms' Contacts	% Of Firms Which Have Developed a Closer Contact to a High Extent or Some Extent
Customers	91
Suppliers	79
Consultants	33
Research institutions	23

Source: PIE survey.

the development process. Customer relevant input at the beginning of the process was referred to above in Section 4 concerning the *idea* for changing a product or developing a completely new product.

During the process the developers might contact (potential) customers to get a more solid base for a choice between alternative product possibilities. At the end of the development process when a prototype or a zero series had been produced, the development and sales people would often contact a key customer and ask him to try the product. The developers could give examples of learning from such so-called field tests both regarding the technical parts of the products and the manual to be used by the customer. In the food machinery factory the manager responsible for deliveries would see to it that production by the customer was registered and the data diffused to the developers and people from his own division. He underlined that such information was not given to many employees, but to those who could use it.

The developers had an ambiguous attitude toward customer contacts. On the one hand they saw advantages of such contacts for their own learning about the product and to show the importance the firm felt for its product and use. On the other hand such contacts took time from other tasks, which the developer was expected to carry out. Through experiences the developers went through learning processes with regard to administer such customer relationships.

During full production customer complaints and experiences from service employees would be part of the input to new product developments. Such input would be discussed at meetings within the sales department together with experiences from sales people and raised in other fora as well.

For technical and manpower reasons the visited firms used *suppliers* incl. sub-contractors to a certain extent. In relation to learning and knowledge some such input took the shape of technologies, but at the same time the developers learnt about the use of the products by the suppliers and by related experiments together with suppliers. It was the opinion among the developers that suppliers could come up with solutions that the developers had not thought themselves. In relation to some equipment, which was bought by a developer in the metal firm the necessary software demanded a good deal of learning by the developer.

The graphical firm sometimes hired in employees from their suppliers for a period and at a certain stage of the development for two reasons. Firstly, the managers at the electronic firm expected that the supplier's employee would see to it that the firm got a new product development, which would give no delivery trouble with his own firm. Secondly, the visited firm's employees learnt more by having the employee from the other firm nearby to see how he solved upcoming problems and by having extensive interaction with him along diverse tasks.

Part of the learning regarding suppliers had a social dimension. In relation to the investigated product developments, the developers could tell the researchers about two cases where they had to *renegotiate* the contracts with sub-contractors. They could tell that they had learnt to be more careful and be more specific when negotiating contracts. Other cases stemmed from the handling of problems with quality of deliveries and the ability to keep to time limits. Information on such issues would be recognized by logistics people and communicated to those responsible for quality. In case of dissatisfaction with a supplier various measures to change the situation could be taken, and as examples given during the interviews are written warnings to suppliers of discontinuation of business.

The support from *knowledge institutions* such as universities and technical and commercial high schools comprised both formal educational courses, cooperation on projects and ad hoc advice on technical and commercial matters. Furthermore some learning took place through the relationships to the technological institutes which provided authorization as required by public authorities regarding environment protection, fire risks etc.

In the graphical firm the technical director stated that he had an educational plan for the employees, and this plan was related to the strategic plan. Another manager from within the director's department modified this impression. He had no formalized educational plan in his section, but written information about the employees' courses and wishes for further education. The main impression from the other four firms was that the management had chosen an adaptation strategy in relation to learning by formal education. To the extent new tasks were to be carried out or an employee should change his job, the management would initiate the necessary education. The form could be learning on the job by the help of a colleague or an external course.

In the PIE survey it was found that long term educational planning took place in 53% of the firms with product development. Custom made courses were used by 65% of the product developing firms.

In the five firm's development departments the educational background was characterized by medium or higher education. Most product developers were civil engineers or engineers educated at polytechnics even though a few were skilled workers who had supplemented their craft background with supplementary courses.

All the firms' product developers had participated in various forms for relevant courses. They showed much interest in supplementary courses because of continuous changes in their area of work, but also based on a wish for new contacts and wider horizons. The technicians working on tests, construction tasks etc. usually had a formalized technical education, but again you could find skilled workers who had supplemented their training with relevant courses.

The firms' external contacts concerning research and development covered both Danish and foreign institutions. The motives for such contacts were based on the new possibilities which opened up due to new knowledge and extra capacities, economic advantages and motivation of the employees.

The machine firm which produced new products for the metal industry and transport drew upon the Danish FORCE institutes as well as foreign institutes. Moreover the firm had good contacts to Danish universities. The firm did also participate in some projects supported by EU. By these contacts the firm sought to be in front regarding new processes of importance for its products. To this were added the economic advantages of EU projects and the possibilities for the management to present more interesting tasks to its employees with the hope of keeping a motivated work force.

The electronics firm worked together with a Technological Institute and other consultants who provided expertise concerning design and compensated for the firm's shortage of manpower in other new product development areas.

The metal firm was part of a foreign concern which meant cross firm development work. So the concern's managers of development defined a joint product development project during the interviewing period. Also the metal firm worked together with the Technological Institute concerning areas where the firm lacked the necessary competence. Some projects were supported by public funds.

The machine firm, which delivered products to the food industry cooperated with a technological institute concerning the use of the institute's machines. Regarding some construction tasks the firm had the support from consultants. One of the projects investigated by the PIE researchers got public support because of the new product's contribution to energy savings.

The graphical firm exchanged knowledge with one of the universities and a couple of research centres.

8. RESTRAINTS ON LEARNING

The previous sections have described *learning situations* and related *promoting factors* connected to new product developments as experienced by the actors of the five visited firms. An overview was given in Table 1 in Section 3. Briefly the situations have comprised the following.

- Contacts with customers and other relationships with the product market such as fairs and visits to potential customers.
- The product committee.
- Experiments and tests.

- On-the-job learning.
- Gate meetings, formal and informal.
- Contacts with suppliers and people from knowledge institutions.
- Formal training and education.

The management of the visited firms were clearly trying to strengthen several factors which could improve learning and competence during the above mentioned situations. On the other hand these learning situations still were hampered by restraining factors due to strategic decisions, structural features, opposing processes and cultural features related to these factors. In the following we report observed restraints, found in each of the learning situations. These restraints are summarized in Table 3.

Starting with the firms' *contacts with customers and other relationships with the product market*, the researchers were told in two of the firms that the management put limits to the learning which would imply the crossing of market borders that might activate their competitors to start retaliations.

Another limit to the learning from the market concerned the feedback from the sales staff. The developers thought sales staff were sometimes biased because they paid too much attention to agents instead of going to the end-consumer. The sales staff were not totally denying this statement, but explained that they had to

Table 3. An Overview of the Learning Situations and Related Restraints.

Learning Situation	Restraints
Contacts with customers and the product market.	Fear of retaliations from other businesses. Limited feedback.
The product committee.	Strategic choices. Strategic ambiguities. Priority to reuse.
Experiments and tests.	Time pressure. Unrealistic plans.
On-the-job learning.	Old routines. Limits to communication. Subconscious knowledge. Lack of capacity, opposing attitudes.
Gate meetings.	Participants' lack of interest. Technological bias. Unsatisfactory minutes of meetings. Lack of openness and mutual trust.
Contacts with suppliers and knowledge institutions. Formal training and education.	Lack of personal relationships. Ad hoc decisions by the management. Limitations of supply. Lack of motivation among employees.

listen to the agents who were the ones with which they did business. Marketing would criticize development staff for not listening to them and learn from their experiences. So, the quality and quantity of the feedback had its limitation. This was clearly shown when a project group at the food machine factory wanted to get information about production cost in user units. Such figures were not at hand and the project group had to find out for itself. All in all fragments of input could be found in the firm, but learning from the results of product development with regard to more development was not systematized and accumulated.

The actors in *the meetings of the product committee* insisted upon the firm's *strategic pattern*. An important strategic signal from the management concerned the priority given to the market and the weakening of the teams put on technological developments. For example one of the members of the product committee stated.

> We try to make those development people much more market oriented. Much more involved in the business part of the project . . . (and later) . . . I think it is very important not to promote technology too much during the single development project, because then you cannot control it (B1.5.17).

It meant that learning initiatives trespassing this strategic orientation would be stopped, and the managers were much aware of holding their developers away from experiments, which would deviate from the managements' orientations. This attitude by management was a reaction to experiences with technological developments of products, which demanded too many resources for too long time. So, a change in business culture had taken place or rather was under its way during the PIE research. On the other hand the management had to balance this strategy giving some concern for the creative ideas of their developers. This was done by giving some leeway to the developers at the beginning of developments. The developers who wanted to stay in their jobs had to accept the managements' orientations. So, when learning brought them off the line defined for a specific new product development, they were ready to stop. Yet, this did not exclude the possibility that the new knowledge might be of use when the developers later on worked on another new project.

The strategic orientations of management were in some cases felt to be too ambiguous according to the developers and sales staff. This ambiguity was given as a reason for difficulties in reaching common understanding of product development across sales and development.

In the graphical firm the management's strategy placed much weight on reuse of components as part of a system called Design for Manufacturing. This strategy resulted in problems for the project leader of the project which the PIE group studied. The reason was that only by creating new components he thought he could stick to the promised measures of small size, but this meant a deviation from the percentage of reuse and the planned costs of the new product. Part of the problem in this case could be seen as coming from development who had reduced the expected costs by promising too much reuse when negotiating the new product development with top management.

Experiments and tests were hampered by adherence to a norm of giving priority to the time factor. The strong negative effect of this factor is illustrated by the following excerpt from the interviewing.

> Interviewer: If you should mention something, which could impede or raise barriers for the development process and later on for the profit, what would you point to?
> Manager: Time pressure.
> Interviewer: Time pressure?
> Manager: Time pressure and unrealistic plans. That is the biggest clog on our department by which we can destroy everything completely. Cases where we take an optimistic viewpoint and forget everything we have around us. Time plans which collapse. You can say time pressure in the creative part of the project. In that case the result will be meagre. Poor preliminary work can also destroy a project. Therefore I have really also tried to make a good preliminary work to get all functions involved before we start up (E1).

In the metal firm one of the developed products gave problems for some of the customers. By his visit the developer found out that his new product was not compatible with a new product used in the same process developed by another company. After adjustment of the new product, compatibility was established. It was his opinion that with a sufficient number of experiments and modelling he could have foreseen the possibility of the other firm's new product and its consequences, but the time loss in his development would not have been rational for his firm.

Both in the electronics firm and the metal firm the developers regretted that production workers sometimes followed old routines instead of *learning-on-the-job* the new ways of work which the developers had announced recommended. In the electronic firm this kind of behavioural inertia damaged the learning of the developer when a zero series went wrong. By taking countermeasures with regard to control of the process he succeeded in getting the necessary information for changing the product.

In the food machinery factory the issue of old routines to the detriment of learning-on-the-job showed itself in the relationship between development and the group responsible for electric equipment. The electric group did not want to involve themselves in new product development. They just demanded the developers to present their prototype and what they thought was necessary with regard to electronics and the electric group would solve the problems. For the developers such behaviour had been acceptable when electric problems were simple, but the content of new product development today would gain from creative work on the part of the electric group. The reluctance by the electric group was a clear hindrance for the developers and new product development across functions.

Limits to communication hampered learning-on-the-job in a number of cases. For instance the assembly worker in one of the electronic firms would tell about her satisfaction with information on the product, which the PIE group investigated but add that such satisfactory information from the developers was lacking in the work of another group. In other cases praise to one developer was followed by making reservations towards other developers with regard to exchange of information. Even though some developers often went to the production shop, others were seen more seldom which restrained their possibility from learning from production. In the metal factory a production manager criticised the developers for not answering suggestions by production and he also pointed to the business culture of physical division between production and development.

A part of the individuals' knowledge was difficult to communicate. So, production people and developers each had their own thoughts about how to use the materials, reduce waste, find the right measures. All those things, a manager explained, was part of each one's subconsciousness. The firm tried to put such knowledge into the quality handbook, but still something would stay as implicit knowledge, which was only brought into play by direct face-to-face interaction.

The managements wanted to change the work roles of both developers and technicians in such a way that technicians got more responsibility by taking over some engineering tasks and the developers got room for more creative work in accordance with their formal education. The experience by the management was that such a change was difficult. Firstly, learning their new role was difficult for the technicians on the background of their previous education and training, which had stressed the execution of specific tasks. So some of them hesitated regarding taking over the responsibility for a full task including taking contact with production staff. Secondly, both the technicians and developers had to change their attitudes and norms i.e. a part of their business culture, which demanded more than just a signal from top management. The relationship between attitude towards change and education is also found in the quantitative data.

According to the PIE survey data an increase in employee responsibility and technical demands is more widespread in product developing firms than other firms; but with variations according to educational levels (cf. Table 4). At the same time lack of qualifications among both middle managers/supervisors and employees is found to hamper organizational changes in product developing firms, but not to the same extent as in firms without product development.

The gate meetings were established to control the product development process but also to integrate the knowledge of the different functions. As mentioned in

Table 4. Some Changes in Work Demands and Acknowledged Qualification Problems.

Change	Product Developing Firms %	Other Firms %
Increased independence and responsibility for employees with higher education.	58	29
Ditto for employees with vocational training.	56	29
Ditto for other employees.	34	18
Middle managers' and supervisors' qualifications as a hampering factor for organizational development.	17	11
Qualifications of employees with no real management responsibility as a hampering factor for organizational development.	17	12

Source: PIE survey.

Section 6 the gate meetings also had their negative sides. One problem was the participants' lack of interest in listening to other's functional input. A solution in the metal factory with specific meetings for each function had a drawback concerning cross-functional learning. The same problem was tackled more satisfactory in the other firms because their management saw the lack of interest as a problem of learning a new culture of increased mutual understanding across different functions.

Another problem was the bias at the gate meetings with regard to a focus on blueprints or the physical model at the expense of market consideration. In the machinery firm which produced for the iron and metal industry, the management would strengthen focus on knowledge on the business conditions by introducing separate meetings before gate meetings for discussion of the technical problems whereas the gate meetings should be made shorter and concentrate on business conditions. By this change the product development process would also become a more continuous one.

A third problem was the accumulation of knowledge from the meetings. The discussions at the meetings were registered in the minutes of the meeting which were written by the project leader but they were directed towards the immediate tasks. So, much information was owned only by the participants. The result was that if knowledge based on gate meetings should get activated, it was necessary to go directly to the participants of the meetings. By a direct question from the PIE researchers about this problem, the manager of development in the machine factory, which delivered to the iron and metal industry suggested to have meetings with the relevant project leader if one thought it fruitful for a specific new product development.

Gate meetings might be used by the different functions to relieve themselves from responsibility. One tactic, which had been used by the actors, was to get their specific task in each stage meticulously defined. But this was to the detriment of a creative solution across functions based upon an open discussion of next steps without blaming each other. At the time of interviewing the management saw it as important to change the culture towards more openness and mutual trust.

Contacts with suppliers and people from knowledge institutions rested to some extent on personal relationships for example built through common educational background or former job experiences. Lack of such relationships or forgetting to cultivate them restrained the contacts with external knowledge institutions.

Formal training and education was strongly circumscribed by the management's human resource strategy putting weight on ad hoc decisions regarding education and training whereas formal continuous education was put into the background. The supply of formal training or education was also experienced as a restraint. In some cases the developers had wanted to follow a specific course, but could not find one at the time they had chosen or courses were suspended because of lack of interest.

Among the interviewees a few expressed a lack of motivation for more formal education as they found they had acquired much knowledge from their previous work and still saw current development tasks as the best way of relevant learning.

9. DISCUSSION

The analysis of the information on new product development activities of managers, developers and other actors working on new products has focussed upon *learning situations and their promoting and hampering factors*. The result has been seven learning situations and a number of positive and negative factors as summarized in Table 1 (Section 3) and Table 3 (Section 8). In this section our findings concerning learning are put in relief on the basis of issues extracted from the organizational literature. The issues are selected from three outstanding summaries of organizational research on learning and knowledge by Levitt and March (1988), Dodgson (1993) and Weick and Westley (1996). To some extent I also call attention to research done by co-authors of this book.

A reminder regarding the PIE cases has to be made at this point, cf. Section 2 in this chapter. The firms were within the range of 100–400 employees. The number of people in the development function varied between 10 and 50. The competitive strategy was one of adaption to more or less well known markets and customers. This meant priority to incremental innovation with no ambition of developing radical product innovations. Projects were carried through within a development period of one to two years. The management style was oriented towards openness and flat hierarchy. The managers of development were all much in favour of extended cross-level and cross-functional communication. Quite clearly these traits of the investigated firms have coloured our results on learning as discussed below.

9.1. Definition of Learning

Our interviews were not bounded by a specific *definition of learning*, but the analysis of the interviews has resulted in the crystallization of *the term "learning situation"* which by the chosen content points to learning from interaction as central among actors from the visited organization and/or between these actors and external contacts. These interactions take a number of forms such as formal and informal meetings, joint tasks, contacts with external partners and training and educational situations. The interactions accounted as learning to the extent that they showed new ideas and understandings, problem solutions and new ways of doing tasks. In some cases restraints blocked such results as highlighted in Section 8. In such cases the learning situation can only be seen as potential.

Levitt and March (1988, p. 320) stated that "organizations are seen as learning by encoding inferences from history into routines that guide behaviour." A comparison of our definition with the definition by Levitt and March shows that they just highlight one aspect of learning i.e. encoding inferences. So we shall return to this difference below. Dodgson's (1993, p. 377) definition of learning said: It's "the ways firms build, supplement and organize knowledge and routines around their activities and within their cultures, and adapt and develop organizational efficiency by improving the use of the broad skills of their workforces." On this background Dodgson (1993, p. 377) stated: "Encouraging and coordinating the variety of interactions in learning is a key organizational task." This viewpoint is similar to the one which characterizes our definition, and will make the issue of interaction topical. Weick and Westley (1996, p. 440) do not give a definition of learning along the same lines as those found above, but instead made the provocative statement: "To learn is to disorganize and increase variety!" This statement calls upon further consideration about organizing for learning which was a major issue during our interviews. Another point made by Weick and Westley (1996, pp. 442, 456) referred to the connection between learning and culture by saying that "learning is inherent in culture" and that "organizations have multiple cultures." On this background we shall discuss our results regarding the importance of interaction, the problem of organizing and creation of variety, the problem of interpreting one's experiences, and cultural traits connected to learning.

9.2. Interaction

Processes of interaction between actors have shown themselves as important for learning in connection with new product development. The small size of the firms was explicitly mentioned by some interviewees as important for their many opportunities to talk to each other, even though certain barriers also existed as mentioned below regarding culture. The crystallized learning situations and the related promoting factors pointed to such learning which resulted from interactions with customers, suppliers, and knowledge institutions, joint experiments carried out by developers, technicians and workers, as well as face-to-face communication at gate meetings. At the same time such interaction was also seen to be restrained during on-the-job learning by lack of capacity, and by lack of interest during gate meetings. The weight put on interaction is in accordance with other research stressing "learning by doing" (Levitt & March, 1988, p. 321) "across the development/manufacturing interface..." and supplemented with "learning by using" (Dodgson, 1993, p. 379), not to mention the research carried out by Lundvall (1992) who has focussed upon "interactive learning" especially "user-producer interaction" (see also Chap. 5 on this point). Regarding lack or no lack of capacity for learning, the research on "absorptive capacity" has developed this viewpoint with regard to interaction with external partners. Dodgson (1993, p. 379) referred to results showing improved absorptive capacity as the result of research and development. Vinding (2002) analysed the impact of absorptive capacity upon innovative performance from a human capital viewpoint and concluded "that interaction with knowledge institutions is dependent on both absolute absorptive capacity and social capital" (Vinding, 2002, p. 212). Our research results supplement these other results by exemplifying the concrete processes of interaction regarding e.g. "doing" in experiments, "using" in field situations and "interacting" with suppliers as part of the new product development activities. Regarding "absorptive capacity" we have seen how a combination of personal relationships and joint educational background was part of the explanation of the successful interaction between the firms and the knowledge institutions.

9.3. Organizing and Variety

Our results point to the importance of organizing learning situations such the stage-gate meetings and creating a role of new product development leader who could take care of the procedure. The structures were followed up by processes of communication and consultation and cross-functional integration of learning and distributed knowledge. In this connection the general climate of openness and flat hierarchies mentioned above was of importance. At the same time it has also been recognized that the formalization of the new product development process raised motivation problems for the developers.

Dodgson (1993, pp. 384, 388) pointed to literature which considered the positive role of organizational structure and strategy and treated "the importance of key individuals in organizational learning" which included "boundary spanners" and "technological gatekeepers". Our cases have shown the important role of the product development leader. This role is highlighted in Chap. 10 regarding getting the development process going, securing communication and holding gate meetings. In Chap. 6 the project leader's contribution to learning has been demonstrated in connection with his promotion of communication and consultation to the benefit of cross-level and cross-functional learning. In this task he had the full support of top management as stated above. Moreover, top management saw to it that the project leaders were ready to extended communication and manifested sociability. This trait was also developed as part of the role as mentioned in Section 5. In the learning literature this trait is part of the social qualifications seen as important for learning in two respects (Illeris, 1999). It helps spreading experiences among actors by pure and simple interaction, but it also provides the sounding-board for joint reflection.

Weick and Westley (1996) make it a central point in their exposition of the learning literature that there is a dilemma with regard to the weight placed respectively on organization and learning. There has to be a balance between stubborn routine and excessive renewal. Our results showed that old routines stood in the way of learning-on-the-job, but trial-and-error without registration was also a nuisance to learning, cf. Section 5. In the same way the priority given to reuse acted against learning, as did unrestricted technological creativity. We were told that some engineers were more interested in their engineering features than reaching a result of interest to the market. Here the management tried to strike a balance by giving some leeway to the engineers, but also securing that the market focus was upheld. In this way the management also kept a distance to a competence trap (Levitt & March, 1988, p. 322), which could develop because the engineers might become more and more specialized concerning their "fancy features" but to the detriment of more attractive user characteristics regarding new products. Keeping to the middle of the road was also chosen by the developers when they loosened their grip on the administration of gate meetings without loss of the meaning of the meetings. So, compared with other research our results have pointed to valid methods used by the management and the developers concerning the avoidance of unrestricted variety as well as too much emphasis on rules. This orientation among the actors can also be seen as quite natural as a corollary to a strategy of adaptation and incremental innovation, whereas our results say much less about best practice in case of a desire for radical innovations.

9.4. Interpretation

During our data gathering both managers and developers called attention to their problems concerning how to interpret diverse information from external contacts or experiments and tests. Among the restraints, which we recognized were strategic ambiguities, time pressure and the difficulties to come to terms with subconscious knowledge as well as unsatisfactory minutes of meetings. Strategic ambiguities were founded on turbulent environments and/or divergent opinions among top managers. The reactions of the subordinates showed that they were insecure concerning what and how to learn from such ambiguity. From a learning theory point of view one could emphasize the fruitfulness of conflicting opinions and the opportunity for seeking an optimal compromise (Weick & Westley, 1996, p. 448). These observations also show deficiencies with respect to the encoding of experiences and call attention to learning as an encoding process as stated by Levitt and March (1988, p. 320). The interpretation of data relates to the issue of single-loop and double-loop learning and diversity of paradigms (Levitt & March, p. 324). In our data we saw these interpretative issues raised in connection with the different paradigms expressed by sales people and developers, and with developers looking for double-loop learning. At the same time it was clear that the management in the five firms pressed for a market orientation as its major paradigm. This orientation is supported by the literature referred to by Dodgson (1993, p. 386) who wrote: "Particularly important for innovation in firms is learning from customers and users." The restraint of subconscious knowledge has been discussed under the term of "tacit knowledge." Here Levitt and March (1988, p. 327) pointed to results, which showed that such knowledge was more frequent in craft situations and complex environments. Our example was also drawn from a learning situation based on craft work necessary for the construction of the first models of the new product.

9.5. Culture

The learning taken place in the five firms was at the same time promoted and restrained by the change in business culture which meant more market orientation to the benefit of customer contacts and to the detriment of free technical experimentation by the engineers during new product development. Another cultural change concerned the management's wish for giving the employees more responsibility. These cases of cultural change were to some extent met with lack of capacity and opposing attitudes, and from the management's side was seen a more or less strong recognition of the necessity of introducing more formal training and education to support the changes. In the literature is found divergent statements on learning and culture. On the one hand it is said that shared culture facilitates learning (Dodgson, 1993, p. 382). Along the same line is seen corporate strategy which aims at learning by creating a corporate culture which can influence structures conducive of learning. (Dodgson, p. 388). On the other hand, cultural differentiation may be seen as significant for learning. This is mirrored in the literature summarized by Weick and Westley (1996). So, central statements by Weick and Westley (1996, p. 442) concerned "learning is inherent in culture" and "organizations have multiple cultures" (Weick & Westley, p. 456). This implies that a cultural approach directed attention to learning as it goes on in the practices of groups and by reciprocal comparisons, but is restrained by cultural systems which were characterized by too much weight on identity and routines instead of giving room for ambivalence and serendipity (Weick & Westley, 1996, p. 450). The interest of the management of the five firms in more openness and trust can be seen as an attempt to combine a common culture based on market orientation with a modern human resource management style. In this way top management gave signals regarding product innovation but it also believed in the knowledge owned by the employees. By putting the new product development leaders in a pivotal role they supported a middle-up-down role regarding knowledge creation (Nonaka & Takeuchi, 1995, pp. 130, 240, 241).

10. CONCLUSIONS AND PERSPECTIVES

By analysing a number of specific product developments within five manufacturing firms it was possible to crystallize seven *learning situations*. The learning element related to interactions producing new ideas and understandings, problem solutions and new ways of doing tasks. These interactions took four major forms: (1) formal and informal meetings e.g. product committees and gate meetings; (2) joint tasks e.g. experiments and tests; (3) contacts with external partners i.e. customers, suppliers and knowledge institutions; and (4) training and educational situations e.g. on-the-job-learning and courses. From the interview data have been extracted a number of promoting factors concerning learning (cf. Table 1) as well as a number of restraints (cf. Table 3).

In line with PIE survey results cooperation with customers e.g. in field tests and cooperation with suppliers and knowledge institutions were found among the important *promoting factors*. The importance of integrating the product development processes was clearly demonstrated by the positive effect of scrutiny processes carried out jointly by actors from different functions, project leaders' cross functional coordinating and motivating activities, and technicians' and workers' active involvement based on delegation and participation in the project during its different stages and related gate meetings.

Important *restraining factors* comprised strategic patterns concerning the priority given to the market forces and tight time planning, inertia with regard to old routines hampering cross functional coordination, communication difficulties, changing of roles, ad hoc decisions on training and education and some employees' lack of motivation for creative contributions to product development.

Taken together the promoting and restraining factors put problems of interactive learning, the dilemma attached to organizing for both innovation and routines and subconscious knowledge and cultural heterogeneity at the fore. These challenges for improved learning in connection with product development were shortly discussed in relation to some organizational research on learning and knowledge. An important result of this analysis has been the weight given by the firms' actors to collective learning activities. It is worth noticing the interactive learning across the hierarchy of managers and non-managerial personnel and the inclusion of external partners. This result paints a *perspective* for extended interactive learning based on flat organizational hierarchies, construction and extension of networks and conscious organization of learning situations, and last but not least more weight attached to integrative product development, something which is explored even more in Chap. 10.

Another perspective relates to the discussion of culture and its differentiation. The visited firms showed to some extent different norms which made mutual understanding of product development activities difficult. An example was the opposite views upon construction and production of a new product. This example together with others go beyond pure learning problems as it is related to work interests and understanding of work. In future research on learning such questions of cultural founded view points on organizing with regard to coordination and cooperation should be given more attention.

NOTE

1. Several places in this chapter reference is made to the survey part of the PIE-data (see explanation in Vinding's chapter). Frequencies referred to may be found on http://www.business.aau.dk/PIE or, if calculations are made on these data, they will be published in Christensen et al. (2005).

ACKNOWLEDGMENTS

I am grateful to Alice Lam and Jesper Lindgaard Christensen for stimulating comments to this chapter.

REFERENCES

Christensen, J. L., Lund, R., Reichstein, T., & Vinding, A. L. (2005). *Produkt innovation, læring og økonomisk performance i danske virksomheder.* Aalborg: Aalborg Universitetsforlag.

Cooper, R. G. (1993). *Winning at new products.* Reading, MA: Addison-Wesley.

Dodgson, M. (1993). Organizational Learning: A review of some literatures. *Organization Studies, 14,* 375–394.

Illeris, K. (1999). *Læring – aktuel læringsteori i spændingsfeltet mellem Piaget, Freud og Marx.* Roskilde: Roskilde Universitetsforlag.

Levitt, B., & March, J. G. (1988). Organizational learning. *Annual Review of Sociology, 14,* 319–340.

Locke, K. (2001). *Grounded theory in management research.* London: Sage.

Lundvall, B. Å. (1992). User-producer relationships, national systems of innovation and internationalization. In: B. Å. Lundvall (Ed.), *National Systems of Innovation* (pp. 45–67). London: Pinter.

Nielsen, P., & Lundvall, B. Å. (2003). Innovation, learning organizations and industrial relations. DRUID Working Paper 2003-7. Aalborg: Department of Business Studies, Aalborg University.

Nonaka, I., & Takeuchi, H. (1995). *The knowledge-creating company.* Oxford: Oxford University Press.

Sanchez, R. (Ed.) (2001). *Knowledge management and organizational competence.* Oxford: Oxford University Press.

Vinding, A. L. (2002). *Interorganizational diffusion and transformantion of knowledge in the process of product innovation.* Ph.D. Thesis. IKE Group/DRUID. Department of Business Studies, Aalborg University.

von Krogh, G., Roos, J., & Kleine, D. (Eds) (1998). *Knowing in Firms.* London: Sage.

Weick, K. E., & Westley, F. (1996). Organizational learning: Affirming an oxymoron. In: S. R. Clegg, C. Hardy & W. R. Nord (Eds), *Handbook of Organization Studies* (pp. 440–458). London: Sage.

HUMAN RESOURCES; ABSORPTIVE CAPACITY AND INNOVATIVE PERFORMANCE

Anker Lund Vinding

ABSTRACT

In relation to firms' innovative performance this study investigates the importance of human capital for the firm's absorptive capacity. The estimation of an ordered probit model including 1938 firms from the private manufacturing and non manufacturing sectors shows that the share of highly educated employees, development of a closer relationship with both vertically related actors and knowledge institutions and, application of human resource management (HRM) practices within the firm, not only promote the ability to innovate but also reduce the degree of innovative imitation. Finally, estimations according to size show that development of a closer relationship with a complete network of actors is especially important for firms with less than 50 employees.

1. INTRODUCTION

In Chapter 5 by Lundvall and Vinding we gave the analytical arguments for, why firms engage in interactive learning and establish network relationships with suppliers and customers. In Chapter 6 by Reinhard Lund the importance of managing knowledge flows, both within the firm and through interaction with

Product Innovation, Interactive Learning and Economic Performance
Research on Technological Innovation and Management Policy, Volume 8, 155–178
Copyright © 2004 by Elsevier Ltd.
ISSN: 0737-1071/doi:10.1016/S0737-1071(04)08007-2

external parties, was illustrated at a very detailed level for a small number of Danish firms. In this chapter, we use survey data and econometric methods to demonstrate the general empirical relevance of these results. In relation to Chapter 5 we show that wider networks including knowledge institutions need to be taken into account as factors that promote innovation and we argue that this should be seen in the light of "the learning economy" as it was developed in Chapter 2 by Lundvall. In relation to Chapter 6 we show that there is complementarity between internal knowledge and external networking.

It is generally recognized that, in the current economic context, the technological element is of crucial importance in securing competitive advantage for the individual firm, nation and the world economy as a whole. Scholars dealing with technological change may use different approaches, but they tend to agree upon the fact that inter-firm relations are of crucial importance to technological development.

Although knowledge received from external partners seems to be important and widespread among firms, managing external relationships is a difficult task. Besides the problem of finding the right person/partner – "know-who" – difficulties in assimilating and exploiting the information is also a problem. One of the most comprehensive and well-known contributions to this issue refers to the concept "absorptive capacity," in which internal capability and external collaboration are viewed as complementary (Cohen & Levinthal, 1989, 1990).

In this chapter the concept is investigated through four indicators – the share of highly educated employees, work experience among top management, the application of human resource management practices and development of a closer relationship to external actors. All indicators have been argued to have an influence on absorptive capacity but have mainly been examined separately. Using data from Danish manufacturing and service sectors the purpose is to clarify how these four indicators contribute to absorptive capacity.

In the original work Cohen and Levinthal argued that, doing one's own R&D produces not only new knowledge in the sense of innovations, but also contributes to the firm's absorptive capacity by increasing its stock of knowledge. An increased knowledge base will create opportunities to exploit new technical developments by increasing the ability to assimilate and utilize external knowledge. This explains why some firms may invest in basic research, even though the findings will spill over to the public and competitors (Cohen & Levinthal, 1990; Rosenberg, 1990). Absorptive capacity may be seen as cumulative in nature – previously accumulated knowledge makes it easier to assimilate new knowledge. Moreover, the existence of a certain level of knowledge in a particular field will provide a stronger capability to read signals and exploit new technological opportunities, especially important in uncertain environments.

The complementarity between internal capability and external collaboration has been illustrated in a number of studies, mostly by using traditional science indicators such as R&D or patents. Arora and Gambardella (1990) found complementarity between patents of 61 large biotechnology firms in the U.S., Japan and Europe and their number of agreements with other firms and universities. Gambardella (1992) found similar evidence from 14 case studies of large U.S. drug manufacturers and from statistical analysis using patent data as output indicator. Firms that had strong in-house scientific capabilities (measured by scientific publications) were able not only to make more efficient use of internal knowledge, but also to exploit external knowledge more effectively. Tripsas (1997) in a case study of the typesetting industry found that a combination of internal R&D investment in the firm's absorptive capacity and an external communication infrastructure to facilitate the transmission of external knowledge enables firms to successfully integrate knowledge from outside their boundaries.

Other studies have moved away from the traditional indicators and focused instead on the human capital involved in the processes. Cohen and Levinthal were aware of the fact that absorptive capacity is dependent on individuals working in the organization. They argue for instance that absorptive capacity may be developed "directly by sending employees to monitor and read the technical literature in their areas of expertise" (Cohen & Levinthal, 1994, p. 227). This is especially the case for people located at the interface of either the firm or its environment or at the interface between subunits within the firm. These "gatekeepers" are essential; Tushman and Katz (1980) also emphasize that "gatekeepers" are able to reduce the mismatch in language and cognitive orientation between two systems, which is especially important in development projects. Inside the firm, an important task for the "gatekeeper" is to transmit the information to the rest of the organization, and if the other members of the organization have high levels of expertise, the transmission process will become easier.

This is in line with Mangematin and Nesta (1999). They argue that highly educated employees in particular, through their daily tasks, will increase the stock of knowledge of the organization. They will also encourage relationships with other individuals with similar competencies outside the firm, thus facilitating access to external networks of knowledge, especially in the case of utilizing scientific knowledge (Rothwell & Dodgson, 1991). Carter (1989) argues that employees with high levels of education are the main contributors to know-how trading due to the high levels of knowledge embodied in these people. The high level of knowledge implies that they will be in a better position to recognize and value new external knowledge.

Besides formalized knowledge, tacit knowledge is an important component of innovation (Dosi, 1988; Rosenberg, 1982; Senker, 1995). Cohen and Levinthal also point out that absorptive capacity may be developed through "the accumulation of manufacturing experience" (Cohen & Levinthal, 1994, p. 229). This kind of firm-specific knowledge, that is, knowledge established through learning by doing, may be measured by work experience of the employees. Albaladejo and Romijn (2000) finds that work experience obtained in either multinational or large domestic firms in the UK by founder/manager(s) has an influence on firms' innovative capabilities. But prior work experience in public R&D institutions and having a degree in science and engineering were also shown to have an impact.

A third element, on which Cohen and Levinthal placed less emphasis, is the organizational setting within which the employees operate. They point out that cross-function interfaces such as those connecting R&D, design, manufacturing and marketing increase the absorptive capacity. Also, practices such as rotating R&D personnel through other units within the firm are important. In general terms, restructuring of employment relations in the form of Human Resource Management practices (HRM) has been shown to have positive linkages to innovative performance (Michie & Sheehan, 1999). Laursen and Foss (2000) go one step further and find that complementarities between HRM practices have a positive influence on innovative performance.

Finally, Cohen and Levinthal (1994) recognize the importance of the strength of the external relationships in the development of absorptive capacity. Development of closer relationships may contribute to a firm's absorptive capacity because such relationships may create and strengthen information channels and "thicken" the knowledge flow, hence increasing the efficiency of the transfer of tacit knowledge. Moreover, the argument may be sector-specific in the sense that some sectors may be more sensitive to some of the external actors; for example, development of closer relationships with universities may be more important for high-tech sectors than for low-tech sectors.

According to the above discussion, general knowledge in terms of formal education, firm-specific knowledge in terms of work experience, the organizational set-up and, finally, development of a closer relationship with external actors are all factors that matter for absorptive capacity. This leads us to a widening of the concept giving more emphasis to the importance of human capital.

Besides incorporating a fourfold approximation of absorptive capacity, this study goes further. Instead of focusing on intermediary outcomes such as citations or patents, we capture measurement on innovative activity, which, according to Acs and Audretsch (1988), is the most direct measure of innovative activity. Finally, the whole private economy is analyzed, thus making it possible to check for sectoral differences.

The rest of the chapter is organized as follows: Section 2 describes the data set; Section 3 outlines the model while Section 4 presents the results. Finally, conclusions and implications are provided in Section 5.

2. DATA

Two databases have been combined in order to carry out the analysis. One is a survey on organization, employee skills and development of new products (1998–2000). The survey was carried out in 2001 and was submitted to 6,975 firms from the manufacturing and service sectors, where firms with 20 employees or more were selected. The sample thus covered the total population of firms with more than 25 employees whereas firms with 20–25 employees were selected randomly based on two-digit industry classification. The overall response rate was 28.7% (2,007 firms), and in the manufacturing and service sectors the response rates were 29% and 28% respectively. The second database is the integrated database on the labour market (IDA), which includes register data on each individual in Denmark for the period 1980–1999. The two databases were merged, and along with data for the period 1998–2000, IDA data for 1998–1999 covering 271,154 persons who have been in contact with the firms were included.

3. MODEL

On the basis of the theoretical and empirical discussion, a model is estimated in which a firm's ability to innovate is used as dependent variable, and absorptive capacity and traditional control variables as independent variables. The basic structure of the model may be specified as follows:

$$y = f(\beta_1 z + \beta_2 q)$$

y represents the innovative activity of the firm; z and q are vectors containing proxies for absorptive capacity and other standardized variables used in the literature explaining the innovative activity of the firms. See Appendix A for descriptive statistics.

y expresses the innovativeness of the firm on an ordered scale from 0–3. 0 is equal to a non-innovator firm (1163), 1 indicates that the firm has introduced a product/service in the period of 1998–2000 that is new to the firm only (673), 2 indicates that the firm has introduced an innovation that is new in the Danish context (117), and, finally, 3 indicates that the firm has introduced an innovation that is new to the world (54). Thus category 1 and 2 measures the degree of imitative innovations while category 3 measure innovation in the strict sense.

z can be decomposed into four variables representing measures needed in the organization in order to assimilate and utilize external knowledge. First, *HIEDU* measures the share of employees who have an academic degree. Second, EXPE measures the average work experience of the employees. EXPE is measured according to how long the employees have been in the labour market. In order to focus upon those employees in the organization who are the most influential in the development process, managers and heads of departments as well as workers at the managerial level have been taken into account. Third, an *HRM* index originally developed in Lund and Gjerding (1996) is applied. This includes *HRM*-practices such as: (i) interdisciplinary workgroups; (ii) quality circles; (iii) planned job rotation; (iv) delegation of responsibility; (v) integration of functions; and (vi) performance related pay. Firms using 0–2 practices are considered as having a low level of development, 3–4 practices as medium, and 5–6 as a high level of HRM practices. Finally, *EXTERN* takes on three values and indicates the degree to which firms have developed closer relationships with external actors such as customers/suppliers on the one hand and knowledge institutions on the other hand.[1] The first category of firms includes those that have not established closer links to any of the external actors. The second category represents firms that have developed closer relationships with either customers/suppliers, as pointed out by (Lundvall, 1988; von Hippel, 1988), or with knowledge institutions.[2] The final category includes those firms that have developed closer relationships with both types of actors and thus have developed closer relationships with a more complete network of actors.

q represents four standard control variables in the model. The first is sectoral affiliation (*SECTOR*). Although there are different taxonomies, i.e. Schumpeter's Mark I and Mark II, sectoral patterns of technical change – Pavitt's taxonomy – with four sectors representing the manufacturing sector and five sectors representing service firms, is applied.[3] One of the criteria in the classification – sources of main knowledge inputs in the process of innovation i.e. internal versus external – is important with respect to the discussion of absorptive capacity.

One Schumpeterian hypothesis concerns innovation and *SIZE*. The late Schumpeter argued that innovative activity was positively correlated with firm size due to the existence of R&D departments. Although there have been contradictory results concerning this issue over the decades, the results seem to be in favour of a positive relationship (Brouwer & Kleinknecht, 1996).[4] The third control variable concerns competition (*COMP*). Several measures have been applied, mostly the level of competition in terms of different ratios concerning concentration, and, over the last decades, contradictory results have been obtained. Schumpeter was in favour of concentrated industries being more innovative. Others have found that competition doesn't matter (Arvanitis & Hollenstein, 1996), while still others have found that increased competition favours innovation (Geroski, 1990). Alternatively, competition may become non-linear, where markets with an intermediate degree of market power, favour innovation (Kleinknecht & Verspagen, 1989). *COMP* is measured in a slightly different way since the firms are asked about the rate of change in the level of competitive pressure within the period; thus, this study deals with intensification in competition instead of level of competition. Finally, the study controls for whether or not the firm is a subsidiary of a larger firm – *SUBSID*. Again, contradictory results exist, although the most recent studies tend to argue that a positive relationship exists due to the fact that subsidiary firms have access to the parent firm's larger resource base and thus benefit in terms of innovative activity.

4. RESULTS

4.1. All Firms

As mentioned previously, the dependent variable takes four discrete ordered values. Hence, an ordered probit model is applied as the means of estimation where maximum likelihood is the method used.

In Table 1 the estimations of equation 1 with and without sectors are reported.[5] Besides coefficients the table shows marginal effects as well.[6]

Table 1 shows that the average share of highly educated employees (HIEDU) is significant in both types of models. A change in the share of academic employees will decrease the probability for no innovation and increase the probability for an innovation. Especially product innovation which is new for the firm only, but also the likelihood for producing more radical product innovations will be effected positively although the magnitude decreases the more radical the product innovation becomes. The significant estimate for the second model shows that the share of highly educated employees is important within each sector, as well.

However, the average work experience among top management (EXPE) is less convincing, thus questioning the importance of the learning-by-doing effect. The specific knowledge through work experience does not show any significant effect on the degree of innovative activity. One reason may be that younger people are educated with the most recent knowledge about technology and management practices, whereas older people due to the increasing speed of change may have difficulties in acquiring the latest advances in information technology. Older people may moreover have difficulties with knowledge destruction. Some knowledge needs to be forgotten before applying new knowledge. Last but not least, developing new products/services may be argued to have a certain degree of craftsmanship. In order to cope with these challenges, a combination of old and young employees may be preferred. Older employees may have the practical experiences while younger employees may have the ideas. However, one explanation may be found in the set-up of the questionnaire that the study does not take into account that some

Table 1. Ordered Probit Estimation of Innovative Performance and Absorptive Capacity, Weighted.

Variables	Model I Marginal Effects						Model II Marginal Effects					
	Coef.	Std. Err.	None	New to Firm	New in DK	New to World	Coef.	Std. Err.	None	New to Firm	New in DK	New to World
Intercept	-1.040	0.069	0.407	-0.274	-0.087	-0.046	-0.781	0.105	0.304	-0.212	-0.063	-0.029
HIEDU – share of academic employees	1.495**	0.226	-0.582	0.391	0.125	0.066	1.203**	0.285	-0.468	0.327	0.097	0.045
EXPE – work expe. of top–manag.	0.005	0.004	-0.002	0.001	0.000	0.000	-0.001	0.004	0.001	0.000	0.000	0.000
HRM – Human ressource management												
High	0.772**	0.071	-0.301	0.203	0.065	0.034	0.766**	0.070	-0.298	0.208	0.062	0.029
Medium	0.432**	0.056	-0.169	0.114	0.036	0.019	0.398**	0.058	-0.155	0.108	0.032	0.015
Low	Benchmark						Benchmark					
EXTERN – closer relat. with extern. actors												
Both vertical/know.inst.	0.294**	0.077	-0.115	0.077	0.025	0.013	0.219**	0.078	-0.086	0.060	0.018	0.008
Either vertical/know.inst.	0.268**	0.053	-0.105	0.070	0.022	0.012	0.223**	0.053	-0.087	0.061	0.018	0.008
None	Benchmark						Benchmark					
SUBSID – belonging to a sub. firm. Binary												
Yes	0.209**	0.051	-0.082	0.055	0.018	0.009	0.183**	0.050	-0.071	0.050	0.015	0.007
COMP – Experi. Increased Comp. Binary												
Yes	0.147**	0.054	-0.058	0.039	0.012	0.007	0.165**	0.055	-0.064	0.045	0.013	0.006

SIZE – size of the firm						
>50	0.211**	0.069	-0.082	0.055	0.018	0.009
25–50	0.006	0.057	-0.002	0.002	0.001	0.000
<25	Benchmark			Benchmark		
N	1938					
% of correct predictions	61					
Log likelihood	-1702					
Restricted log likelihood	-1880					
Likelihood ratio test	355.61					

SECTORS						
Supplier–dominated	0.193	0.108	-0.075	0.052	0.016	0.007
Scale intensive	0.081	0.102	-0.032	0.022	0.007	0.003
Specialised suppliers	0.490**	0.111	-0.191	0.133	0.039	0.018
Science based	0.394*	0.182	-0.154	0.107	0.032	0.015
Crafts	-0.520**	0.119	0.202	-0.141	-0.042	-0.020
Wholesale trade	0.004	0.104	-0.001	0.001	0.000	0.000
Specialised services	-0.361**	0.107	0.141	-0.098	-0.029	-0.014
Scale intensive services	-0.320	0.175	0.125	-0.087	-0.026	-0.012
ICT intensive services	Benchmark			Benchmark		
N	1938					
% of correct predictions	61					
Log likelihood	-1658					
Restricted log likelihood	-1880					
Likelihood ratio test	444.15					

Notes: There is no serious sign of multicollinearity between the independent variables. The multicollinearity is estimated by using the predicted probabilities of the dependent variable.

These predicted values are then used to contruct a weight variable which are applied in a weighted least squares regression.

A tolerance is computed by regressing each variable on all the other explanatory variables.

* Significance at 5% level.

** Significance at 1% level.

innovations are more dependent on accumulation of knowledge. Although the sectoral classification partly takes this matter into account, another classification or another variable that treat this issue more carefully may be needed.

For both models, the use of HRM practices is significant. Firms that apply HRM practices to a high degree are in a better position to innovate. The result is also in line with Michie and Sheehan (1999), who find that the application of HRM practices is more effective in influencing the innovative performance when these practices are applied together rather than alone. Hence, HRM practices are complementary. In addition, the estimation within each of the nine Pavitt sectors (see Appendix 4) gives rise to interesting results. The marginal effect for high involvement in HRM practices is lower for more low-tech oriented sectors like *supplier-dominated* (0.197), *scale-intensive* (0.307), *craft* (0.192), *wholesale trade* (0.239), whereas high-tech oriented sectors like *specialized suppliers* (0.505), *science-based* (0.439) and *ICT intensive* firms (0.301) experience larger effect by applying a high degree of HRM practices compared to firms in same sectors which have not applied these types of HRM practices. For these high-tech oriented sectors the frequency and speed of new knowledge, besides of being sophisticated and complex, is more widespread compared to low-tech sectors. In order to deal with these facts, HRM practices like enhanced cross-functional interaction as well as increasing the motivation of employees i.e. performance-related pay, may promote the participation of employees in innovation processes. In general, HRM may be understood in two dimensions – employee ability and employee motivation – and these may be argued to be complementary.

Development of closer external relationships of the firm (EXTERN) and hence increasing the potential effect of transferring information as well as tacit knowledge is significant for both models. Firms that have developed closer relationships to vertically related actors such as customers and suppliers, but also to knowledge institutions such as universities, and consultants do significantly better in terms of innovative performance compared to firms that have not developed closer relationships to their external actors.

The result is not surprising – it is a well-known fact that external interaction matters (De Propris, 2000; Tether, 2002) – but the evidence highlights one interesting point. The significant relationship with knowledge institutions indicates that "interactive learning" should be extended to include actors that are not located in the value chain of the product/service. It is a wider set of organizations that form the networks that matter for innovation. This is in line with Foray and Lundvall (1996), who argue that we are moving toward a networked learning economy where networks determine the relative success of the firms. This is in line with the result presented by DeBresson (1999) that firms interacting with many rather than few external actors, are the most successful innovators. Kaufmann and Tödtling

(2001) emphasize that the risk for lock-ins can be reduced when the range of external sources of knowledge is diverse. The increasing importance of complete networks may also be seen as reflecting the increasing specialisation and speed-up of change in the learning economy.

The degree of increased competition (COMP) comes out with a positive sign and is significant for all models. Firms exposed to increased competition are, ceteris paribus, more likely to innovate.

Firms belonging to a subsidiary firm (SUBSID) show significant results in general and subsidiary firms are hence more likely to increase innovative performance due to access to the larger resource base of the parent firm.

The SIZE variable is significant although the estimates are not as clear-cut as expected. Firms with fewer than 25 employees are less likely to produce innovations in the strict sense compared to firms with more than 50 employees. The argument is well known since larger firms can more easily devote resources to the innovation process.

Finally, sector variables show that the service sector is more heterogeneous in terms of innovative performance than manufacturing. One explanation may be that innovations play a more important role in earlier stages of the value chain where we find both *ICT intensive services* and manufacturing firms. Further down the value chain, where the rest of the service firms are located, other elements such as personal contacts with customers are more important for success than innovations. Instead, these firms rely on receiving innovations/knowledge from manufacturing and knowledge intensive service firms, as argued in Drejer (1998).

4.2. Size Estimations

The four proxies for absorptive capacity may behave differently depending upon the size of the firm, e.g. that HRM is more important for large firms or that closer relationships within a complete network of external actors is more important for small firms.

Table 2 shows probit estimation for the ability to innovate for firms with less than and more than 50 employees. As can be seen from Table 2, the share of highly educated employees (HIEDU) is significant for both types of size categories whereas work experience for top-management (EXPE) remains insignificant.

High involvement of human resource management practices (HRM) is conducive for the innovative performance for both size categories.

Among the small firms developing a closer relationship with external actors (EXTERN) is a significant, while the estimate is insignificant for larger firms, hence indicating that the variation is bigger among small firms. Developing a

Table 2. Probit Model of the Ability to Innovate Yes/No and Absorptive Capacity by Size, Weighted.

Variables	Less Than 50 Employees			More Than 50 Employees		
	Coef.	Std. Err.	Mar. Eff.	Coef.	Std. Err.	Mar. Eff.
Intercept	−0.775	0.251	−0.307	−0.753	0.184	−0.282
HIEDU – share of academic employees	1.596*	0.810	0.633	1.527*	0.637	0.572
EXPE – work expe. of top-manag.	0.002	0.010	0.001	−0.004	0.006	−0.001
HRM – human ressource management						
High	0.758**	0.134	0.301	0.814**	0.122	0.305
Medium	0.279*	0.127	0.111	0.394**	0.090	0.148
Low	Benchmark			Benchmark		
EXTERN – closer relat. with extern. actors						
Both	0.587**	0.160	0.233	0.011	0.141	0.004
Either vertical/know. inst.	0.135	0.102	0.054	0.195*	0.089	0.073
None	Benchmark			Benchmark		
SUBSID – belonging to a sub. firm, binary						
Yes	0.234*	0.100	0.093	0.192*	0.083	0.072
COMP – experi. increased comp., binary						
Yes	0.030	0.097	0.012	0.405**	0.088	0.152
Sectors						
Supplier–dominated	0.426*	0.216	0.169	0.157	0.193	0.059
Scale intensive	0.147	0.205	0.058	0.007	0.196	0.003
Specialised suppliers	0.518*	0.238	0.206	0.273	0.213	0.102
Science based	0.523*	0.274	0.208	−0.002	0.348	−0.001
Crafts	−0.564*	0.246	−0.224	−0.565**	0.186	−0.212
Wholesale trade	0.124	0.201	0.049	−0.022	0.176	−0.008
Specialised services	−0.1418653869	0.228	−0.056	−0.464*	0.181	−0.174
Scale intensive services	0.018	0.279	0.007	−0.639*	0.281	−0.239
ICT intensive services	Benchmark			Benchmark		
N	811			1127		
% of correct predictions	66			70		
Log likelihood	−493			−649		
Restricted log likelihood	−558			−747		
Likelihood ratio test	130.1			194.8		

Notes: There is no serious sign of multicollinearity between the independent variables.
The multicollinearity is estimated by using the predicted probabilities of the dependent variable. These predicted values are then used to construct a weight variable which are applied in a weighted least squares regression. A tolerance is computed by regressing each variable on all the other explanatory variables.
* Significance at 5% level.
** Significance at 1% level.

closer relationship with a complete network of external actors is thus more likely to promote innovation for small firms than for large firms. One reason could be that there is a lack of resources inside small firms that may be compensated by developing a closer relationship with complete networks, hence increasing the likelihood of locating and, eventually, absorbing tacit knowledge. Larger firms, on the other hand, have more resources available and are therefore not as dependent on external interaction. Another interpretation could be that large firms already have established close relationships to external partners and, therefore, a marginal increase would not have any effect on innovation activities.

Whereas belonging to a subsidiary firm (SUBSID) is of importance for both small and large firms, increased competition (COMP) is significant only for large firms' probability to innovate.

5. CONCLUSIONS

Over the past decades the use of external knowledge in the innovation process has grown in importance. Research has also shown that increasing the firm's internal capability is a prerequisite for effectively assimilating and utilizing this knowledge from the outside.

The estimation of an ordered probit model shows that the share of highly educated employees, the application of HRM practices within the firm, and development of closer relationships with both vertically related actors and knowledge institutions, not only improves a firm's ability to innovate, but also to produce more radical innovations, thus indicating an improved ability to deal with complexity (OECD, 2000).

An implication for policy as well as management strategies, of the significance of HRM, is that one of the most efficient ways to promote innovation is to stimulate the development of human resources. This can be done by developing the organizational structure and the corporate culture and by motivating employees – for instance through decentralization of responsibility.

The positive effect of the share of highly educated employees on innovative performance indicates that updating the skills and/or employing highly educated candidates is important for the competitiveness for the firm.

The results referring to external actors show that learning by interacting needs to be broadened to include knowledge institutions. A development of a closer relationship with a network of actors can be beneficial in several ways. The uncertainty of technological development as well as opportunism will be reduced (DeBresson & Amesse, 1991). The learning economy will further increase the need for more efficient and trustworthy information. According to Powell (1990) this may be achieved through networks since information that passes through networks is "thicker" than information obtained in the market due to the fact that participants know each other. Further, the information will be "freer" than that communicated in a hierarchy, which is characterized by being more formalized.

With respect to knowledge institutions, it may be argued that firms that are able to utilize and assimilate this kind of sophisticated knowledge will be in a better position to adjust more rapidly to the changing environment. One problem with knowledge institutions is that firms may have especially big difficulties with determining the intrinsic value of the information they buy. In the case of choosing a supplier of a tangible product, it is easier for the firm to know what it actually gets. Thus, an important task is to increase the transparency of the market for knowledge intensive services (Christensen et al., 2001).

Neither the work experience of managers nor that of workers at the managerial level shows significant results.

An explanation might be that, in the learning economy, due to the rapid speed of change, the knowledge and skills of employees might become outdated more quickly. Although experienced employees may have an advantage in some respects, they are not necessarily aware of the latest technologies and management practices and not trained in the latest advances in information technology. In this respect they are disadvantaged compared to employees who have just graduated from universities or other educational institution. Experienced employees may have difficulties in "forgetting" old knowledge that may hamper acquiring new knowledge. However, more research is needed in order to get a better understanding of the impact of work experience on innovative performance.

Finally, sectoral differences appear, where *specialized suppliers, science-based* and *ICT intensive services* are the most conducive to innovation, while *craft and specialized services* are the least conducive. One could put forward a hypothesis that industries in the beginning of the value chain of the product are more dependent on innovative activity. Industries at the end of the value chain, like most of the service industry, are less dependent on innovation but more dependent on other factors such as personal contact with customers etc. Another argument, which is well documented, concerns the relatively low level of competition in the service industry, which is further supported by the estimates at the sector level. Increasing the level of competition in the service industry may have a positive impact upon innovation. A further implication would be that the increased competitive pressure in services could have a positive impact upon the rest of the economy through forward and backward linkages.

Although this chapter has brought a better understanding of how different elements associated with absorptive capacity behave, some limitations still remain. Most of the variables in the estimation are survey specific. The lack of a time dimension in these variables makes it difficult to take the problem of causality into account.

Despite this problem, the chapter indicates that human capital matters for determination of absorptive capacity of the firm. Further research is, however, necessary in order to get a deeper understanding of the relationships. For instance are certain types of education more conducive to innovations than others? Are some types of work experience more important than others? Are some types of human resource management practices more conducive to innovation than others?

NOTES

1. Regardless of innovative activity the firms are asked: "To which extent has the firm developed a closer relationship with the following actors during 1998–2000."

2. Knowledge institutions express whether the firm had developed a closer relationship with institutions such as technical support institutions or universities, or with consultants. Information from these partners requires higher absorptive capacity due to the higher level of sophistication.

3. The categorization of the service firms is taken from Laursen (2000). For further details on the categorization, see Appendix 2 and 3.

4. See Cohen (1995) for an empirical review.

5. Size was included in the model with sector estimation according to Pavitt, but became insignificant. As argued in Laursen (2000), the additional variance explained by size is removed when sector is included. Thus, the size of firms between the sectors differs, but the effect of the variance in size is not that important within each sector. Further, size is also one of the criteria behind the Pavitt taxonomy and one could therefore argue that the size variable should be omitted from the estimations.

6. One of the problems of coefficients in probit models is their immediate interpretability. The level of significance is meaningful, but the sign and the magnitude may not be, the latter in particular, when the variables are in different metrics. One way to deal with the problem is calculation of the first partial derivatives of the probability function with respect to each variable. The partial change or marginal effect is then the slope of the curve holding all other variables constant, normally at their means. Hence, the interpretation is very close to linear regression models. However, since dummy variables can only change in discrete amounts, it may be argued (Long, 1997) that these effects should be calculated by calculating the percentage predicted evaluated at the discrete change in the dummy variable. Since there was little difference in these two sets of calculations, we have therefore reported the usual effect calculations provided by Limdep.

ACKNOWLEDGMENTS

I would like to thank Associated Professor Jesper Lindgaard Christensen, Professor Bengt-Åke Lundvall, Professor Emeritus Reinhard Lund, research fellow Toke

Reichstein and Associated Professor Peter Nielsen, who are the persons behind the PIE (Product innovation and Economic performance) project for comments as well as giving me the opportunity to work on the data.

REFERENCES

Acs, Z. J., & Audretsch, D. B. (1988). Innovation in large and small firms: An empirical analysis. *The American Economic Review, 78*, 678–690.
Albaladejo, M., & Romijn, H. (2000). Determinants of innovative capability in small UK firms. Eindhoven Centre for Innovation Studies, Working Paper.
Arora, A., & Gambardella, A. (1990). Complementarity and external linkages: The strategies of the large firms in biotechnology. *Journal of Industrial Economics, 38*, 361–379.
Arvanitis, S., & Hollenstein, H. (1996). Industrial innovation in Switzerland: A model-based analysis with survey data. In: A. Kleinknecht (Ed.), *Determinants of Innovation* (pp. 13–62). London: Macmillan.
Brouwer, E., & Kleinknecht, A. (1996). Determinants of innovation: A microeconometric analysis of three alternative innovation output indicators. In: A. Kleinknecht (Ed.), *Determinants of Innovation* (pp. 99–125). London: Macmillan.
Carter, A. P. (1989). Know-how trading as economic exchange. *Research Policy, 18*, 1–9.
Christensen, J. L., Schibany, A., & Vinding, A. L. (2001). Collaboration between manufacturing firms and knowledge institutions on product development: Evidence from harmonised surveys in Australia, Austria, Denmark, Norway and Spain. Paris: OECD.
Cohen, W. (1995). Empirical studies of innovative activity. In: P. Stoneman (Ed.), *Handbook of Economics of Innovation and Technological Change* (pp. 182–265). Oxford: Basil Blackwell.
Cohen, W., & Levinthal, D. (1989). Innovation and learning: The two faces of R&D. *The Economic Journal, 99*, 569–596.
Cohen, W., & Levinthal, D. (1990). Absorptive capacity: A new perspective of learning and innovation. *Administrative Science Quarterly, 35*, 128–152.
Cohen, W., & Levinthal, D. (1994). Fortune favors the prepared firm. *Management Science, 40*.
DeBresson, C. (1999). An entrepreneur cannot innovate alone: Networks of enterprises are required. In: *DRUID Conference on Systems of Innovation*. Aalborg: Rebild.
DeBresson, C., & Amesse, F. (1991). Networks of innovators: A review and introduction to the issue. *Research Policy, 20*, 363–379.
De Propris, L. (2000). Innovation and inter-firm co-operation: The case of the West Midlands. *Economics of Innovation and New Technology, 9*, 421–446.
Dosi, G. (1988). The nature of the innovative process. In: G. Dosi, C. Freeman, R. Nelson, G. Silverberg & L. Soete (Eds), *Technical Change and Economic Theory*. London: Pinter.
Drejer, I. (1998). Den Vidensbaserede Økonomi. *DISKO rapport, 4*(Maj), Erhvervsudviklingsrådet.
Foray, D., & Lundvall B. Å. (1996). The knowledge-based economy: From the economics of knowledge to the learning economy. In: *Employment and Growth in the Knowledge-based Economy*. Paris: OECD.
Gambardella, A. (1992). Competitive advantages from in-house scientific research: The U.S. pharmaceutical industry in the 1980s. *Research Policy, 21*, 391–401.
Geroski, P. A. (1990). Innovation, technological opportunity, and market structure. *Oxford Economic Papers, 42*, 586–602.

Gjerding, A. N. (1997). *Den fleksible virksomhed: Omstillingspres og fornyelse i dansk erhvervsliv.* Copenhagen: Erhvervsudviklingsrådet.

Kaufmann, A., & Tödtling, F. (2001). Science-industry interaction in the process of innovation: The importance of boundary-crossing between systems. *Research Policy, 30,* 791–804.

Kleinknecht, A., & Verspagen, B. (1989). R&D and market structure: The impact of measurement and aggregation problems. *Small Business Economics,* 297–301.

Laursen K. (2000). The importance of sectoral differences in the application of new HRM practices for innovation performance. LINK Working Paper.

Long J. S. (1997). *Regression models for categorical and limited dependent variables.* Thousand Oaks: Sage.

Lund, R., & Gjerding, A. N. (1996). The flexible company innovation, work organisation and human resource management. In: DRUID Working Paper No. 17. Aalborg: IKE/DRUID, Department of Business Studies.

Lundvall B. Å. (1988). Innovation as an interactive process: From user-producer interaction to national systems of innovation. In: G. Dosi, C. Freeman, R. Nelson, G. Silverberg & L. Soete (Eds), *Technical Change and Economic Theory.* London: Pinter.

Mangematin, V., & Nesta, L. (1999). What kind of knowledge can a firm absorb? *International Journal of Technology Management, 18,* 149–172.

Michie, J., & Sheehan, M. (1999). HRM practices, R&D expenditure and innovative investment: Evidence for the UK's 1990 workplace industrial relations survey. *Industrial and Corporate Change, 8,* 211–234.

OECD (2000). Working group on innovation and technology policy, science, technology and industry. *Outlook 2000* (Chap. VII), Innovation Networks.

Pavitt, K. (1984). Sectoral patterns of technical change: Towards a taxonomy and a theory. *Research Policy, 13,* 343–373.

Powell, W. (1990). Neither market nor hierarchy: Network forms of organization. *Research in Organization Behaviour, 12.*

Rosenberg, N. (1982). *Inside the black box: Technology and economics.* Cambridge: Cambridge University Press.

Rosenberg, N. (1990). Why do firms do basic research (with their own money). *Research Policy, 19.*

Rothwell, R., & Dodgson, M. (1991). External linkages and innovation in small and medium-sized enterprises. *R&D Management, 21,* 125–137.

Senker, J. (1995). Tacit knowledge and models of innovation. *Industrial and Corporate Change, 4.*

Tether, B. (2002). Who co-operates for innovation, and why an empirical analysis. *Research Policy, 31,* 947–967.

Tripsas, M. (1997). Surviving radical technological change through dynamic capability: Evidence from the typesetter industry. *Industrial and Corporate Change, 6,* 341–377.

Tushman, M., & Katz, R. (1980). External communication and project performance: An investigation into the role of gatekeepers. *Management Science, 26,* 1071–1085.

von Hippel, E. (1988). The sources of innovation. New York: Oxford University Press.

APPENDIX A

Variable Definition and Descriptive Statistics, Weighted.

Continuous Variable	N	Mean	Stand. Dev.	Min.	Max.
HIEDU – The average share of employees with an academic degree from 1990 to 1995	1938	0.032	0.078	0	0.646
EXPE – The average work experience of managers, head of departments and workers at the managerial level	2007	11243.3	6616.73	0	19500

Discontinuous Variables	N	Percent
Innovative performance	2006	100
Non-innovator	1163	58
Product/service innovation new to the firm	673	34
Product/service innovation new in the Danish context	117	6
Product/service innovation new to the world	54	3
HRM – The application of Human Resource Management practices	2006	100
Low	665	33
Medium	879	44
High	462	23
EXTERN – Development of a closer relationship with external actors:	2006	100
None	1125	56
Either vertical/knowledge institutions	665	33
Both types	215	11
SUBSID – Belonging to a subsidiary firm, binary	2006	100
Yes	1069	53
COMP – Experienced increased competition, binary	2006	100
Yes	690	34

APPENDIX A   *(Continued)*

Discontinuous Variables	*N*	Percent
SIZE – Size of the firm	2006	100
<25	568	28
25–50	762	38
>50	677	34
SECTOR	1983	100
Supplier dominated firms	248	13
Scale intensive firms	256	13
Specialised suppliers	143	7
Science-based firms	56	3
Crafts	337	16
Wholesale trade	348	17
Specialised services	330	17
Scale intensive services	87	4
ICT intensive services	197	10

APPENDIX B
SECTORAL CLASSIFICATION.

Making use of the SPRU database, Pavitt (1984) developed a taxonomy of sectoral patterns of innovation based primarily on information about main knowledge inputs into the innovation processes, requirements of users and means of appropriation. These characteristics and variations are classified according to four sectors: *Supplier dominated*, two kinds of production intensive (*scale-intensive* and *specialized suppliers*) and *science-based*. Firms in the *supplier-dominated* sector are traditionally characterized as manufacturing firms that are small in size and have a low technology orientation. Technological progress is therefore dependent on external actors such as suppliers of equipment and materials and, in some cases, large customers and government-financed research and extension services. Firms in the *scale-intensive* sector are low technology-oriented as well, but they do have some in-house development capability. Besides being large in size, those firms interact primarily with firms in the second part of the production-intensive sector – *specialized suppliers* – where the level of technology is higher and the firm size is smaller. For specialized suppliers, the pattern of interaction is more based on the user-producer relationship. In the *science-based* sector, the main sources of technology (which is quite high) are in-house development together with the underlying science developed in universities.

Since the empirical material covers the whole economy, Pavitt's taxonomy has to be extended. For this propose, the categorization in Laursen and Foss (2000) is applied. In their categorization, five additional sectors were added to Pavitt's taxonomy – ICT– (Information and Communication Technology) intensive services, wholesale trade, scale intensive services, specialized services and crafts. See Appendix C for a detailed assignment of all industries into the nine sectors.

APPENDIX C

The Assignment of Industries Into Nine Sectoral Categories.

No.	Industry	Sector
1	Production etc. of meat and meat products	SCAI
2	Manufacture of dairy products	SCAI
3	Manufacture of other food products	SCAI
4	Manufacture of beverages	SCAI
5	Manufacture of tobacco products	SCAI
6	Manufacture of textiles and textile products	SDOM
7	Mfr. of wearing apparel; dressing etc. of fur	SDOM
8	Mfr. of leather and leather products	SDOM
9	Mfr. of wood and wood products	SDOM
10	Mfr. of pulp, paper and paper products	SDOM
11	Publishing of newspapers	SDOM
12	Publishing activities, excl. newspapers	SDOM
13	Printing activities etc.	SDOM
14	Mfr. of refined petroleum products etc.	SCAI
15	Mfr. of chemical raw materials	SCIB
16	Mfr. of paints, soap, cosmetics, etc.	SCAI
17	Mfr. of pharmaceuticals etc.	SCIB
18	Mfr. of plastics and synthetic rubber	SCAI
19	Mfr. of glass and ceramic goods etc.	SDOM
20	Mfr. of cement, bricks, concrete ind. etc.	SCAI
21	Mfr. of basic metals	SCAI
22	Mfr. Construction materials of metal etc.	SCAI
23	Mfr. of hand tools, metal packaging etc.	SDOM

APPENDIX C   (*Continued*)

No.	Industry	Sector
24	Mfr. of marine engines, compressors etc.	SPEC
25	Mfr. of other general purpose machinery	SPEC
26	Mfr. of agricultural and forestry machinery	SPEC
27	Mfr. of machinery for industries etc.	SPEC
28	Mfr. of domestic appliances n.e.c.	SCAI
29	Mfr. of office machinery and computers	SCIB
30	Mfr. of radio and communication equipment etc.	SCIB
31	Mfr. of medical and optical instruments etc.	SPEC
32	Building and repairing of ships and boats	SCAI
33	Mfr. of transport equipment excl. ships, etc.	SCAI
34	Mfr. of furniture	SDOM
35	Mfr. of toys, gold and silver articles etc.	SDOM
36	General contractors	CRAF
37	Bricklaying	CRAF
38	Install. of electrical wiring and fittings	CRAF
39	Plumbing	CRAF
40	Joinery installation	CRAF
41	Painting and glazing	CRAF
42	Other construction works	CRAF
43	Sale of motor vehicles, motorcycles etc.	SSER
44	Maintenance and repair of motor vehicles	CRAF
45	Service stations	SSER
46	Ws. of agricul. Raw materials, live animals	WTRA
47	Ws. of food, beverages and tobacco	WTRA
48	Ws. of household goods	WTRA
49	Ws. of wood and construction materials	WTRA
50	Ws. of other raw mat. and semimanufactures	WTRA
51	Ws. of machinery, equipment and supplies	WTRA
52	Commission trade and other wholesale trade	WTRA
53	Re. Sale of food in non-specialised stores	SCIS
54	Re. Sale of food in specialised stores	SSER
55	Department stores	SCIS
56	Retail sale of phar. goods, cosmetic art. etc.	SSER
57	Re. Sale of clothing, footwear etc.	SSER
58	Re. Sale of furniture, household appliances	SSER

APPENDIX C   *(Continued)*

No.	Industry	Sector
59	Re. Sale in other specialised stores	SSER
60	Repair of personal and household goods	SSER
61	Hotels etc.	SSER
62	Restaurants etc.	SSER
63	Transport via railways and buses	SCIS
64	Taxi operation and coach services	SSER
65	Freight transport by road and via pipelines	SSER
66	Water transport	SCIS
67	Air transport	SCIS
68	Cargo handling, harbours etc.; travel agencies	SCIS
69	Monetary intermediation	ITIS
70	Other financial intermediation	ITIS
71	Insurance and pension funding	ITIS
72	Activities auxiliary to financial intermediates	ITIS
73	Letting of own property	SSER
74	Real estate agents etc.	SSER
75	Renting of machinery and equipment etc.	SSER
76	Computer and related activity	ITIS
77	Research and development	ITIS
78	Legal activities	ITIS
79	Accounting, book-keeping and auditing activities	ITIS
80	Consulting engineers, architects etc.	ITIS
81	Advertising	ITIS
82	Building-cleaning activities	SCIS
83	Other business services	ITIS

Note: SCAI = scale intensive firms; SDOM = Supplier dominated firms; SCIB = Science based firms; SPEC = Specialised suppliers; CRAF = Crafts; WTRA = Whole sale trade; SSER = Specialised services; SCIS = Scale intensive services; ITIS = ICT intensive services.
Source: Laursen and Foss (2000, p. 16).

APPENDIX D

Probit Model of the Ability to Innovate Yes/No and Absorptive Capacity by Sector, Weighted.

Variables	Supplier Dominated			Scale Intensive			Specialized Suppliers			Science Based		
	Coef.	Std. Err.	Mar. Eff.	Coef.	Std. Err.	Mar. Eff.	Coef.	Std. Err.	Mar. Eff.	Coef.	Std. Err.	Mar. Eff.
Intercept	0.034	0.292	0.013	−0.881	0.288	−0.351	−0.850	0.508	−0.318	0.833	1.144	0.301
HIEDU – share of academic employees	2.263	3.134	0.892	6.184	3.663	2.467	8.693*	4.323	3.257	−2.333	3.819	−0.843
EXPE – work expe. of top-manag.	−0.027	0.014	−0.011	0.004	0.014	0.002	0.035	0.025	0.013	−0.092	0.060	−0.033
HRM – human ressource management												
High	0.500*	0.245	0.197	0.769**	0.228	0.307	1.348**	0.356	0.505	1.214*	0.512	0.439
Medium	0.043	0.201	0.017	0.606**	0.213	0.242	0.687*	0.289	0.257	0.956	0.508	0.346
Low	Benchmark			Benchmark			Benchmark			Benchmark		
EXTERN – closer relat. with extern. actors												
Both	0.302	0.267	0.119	0.337	0.272	0.135	0.362	0.382	0.136	−0.041	0.461	−0.015
Either vertical/know.inst.	0.048	0.193	0.019	0.132	0.179	0.052	−0.115	0.254	−0.043	0.135	0.401	0.049
None	Benchmark			Benchmark			Benchmark			Benchmark		
SUBSID – belonging to a sub. firm, binary												
Yes	0.126	0.172	0.050	0.105	0.182	0.042	0.302	0.241	0.113	0.514	0.408	0.186
COMP – experi. increased comp., binary												
Yes	0.071	0.176	0.028	0.374*	0.186	0.149	0.269	0.251	0.101	−0.094	0.385	−0.034
SIZE – size of the firm												
>50	0.348	0.251	0.137	0.055	0.226	0.022	−0.372	0.395	−0.139	−0.150	0.689	−0.054
25–50	0.007	0.238	0.003	−0.125	0.236	−0.050	−0.611	0.389	−0.229	−0.795	0.726	−0.287
<25	Benchmark			Benchmark			Benchmark			Benchmark		
N	235			252			154			69		
% of correct predictions	63			64			74			72		
Log likelihood	−151			−158			−84			−37		
Restricted log likelihood	−160			−174			−101			−44		
Likelihood ratio test	16.9			31.8			33.9			14.5		

APPENDIX D (Continued)

	Craft			Wholesale trade			Specialized services			Scale Intensive Service			ICT Intensive Services	
	Coef.	Std. Err.	Mar. Eff.	Coef.	Std. Err.	Mar. Eff.	Coef.	Std. Err.	Mar. Eff.	Coef.	Std. Err.	Mar. Eff.	Coef.	Mar. Eff.
Intercept	-1.320	0.198	-0.346	-0.411	0.252	-0.164	-1.412	0.224	-0.470	-0.690	0.483	-0.232	-1.450	-0.564
HIEDU – share of academic employees	-0.264	5.935	-0.069	4.007**	1.470	1.626	3.499	2.628	1.165	8.142	9.274	2.740	0.910	0.354
EXPE – work experience of top-management	0.003	0.012	0.001	-0.001	0.013	0.000	-0.012	0.011	-0.004	0.005	0.022	0.002	0.038	0.015
HRM – human ressource management														
High	0.732**	0.264	0.192	0.599**	0.222	0.239	1.108**	0.249	0.369	0.926*	0.493	0.312	0.902**	0.351
Medium	0.274	0.184	0.072	0.152	0.171	0.061	0.513*	0.193	0.171	0.297	0.395	0.100	0.411	0.160
Low	Benchmark			Benchmark			Benchmark			Benchmark			Benchmark	
EXTERN – closer relat. with extern. actors														
Both vertical/know.inst.	0.339	0.295	0.089	0.104	0.252	0.041	0.145	0.293	0.048	0.275	0.245	0.054	0.179	0.070
Either vertical/know.inst.	0.383*	0.190	0.101	0.120	0.157	0.048	0.286	0.187	0.095	-0.124	0.365	-0.042	0.365	0.142
None	Benchmark			Benchmark			Benchmark			Benchmark			Benchmark	
SUBSID – belonging to a sub. firm, binary														
Yes	0.255	0.180	0.067	-0.129	0.157	-0.051	0.153	0.167	0.051	0.419	0.354	0.141	0.615**	0.239
COMP – experienced increased comp., binary														
Yes	0.362	0.194	0.095	0.246	0.148	0.098	0.472*	0.171	0.157	-0.111	0.335	-0.037	0.066	0.026
SIZE – size of the firm														
>50	-0.202	0.261	-0.053	0.092	0.190	0.037	0.382	0.239	0.127	-0.238	0.486	-0.080	0.038	0.015
25–50	-0.203	0.192	-0.053	-0.030	0.179	-0.012	0.127	0.200	0.042	-0.840	0.482	-0.282	0.214	0.083
<25	Benchmark			Benchmark			Benchmark			Benchmark			Benchmark	
N	321			330			296			78			185	
% of correct predictions	80			63			74			72			69	
Log likelihood	-147			-213			-156			-42			-108	
Restricted log lokelihood	-161			-228			-180			-49			-124	
Likelihood ratio test	29.3			30.4			48			14.1			-31.5	

Notes: There is no serious sign of multicollinearity between the independent variables. The multicollinearity is estimated by using the predicted probabilities of the dependent variable. These predicted values are then used to construct a weight variable which are applied in a weighted least squares regression. A tolerance is computed by regressing each variable on all the other explanatory variables.

*Significance at 5% level.

**Significance at 1% level.

PART III:
INDUSTRIAL RELATIONS, HRM
AND THE ORGANIZATION OF
PRODUCT INNOVATION

HRM COMPLEMENTARITIES AND INNOVATIVE PERFORMANCE IN FRENCH AND BRITISH INDUSTRY

Edward Lorenz, Jonathan Michie and Frank Wilkinson

ABSTRACT

A dominant theme in the high performance HRM literature concerns complementarities among individual practices and the positive performance benefits associated with adopting simultaneously a bundle of HRM practices. While there is little consensus over what practices should be included under the "high performance" label, most authors see employee representation and consultation as representing a traditional management approach. Moreover enterprise performance is commonly measured as financial performance and relatively little attention has been given to innovative performance. In contrast to the mainstream view, we argue that employee representation can be highly complementary to the training and incentive devices focused on in the high performance HRM literature. This proposition is empirically tested for the innovative performance of comparable populations of U.K. and French private sector establishments. The chapter constitutes one of the first major comparative empirical investigations of the HRM/innovative performance link.

Product Innovation, Interactive Learning and Economic Performance
Research on Technological Innovation and Management Policy, Volume 8, 181–210
ISSN: 0737-1071/doi:10.1016/S0737-1071(04)08008-4

1. INTRODUCTION

In Chapter 7 by Anker Lund Vinding it was shown that firms applying HRM-practices are more innovative while Chapter 3 by Alice Lam gave analytical arguments for why the organization of firms will reflect the broader institutional setting around national labour markets and education systems. This chapter combines these two perspectives. In relation to Chapter 7 it shows that the industrial relations affect to what degree HRM-practices will have an impact on innovation. In relation to Chapter 3 it is shown that formal rules regarding worker's representation and the role of trade unions will be reflected in how specific organizational patterns affect innovation.

The starting point for the chapter is the widely held view that increasing international competition based on such non-price factors as quality, design and innovation is encouraging firms to adopt a variety of new work practices which serve to involve employees more fully in production related decision-making. Often labelled "high involvement work practices" (HIWP) or "high performance work practices" (HPWP), these new organizational forms typically include the use of quality circles or problem-solving groups, the use of self-managed work teams, enhanced use of job rotation and job enlargement, and individual or group responsibility for quality control (see for example, Clegg et al., 1996; Deutouzos et al., 1989; Gittleman et al., 1998; Guest, 1997; Guest et al., 2003; Lawler et al., 1992; Michie & Sheehan, 1999a, 2003; Osterman, 1994, 2000; Womack et al., 1990).

There is little consensus in the literature over what practices should be included under the label of "high involvement" or "high performance."[1] Much of the early literature, and notably that inspired by work on the "lean production" model coming out of the MIT auto project, focussed on the diffusion of a limited set of core work practices (Womack et al., 1990; MacDuffie & Krafcik, 1992). Osterman (1994), for example, measured the move towards the "transformed" organization in terms of the level of penetration of four practices: TQM, job rotation, quality circles and team work. In the more recent literature the emphasis has been increasingly on analysing the performance effects of adopting a wider set of human resources management (HRM) practices, including policies around pay, training and careers (Becker & Gerhart, 1996; Becker & Huselid, 1998; Huselid et al., 1997). Applebaum et al. (2000), for example, identify three basic components of the high performance work system: organizational practices which provide opportunities to participate (e.g. quality circles, team work etc.); training practices providing the necessary skills to participate; and pay and promotion policies providing the appropriate incentives to participate (e.g. profit sharing and performance appraisal).

A central question raised in this more recent literature is whether there exist complementarities among the individual HRM practices resulting in performance benefits from adopting a set or bundle of practices simultaneously. Underlying this notion of HRM complementarities is the idea that the core high involvement work practices (quality circles, team organization, etc.) are more likely to be effective if they are supported by substantial investments in training and by forms of pay linking employees' compensation to their effort and to company performance. Training can be seen as a natural complement to work arrangements that provide increased opportunities for employee participation in decision-making. Collective incentive schemes, as profit sharing and gain sharing, and individual incentive schemes, as pay for knowledge and compensation for suggestions, are seen as complementary pay devices which encourage employees to commit themselves to the goal of improving company performance. Such payment arrangements promise employees a share of the increased returns from their enhanced effort (Applebaum et al., 2000; Becker & Gerhart, 1996; Guest, 1997; Huselid et al., 1997; Ichiniowski et al., 1997; Whitfield, 2000). It has also been argued that such practices are more likely to be effective if they are complemented by commitment incentives in the form of job security that serve to increase employees' time horizons thus encouraging them to invest in firm-specific skills (Doeringer et al., 2003; Levine & Tyson, 1990).

Most authors see negotiation and consultation as representing a traditional personnel management approach rather than an innovative one that is central to achieving the performance gains associated with increased employee involvement. In contrast to this view, and in keeping with previous work by Michie and Sheehan (1999b) and Lorenz (1999), we argue that employee representation can be highly complementary to the training, and incentives devices focussed on in the mainstream HPWP literature. For example, formal systems of employee representation can increase employees' confidence that disputes around the design or operation of the pay and promotion system will be resolved in a way that respects their interests. Representation can also increase employee confidence that implicit guarantees around employment security will be respected. One of the key objectives of this chapter is to test for the presence of performance enhancing complementarities between systems of employee representation and the more conventional set of HRM practices identified in the HPWP literature.

Enterprise performance in the HRM literature has for the most part been measured as financial performance. This chapter contributes to the literature on HRM complementarities by investigating the relation between the firm's capacity to innovate new products and services and the nature of the organizational devices it uses to manage its competencies and internal knowledge flows. Relatively little attention has been given to the impact of HRM practices and their bundling on innovative performance.[2] Yet, there are good reasons to suppose that the firm's capacity for innovation can be increased by the use of such practices as job rotation, quality circles, and shop or service meetings. For example, such devices can positively contribute to the sort of interdepartmental information flows and feedbacks which studies in the spirit of Kline and Rosenberg's (1986) well-known chain-link model of innovation have identified as critical to the firm's capacity for technological innovation.[3] Another key idea in the literature on innovation is that there exist knowledge development cycles, in which tacit knowledge is transformed into more explicit and codified forms that are then embodied in new products and services (Nonaka & Takeuchi, 1995; Nooteboom, 2000, Ch. 9). HRM practices such as team organization, quality circles, suggestion schemes and shop meetings can be mobilised in order to provide a framework within which employees can articulate and make more explicit tacit knowledge that subsequently may be integrated into the process of new product design and development.

This chapter is also one of the first major internationally comparative empirical investigations of the HRM/performance link.[4] By drawing on comparable data sets of private sector establishments in the U.K. and France, this chapter provides a more solid basis for investigating the way the wider institutional environment may support and constrain the design of firm level organizational forms and governance mechanisms. This part of the analysis pertains to the question of market selection dynamics and to possible limits to the diffusion of "best-practice" organizational forms (Becker & Huselid, 1998). Regulatory factors impacting on company polices include the character of union policy on matters of pay and job content, the content, coverage and degree of coordination of collective bargaining, and the nature of national labour legislation prescribing certain forms of remuneration and employee representation. Our view of the matter is that unconstrained competition in the labour market does not necessarily constitute the ideal environment for the diffusion of new work and pay practices. It can plausibly be argued that employers left to their own devices will under-invest in potentially superior forms of work organization. Levine and Tyson (1992), for example, have argued that externalities transmitted through labour and product markets may impact on the effectiveness of the various personnel policies that support high involvement work organization. For example, companies using commitment incentives in the form of employment guarantees may be penalised in periods of recession relative to firms that can readily adjust their labour costs through layoffs. Moreover, while fluid labour markets may facilitate the rapid reconfiguration of the firm's competence base, they may also lead to an underinvestment in skills due to the risk of labour poaching. On the other hand, more general restraints on a numerical flexibility response to crisis could induce more innovative employment policies to enhance performance.[5]

The regulatory settings in France and the U.K. differ in a number of important respects. France ranks relatively high among OECD countries in terms of employment protection legislation (OECD Employment Outlook, 1999). While the rate of unionisation is low in France, collective bargaining coverage is amongst the highest in Europe due to legislation providing for the extension to all firms in the relevant industrial branch of agreements (conventions collectives) negotiated between regional employers' associations and the unions. Legislation in France also provides for various non-union forms of legally mandated employee representation, including works councils (*comité d'entreprise*) and *délégués du personnel*. The highly regulated labour market setting in France is a far cry from that found in the U.K. The 1990s witnessed an important decline in multi-employer bargaining and declining levels of unionisation in the U.K. Compared to their French counterparts, U.K employers face few legal restrictions on hiring and firing. These important differences in the French and U.K. institutional settings make a comparison of these two countries especially suitable for an investigation of the impact of local context conditions on the HRM/performance link.

2. DATA AND RESEARCH DESIGN

Our comparative analysis is based on two nationally representative samples of public and private sector establishments: the WERS98 survey which covers U.K. workplaces with 10 or more employees, and the REPONSE98 survey which covers French establishments with 20 or more employees. The response rates for WERS98 and REPONSE97 were 83 and 65% respectively. These rates compare well to those achieved for most U.S. based surveys which rarely top 25%. The analysis in this chapter is restricted to the trading sector and excludes public services (government, health, education, etc) resulting in samples of 2,086 establishments for France and 1165 establishments for the U.K.[6] In both cases the samples of workplaces were arrived at through a process of stratified random sampling using variable sampling fractions.[7] The survey designs involve over-sampling of large establishments and establishments in such industrial sector classifications as construction and financial services which contain relatively few establishments compared to manufacturing or trade.[8] In order to compensate for the over-sampling bias this generates and to create unbiased population estimates, weights equal to the inverse of the probability of selection for an establishment can be applied. All descriptive statistics and point estimates reported in this chapter are based on the weighted data for each survey sample.

2.1. HRM Variables

The selection of comparable HRM variables for the analysis was constrained by the only partial overlap of WERS98 and REPONSE98 surveys. Questions pertaining

Table 1. Use of HRM Practices in U.K. and French Establishments.

U.K. Establishments		French Establishments	
Practice or Policy	% Using the Practice or Policy	Practice or Policy	% Using the Practice or Policy
Opportunity to participate			
Team organization where members jointly decide how the work is to be done[a]	36.0	Self-Managing Teams[d]	15.2
Employees have a lot of variety in their work[b]	39.8	Job Rotation[d]	31.7
Suggestion scheme	22.9	Suggestion scheme	24.5
Quality circles used over the last 12 months[c]	15.9	Quality circles[d]	15.5
Regular meetings with the entire workforce present	33.1	Regular shop, office or department meetings[a]	39.4
Skills			
Formal off-the-job training over the last 12 month[a]	26.1	Training expenditures = 3% or more of wage bill	26.9
Incentives/motivation			
Use of performance pay[c]	19.9	Use of individual or group performance pay for non-managerial employees	72.6
Formal performance appraisal[c]	47.6	Periodic evaluation of non-managerial employees by superiors	44.9

Regular diffusion of information on staffing plans	53.8	
Regular diffusion of information on the financial position of the establishment	63.2	
Regular diffusion of information on employment prospects		42.7
Regular diffusion of information on the establishment's economic situation		55.1
Representation		
Negotiations or consultation with union of non-union representatives over pay or conditions of employment	17.8	
Negotiations or consultation with union of non-union representatives over staffing or manpower planning	10.7	
Negotiations or consultation with union of non-union representatives over training of employees	11.3	
Discussions or negotiations on working conditions over the last 3 years		48.7
Discussions or negotiations on employment (hiring/firing) over the last 3 years		33.5
Discussions or negotiations on training over the last 3 years		51.8
No. of establishments	1165	2086

[a] Over 40% of largest occupational group involved.
[b] The largest occupational group.
[c] Over 40% of non-managerial employees involved.
[d] Over 50% of employees involved.

to 13 HRM practices were chosen as a basis for the measures presented in Table 1.[9] All multiple response items were rescaled to dichotomous yes/no responses as described in more detail in the appendix. The questions, as can be seen, are not phrased in exactly the same manner in the two surveys. A number of the questions which in REPONSE98 pertain to all employees or to all non-managerial employees pertain only to the largest occupational group in WERS98. Further, while in REPONSE98 the respondent was typically asked to identify whether a particular practice was in use, in WERS the respondent was in certain instances asked whether the practiced had been in use during the last 12 months (e.g. quality circles). The least degree of overlap between the two questionnaires concerns the training policies. A single question was posed in REPONSE98. It asked the respondent to identify the amount spent on training as a percent of the total wage bill. French enterprises are legally required to make training expenditures equal to 1.5% of the wage bill and we have used the 3% level of expenditures as a measure of high employer commitment to training. As no comparable question was posed in WERS98, we used the criterion of 40% or more of the largest occupational group receiving off-the-job training as a measure of high employer commitment to training.

The questions on employee representation do not merely seek to identify whether some such system exists but also whether representatives have been actively engaged in discussions, consultations or negotiations with management. The measures allow for both union and non-union forms of representation. In the French case, the range of non-union forms identified include legally mandated employee delegates (*délégués du personnel*), elected members of the legally mandated works councils (*comités d'entreprise*), elected members of the health and safety committees, and employee representatives elected or nominated independently of any legally mandated procedure.[10]

As can be seen from Table 1, the utilisation rates of the practices providing opportunities to participate are comparable across the two countries with the exception of team organization which is more highly adopted in the U.K. Moreover, if we focus on the five practices measuring opportunities to participate, the results indicate that a minority of the establishments in each country are "transformed," in the sense that the term has been used by Osterman (1994). This is in keeping with the results of other studies on the diffusion of HPWP in France and the U.K. (DARES, 2000, p. 5; Guest et al., 2003, pp. 302–303).

The most striking differences between the two populations are in the areas of performance pay and employee representation. The explanation for the high utilisation rate of performance pay in France is legislation which offers fiscal advantages to firms that negotiate agreements with a local union or with the *comité d'entreprise* for the universal coverage of employees in profit or gain sharing plans.[11] The striking differences in the extent to which employees benefit from representation also reflect the different regulatory contexts in each country. French employers are not only required to negotiate pay at the plant or enterprise-level with a local union or unions on an annual basis, but they also have multiple obligations in the area of employee representation, including the requirement to establish *comité d'entreprise*, to hold elections for the appointment of *délégués du personnel*, and the obligation to establish employee direct expression groups via negotiations with local union representatives. None of these requirements exist for firms operating in Britain, where the 1990s were marked by declining union strength and a significant decline in multi-employer bargaining (Brown et al., 1998; Claydon, 1996).

2.2. Performance Variables

The performance measures for innovation are based on a question asking management whether the establishment had introduced a new product or service over the previous five years in the case of the U.K. and over the previous three years in the case of France. The filter in the French case is evidently more restrictive and while somewhat over 37% of the French establishments are innovative on this measure, slightly over 53% of the U.K. establishments are innovative (see Appendix for mean values).

2.3. Control Variables

As in the case of most previous studies examining the HRM/performance link, sector and establishment size controls are used in the logistic regression analysis. The population of establishments is classified according to seven sectors: manufacturing; construction, electricity, gas and water; trade; transport; financial services; business services; and other. The key differences in the industrial structure between the two countries are the greater importance of the manufacturing sector in the French economy and the relative importance of the wholesale and retail trade sector in the U.K. economy. The size distribution of establishments as measured by the number employed is approximately the same (see Appendix for variable means).

2.4. Research Design

As noted above, there are different views over the set of practices that make up the HPWP system, and there are different views regarding the likely performance affects of bundling practices in particular ways. The approach we adopt to identify HRM bundles or systems follows that used by Wood (1999) and by Laursen and Foss (2002) in letting the form of bundling emerge directly from the statistical analysis rather than constructing ideal combinations of practices on *a priori* grounds and then determining to what extent these preconceived forms can be observed in practice. To do this, we use factor analysis to identify the underlying associations that exist among the 13 practices identified in Table 1. We then use the factor scores or the coordinates of the observations on the first five factors as a basis for clustering the establishments into distinct groups, using a single-link hierarchical clustering method known as the nearest neighbour method.[12] Finally we use logit regression analysis to estimate the impact of different HRM practices or clusters of HRM practices on innovative performance. By comparing the size of the point estimates for the different clusters it is possible to test for the presence of positive system or bundling effects on innovative performance.

The factor analysis method used is multiple correspondence analysis, a mathematical technique similar in spirit to principal components analysis in that it similarly transforms a set of correlated response variables into a smaller set of uncorrelated variables called principal factors or axes. It is suitable for analysing the associations between more than two categorical variables that can be presented in multi-way contingency tables. While in principal components analysis the total variance is decomposed along the principal factors or components, in correspondence analysis the total variation of the data matrix is measured by the usual chi-squared statistic for row-column independence and it is the chi-squared statistic which is decomposed along the principal factors.[13] Some information is usually lost in the data reduction process; the accuracy of the display is measured by the percentage of the chi-squared statistic or "inertia" of the original data matrix that the principal factors account for.

3. HRM AND INNOVATIVE PERFORMANCE

3.1. Identifying HRM Systems

One type of information that is commonly used in interpreting the results of a multiple correspondence analysis is the percentage contributions of the variables to the part of the total inertia or chi-squared statistic accounted for by each factor. This shows which variables contribute most to the construction of the factors and it plays a role in interpreting the results that is similar to that played by factor loadings in principal components analysis.

Table 2. Factor Analysis for French and U.K. Establishments.

Variable	U.K. Contributions					France Contributions				
	1	2	3	4	5	1	2	3	4	5
Self-managing teams	5.2	4.1	**21.0**	0.0	4.6	1.8	0.6	**31.4**	0.3	6.2
Job rotation/Variety	0.8	6.7	**31.2**	0.9	19.9	0.2	0.5	**33.9**	0.0	1.1
Suggestion scheme	6.0	2.2	13.5	**15.2**	7.5	5.7	0.1	2.6	0.6	6.6
Quality circles	5.2	3.3	3.5	4.2	0.0	6.5	4.9	**12.9**	4.9	7.8
Meetings	9.5	4.1	6.5	3.5	**15.2**	**13.4**	3.6	0.0	6.3	13.4
Training	**8.9**	5.4	2.6	3.3	4.7	**10.1**	2.1	5.7	10.1	0.2
Performance pay	2.6	0.7	0.9	**72.5**	2.6	2.2	0.5	3.9	5.7	**62.3**
Performance evaluation/appraisal	5.1	11.1	0.0	1.0	**20.2**	**14.4**	3.2	7.5	5.8	0.0
Diffusion of information on hiring and firing/staffing	**12.2**	0.9	0.2	2.6	6.0	14.9	0.2	0.0	**36.9**	0.3
Diffusion of information on economic situation/financial position	**13.9**	2.0	6.9	0.0	11.8	17.7	0.9	0.6	**27.3**	0.1
Consultation or negotiations on working conditions/pay	9.9	**21.8**	0.1	0.0	0.1	3.0	**29.6**	1.5	0.7	0.0
Consultation or negotiations on employment/staffing	12.8	**17.1**	1.5	0.0	1.0	5.5	**25.4**	0.0	0.8	1.8
Consultation or negotiations on training	13.0	**19.1**	0.5	0.1	0.0	4.9	**28.3**	0.0	0.5	0.2

The percentage contributions of the HRM variables to the first five factors for the U.K. and French samples of enterprises are shown in Table 2. In the case of the U.K., the first five factors account for approximately 56% of the total variation of the data matrix. Factor 1 is constructed primarily by the two measures of information sharing and by the variable measuring commitment to training. The second factor is formed from the three variables measuring the presence of employee representation. The third factor is constructed from the variables measuring team organization and diversity in work. The fourth is constructed from the measures of performance and suggestion schemes while the fifth factor is formed from the variables measuring performance appraisals and meetings.

Despite the underlying associations that exist among certain sub-groups of variables, the analysis suggests that the U.K. HRM system is highly fragmented. There is no evidence for the population of establishments as a whole that the majority of the practices are linked in a systematic way. Thus while teams and variety in work tended to be associated, the firms that use these practices together do not necessarily use them in conjunction with pay incentives, significant investments in training or systems of employee representation. Moreover, the variable measuring quality circles is not highly associated with any of the other measures, suggesting that it forms a separate factor in the U.K. case.[14]

In the case of France, the first five factors account for approximately 53% of the total variation of the data matrix. The first factor, which corresponds roughly to the fifth factor in the U.K. case, is constructed primarily from the variables measuring the use of meetings and systems of employee evaluation. The variable measuring commitment to training makes equal contributions to the first and fourth factors. The second factor is constructed from the variables measuring employee representation and corresponds to the second factor in the U.K. analysis. The third factor is constructed mainly from three of the core high performance work practices: teams, job rotation and quality circles. Suggestion schemes are not strongly associated with these three variables and make only a small contribution to any of the first five factors. The two measures of information sharing are the main contributors to the fourth factor, while the fifth factor is constructed almost entirely from performance pay.

The results for the French case, much as those for the U.K., point to a fragmented HRM system, where only sub-groups of variables are systematically associated. The results are in many respects similar to those for the U.K. In particular there is little evidence that policies in the areas of incentives, training and employee representation are systematically associated with the use of the core high involvement work practices. It needs to be appreciated, however, that these results do not demonstrate the absence of a sub-group of establishments that cluster all, or the majority, of the 13 HRM practices identified. The results simply show that the observed variation of all – or the majority of – practices cannot be accounted for by a single unobserved latent variable for either of the country samples.

The hierarchical clustering analyses allow us to demonstrate that different sub-groups of enterprises cluster the HRM practices in different ways in each country. Table 3 presents the results of the cluster analysis for the U.K., which resulted in the grouping of establishments into four organizational categories. The first two clusters (Columns 1 and 2), which group 28.3 and 13.9% of the total population respectively, come the closest to corresponding to the HPWP model, in the sense of Applebaum et al. (2000) or Ichiniowski et al. (1997). Relative to the population as a whole, these clusters are characterised by an over-representation of the variables measuring opportunities, ability and incentives to participate. This is notably the case for the variables measuring information diffusion. The two clusters can be distinguished primarily on the basis of performance pay, which is used by almost all of the enterprises grouped in UKHPWP2 and by virtually none of those grouped in UKHPWP1. The UKHPWP1 cluster is also distinguished from the UKHPW2 cluster by the greater importance of quality circles.

Table 3. HRM Cluster Analysis: U.K. Firms.

Practice or Policy	Percentage of Establishments in the Cluster Using the Practice				
	HPWP1	HPWP2	Hybrid	Traditional	All
Team organization where members jointly decide how the work is to be done	**47.9**	**45.9**	33.6	25.8	36.0
Employees have a lot of variety in their work	**47.5**	**50.2**	26.9	35.5	39.8
Suggestion schemes	43.3	**27.6**	24.1	7.5	22.9
Quality circles used over the last 12 months	**28.8**	16.3	**22.0**	5.2	15.9
Regular meeting with the entire workforce present	**50.6**	**54.0**	**39.7**	13.4	33.1
Formal off-the-job training over the last 12 month	**39.4**	**43.9**	**29.7**	10.7	26.1
Use of performance pay	0.8	**99.9**	24.8	7.4	19.9
Formal performance appraisal	**76.4**	**73.2**	41.1	22.5	47.6
Regular diffusion of information on staffing plans	**78.8**	**77.7**	**73.6**	24.0	53.8
Regular diffusion of information on the financial position of the establishment	**86.2**	**99.2**	**88.2**	31.5	63.2
Negotiations or consultation with union of non-union representatives over pay or conditions of employment	5.2	4.7	**79.1**	11.7	17.8
Negotiations or consultation with union of non-union representatives over staffing or manpower planning	0.5	0.1	**75.8**	1.2	10.7
Negotiations or consultation with union of non-union representatives over training of employees	3.5	1.0	**70.6**	1.6	11.3
Percentage of total population	28.3	13.9	23.0	34.8	100.0

Note: Figures in bold indicate that the percentage of the enterprises in the class characterised by the practice is significantly greater (5% level or better) than the percentage of the total population characterised by the practice.

We refer to the third cluster, which accounts for 23% of the population, as a Hybrid organizational form. It can be distinguished from the other three clusters by an over-representation of the variables measuring systems of employee representation. A large majority of the establishments which make use of systems of employee representation are grouped in this cluster. This feature is combined with above average use of information diffusion practices, meetings, quality circles, training and performance pay. Team and work variety are under-represented in this cluster, while the use of suggestion schemes is about average. We refer to the fourth or residual cluster as "traditional." It corresponds to Osterman's non-transformed organizational category, as all of the HRM practices are under-represented. It is the largest of the clusters, accounting for approximately 35% of the total population.

The French cluster analysis, which also resulted in a grouping of establishments into four organizational types, displays a number of differences from those for the U.K. analysis. Firstly, a smaller part of the population, only 17.8%, are grouped in a cluster which corresponds to the HPWP model – in the sense of an over-representation of the practices measuring opportunities, ability and incentives to participate. Secondly, as might be anticipated from the distinctive features of the French regulatory context referred to above, employee representation is much more evenly distributed across the entire population of enterprises than is the case in the U.K., where a large fraction of the population is characterised by an absence of any of the three forms of representation identified. FRHybrid1 and FRHybrid2, which are both characterised by an over-representation of systems of employee representation, can be distinguished by differences in their incentives systems. FRhybrid1 is notable for the emphasis placed on information diffusion; while in FRHybrid2 the key incentive devices are performance pay combined with periodic employee evaluation. As in the U.K., the largest cluster is the traditional or non-transformed one, which accounts for about 40% of the French population (Table 4).

3.2. Differences in HRM Systems According to Size and Sector

Tables 5 and 6 show that size plays a role in the likelihood of adopting the different HRM systems. In both the U.K. and France, the smallest size category of establishment is over-represented in the traditional cluster while establishments with 200 employees and over are under-represented.

Large establishments are over-represented in UKHPWP2 while they are under-represented in UKHPWP1, suggesting a positive link between size and the use of performance pay. Large establishments are also over-represented in UKHybrid and FRHybrid2, pointing to a positive relation between establishment size and the use of systems of employee representation.

Tables 7 and 8 show differences in the sector distribution of the HRM clusters. In both the U.K. and France establishments in the trade sector and to a lesser extent in financial and/or business services are more likely to adopt the

Table 4. HRM Cluster Analysis: French Firms

Practice or Policy	HPWP	Hybrid1	Hybrid2	Traditional	All
Self-managing teams	**31.4**	18.9	7.6	9.5	15.2
Job rotation	**43.8**	**38.6**	14.1	30.9	31.7
Suggestion scheme	43.3	**28.0**	**30.8**	11.3	24.6
Quality circles	**51.5**	4.8	14.0	6.4	15.5
Regular shop, office or department meetings	**87.5**	15.5	**62.1**	20.8	39.4
Training expenditures = 3% or more of wage bill	**55.0**	6.9	**52.3**	13.9	27.0
Use of individual or group performance pay for non-managerial employees	**83.5**	67.8	**84.1**	65.1	72.6
Periodic evaluation of non-managerial employees by superiors	**83.4**	24.7	**77.9**	23.7	44.9
Regular diffusion of information on employment prospects	69.4	**82.7**	46.5	6.2	42.7
Regular diffusion of information on the enterprise's economic situation	**86.6**	**89.8**	**67.4**	15.4	55.1
Discussions or negotiations over the last 3 years on working conditions	35.1	**55.2**	**79.3**	36.5	48.7
Discussions or negotiations over the last 3 years on employment	18.4	**40.3**	**76.6**	15.9	33.5
Discussions of negotiations over the last 3 years on training	34.9	**62.8**	**92.4**	33.7	51.8
Percentage of total population	17.8	23.0	19.1	40.1	100.0

Table 5. Size Composition of U.K. HRM Clusters.

Size in Terms of Number of Employees	HIWP1	HIWP2	Hybrid	Traditional	All
20–49	63.05	56.74	39.59	68.41	61.47
50–99	19.53	23.83	24.56	17.62	19.92
100–199	8.29	9.84	16.18	8.55	9.65
200–499	7.71	6.90	13.36	4.32	6.86
500–999	1.09	2.03	4.39	0.90	1.57
>999	0.33	0.67	1.92	0.21	0.54

Table 6. Size Composition of French HRM Clusters.

Size in Terms of Number of Employees	HIWP	Hybrid1	Hybrid2	Traditional	All
20–49	66.34	61.79	50.89	70.01	63.82
50–99	16.32	22.73	21.79	16.36	18.85
100–199	8.88	9.88	14.63	8.76	10.16
200–499	6.16	4.59	8.71	4.03	5.43
500–999	1.65	0.66	2.71	0.70	1.24
>999	0.66	0.35	1.26	0.14	0.49

Table 7.   Sector Composition of U.K. HRM Clusters.

Sector	HPWP1	HIWP2	Hybrid	Traditional	All
Manufacturing	13.54	8.11	33.23	31.48	23.33
Construction, electricity, gas and water	2.65	1.49	6.06	8.62	5.58
Trade	40.21	50.67	12.52	25.82	31.59
Transport	4.57	4.96	19.53	7.80	8.03
Financial services	6.76	11.15	3.72	2.41	5.02
Business services	16.79	16.79	17.27	13.20	14.69
Other[a]	15.47	15.47	7.67	10.67	11.76

[a] Includes hotels and restaurants, domestic services and personal and other community services.

Table 8.   Sector Composition of French HRM Clusters.

Sector	HPWP	Hybrid1	Hybrid2	Traditional	All
Manufacturing	25.77	44.81	28.90	33.95	34.02
Construction, electricity, gas and water	11.82	8.70	10.70	14.32	11.89
Trade	27.15	18.20	25.22	21.29	22.37
Transport	2.57	10.92	6.35	8.84	7.73
Financial services	7.41	2.95	7.22	3.53	4.80
Business services	17.74	10.58	14.41	11.66	13.02
Other[a]	7.54	3.84	7.20	6.41	6.17

[a] Includes hotels and restaurants, domestic services and personal and other community services.

HPWP model. UKHybrid, distinguished by the relative importance of systems of employee representation, is especially characteristic of the manufacturing and transport sectors, while the trade sector is clearly under-represented in this cluster. Traditionally organised firms in the U.K. tend to be concentrated in the manufacturing sector and in construction, electricity, gas and water.

FRHybrid1 is similar to UKHybrid in being especially developed in the manufacturing and transport sectors. However, there is little difference between the sector breakdown of FRHybrid2 and the population as a whole. Traditionally organised establishments in France, as in the U.K., tend to be concentrated in construction, electricity, gas and water.

3.3. HRM Complementarities, Employee Representation and Innovative Performance

Tables 9 and 10 present the estimations of the models predicting innovative performance for the U.K. and French establishments. Some of the variables

Table 9. Logit Regressions: HRM Practices and Innovative Performance.

	U.K. Establishments (Without Controls)		U.K. Establishments (With Controls)		French Establishments (Without Controls)		French Establishments (with Controls)	
	Model 1	Model 2	Model 1	Model 2	Model 1	Model 2	Model1	Model 2
Team organization	−0.022		0.042		0.301		0.389*	
Job rotation/variety	0.352		0.358		0.253		0.351*	
Suggestion schemes		−0.037		−0.161		0.434**		0.431**
Quality circles	0.123		0.071		0.207		0.210	
Meetings	−0.544*		−0.558*			−0.058		−0.083
Performance pay	0.158		0.167		0.094		0.111	
Performance appraisal/periodic evaluation		−0.108		−0.145		0.141		0.155
Diffusion of financial information	0.897*		0.832**		0.310*		0.275*	
Diffusion of information on staffing	0.120		0.188			0.387**		0.379**
Training		0.415		0.409	0.226		0.179	
Negotiation/discussion on staffing		0.558		0.582		0.275*		0.273*
Negotiations/discussions on pay/working conditions	0.176		0.065		0.175		0.175	
N	1165	1165	1165	1165	2086	2086	2086	2086
Pseudo χ^2	0.045		0.012		0.027		0.016	

* Significant at the 0.05 level.
** Significant at the 0.01 level.

Table 10. Logit Regressions: HRM Systems and Innovative Performance.

	U.K. Establishments			French Establishments	
	Model 3 (Without Controls)	Model 3 (with Controls)		Model 3 (Without Controls)	Model 3 (with Controls)
UKHPWP1	0.358	0.319	FRHPWP	0.609**	0.572**
UKHPWP2	0.359	0.309	FRHybrid1	0.557**	0.543**
UKHybrid	0.748*	0.711*	FRHybrid2	0.407*	0.372*
Size			Size		
50–99		0.078	50–99		−0.163
100–199		0.233	100–199		−0.002
200–499		0.519*	200–499		0.147
500–999		0.745*	500–999		0.268
>999		0.216	>999		0.473
Sector			Sector		
Construction, electricity, gas water		−1.165*	Construction, electricity, gas water		−0.720**
Trade		−0.313	Trade		−0.061
Transport		−0.593	Transport		−0.120
Financial services		0.091	Financial services		0.371
Business services		−0.387	Business services		0.084
Other		0.484	Other		−0.262
N	1165	1165	N	2086	2086
Pseudo χ^2	0.012	0.039	Pseudo χ	0.012	0.025

* Significant at the 0.05 level.
** Significant at the 0.01 level.

measuring HRM practices are strongly correlated and for this reason we test two models of the impact of individual practices on innovative performance (Models 1 and 2). In Model 3 the predictors of innovative performance are the different HRM systems that emerged from the cluster analyses undertaken for the U.K. and French populations. Results both with and without sector and establishment size controls are presented.

The results for both the U.K. and France can be seen as providing support for the thesis that HRM complementarities count for innovative performance. Moreover, they point to striking differences in the form taken by these complementarities. In the U.K. case we find strong support for the view that systems of employee representation are not only complementary to the HRM practices focused on in the mainstream HPWP literature, but also are a precondition for realising the benefits associated with the use of these practices. The results for France, while making it clear that employee representation does not constitute a serious obstacle to realising the gains from using HPWPs, provide support for the view that HRM complementarities can be realised independently of the existence of some system of employee representation.

Turning to the U.K. case first, as shown in Table 9 only one of the 12 individual HRM practices considered – the diffusion of financial information – is a positive and significant predictor of innovative performance. This suggests that in the U.K. context an incremental approach to the introduction of HRM practices is unlikely to deliver substantial benefits in terms of innovative performance. The analysis of system effects in Table 10 shows that of the three HRM systems only UKHybrid, which combines employee representation with a subset of the other HRM practices, is a positive and significant predictor of innovative performance. We take this as strong support for the view that the benefits in terms of innovation from bundling HRM practices will not be realised in the absence of employee representation.

In the French case, seven of the 12 HRM practices individually have a positive effect on innovative performance. However, team organization and job rotation are barely significant at the 5% level and only two of the practices – suggestion schemes and the diffusion of information on staffing – are significant at the 1% level or better. Moreover, Table 10 shows that all three of the HRM systems examined are positive and significant predictors of innovation. The strongest effects, however, are achieved by FRHPWP, which is distinctive for the weak presence of employee representation and the over-representation of the other HRM practices. Only a slightly smaller positive effect is registered for FRHybrid1 which combines employee representation with an emphasis on the diffusion of information, job rotation and suggestion schemes. Here we take the larger size of the coefficients on FRHPWP and FRHybrid1 relative to those on the individual practices, as well as the fact that only two of the practices individually are significant at the 1% level, as support for the importance of HRM complementarities for innovative performance in the French context. Unlike the U.K. case, however, the results suggest that in France employee representation is at best neutral as regards reaping these system benefits.

4. CONCLUSION

What accounts for the striking differences between the U.K. and France in the role played by employee representation in realising the positive effects of HRM bundling on innovative performance? Here we can only offer some tentative hypotheses, since the data will not allow us to resolve the issue. We will suggest the following hypothesis, which might appear somewhat paradoxical. The more decisive role played by employee representation in the U.K. is linked to the U.K.'s relatively deregulated labour market setting, characterised by a low level of legislative protection and a very limited capacity on the part of employers for collective coordination around wages and skill provision. In such an institutionally impoverished setting, the willingness of some employers to engage representatives in discussions and negotiations around working conditions and labour force planning issues can play a crucial role in eliciting from employees the forms of commitment and cooperation that we have argued are central to strategies of incremental innovation.

As a number of authors have observed (Streeck, 1992; Thelen, 2001; Wilkinson, 2002) collective coordination of the labour market provides a favourable institutional setting for the successful pursuit of incremental innovation. There are at least two reasons for this. First, employer coordination around wage-setting serves to buffer the establishment from distributional conflict which can easily spill-over into areas of labour/management cooperation that are vital for competing through strategies of incremental innovation. Secondly, the collective provision of skills helps reduce problems of labour poaching, thus providing a more solid foundation upon which to make extensive investments in training. Moreover, a high level of employment protection, be it legally mandated or otherwise, serves as an important complement to such collective labour market coordination since it increases employees' time horizons and encourages them to invest in firm-specific skills

While it is true that French employers face fewer restrictions around individual and collective layoffs today than they did in the 1970s and early 1980s, the differences in the degree of labour market regulation between France and the U.K. are nonetheless striking. In terms of legislative employment protection, the U.K. ranks near the bottom amongst OECD countries while France ranks near the top

(OECD Employment Outlook, 1999).[15] In terms of such factors bearing on unemployment protection as the generosity of benefits and the definition of what constitutes a suitable job, the U.K. ranks near the bottom of OECD countries while France ranks near the mean (Estevez-Abe et al., 2001, p. 168). While references to the relatively fluid U.K. labour market might suggest that the cost of job loss is lessened by the relatively high probability of finding suitable alternative employment, in fact OECD figures reported in Esping-Andersen (1999, p. 22) indicate that net unemployment replacement rates in the U.K. are well below the OECD average and below those pertaining in France. Thus, on average, job loss imposes substantially higher costs on U.K. workers than it does on workers in most other OECD nations and notably on workers in France.

In the past, in many U.K. sectors, strong union organization and broad collective bargaining coverage may well have compensated for the relatively low level of legislative guaranteed social protection. The other critical aspect of deregulation in the U.K., however, has been declining union influence at all levels in the 1980s and 1990s. Moreover, this has gone hand in hand with a decline, or in some case a virtual collapse, of multi-employer bargaining, undermining the capacity of employers for coordinated action around issues of wages and other conditions, including training. In the deregulated U.K. context, as Thelen (2001) has argued, success in achieving the forms of cooperation and employee commitment will depend almost exclusively on the individual employer's capacity to put in place firm-specific internal labour markets that serve to structure careers and provide appropriate incentives for skill acquisition and employee involvement. The risk employers face is that in the absence of supporting external coordinating mechanisms these firm-specific governance mechanisms will prove to be unstable. Distributional conflict at the plant or enterprise level may prove inimical to securing labour's commitment to progressive improvements in product quality, while the risk of loss of skilled labour to competitors will encourage firms to under-invest in the provision of training. Moreover, faced with a temporary decline in product market demand, employers may be under considerable pressure to lower their costs through collective layoffs, thus reneging on their formal or informal commitments to employment security.

We would argue that in the deregulated U.K. setting the all too exceptional commitment of individual employers to substantial forms of employee representation can play a crucial role in eliciting the forms of employee involvement and cooperation that support strategies of incremental innovation. The willingness of employers to consult or negotiate with representatives around workforce planning issues can increase workers' confidence that implicit commitments around employment security will be respected (Lorenz, 1995). In a like manner, the willingness of employers to engage representatives around pay and conditions can increase employees' confidence that disputes around issues of promotion and access to training will be resolved in a manner that respects their interests (Eaton & Voos, 1992; Freeman & Lazear, 1995).

To avoid possible misunderstanding, we are not suggesting that systems of employee representation in France constitute an obstacle to achieving the forms of cooperation and information sharing that support strategies of incremental innovation. The coefficient estimates on the FRHybrid1 and FRHybrid2 clusters are only slightly smaller than that on FRHPWP implying a near neutral effect on performance. A possible explanation of this is simply that since representation is a legal requirement in France all or most firms will have it, while commitment to involving employees in decision-making will vary much more widely and in many cases may be quite low. On the other hand, where representation is not a legal requirement, as in the U.K., only those firms that are seriously concerned to involve their employees in decision-making are likely to have it.

This reading of the statistical results is necessarily provisional and confirmation for our line of interpretation would require more qualitative evidence based on case study research. Regardless of the degree to which our interpretation for the striking differences between the U.K. and France is correct, on one key point our results are unambiguous. Indirect forms of employee participation constitute no obstacle to instituting direct forms of participation and they are fully compatible with reaping the performance gains that direct forms of participation can deliver.

NOTES

1. For useful discussions of the literature, see Michie, 2001; Ramsay et al., 2000; Truss, 2001; Wood, 1999.

2. The key survey-based studies focusing on innovative performance are Michie and Sheehan (1999a, 2003) and Laursen and Foss (2003).

3. For a detailed presentation of the Chain-linked model see Chapter 12 by Ina Drejer and Birte Holst Jørgensen.

4. Despite the large number of surveys undertaken on the diffusion and impact of HRM practices in both France and the U.K., differences in survey design and conception preclude making reliable cross-country comparisons. For example, the ESRC sponsored study of new work practices in manufacturing undertaken by Clegg et al. (1996) seeks to determine the extent of utilisation within the firm by means of a four point subjective scale ranging from "a little" to "entirely." The meaning of such subjective judgements is difficult to interpret and provide a poor basis for solid international comparisons. For a general discussion of European survey evidence, see Lhuillery (1997) and Coriat (1998).

5. Our analysis confirms the general idea put forward by Alice Lam in Chapter 3 that the national institutional setting has an impact on the way firms organise themselves and that this can be documented by comparing different countries.

6. U.K. workplaces in the 10–19 employee size range were excluded from the descriptive statistics and econometric analysis.

7. For detailed discussions of the sampling designs, see Purdon and Pickering (2001) for WERS and Coutrot et al. (2003) for REPONSE.

8. The use of variable sampling fractions is due to the fact that in both countries the population of workplaces is dominated by small workplaces and there are many more workplaces in manufacturing as compared, for example, with construction or financial services. The use of a simple random sampling procedure would not result in a sample with sufficient large workplaces or sufficient workplaces in financial services to permit reliable inferences to be drawn for such groups.

9. See Appendix for a more a more complete presentation of the survey questions upon which the measures are based.

10. Of course in the vast majority of cases the *délégués du personnel* and members of the *comités d'entreprise* are elected from official union lists.

11. The ordinance of 4 January 1959 provided financial incentives for firms to link employee compensation to company profits while the ordinance of 17 August 1967 made such pay system obligatory. See Reynaud (1975, p. 252).

12. For a description of this technique, see Johnson (1998, pp. 323–326).

13. It is common to refer to the percentage of the "inertia" accounted for by a factor. Inertia is defined as the value of the chi-squared statistic of the original data matrix divided by the grand total of the number of observations. See Greenacre (1993).

14. See Wood (1999) for a similar conclusion concerning the use of quality circles in the U.S.

15. The OECD's overall index of employment protection legislation places France near the top at 2.8 and the U.K. close to the bottom at 0.8.

REFERENCES

Applebaum, E., Bailey, T., Berg, P., & Kalleberg, A. (2000). *Manufacturing competitive advantage: The effects of High Performance Work Systems of plant performance and company outcomes.* Ithaca, NY: Cornell University press.

Becker, B., & Gerhart, B. (1996). The impact of Human Resource Management on organisational performance: Progress and prospects. *Academy of Management Journal, 39,* 779–801.

Becker, B., & Huselid, M. (1998). High-Performance Work Systems and firm performance: A synthesis of research and managerial implications'. In: G. Ferris (Ed.), *Research in Personnel and Human Resources* (Vol. 16, pp. 53–102). Greewick, CT: JAI Press.

Brown, W. et al. (1998). *The individualisation of employment contracts in Britain.* Research paper. London: Department of Trade and Industry.

Claydon, T. (1996). Union de-recognition: A re-examination. In: I. Beardwell (Ed.), *Contemporary Industrial Relations,* Oxford: Oxford University Press.

Clegg, C., Axtell, C., Damodaran, L., Farby, B., Hull, R., Lloyd-Jones, R., Nicholls, J., Sell, R., Tomlinson, C., Ainger, A., & Stewart, T. (1996). The performance of Information Technology and the role of human and organisational factors. Report to the ESRC, U.K.

Coriat, B. (1998). L'innovation organisationnelle dans les firmes Européennes. Rapport Final pour le DGIII, Commission Européenne.

Coutrot, T., Malan, A., & Zouary, P. (2003). La boîte noire des relations sociales dans l'entreprise. *Travail et Emploi, 93*(Janvier).

DARES (2000). Les salariés industriel face au changement organisationnel en 1997. *Premières Synthèses, Ministère de l'Emploi et de la Solidarité, 09*(3), Paris.

Deutouzos, M., Lester, R., & Solow, R. (1989). *Made in America.* Cambridge, MA: MIT Press.

Doeringer, P., Lorenz, E., & Terkla, D. (2003). National hybrids: How Japanese multinationals transfer workplace practices to other countries. *Cambridge Journal of Economics* (March), 265–286.

Eaton, A., & Voos, P. (1992). Unions and contemporary innovation in work organisation, compensation and employee participation. In: L. Mishel & P. Voos (Eds), *Unions and Economic Competitiveness.* Armonk, ME: Sharpe.

Estevez-Abe, M., Iversen, T., & Soskice, D. (2001). Social protection and the formation of skills: A re-interpretation of the welfare state. In: P. Hall and D. Soskice (Eds), *Varieties of Capitalism,* Oxford: Oxford University Press.

Esping-Andersen, G. (1999). *Social foundation of post-industrial societies.* Oxford: Oxford University Press.

Freeman, R., & Lazear, E. (1995). An economic analysis of works councils. In: J. Rogers & W. Streeck (Eds), *Works Councils.* Oxford: Oxford University Press.

Gittleman, M., Horrigan, M., & Joyce, M. (1998). Flexible, workplace practices: Evidence from a nationally representative survey. *Industrial and Labour Relations Review, 52*(1).

Greenacre, M. J. (1993). *Correspondence analysis in practice.* New York: Academic Press.

Guest, D. (1997). Human resource management and performance: A review and research agenda. *International Journal of Human Resource Management, 8*(3), 226–263.

Guest, D., Michie, J., Conway, N., & Sheehan, M. (2003). Human resource management and corporate performance in the U.K. *British Journal of Industrial Relations, 41*(2), 291–314.

Ichiniowski, C., Shaw, K., & Prennushi, G. (1997). The effects of human resource management policies on productivity: A study of steel finishing lines. *American Economic Review* (June).

Kline, S., & Rosenberg, N. (1986). An overview of innovation. In: R. Landau & N. Rosenberg (Eds), *The Positive Sum Strategy: Harnessing Technology for Economic Growth.* Washington, DC: National Academy Press.

Laursen, K., & Foss, N. (2003). New HRM practices, complementarities, and the impact on innovation performance. *Cambridge Journal of Economics.*

Lawler, E., Mohrman, S., & Ledford, G. (1992). *Employee involvement and total quality management: Practices and results for fortune 1000 companies.* San Francisco: Jossey-Bass.

Levine, D., & Tyson, L. (1990). Participation, productivity and the firm's environment. In: A. Blinder (Ed.), *Paying for Productivity.* Washington, DC: Brookings.

Lhuillery, S. (1997). Les enquêtes nationales sur l'innovation organisationnelle. Working Paper CREI No. 98-03, University of Paris 13.

Lorenz, E. (1995). Policies for participation: Lesson from France and Germany. *The German Journal of Industrial Relations, 2*(1), 46–63.

Lorenz, E. (1999). Organisational innovation, governance structure and innovative capacity in British and French Industry. DRUID Working Paper Series, http://www.druid.dk/wp/wp.html.

MacDuffie, J. P., & Krafcik, J. (1992). Interacting technology and human resources for high performance manufacturing: Evidence from the international auto industry. In: T. Kochan & M. Useem (Eds), *Transforming Organisations.* New York: Oxford University Press.

Michie, J. (2001). High Performance Work Systems. In: J. Michie (Ed.), *A Reader's Guide to the Social Sciences.* London & New York: Fitzroy Dearborn & Routledge.

Michie, J., & Sheehan, M. (1999a). HRM practices, R&D expenditure and innovative investment: Evidence from the UK's 1990 workplace industrial relations survey. *Industrial and Corporate Change, 8*, 211–234.

Michie, J., & Sheehan, M. (1999b). No innovation without representation? An analysis of participation, representation, R&D and innovation. *Economic Analysis, 2*(2), 85–97.

Michie, J., & Sheehan, M. (2003). Labour market deregulation, flexibility' and innovation. *Cambridge Journal of Economics, 27*(1), 123–143.

Nonaka, I., & Takeuuchi, H. (1995). *The knowledge creating company.* Oxford University Press.

Nooteboom, B. (2000). *Learning and innovation in organizations and economics.* Oxford University Press.

Osterman, P. (1994). How common is workplace transformation and who adopts it? *Industrial and Labor Relations Review, 47.*

Osterman, P. (2000). Work reorganization in an era of restructuring: Trends in diffusion and effects on employee welfare. *Industrial and Labor Relations Review, 53*, 179–196.

Purdon, S., & Pickering, K. (2001, July). *The use of sampling weights in the analysis of the 1998 Workplace Employee Relations Survey.* National Centre for Social Research.

Ramsay, H., Scholarios, D., & Harley, B. (2000). Employees and High-Performance Work Systems, testing inside the black box. *British Journal of Industrial Relations, 38*(4), 501–531.

Streeck, W. (1992). On the institutional conditions for diversified quality production. In: E. Matzuen & W. Streeck (Eds), *Beyond Keynesianism: The Socio-Economics of Production and Employment.* London: Edward Elgar.

Thelen, K. (2001). Varieties of labour politics in developed democracies. In: P. Hall & D. Soskice (Eds), *Varieties of Capitalism* (pp. 71–103). Oxford: Oxford University Press.

Truss, C. (2001). Complexities and controversies in linking HRM with organisational outcomes. *Journal of Management Studies, 38*(8), 1120–1149.

Whitfield, K. (2000). High-performance workplaces, training and the distribution of skills. *Industrial Relations, 39*(1), 1–25.

Wilkinson, F. (2002). Productive systems and the structuring role of economic and social theory. In: B. Burchell, S. Deakin, J, Michie & J. Rubery (Eds), *Systems of Production: Markets, Organisations and Performances.* London: Routledge.

Wood, S. (1999). Getting the measure of the transformed high-performance organisation. *British Journal of Industrial Relations, 37*(3), 391–417.

Womack, J. P., Jones, D. T., & Roos, D. (1990). *The machine that changed the world.* New York: Rawson.

APPENDIX

Variable Definitions

Variable		Mean
U.K. HRM variables		
Team organization	1 if over 40 employees in the largest occupational group work in formally designated teams and team members jointly decide how the is to be done; 0 otherwise	0.360
Variety in work	1 if the employees in the largest occupational group have a lot of variety in their work; 0 otherwise.	0.398
Suggestion scheme	1 if management uses suggestion schemes to communicate or consult with employees; 0 otherwise	0.229
Quality circles	1 is over 40% of non-managerial employees have involved in quality circles in the last 12 months; no otherwise	0.159
Performance pay	1 if over 40 of non-managerial employees have received performance-related pay in the last 12 months; 0 otherwise	0.199
Performance appraisal	1 if over 40% of non-managerial employees have had their performance formally appraised; 0 otherwise	0.476
Training	1 if over 40% of the largest occupational group have had formal off-the-job training over the last 12 months; 0 otherwise	0.261
Meetings	1 if management communicates or consults employees with regular meetings with the entire workforce present; 0 otherwise	0.331

Variable		Mean
Information diffusion on staffing plans	1 if management regularly gives employees, or their representatives, information about staffing plans; 0 otherwise	0.538
Information diffusion on financial position	1 if management regularly gives employees, or their representatives, information about the financial position of the establishment: 0 otherwise	0.631
Negotia-tion/consultation over pay/conditions	1 if management negotiates or consults with union of non-union employee representatives over pay or conditions of work; 0 otherwise	0.178
Negotia-tion/consultation over staffing	1 if management negotiates or consults with union of non-union employee representatives over staffing or manpower planning; 0 otherwise	0.107
Negotia-tion/consultation over training	1 if management negotiates or consults with union of non-union employee representatives over training; 0 otherwise	0.113
French HRM variables		
Team organization	1 if over 50% of the employees work in autonomous teams; 0 otherwise	0.152
Job Rotation	1 if over 50% of the employees normally move from one job to another while working; 0 otherwise	0.317
Suggestion scheme	1 if the employer use suggestion schemes as a means of motivating employee involvement; 0 otherwise	0.246
Quality circles	1 if over 50% of employees are involved in quality circles or problem-solving groups; 0 otherwise.	0.155
Performance pay	1 if non-managerial employees receive bonus payments linked to either individual or group performance; 0 otherwise.	0.726

Variable		Mean
Performance appraisal	1 if non-managerial employees regularly meet with their superiors for a performance evaluation; 0 otherwise.	0.449
Training	1 if training expenditures constituted over 3% of the wage bill in 1998; 0 otherwise.	0.270
Meetings	1 if over 50% of the employees regularly participate in shop, office or departmental meetings; 0 otherwise.	0.394
Information diffusion on employment	1 if the employer regularly makes available to the entire workforce information on the establishment's employment prospects; 0 otherwise.	0.427
Information diffusion on economic situation	1 if the employer regularly makes available to the entire workforce information on the establishment's economic situation; 0 otherwise.	0.551
Negotiation/discussions over working conditions	1 if during the last 3 years there have occurred negotiations or discussions with employee representatives over working conditions; 0 otherwise.[a]	0.487
Negotiation/consultation over hiring/firing	1 if during the last 3 years there have occurred negotiations or discussions with employee representatives over hiring/firing; 0 otherwise.[a]	0.335
Negotiation/consultation over training	1 if during the last 3 years there have occurred negotiations or discussions with employee representatives over training; 0 otherwise.[a]	0.518

[a] Representation may be provided by: union delegates, personnel delegates (délégués du personnel), members of the "comité d'entreprise" or the health and safety committee, or an unofficially elected employee.

Variable		Mean
U.K. performance variable		
Innovation	1 if over the last 5 years management has introduced a new product or service: 0 otherwise.	0.531
French performance variable		
Innovation	1 if during the last 3 years the establishment has introduced a new product or service, 0 otherwise.	0.373

Variable	Mean
U.K. establishment control variables	
Establishment size in number of employment	
20–49	0.615
50–99	0.199
100–199	0.096
200–499	0.068
500–999	0.016
Over 999	0.005
Sector	
Manufacturing	0.233
Construction, electricity, gas and water	0.055
Trade	0.316
Transport	0.080
Financial service	0.050
Business services	0.147
Other[a]	0.118
French establishment control variables	
Establishment size in number of employment	
20–49	0.638
50–99	0.189
100–199	0.102
200–499	0.054

Variable	Mean
500–999	0.012
Over 999	0.005
Sector	
Manufacturing	0.333
Construction, electricity, gas and water	0.126
Trade	0.224
Transport	0.077
Financial service	0.048
Business services	0.130
Other[a]	0.062

[a] Includes hotels and restaurants, domestic services and personal and other community services.

LEARNING, KNOWLEDGE AND COMPETENCE BUILDING AT EMPLOYEE LEVEL IN THE U.K.

Mark Tomlinson

ABSTRACT

Using the Employment in Britain dataset (a representative sample of employees in Britain in 1992) we analyse the determinants of learning within organizations at employee level. Questions were asked about the role of learning new skills in the respondent's job. Various determinants of learning are explored such as human resource management practices, career patterns etc. These results are set within the context of a "competence building system" and related to current debates within the national systems of innovation literature.

1. INTRODUCTION

The National Innovation Systems (NIS) literature (e.g. Edquist, 1997; Freeman, 1995; Lundvall, 1992) has made a good deal of headway in analysing the R&D system and the science base and its role in building competence at national and sectoral levels. However, relatively little attention has been paid to the wider institutional frameworks required for building competence and generating knowledge such as education and training systems, labour markets and organizational practices. The ways that these subsystems fit together, generate

Product Innovation, Interactive Learning and Economic Performance
Research on Technological Innovation and Management Policy, Volume 8, 211–228
ISSN: 0737-1071/doi:10.1016/S0737-1071(04)08009-6

knowledge and interact within the NIS have been relatively little explored. For example, within firms, different procedures and routines may foster learning and knowledge generation at different rates and mechanisms may vary in different national contexts. Thus argued by Alice Lam in Chap. 3, different labour market set-ups may also have a bearing on the way people learn new skills and competences as well as the individual's access to education and training (whether through work or through public access).

As was raised in Chap. 2 by Lundvall in this volume, research is only now beginning to raise the fundamental issue of learning and relate it to research on economic development in general. The traditional methodologies of economics need to be broadened to encompass tools traditionally associated with sociology, psychology, anthropology etc. in order to enhance our understanding of competence building systems. The link between competence building and learning at different levels (individual, organizational, national etc.) and innovation systems will then be revealed more fully.

This chapter is set within the context of the learning economy framework proposed by Lundvall and Johnson (1994). Lundvall separates the concept of a knowledge economy from a learning economy – see Chap. 2. Though they are closely linked, the learning economy is not only connected to the flow of objects from the "stock of knowledge," but also the generation of new knowledge, particularly through innovation. This, argues Lundvall, allows us to expand the range of objects of study beyond the knowledge institutions, such as universities and laboratories, to the more general arena of routinised learning (for example, learning-by-doing or learning-by-using – see Arrow (1962), Rosenberg (1982) "which emphasise knowledge creation as a by-product of routine activities" (Lundvall, 1998, p. 35). The innovative capacity of an economic system is enhanced by the increases of skills and competence of its individual members.

In order to understand some of the mechanisms that lead to this increase in skills and learning, there follows analysis of the Employment in Britain dataset (a representative sample of employees in Britain in 1992). The determinants of learning within organizations at employee level are explored using multivariate statistical techniques. First of all, there is a wealth of information in the dataset on the use of skills and responsibilities. Second, questions were asked about the role of learning new skills in the respondent's job. Before getting to the empirical analysis, a discussion of the organization of labour is pursued. This is followed by a brief overview of Japanese systems of labour organization that sets the context for the statistical exploration. This chapter differs from most of the other chapters in this volume since the focus is on individual learning among those active in the labour market as a performance variable rather than on the innovation at the firm level.

2. THE ORGANIZATION OF LABOUR WITHIN THE FIRM

Many organizations in modern economies are said to have shifted from Taylorist to "postfordist" regimes. Gjerding (1992), for example, argues that this is a move from closed to open systems of production. This form of organization is said to involve flattening hierarchies within organizations, allowing more employee participation and communication with management, coupled with more responsibility and flexibility in the work task. This is commonly associated with the type of work structure prevalent in Japan.

Gjerding thus calls this type of system in general the Japanese Management System (JMS) and it is widely accepted that these "Japanese" techniques are adopted by Western organizations with good effect. The human resource management literature is full of praise for this type of flexible work structure and it is said to lead to significant benefits in terms of competitive advantage over more rigid organizational forms. With respect to National Innovation Systems and the learning economy, the adoption of these types of practices may help to improve the overall efficiency of employees and firms, but there has been little systematic analysis of the real impact of such human resource management practices in innovation systems research.

The analysis proceeds from the assumption that although the JMS is not directly applicable to the U.K., in the sense that it has been directly imposed, certain features of the JMS have been used in some British firms. We use the Japanese system as a metaphor for the adoption of some of these typical work practices and assess whether there are real benefits to organizations from their adoption. There is a general assumption in the literature that these techniques promote learning and co-operation among employees and that this will enhance innovative capacity, coordination and productivity. Using employee level data allows us to test whether this is likely to be true. There is also a tradition in the literature on national systems that makes reference to the Japanese innovation system (see for example, Freeman, 1987). It is thus interesting to observe the effects of "Japanese" style practices within a somewhat different setting.

3. WHAT IS THE JAPANESE MANAGEMENT SYSTEM?

The JMS is generally assumed to consist of an integrated model of employee organization rather than a confrontational one. Although a hierarchy still exists, there is more communication between layers in the organization and recognition that team working produces better performance than the individuated and invariable human activity associated with Fordist production systems (Gjerding, 1992; Itami, 1988). Itami (1988) has coined the term "peoplism" to describe the increased levels of equality and discretion allowed within these systems.

Urabe (1988) and Aoki (1990) have also emphasized the advantages of the *kanban* system, a form of the JMS where there are only tentative planning guidelines for production, but local control allows flexibility in how the work group meets its targets. This form of just-in-time technique fosters information flows horizontally and allows for "productive search" (Gjerding, 1992, p. 104) where units are allowed to solve local problems as and when required. Shimada (1991) emphasizes that this is very much a demand-pull system rather than a centrally dominated (Fordist) demand push system. One of the consequences of this is that process innovations and learning by employees can take place in a spontaneous way at the point of production without having a centrally dominated planning mechanism. This fosters a learning and innovative culture among employees which benefits the organization as a whole. Learning by doing and learning by interacting become central features of this kind of system, as new problems have to be solved repeatedly. The nature of the job and the employees' responsibilities are said to become more fluid. There may also be downsides to this type of approach. A situation may arise where there are too many managers and a small-scale bureaucracy may arise which is not terribly efficient.

There are also significant benefits associated with the JMS at the more general level of the firm. For example, the organizational culture of the firm fosters flattened hierarchies. Blue- and white-collar workers are seen as essential components of an efficient system rather than separate and different parts of a hierarchy (Urabe, 1988). Thus the broad aims of the organization and those of the individual are fused. Systems such as *nemawashi* (an informal consultation process at all levels), *ringi* (the circulation of information and proposals to employees) and "quality circles" all combine to create a cultural atmosphere of mutual trust and responsibility. Communication is therefore a vital part of the JMS.

It must be considered now that the Japanese system may not necessarily be as bright as many commentators thought. Especially since the bubble burst, Japanese firms have to come to terms with several problems and there is a transitional period underway in Japan itself where many of these work practices are changing (see for example, the collection in Sako & Sato, 1997). However, despite downsizing, many Japanese firms are still keen to invest in the development of their employees (although at a reduced level), and are even keener to de-layer their organizations and generate multi-skilled employees (see for instance, Kawakita, 1997). In some senses the JMS style is becoming intensified in Japan, although firm welfare benefits and promotion prospects are being reduced from their bubble period high-points. This chapter proceeds on the assumption that it is still a useful metaphor for exploring the British situation.

4. THE JMS, LEARNING ECONOMIES AND INNOVATION

Knowledge, which is essential to improving the economic performance of modern organizations, is the outcome of learning. In terms of the "learning economy" there are several ways in which different organizational forms could foster an enhanced learning environment. As much of the knowledge in the economy is of a tacit nature and as such resides for the most part in the minds of people, for HRM to be of real benefit to organizations it follows that it should enhance learning by interacting. Employees of firms using "Japanese" methods of work organization should be enhancing their personal capabilities at many levels by being able to put their tacit knowledge into practice more often and to pass on such knowledge to others. These learning processes will be felt throughout the organization as a whole. They will not be restricted to small sections of the workforce. The flattened hierarchies and enhanced communication channels between workers and departments are essential to foster an increase in the overall level of performance.

If the routines operating in an organization implementing a JMS really are of benefit then a substantial impact should be felt on both the innovative performance of the firm and the capabilities of the firm's employees. This impact should be felt irrespective of considerations of the size or sector of the firm or the occupational composition of the firm. Even firms in fairly low-technology or lesser-skilled industries should be able to benefit from enhancing their employees involvement in the process of work. Commitment to the organization should also be enhanced by these methods.

If a significant number of organizations within a national system adopt such beneficial procedures then the competitiveness of the economy at a national level could be enhanced. As stated above, there are more pressing reasons to incorporate the type of analysis proposed here within a national systems perspective. Recent pronouncements by innovations systems researchers are suggesting that the "human resource development" aspects of innovation systems have been somewhat neglected in the literature (see Lundvall & Christensen, 1999). Following the work of Boyer et al. (1997), an important strong human resource element was identified within national systems. This includes labour market flexibility, skill levels and educational achievements.

4.1. A Simple Model of a Competence Building System Within a National Innovation System

From what has been said so far we can separate some of the different elements of a competence building system and suggest some additional components. This is illustrated in Fig. 1.

Bearing this overall scheme in mind we now attempt, at employee level, to statistically model learning behaviour based upon independent effects from this system. The data used for this are now described.

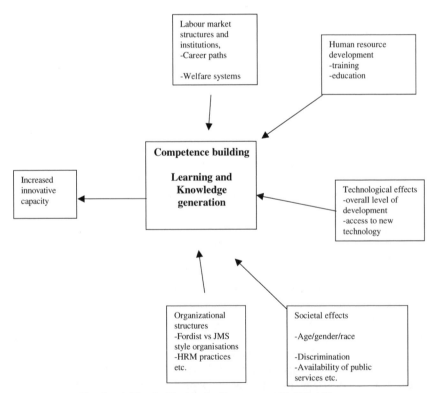

Fig. 1. A Simple Model of a Competence Building System.

5. THE DATASET

The *Employment in Britain* survey (EIB) was a survey of the British labour market in 1992. Data were generated from a random sample of employed and self-employed people aged between 20 and 60. Information was collected from 3,855 respondents including complete career histories. The dataset has several sections of information about the nature of work and employment that are particularly appropriate for the study of skills and obsolescence of skills. Questions were asked about the nature of the work task, whether skills were increasing of decreasing, whether flexibility was declining or increasing, communication within the organization, hierarchies etc. Some questions were also asked relating to how the respondent felt about the innovativeness of the organization and also how the employees' tasks and abilities had been changing over time. A detailed sociological analysis of this dataset can be found in Gallie, White, Cheng and Tomlinson (1998).

In what follows the dependent variable is based on whether the respondent answered that he or she felt strongly that he/she had to keep on learning new things in their current main job. The independent variables are a set of dummies representing the occupation of the respondent (these are based on the 1 digit level of the Standard Occupational Classification (see Appendix). As well as occupation, independent variables are entered in blocks relating to the above discussion. They are discussed in the following order.

(1) Demographic and human capital.
(2) Organizational factors.
(3) Career and labour market factors.

In all cases the models are logistic regressions predicting the learning outcome.

6. DEMOGRAPHIC EFFECTS AND EXTANT HUMAN CAPITAL

Tables 1 and 2 show the determinants of learning based on demographic factors and human capital variables. That is certain extant characteristics of employees as they were at the time of interview. Turning to Table 1 first we see that after controlling for occupation (which in all models here demonstrate the advantages of middle class occupations such as professionals and managers over others) that gender and age are significant factors influencing learning in the workplace. It appears that people in their 20's learn at a significantly greater rate than all other age categories. This may not be surprising as someone embarking on a career will

Table 1.   Logistic Regression Predicting Learning Based on Demographic
Factors.

Independent Variables	Model
Occupational groups	
Managers	2.07** (0.28)
Professionals	2.66** (0.28)
Technical associate professionals	2.77** (0.29)
Administrative and clerical	1.56** (0.28)
Skilled trades	1.30** (0.30)
Personal service workers	1.62** (0.29)
Sales workers	1.11** (0.32)
Process/plant and machine operatives	1.08** (0.30)
Ethicity = Non-white	0.12 (0.19)
Gender = Female	−0.28** (0.09)
Age 20–29	0.43** (0.14)
Age 30–39	0.15 (0.14)
Age 40–49	0.09 (0.14)
Constant	−2.89** (0.29)
Chi square	328.7**

Note: Base categories are unskilled workers, white, male, aged 50–60.
   Table shows regression coefficients with standard errors in brackets.
** Significant at 1%.

have to learn lots of new skills in the beginning. What is more surprising is that
apart from this age group there were no significant effects, so according to this
model people in their 30's learn just as fast as people in their 50's after taking
occupation into account. This may have a bearing on organizations reluctant to
recruit older people on the grounds that they are no longer useful.

The other significant effect was gender. Women are significantly less likely
to learn than men. The most likely explanation for this result is discrimination.
It is well known that women are paid significantly less than men for the same
occupations. It may also be the case that women are more often placed in
less demanding roles than their male colleagues which in turn requires less
learning and competence building to perform the required tasks. Whether this
is just an effect pertinent to the U.K. is difficult to tell, although an analysis of
similar data in three east European countries found no such effect (Tomlinson,
2003). It is interesting to note that there was no significant racial effect. Non-
white workers are no different from their white counterparts with respect to
learning.

Turning to human capital (Table 2) we find, that after taking occupation
into account, there are significant benefits to both educational qualifications and

Table 2. Logistic Regressions Predicting Learning Based on Human Capital.

Independent Variables	Model 1
Occupational groups	
Managers	1.22** (0.32)
Professionals	1.59** (0.33)
Technical associate professionals	1.82** (0.32)
Administrative and clerical	1.08** (0.31)
Skilled trades	0.81* (0.32)
Personal service workers	1.18** (0.31)
Sales workers	0.96** (0.34)
Process/plant and machine operatives	1.09** (0.33)
Ordinary level (usually aged 16)	0.25 (0.13)
Advanced level (usually aged 18)	0.61** (0.17)
Further education (post aged 18)	0.42** (0.16)
Degree (university)	0.69** (0.17)
Training < 1mth	0.69** (0.15)
Training 1–3mth	0.61** (0.18)
Training 4–6mth	0.62** (0.22)
Training 7–12mth	0.69** (0.19)
Training 1–2yr	1.22** (0.18)
Training > 2yr	1.42** (0.13)
Constant	−3.24** (0.29)
Chi square	491.2**

Note: Base categories are unskilled, less than ordinary level education, no training.
      Table shows regression coefficients with standard errors in brackets.
* Significant at 5%.
** Significant at 1%.

vocational training. Anyone educated to Advanced level (usually at 18 years of age) or above is more likely to learn than those with lesser qualifications. Thus a manager with a degree is more likely to learn than a manager with fewer qualifications. The other interesting finding here is that even a small degree of training has an effect on learning. Even those respondents who claimed to have received less than four weeks training were significantly more likely to be learners than those who received no training at all. There were very substantial effects for those who had received extensive training of over one year's duration.

7. ORGANIZATIONAL/HRM EFFECTS ON LEARNING

The EIB data allows us to identify which workers are involved in the types of employment practices typical of the JMS or post-Fordist regimes discussed above.

Table 3. Variables in the EIB Dataset Used as Proxies for JMS Practices.

1. Whether the respondent works in a group or individually.
2. Whether the respondent has any say regarding changes in the job.
Whether management gives out information, posts notices etc. about work.
Whether management gives out information via meetings.
Whether management holds meetings where employees can express views.
3. Whether the employee has had any training/education in the past 3 years.
Whether there is a career ladder associated with the current job.

We have several variables to choose from (Table 3). These are divided into three groups. The first is simply whether teamwork or individual work is the norm. The second is a set of variables relating to communication mechanisms within the firm. That is whether there is information flow, whether the worker has any say at work etc. The third group relates to the employer's investment in the worker (whether there is a career structure within the job or whether the worker has been invested in via education or training for the job). In a lifelong learning environment we would expect the employee to answer yes to both of these questions.

Just how prevalent these practices are can be seen in Table 4. Clearly around half or more of the sample have some form of practice at work that falls within the ambit of a JMS. Around two thirds of the respondents had some formal meetings where they could express their views and information flows seem quite high with three quarters reporting information posted via notices etc. and 70% reporting information via meetings. Furthermore at least half the sample said they had some say at work, had training and had some form of career structure.

Does the prevalence of these practices in the workplace lead to any gains for the organization in terms of learning, and hence innovation? In all the models below we control for occupational class as usual. It is desirable to control for occupation here, as there will not be equal access to the outcomes of the system suggested by the variables in Table 4 across the occupational spectrum. We wish to know whether these JMS type activities make a difference over and above that expected by the general occupational structure of the British economy. The JMS variables

Table 4. Percent of Employees Responding "Yes" to the JMS Variables.

Whether the respondent works in a group or individually 48%
Whether the respondent has say regarding changes in the job 51%
Whether management gives out information, posts notices etc. about work 75%
Whether management gives out information via meetings 70%
Whether management holds meetings where employees can express views 63%
Whether the employee has had any training/education in the past 3 years 54%
Whether there is a career ladder associated with the current job 58%

Table 5. Logistic Regressions Predicting Learning Based on Organizational Factors.

Independent Variables	Model 1	Model 2	Model 3
Occupational group			
Managers	2.68** (0.20)	2.29** (0.21)	2.15** (0.21)
Professionals	3.23** (0.24)	2.80** (0.25)	2.32** (0.25)
Technical associate professionals	3.09** (0.25)	2.81** (0.25)	2.31** (0.26)
Administrative and clerical	1.52** (0.15)	1.31** (0.16)	1.02** (0.16)
Skilled trades	1.59** (0.17)	1.61** (0.17)	1.44** (0.18)
Personal service workers	1.33** (0.16)	1.18** (0.17)	0.98** (0.17)
Sales workers	1.26** (0.18)	1.13** (0.19)	1.00** (0.19)
Process/plant and machine operatives	0.79** (0.16)	0.68** (0.17)	0.72** (0.17)
Work in a group	0.31** (0.09)	–	–
Has say in job	–	0.32** (0.09)	–
Notices posted	–	0.26* (0.11)	–
Information meetings	–	0.52** (0.14)	–
Views expressed at meetings	–	0.31* (0.13)	–
Had training	–	–	0.97** (0.10)
Career ladder	–	–	0.98** (0.10)
Constant	−0.58** (0.13)	−1.10** (0.15)	−0.96** (0.13)
Chi square	471.5**	570.4**	732.2**

Note: Base category unskilled, work individually, no say, no notices, no meetings, no training, no career ladder.

Table shows regression coefficients with standard errors in brackets.

*Significant at 5%.

**Significant at 1%.

are entered in blocks along with occupation (these are all simply recoded as dummy variables). The results are shown in Table 5.

First of all we see from Model 1 that working in groups rather than individually has a significant impact on learning. This reflects the social aspects of the learning economy. Groups of workers interacting are more likely to progress than those isolated workers involved in, say, production line work where there is little scope for interaction of any meaningful kind. Model 2 shows the importance of the diffusion of information within the organization. It appears that those firms that allow employees to have a say, where notices giving information are posted, and where meetings are organised to give information and receive feedback, all contribute to a better learning environment than those firms that do not. There is also evidence here of a cumulative effect (all four variables were positive and significant). Finally Model 3 shows the importance for employee learning of human capital development and internal career structures of the firm. Those employees who receive training and have a recognised career structure are more likely to learn than those that do not.

The implications of these three models for the current analysis are that first of all human resource management is very important from a learning economy perspective, and also that the types of organizational structures normally associated with post-Fordism have significant benefits to both the employees and the firm at all levels within the occupational hierarchy, assuming that employees who learn have a more fulfilling role at work than those who do not. We finally turn to career structure and its effects on learning.

8. CAREER DATA AND LEARNING

Table 6 shows the effects of different career patterns on employee learning. In all these models we have controlled for job tenure (that is the amount of time spent

Table 6. Logistic Regressions Predicting Learning Based on Career Data.

Independent Variables	Model 1	Model 2	Model 3	Model 4
Occupational group				
Managers	2.10^{**} (0.28)	2.03^{**} (0.28)	2.10^{**} (0.28)	1.94^{**} (0.28)
Professionals	2.74^{**} (0.28)	2.71^{**} (0.28)	2.74^{**} (0.28)	2.67^{**} (0.28)
Technical associate professionals	2.83^{**} (0.29)	2.79^{**} (0.28)	2.84^{**} (0.28)	2.74^{**} (0.29)
Administrative and clerical	1.53^{**} (0.28)	1.48^{**} (0.28)	1.52^{**} (0.28)	1.46^{**} (0.28)
Skilled trades	1.49^{*} (0.29)	1.45^{**} (0.29)	1.49^{**} (0.29)	1.46^{**} (0.29)
Personal service workers	1.68^{**} (0.29)	1.64^{**} (0.29)	1.67^{**} (0.29)	1.63^{**} (0.29)
Sales workers	1.12^{**} (0.32)	1.10^{**} (0.32)	1.12^{**} (0.32)	1.12^{**} (0.32)
Process/plant and machine operatives	1.21^{**} (0.30)	1.16^{**} (0.30)	1.20^{**} (0.30)	1.18^{**} (0.30)
Log tenure	-0.03 (0.03)	0.06 (0.04)	-0.03 (0.03)	0.01 (0.04)
No. of Jobs between 1987–1992	–	0.14^{**} (0.04)		–
No. jobs (not for same employer)	–	–	0.01 (0.03)	–
No. jobs (same employer)	–	–	–	0.16^{**} (0.04)
Constant	-2.76^{**} (0.29)	-3.38^{**} (0.33)	-2.78^{**} (0.31)	-2.95^{**} (0.29)
Chi square	310.2^{**}	326.4^{**}	311.4^{**}	325.8^{**}

Note: Base category unskilled.

Table shows regression coefficients with standard errors in brackets.

*Significant at 5%.

**Significant at 1%.

by the respondent in his or her current job within the current firm). It might be expected that the longer a person spends in the same job, all other things being equal, that there would be gradually less learning taking place, but Model 1 shows this not to be the case.

Models 2–4 show the effects of moving jobs in the last five years (these models necessarily only include people who have been in the labour market for at least five years). It might be expected that people who are highly mobile with respect to their jobs might learn faster. They are often in a new environment, often in a different organization etc. and Model 2 shows that there is a significant positive effect on learning from the number of jobs the respondent has had in the past five years. However, if we delve a little deeper into this we find that the effect is based on intra- rather than inter-firm job shifts. Model 3, which uses the variable of inter-firm job shifts, has no effect while Model 4 shows the significant impact of intra-firm job shifts. It would appear then that there might be substantial benefits to internal labour markets where workers have several jobs within one organization rather than moving between organizations (recalling Doeringer & Piore, 1971).

If one assumes that people moving to different jobs diffuse knowledge around the economy then these results suggest that there may be significant trade-offs between personal human development and competence building and occupational mobility of the external labour market type. Thus the recent pronouncements of the EC and the OECD advocating flexible labour markets as the solution to flagging competitiveness need to be carefully thought through. This has been dealt with in more detail by Tomlinson and Miles (1999).

9. CONCLUSIONS

Set within the National Innovation Systems paradigm a model based around exploring competence building is proposed as a useful way to look at the learning economy. This chapter has concentrated on competence building at the individual level, but work needs to seriously address all aspects of the competence building system, such as labour institutions, technological development, access to technology, cultural influences and, training systems etc. The chapter has dealt mainly with variables inspired by the "Japanese" style of management.

From a learning economy perspective this chapter has sought to identify the characteristics of employees and their organizations that have a bearing on learning and competence building at three levels: personal attributes such as gender and education; organizational factors based on a post-Fordist rationale; and career patterns and labour market trajectories.

Taking personal characteristics first, there appear to be problems for women in terms of competence building and learning. Women appear to be discriminated against in this regard. With respect to learning women in the workplace are shown to have serious disadvantages when compared to their male colleagues. There is relatively little to say about age other than the fact that very young people learn fastest. Apart from this there were no effects. Thus there is evidence that employers should examine their policies with respect to women and older workers within their organizations. If employers want to be competitive in the learning economy then perhaps they should re-examine their attitudes towards the role of women and the recruitment of older workers.

In terms of human capital it is clear that those workers with advanced qualifications are at an advantage, but it is also notable that even a low level of training can go a long way. This has policy implications for both governments and employers. Those employers providing no training are going to be at a serious disadvantage. Governments should encourage employers to at least provide a minimal level of training for all their employees as this may well have greater pay-offs in the future. It must also be restated that those workers who received a substantial amount of training (over one year's duration) had the greatest levels of learning and personal competence building.

The types of organizational structures and HRM practices most conducive to the learning economy are those typified by post-Fordist "Japanese" systems. Workers who operate in teams, who experience flatter hierarchies where communication between different levels in the organization can take place, and where training is provided and career structures are in place, learn more than those who do not have these benefits.

Finally the career data revealed the advantages of internal labour markets as opposed to external labour markets in terms of learning. Clearly organizations that foster the movement and careers of their employees within their organizations will benefit from increased learning and competence building of those individuals. There was no effect on learning from movement between organizations. This has serious implications for those advocating flexible labour markets as a way of diffusing knowledge around the economy as a whole through employee mobility. Basically there may be a price to pay for too much flexibility: not enough learning.

REFERENCES

Aoki, M. (1990). A new paradigm of work organisation and co-ordination? Lessons from Japanese experiences. In: S. A. Marglin & J. B. Schor (Eds), *The Golden Age of Capitalism*. Oxford: Clarendon Press.

Arrow, K. J. (1962). The economic implications of learning by doing. *Review of Economic Studies*, *29*(80), 155–173.

Boyer, R., Amable, B., & Barré, R. (1997). *Les systémes d'innovation a l'ere de la globalization*. Paris: Economica.

Doeringer, P., & Piore, M. (1971). *Internal labour markets and manpower analysis.* ??Heat??, Lexington: Lexington Books.

Edquist, C. (Ed.) (1997). *Systems of innovation: Technologies, institutions and organisations*. London: Pinter.

Freeman, C. (1987). *Technology policy and economic policy: Lessons from Japan*. London: Pinter.

Freeman, C. (1995). The national innovation systems in historical perspective. *Cambridge Journal of Economics*, *19*(1), 5–24.

Gallie, D., White, M., Cheng, Y., & Tomlinson, M. (1998). *Restructuring the employment relationship*. Oxford: Oxford University Press.

Gjerding, A. N. (1992). Work organisation and the information design dilemma. In: B. Å. Lundvall (Eds), *National Systems of Innovation: Towards a Theory of Innovation and Interactive Learning*. London: Pinter.

Goldthorpe, J. H., & Heath, A. (1992). Revised class schema 1992. JUSST Working Paper No. 13. Oxford: SCPR and Nuffield College.

Itami, H. (1988). The Japanese corporate system and technology accumulation. In: Urabe et al. (Eds), *Innovation and Management: International Comparisons*. Berlin: Walter de Gruyter.

Kawakita, T. (1997). Corporate strategy and human resource management. In: Sako & Sato (Eds), *Japanese Labour and Management in Transition: Diversity, Flexibility and Participation* (pp. 79–103). London: Routledge and LSE.

Lundvall, B. Å. (Ed.) (1992). National systems of innovation: Towards a theory of innovation and interactive learning. London: Pinter.

Lundvall, B. Å. (1998). The learning economy: Challenges to economic theory and policy. In: K. Nielsen & B. Johnson (Eds), *Institutions and Economic Change: New Perspectives on Markets, Firms and Technology*. Cheltenham: Edward Elgar.

Lundvall, B. Å., & Christensen, J. L. (1999). Extending and deepening the analysis of innovation systems – with empirical illustrations from the DISKO project. DRUID Working Paper No. 99-12, Denmark: Copenhagen Business School.

Lundvall, B. Å., & Johnson, B. (1994). The learning economy. *Journal of Industry Studies*, *1*(2), 23–42.

Rosenberg, N. (1982). *Inside the black box: Technology and economics*. Cambridge: Cambridge University Press.

Sako, M., & Sato, H. (Eds) (1997). *Japanese labour and management in transition: Diversity, flexibility and participation*. London: Routledge and LSE.

Shimada, H. (1991). Humanware technology and industrial relations. In: *OECD, Technology and Productivity: The Challenge for Economic Policy*. Paris: OECD.

Tomlinson, M. (2003). Learning and career patterns in transition economies: A comparison with Britain. Paper presented to the European Network for the Study of Mobility Workshop (ENMOB), Oslo, 22nd September.

Tomlinson, M., & Miles, I. (1999). The career trajectories of knowledge workers. In: *Mobilising Human Resources for Innovation: Proceedings from the OECD Workshop on Science and Technology Labour Markets* (DSTI/STP/TIP(99)2/FINAL, pp. 152–167). Paris: OECD.

Urabe, K. (1988). Innovation and the Japanese management system. In: Urabe et al. (Eds), *Innovation and Management: International Comparisons*. Berlin: Walter de Gruyter.

Urabe, K., et al. (Eds) (1988). *Innovation and management: International comparisons*. Berlin: Walter de Gruyter.

APPENDIX

The Standard Occupational Coding Scheme

This occupational scheme has a 3-digit code at its most detailed level. For the purposes of this chapter the first digit is used to define the broad occupational groups as follows (see Goldthorpe & Heath, 1992).

Group	Subgroup	Description
1	10	General managers and administrators in national and local government, large companies and organizations
	11	Production managers in manufacturing, construction, mining and energy industries
	12	Specialist managers
	13	Financial institution and office managers, civil service executive officers
	14	Managers in transport and storage
	15	Protective service officers
	16	Managers in farming, horticulture, forestry and fishing
	17	Managers and proprietors in service industries
	19	Managers and administrators nec
2	20	Natural scientists
	21	Engineers and technologists
	22	Health professionals
	23	Teaching professionals
	24	Legal professionals
	25	Business and financial professionals
	26	Architects, town planners, surveyors
	27	Librarians and related professionals
	29	Professionals nec
3	30	Scientific technicians
	31	Draughtspersons, quantity and other surveyors
	32	Computer analysts and programmers

Group	Subgroup	Description
	33	Ship and aircraft officers, air traffic planners and controllers
	34	Health associate professionals
	35	Legal associate professionals
	36	Business and financial associate professionals
	37	Social welfare associate professionals
	38	Literary, artistic and sports professionals
	39	Associate professionals and technical occupations nec
4	40	Administrative, clerical officers, and assistants in civil service and local government
	41	Numerical clerks and cashiers
	42	Filing and records clerks
	43	Clerks not otherwise specified
	44	Stores and despatch clerks, storekeepers
	45	Secretaries, personal assistants, typists, wp operators
	46	Receptionists, telephonists and related occupations
	49	Clerical and secretarial occupations nec
5	50	Construction trades
	51	Metal, machine fitting and instrument making trades
	52	Electrical and electronic trades
	53	Metal forming, welding and related trades
	54	Vehicle trades
	55	Textiles, garments and related trades
	56	Printing and related trades
	57	Woodworking trades
	58	Food preparation trades
	59	Other craft and related occupations nec
6	60	NCOs and other ranks, armed forces
	61	Security and protective service occupations
	62	Catering occupations
	63	Travel attendants and related occupations
	64	Health and related occupations
	65	Childcare and related occupations
	66	Hairdressers, beauticians and related occupations
	67	Domestic staff and related occupations
	69	Personal and protective service occupations nec

Group	Subgroup	Description
7	70	Buyers, brokers and related agents
	71	Sales representatives
	72	Sales assistants and check-out operators
	73	Mobile, market, and door-to-door salespersons and agents
	79	Sales occupations nec
8	80	Food, drink and tobacco process operatives
	81	Textile and tannery process operatives
	82	Chemical, paper, plastics and related operatives
	83	Metal making and treating process operatives
	84	Metal working process operatives
	85	Assemblers/line workers
	86	Other routine process operatives
	87	Road transport operatives
	88	Other transport and machinery operatives
	89	Plant and machine operatives nec
9	90	Other occupations in agriculture, forestry and fishing
	91	Other occupations in mining and manufacture
	92	Other occupations in construction
	93	Other occupations in transport
	94	Other occupations in communication
	95	Other occupations in sales and services
	99	Other occupations nec

SOME DANISH EXPERIENCES RELATED TO THE ORGANIZATION OF NEW PRODUCT DEVELOPMENT

Reinhard Lund

ABSTRACT

This chapter treats new product development in relation to management and organization. The data comprise new product development within four Danish manufacturing firms studied by interviewing the management, product leaders and other employees. The results show how integrated product development procedures have furthered a stronger market orientation. The stage-gate version of integration has fertilized knowledge across functions. The new procedures have made the understanding of cooperation across functions topical and have been followed up by more involvement of the employees. The changes have run into barriers which to a certain extent have been met by organizational changes.

1. INTRODUCTION

This chapter treats the actual course of a number of new product developments in four firms. Some of these developments were studied during the period when they took place, others were studied a very short time after the products were launched. The aim is to present a realistic picture of such product developments, how they are organized, and crystallize promoting and hampering traits concerning a

Product Innovation, Interactive Learning and Economic Performance
Research on Technological Innovation and Management Policy, Volume 8, 229–254
Copyright © 2004 by Elsevier Ltd.
ISSN: 0737-1071/doi:10.1016/S0737-1071(04)08010-2

satisfactory course of action. The economic success or failure of the products is not investigated. Whereas the previous chapters by the present author (Chapters 4 and 6) was focused upon product innovation in respectively a knowledge management and a human resource management/organizational perspective then this chapter is to a greater extent to the management of technology literature. A part of the literature on product innovation offers recommendations as regards successful behaviour and organization as was evident from the chapters by Tomlinson and by Lorenz et al. in this volume. On the other hand empirical investigations show that often such recommendations are not followed. Cooper and Kleinschmidt (1986) (quoted by Dougherty, 1996, p. 424) go as far as writing: "What the literature prescribes and what most firms do are miles apart." In this chapter we shall give a more varied picture as it will be shown that some recommendations are followed, but only as the results of improvements after the first experiences.

The starting point is a few central contributions concerning product innovation from both a normative and empirical point of view. In a Danish setting it is natural to mention the book by Hein and Andreasen (1985) in which they give recommendations concerning "integrated product development" from the standpoint of an idealized model. The central features comprised market orientation and coordinated development across marketing/sales, construction and production. Their recommendations were founded upon their research in cooperation with firms within the iron and metal industry. In an international context Cooper's (1993) Stage-Gate model developed during the period 1972–1985 expresses the same intentions. His model implies an introductory period of market assessment and research and a division of the total development process into multifunctional stages each of which is evaluated at check points called gates. If the evaluation is negative the necessary changes of the product related activities have to be completed before the responsible team is allowed to proceed. Alternatively the product development might be stopped. One of the visited firms had been in contact with representatives for both models, others had heard about Cooper's model. Cooper (1993) refers to a number of positive experiences with the Stage-Gate model, but he mentions also the difficulties with the implementation of the model. Training of the users of the model and selection of persons to take on responsibility of the stage-gate processes were important for success. As said earlier, in this chapter focus is on the product development process, and not the economic success of the product which would demand an analysis of the overarching strategy of the visited firms. In a similar way Cooper (1993) emphasizes that the Stage-Gate model does not tell the whole story but has to fit into the firm's product strategy when it comes to economic success.

Apart from presentations of a totally or partly normative character, a number of authors analyses concrete developments or specific processes during such developments. Brown and Eisenhardt (1995) found in an overview of articles on product developments from an organizational viewpoint, they found viewpoint investigations directed on group processes with special weight given to the importance of communication across groups and in relation to external partners. Such results and others with reference to this chapter's treatment of Danish experiences with the organization of product development processes are commented upon in the conclusion.

With regard to contributions which present results from studies of the total process of new product development, the Van de Ven et al. (1999) major longitudinal study of innovation – not only of products, but also process innovations and new administrative rules – is an outstanding one. Their studies disclose a dozen elements, which were commonly observed among their 14 innovations. On this basis they built a non-linear cyclical process model. It contains divergent and convergent activities, which are promoted by resource investments and structural changes and constrained by external rules and mandates, internal focus and self-organizing. Some of the relationships from this model will be commented upon in the conclusion.

In this chapter product innovation is discussed from an organizational point of view.

2. THE SCOPE OF PRODUCT DEVELOPMENT AND ITS ORGANIZATION

New product development is of course a technical problem, but for some time it has been recognized that product innovation implies important organizational problems. They concern the links to the markets and a smooth internal coordination of the different specialties involved. During the period 1998–2000 half of the Danish private firms carried through important organizational changes (The PIE-project, (www.business.auc.dk/pie) and IDA-DISKO database, cf. Reichstein & Vinding, 2002; and the chapters by Vinding & Reichstein in this volume). Among those firms which made these changes, two thirds of the firms had as their objective to strengthen *inter alia* the ability to develop new products/services. As mentioned above Hein and Andreasen (1985) and Cooper (1993) suggest that product innovation can be strengthened by integrating the functions of development, production and sales and organizing gate meetings. The PIE survey shows that one third of the Danish firms practices such an integration of functions. Three quarters of the firms which develop new products (45.2% of the sample) report that they organize regular meetings during the process of the development of products and services. About three fifths have a meeting at the end of the development process and two thirds answer that documentation will be prepared. Just like its forerunner, the DISKO project (Laursen & Foss, 2000; Lundvall, 1999; Vinding, 2002), analyses of the PIE data show that a broad range of human resource management methods which activate and develop management and employees were conducive to new product innovation (Laursen & Foss, 2000; Vinding, 2002). This chapter is based on the qualitative part of the PIE survey and the aim is to contribute with details regarding the organization of integrative new product development. The presentation is centered around promoting and hampering traits and concerns the following questions.

- aim and organization of the integration of business functions.
- experiences with the stage-gate procedure and the use of documentation.
- the role of employees without management responsibilities.

International research on new product development has provided answers to similar questions. To some extent these results will be commented upon in the conclusion.

3. DATA

The PIE data comprise a quantitative study of 2,007 Danish private firms who answered a questionnaire in 2001. This sample includes 637 firms who also answered the DISKO questionnaire in 1996. This chapter draws upon the qualitative part of the PIE project, which included 11 firms who were asked about new product development. Among these firms I analyse the experiences of four firms investigated by longitudinal studies carried out during the period 2001–2002.

The examined firms were medium sized (100–400 employees) and comprised one electronic firm, one metal firm and two machine firms who produced machines for respectively food industry, and iron, metal and transport industries. The new product developments which were followed by the researchers comprised.

(1) Dimmer. A product for controlling electric light.
(2) Heat Regulation. A product for regulation of room temperature.
(3) Oxygen Control. A product for regulation of heat production.
(4) Automatic Filling. A product for convenient filling of boilers.
(5) Coater. A product for processing food.
(6) Drier. A product for drying food.
(7) Welding machine W1. A product with flexible adjustments.
(8) Welding machine W2. A product with new process control.

The information was gathered by interviewing directors of development, product developers, sales and marketing managers, managers of production, other managers, a few technicians, and in two firms a shop floor worker was also interviewed, resulting in a total of 23 persons. Three of the firms were visited four times, and one firm was visited three times during the period January 2000–December 2001. The total number of interviews amounted to 41 during the two years.

It is clear that the qualitative investigation has some limitations concerning its general use for understanding product development. It has to be recognized that the medium size of the visited firms meant that communications generally were good. In the investigated firms there was a good relationship between the management and the employees. It is moreover to be noticed that the management was very much aware of the importance of organizational conditions concerning product innovation. This will be shown in the following sections regarding new organizational procedures and ongoing work to improve structures and processes. This implies a difference to Dougherty's (1996) summary article on innovation, which is concentrated on large, complex firms. We believe that treating projects or simple organizations result in overlooking "the most problematic relationship between innovation and the organization" (*ibid.*, p. 425). The presentation is centred around tensions such as outside/market versus inside/technology orientation, preferences for new versus old routines during problem solving and balancing freedom versus responsibility to develop commitment to innovation (*ibid.*, p. 431). The discussion to be found in this chapter is just directed towards such organizational problems and so it weakens Dougherty's statement.

The questions considered by the PIE investigation relate to Pavitt's typology of the innovation base in different economic sectors. This will be seen in the chapters which discuss the quantitative results. The qualitative part of the PIE investigation gives no possibility concerning results of interest to the Pavitt typology as the visited firms generally were oriented towards the market and customers and do not include mass production or independent R&D activities.

4. FUNCTIONAL INTEGRATION AND THE DEVELOPMENT OF NEW PRODUCTS

In this section we treat the management's objectives with regard to integration of the various business functions related to new product development. Furthermore, the organization of these activities by teams and project leaders is considered. It will be shown that obtaining integration is not an easy task. So, the actors presented examples of a number of different types of difficulties.

4.1. The Top Managements Objectives and the Organization of Product Development

The top management wanted previous technological orientations to give way to a market orientation among developers. Along this line, the four firms had employed new managers/directors of development within a recent period previous to the PIE investigation. Also the management's preference for an integrated procedure concerning new product development mirrored a wish for a stronger coordination between the viewpoints expressed by respectively sales and development. To this should be added a wish for an improved understanding between the different departments. Previously a more linear process in a segmented organizational structure had meant that each function only focussed upon its own tasks which reduced important input from other departments during the development process.

In three of the firms, the wish for integration took the form of a cross-department top committee to discuss new product proposals, whereas the administrative director of the fourth firm would make his own probing. Nevertheless, it was in this firm that the most radical example of the organization of a product development group took place. To the benefit of both market orientation and integration, the development activities had to follow certain rules. The rules were not identical among the firms but comprised some common elements: (1) The establishment of market, technical, and economic specifications when starting a new product so that the saleability was put in focus, and the market orientation taken seriously; (2) the acknowledgement of stages divided by points of review called e.g. gates or milestones where a decision had to be taken whether or not the process could continue to the next stage; (3) cross-functional participation at the gates and more or less also during stages; (4) the delegation of responsibility to a project leader and possibly the formation of a project group; and (5) a demand for documentation of the process. These common elements can be seen as a good approximation to Cooper's (1993) Stage-Gate model and Hein and Andreasens (1985) ideal model for product development. One firm had not established these rules, but the director of development stressed the importance of building upon information from the sales department, and one of the new products named Drier above was handled by a team organization following a concept similar to the above mentioned rules.

By getting information during the actual processes of the eight new products, it has been possible to observe whether the management's intentions of a stronger market orientation and cross-functional integration were carried through and which events were seen by the actors as positive or negative relative to these objectives.

4.2. Team Management

The daily management of the development activities of the eight projects showed two distinct models. One was team oriented while the other was built around a single project leader.

This section treats the teams which had a major responsibility for the *Drier project* and the two *Welding machines*. In these cases it is seen that the market orientation has a strong hold in the development activities and cross-functional integration is a leading idea. But the cases also show some difficulties concerning full support to cross-functional team work.

The concept which should direct the development of the *Drier machine* was developed by a team, which also followed the project during its later stages. This way of organizing the project was not planned from the start since the new Drier was only thought to be a follow-up based upon an older drier machine; but the designated project leader was given a more urgent task, and when this was finished, and he should start working upon the idea of a new drier, the mother company became interested in the Drier project. Accordingly the mother company took the initiative and chose a German consultant to act as process consultant for a Danish team, which should study the possibilities of a new Drier. The food company did not have specific rules for an integrated product development process, but the consultant stressed the importance of cross functional cooperation and saw to it that all relevant departments were represented in the team and that expertise from the mother company was included. He stressed the necessity of an open dialogue concerning the various production possibilities and saw to it that the team members met with key customers. After some months the team agreed upon a concept specification, and the previously appointed project leader who had been a member of the team was given the task to carry through the construction work together with a colleague, whereas the team would follow the work and act as gatekeeper. The team evaluated the prototype, and a zero series was prepared to be followed by trial production at a customer. The full production and the launching of the product was not followed by the researchers, because the firm withdrew from cooperation during the final stages of the new product.

The experiences of the team members were seen by themselves as both positive and negative. An example.

Interviewer: The good thing (about the team's work), what was that?

Team member: The good thing was the good meetings we had. That was the first meetings ... It was just fine that people found out that it was a good idea just to coordinate the viewpoints before you start.

Interviewer: Why didn't the last meetings not work as well as the first ones?

Team member: Well, we have had meetings where you can say according to my opinion that we met too often . . . then you end up in a situation where people are feeling that you have said the same thing too many times.

Interviewer: Who had the responsibility for preparing introductions for the meetings?

Team member: They had not to be made . . . he (the consultant) would not accept an agenda . . . you had to meet open minded. So that things could be developed (during the meeting).

Interviewer: Did they do that?

Team member: Yes, he was competent . . . one thing is one hundred percent realized by this way of doing it . . . know-how is coordinated much better now than before . . . you know what things cost (and) how we use such a Drier. So that the sales people have a much better understanding of why things look the way they do. And production people, when they start . . . (interview transcript F2:2).

A positive outcome of the team work as a result of the cross functional composition of the team had been that people from production, purchase etc. had raised problems of importance for their part of the development, so solutions had been found, which facilitated their work. The quotation also shows that the sales people had a better idea of the product. The interest of the consultant in involving potential customers in the new product was seen as an advantage from the point of view of the product development people. They welcomed the talks with the customers.

On the negative side was mentioned that the meetings were too unstructured (cf. the quotation). So, it was said that in the future a smaller group would be chosen to carry out the work. In general the researchers had the impression that the members had not had enough experience of team work and the process had implied some conflicts among the members.

The *Welding machine W1* was a spin-off from previous more technology oriented projects, and was only carried through because of a major redefinition, which considered market demands and meant a limitation of the necessary resources. The project was developed by team work. The project leader was head of a broader project group and a smaller core group. This organization was in accordance with the firm's new rules for integrated development and practised for the first time. From the beginning, the broader group consisted of the production manager, development people and persons from engineering, logistics, assembly, and electronics. The project leader had frequent meetings with this group. However, the work was hit by labour shortage because of the economic situation of the firm and changes within the staff due to training needs. This meant that the project leader had to solve some construction tasks which reduced his interaction with other departments, and so he was criticised by these departments. Nevertheless, the team organization meant that the development work was focussed more upon the business as a whole than giving priority to ones own function, cf. the following quotation:

> Project leader: . . . now when both development and sales take part already from the start, and as you focus more on whether the business is OK than which types (of the product in a technical sense) . . . We have to show a more dynamic behaviour on the part of the development division because we shall be ready to change the product (B4:6).

Welding machine W2 was developed according to the same organizational ground rules as *W1*.

4.3. The Role of Project Leader

The management objectives of market orientation and cross functional integration had a strong impact upon the selection of project leaders. The directors of development chose deliberately people who they knew could communicate both internally and externally and who could get things done. An example.

> Interviewer: Are there specific qualifications (to become project leader)?

> Manager of Development: Well, you will always see some people who are able to run their projects and do it well and take care of good communication. And then you see others who are too much of a technician who dig themselves into the task and forget all other things. I believe you must have the capacity to do it. Whether it depends on the ability or the inclination, I haven't found out (D1:13).

In all the eight projects the product developer had to see that the project moved on through the different stages and gate meetings were held. According to one development manager he had to remind the developers of the necessity of holding such meetings as the practice was still new to the firm. The product developers were clearly aware of the importance of market considerations. For themselves they were in favour of such autonomy for the benefit of creative work and choice of internal and external contacts. The development managers recognized the dilemma of the new more detailed development procedures and the developers' wish for autonomy, and tried to combine the two viewpoints by letting the developers have some possibilities to work on their own.

The project developers had many experiences, which could document the difficulties of their task. An example.

> Interviewer: What is your experience (in this firm) concerning what to look for carefully?

> Project leader: Actually, it is the same as from where I come from. It means that it is some of the same problems you meet in the projects. It is an iceberg effect because even if you try to uncover as much as possible, you have to be aware of the things below the surface which you cannot see and which you have to guard against and book for in your project . . . (D1:14).

Among the difficulties that developers met were failing supplies, problems with the terms of deliveries, employees following traditional working methods instead of keeping to the directives of the developer, and labour shortages. The developers' experience disclosed their lack of sufficient negotiation skills. Lack of resources was a general phenomenon, therefore, the project leader had as an important task to secure resources for his project. A common way of solving this problem was to raise the issue at department meetings, whereas individual attempts to force one's task resulted in mutual conflicts, which were generally turned down by everybody. Nevertheless, conflicts might occur if the top managers signalled that a project should get ready, but without caring about how the workload should be handled. In connection with this discussion of the use of resources, one of the developers told the researchers that with regard to getting the tasks done, he would make contact with the people he knew could help him with a given task. His knowledge of the organization and its members was thus seen to be an important factor in his management of the product development process.

5. GATE MEETINGS, OTHER REVIEWS AND DOCUMENTATION

To some extent you could talk about stages and gates before the introduction of the integrated procedure for new product development, cf. the following quotation, which shows that the firm was aware of Cooper's (1993) viewpoints.

> Project leader: In our old model we also had such reviews, but they were not described in the same way. In fact, it depended more upon the single project leader how much you involved the other sections. In fact, you could enclose your work in the project group and finish the work there. You could also have success. If you were more open, you would have many reviews, but the reason might be to secure that the basis for decisions was acceptable before you entered the meetings of the project committee. They might be intense . . . Large changes have happened. It is not us who have invented this model.
>
> Interviewer: It isn't?
>
> Project leader: Yes, you also know it?
>
> Interviewer: Yes. You are thinking at?
>
> Project leader: The model which tell us to run it businesslike . . . it is a model which is called the stage-gate model, which has been made by Cooper (B4:14).

The new procedure was that the number of stages was extended and the content of the stages was explained in detail. Also, the different functions were activated more or less as a parallel and coordinated course of actions. The gate meetings prescribed what to look for, and involved a number of specialists. The information gathered by the PIE researchers on the practice of the integrated stage-gate procedure showed a number of problems which *inter alia* meant that the prescriptions were not followed one hundred percent.

The product development process resulted in many reviews and many choices had to be made. The interviewees distinguished between official reviews and unofficial ones. The unofficial reviews comprised the developers' ongoing contacts to development colleagues and other relevant employees. The official reviews were part of the stage-gate procedures. Among the investigated product developments most of them were subject to several reviews carried out by people from different departments. The exceptions were the *Coater* which was a smaller project and only scrutinized by a sales manager and a couple of developers, and the *Oxygen control project* which was finished as soon as the official tests showed that the product could live up to the specifications laid down by law.

Regarding the official reviews, the interviewees could tell about a number of positive and negative experiences. Among important factors which can be crystallized are: (1) the occupational background of the participants; (2) their feeling of responsibility with regard to the product; (3) their direct involvement; (4) the way the gate meeting was organized; and (5) documentation of the meeting.

The *participants* comprised the project leader as chairman, managers from sales and development as well as employees who had been involved in the previous stage, and those who would be involved in the next stage. The gate meetings were felt to be an important way to acquire new knowledge of importance for product development, cf. the following excerpt from the interviews.

Interviewer: How do you actually work in such a (review group)?

Review participant: Well, in reality you look at the product, that is the product you have, and get it commented upon by he who is responsible for the product. You are looking upon it from an aesthetic point of view and so on and a functional point of view. You look to find out whether it looks nice, whether something has to be changed and so on. In reality you are more like a user when you are looking because it is a product which you have not seen before. We come and look at it from a different point of view (than the developers). And then they get our input. It might also be an input from our division in France . . . you might also call upon an external architect concerning the design . . . The production people take part. They will tell and say OK if you do it this way it is easier from a production point of view. And others may come with their input . . . ask questions which they might not have asked themselves (E2:2).

Concerning another gate meeting the researchers were told that it was a new supervisor who could tell about an alternative component for a new product because he had experience with this component from his previous firm. In an interview with a sales manager one of the difficulties which hampered the gate meetings was highlighted. He could tell that he had pointed to poor design as seen from the customers' point of view, but it was not until he had the physical product that he found out. At an earlier date when he had seen the blueprints he had not recognized the poor design. According to the developers it was often those employees who had worked on a prototype who discovered new possibilities. Therefore it was an advantage to have the participation of these employees and not only their supervisor who would not know everything about the operations which his employees had to carry out. The shopfloor workers themselves also saw a possibility of promoting work environment improvements.

The reviews meant that the different departments could be held *responsible* for the flow of the development process. The reason was that the project through the gate meetings became visible outside the development department, and other departments could find out when they had to join the process and tell about their specific wants. In this way the gate meetings were important means for communication which favoured a smooth process, although this process is dependent upon the participants' input and use of the information.

The participants' *involvement* differed to some extent. According to the developers it could be a problem to get the necessary input. Some participants lost interest in the gate meeting when people with another occupational background discussed the new product. Sales people and production people directed their comments toward different things. Therefore one of the developers had chosen to carry out two gate meetings after a given stage – one with production and one with sales – in spite of the extra time that such a procedure required. According to this developer, one of the reasons for an unsatisfactory involvement by production people had been their low expectations regarding the future sales of the product in Denmark, but such a view he found mistaken because you could not beforehand exclude the possibility of high export sales at a later date. The same developer had received a positive reaction from the sales people because he had found a product solution that fitted with their understanding of the customers' wants. Together with sales, service people, participated in the meeting in question and they had contributed with comments which resulted in changes to the product.

The *organization* of the meeting also had an effect upon the outcome. Instead of following a formalized procedure with a list of questions to be asked from the beginning of the meeting, a product developer explained that it was his experience that the participants took a greater interest in the meeting if they had the chance to talk more broadly about the project, feel it and express their spontaneous reactions. Afterwards he would return to the specific questions, but take care to exclude questions which were not of relevant for the product in question. The positive aspect of the list of questions was that it was a reminder for everybody about what to look for. They pointed both to production issues, sales documentation and customers' manuals. The negative aspect was that they might seem boring as soon as they moved outside the individual participants' occupational interest.

As a *documentation* of the activities during a stage, the project leaders wrote a *status report* explaining the activities e.g. the test problems and their solutions. This report was presented at the gate meeting. The discussions at the gate meeting were similarly recorded and were compared with the results of the next stage to see whether those changes which were wanted at the previous gate had been taken into consideration.

In this regard some interviewees made the point that such reports could be used for shirking the responsibility in the sense that demanded corrections might be made without taking new information in consideration, which might go against such corrections. Those developers who raised this problem and similar questions stressed that it was very important to have an open climate of trust among participants where criticism was seen as positive and not result in loss of face for the individual employees or their departments. In one of the firms it was new for the engineers that the climate was changing towards openness and mutual trust and less bureaucracy. Relating to this issue, an interviewee from production explained that for some people it was difficult to accept that their solution was a poor one. He had production technicians in mind. Some had not been accustomed to other peoples' interference in their work, so in their case it would take some time before they would be cooperative in the process of mutual criticism, but from his experience he judged the process would turn out well.

The official gate meetings were under scrutiny in two of the investigated firms. In one firm the management was starting with shorter official gate meetings carried out in a more business-like manner with more economic information. This meant that the meeting focused upon the status reports, which now also included results from meetings of special review groups.

The management of another firm thought of changing the gate meetings because they were carried out in a mechanical and streamlined way. To compensate for this, it was of importance to establish sub-stages and meetings between these sub-stages with fewer participants so they could discuss the problems in more depth than at meetings with many participants. The sales people had thought of combining such meetings with visits to customers to get a better impression of the expected success of the final product. The researchers got the impression that the sales people might feel at loss in relation to the development department's presentations of new products, and the sales department people explicitly explained that the meetings did not give enough room for investigating market considerations. A negative aspect of changing the procedure was that it would demand time and slow-down development processes.

According to the integrated stage-gate procedures an *evaluation* should take place when the product had been launched. This evaluation should compare results with the original specifications which had stated the reason for starting the project.

But this feature was adjusted to the circumstances, which meant that it could be postponed for a long time, or just passed by without much discussion, or changed towards a discussion of current problems without looking backwards because so many things had changed since the definition of the business case at the start of the project.

6. THE ROLE OF EMPLOYEES WITHOUT MANAGEMENT RESPONSIBILITIES

According to the PIE survey about two fifths of the firms reported that employees with vocational training had increased independence and responsibility, and a similar number responded that these employees had experienced increased technical-professional demands (Reichstein & Vinding, 2002). Both of these tendencies were found in relation to new product development within the four firms, and the managers gave also their reasons for moving in this direction. The visits to these firms gave several examples of how technicians and workers became more involved in tasks, which previously were handled by the developers themselves or had taken the form of difficult adjustments between the developers design proposals and production peoples' way of manufacturing the products. These difficulties were based on lack of efficient communication between the parties of the development process.

6.1. The Role of Technicians and the Integration of Design and Production

In the metal firm and the electronic firm interviews were carried out not only with development engineers and sales people, but also with a draughtsman, and people from production layout, production and assembly. The technicians' role was traditionally to serve the engineers in their design and construction work by helping with drawing and testing, but in the investigated firms a change was going on in the direction of more autonomy for technicians and workers in production and assembly. This autonomy also meant a responsibility for having cleared the task with people from production layout and from production.

At the *metal firm* a machine technician in the development department explained that she had a certain autonomy regarding her work with the product developers after having been employed by the firm for some years.

> Machine technician: No, I have not been here for long that is I have been here for three years. Well, the tasks I get change concurrently with that they find out how much you can and what sort of person you are . . .

Interviewer: It is more independent?

Machine technician: Yes, it goes that way, it is quite clear. For example regarding (this product), well I got permission to start it up. Changes have occurred, but so it is always. . . . Then you have reviews, and you find out, that there are things which can be made more suitable and so on, and then you talk about it with those involved, the supervisors in Xsection and so on, and find out what is most suitable and that is done. Well, there are many things you have to keep an eye on. The product has to become adjusted so it can be produced in a practical way (E4:2).

This autonomy did not mean – as it is also clear from the quotation – that she would abstain from taking help from other employees. On the contrary, she used informal relations to get information from colleagues instead of looking into the quality handbook because she found it easier that way. She talked with supervisors as well as workers concerning the transfer of blue prints into guidelines for production work processes. By such transfer she paid attention to the interests of both construction and production. She mentioned that welders could for instance tell her that a certain process might be difficult to carry out. In such a case they would talk about how to change the drawing to take care both of the production process and the idea of the new product. She found her conversations with the other people valuable, because you could not always see from a computer picture what would be a proper way of arranging the production of the new product.

Her understanding of the firm as an organization with influential actors and their various ways of handling the processes gave an important contribution to smooth the product development.

Her way of filling out her role as technician was seen by the managers as ideal, but directors of development as well as project leaders had experiences with employees who were more passive in their behaviour. One problem seemed to be for technicians to clear their task with people from other departments whereas they had less problems behaving independently as long as they could confine their work to their own department.

At the three firms with integrated product development procedures, those persons who should have the responsibility for a given stage would take part in the gate meeting held before their own stage. For instance, at the gate between the business case specification and construction, a technician would be oriented about work on approaching tests, and at the gate between the prototype and zero series a technician responsible for layout should start thinking about production drawings.

Regarding the *Dimmer project* the technician who was responsible for tests explained that he had taken part in the gate meeting which was held before the construction phase. At this meeting he had heard about the project and its specific importance for his work, cf. the following excerpt from the tape recording.

Technician:...In phase three (the project leader) arranges a M2 meeting. He presents his specifications of demands for the product (the Dimmer), and he presents diagrams, and tells a little about how it works. We do not go directly into the tests. Not much because afterwards we (the technician and the product leader) have a meeting because at the M2 meeting production people and purchase take part also. He presents and goes through the project, and we hear a little about it. Afterwards we get some diagrams. I go through the diagrams, and contact the project leader and then we go through the diagram together. He explains how it works, what it must stand up to, limits, tolerances and such things. And then I work for myself and try to develop a circuit which can test those things which have to be tested. And when I have worked upon it for some time, that is to make some diagrams, then I begin to make some test equipment, some print. And then I get a prototype from the project leader, so I can run some tests on the test equipment...Then the project leader approves it. And then we go to M3 meeting where it has to be delivered and presented for production (D2:1).

The technician had primarily used methods he knew from other tasks, but some new ways of testing had been included. By this work he had drawn upon colleagues instead of getting stuck in written material. Then a number of tests were carried through where the developer and the technician in an informal way exchanged ideas and talked about different solutions. Afterwards he worked on an instruction for the production people who should control their own work. He made contact with the production people and discussed their reactions, and the results were then adjusted to the users and not to those technically oriented. This result was accepted by the developer who made a report on the meeting regarding tests in the production of the *Dimmer* explaining methods and results of the tests. This report was delivered to the gate meeting held between the construction of prototype and the stage of zero series.

At one of the interviews with a production technician at the *metal firm*, the researchers were given an example of the disagreements which could come to the fore at the transmission of the new product from design and construction to production. The people responsible for production layout valued early contact with the development department. But it happened when the developers were pressed by their customers, sometimes the developers finished their work without considering what production might require. The consequence was that the people responsible for production layout most likely would have to ask for changes in the design. Both parties experienced such changes as a nuisance. Could they be avoided, it would save time and interpersonal conflicts. According to a production technician, he and his colleagues did not always experience a positive dialogue with the developers, but it depended upon the individual members of the development department. The production technicians wanted to join the development process at a reasonably early point of time so they could influence the construction of the new product and make it tailored to production.

Interviewer: Is it something you would want (i.e. to be asked in connection with the product specification).

Production technician: Yes we would want to join as early as possible, because we do not ask for production experience among our developers, but this is what we have or ought to have, so we can become active in the process and take care of a smooth process, also when we start production.

Interviewer: What is your part of the job in more details, in such an engineering section?

Production technician: We get some blueprints on which we specify which operations have to be done concerning the various components, where to carry them out in the workshop, and we take care of drawing up the production papers so the flow is in order, so the goods can be moved on to the next work place (E2:07).

As seen from this quotation the technicians' viewpoint concerning influence was also motivated by the fact that it was not a demand when hiring development people whether they had experiences with production. The recent changes at the firm meant that the development department in the case of the *Automatic Filling unit* had cooperated well with the production technicians.

6.2. The Role of Shop Floor Workers and the Position of Production During Development Activities

The shop floor workers were in certain respects assisting the developers and technicians. This was seen by the examples of direct contact between people from production and assembly and the project leaders and as mentioned above in cases where the interviewed machine technician was active. Furthermore, the workers participation in gate meetings had resulted in important contributions regarding information about production problems in relation to the new products.

At the *electronics firm* the assembly worker explained that she had taken part in the gate meeting which finished the construction stage and prepared for the zero series. She worked with print material, which was at the core of the electronic part of the Dimmer. The project leader had given her the necessary information and training with no supervisor between them because she worked in an autonomous assembly group, which had existed during the past year. When working with the new print she had discovered space problems and informed the project leader who had changed the print. She evaluated the relationship with the project leader as an example of good cooperation because she had received all the information she wanted, but she was aware of colleagues who had less positive experiences with other project leaders. She also thought that she had influenced the exchange of information by showing an interest in her work which furthermore might motivate the developer in his work. In the following excerpt from the interview she tells about her work with the *Dimmer*.

> Worker: Yes, it is the first time I work on a zero series.... And I can only speak positively, relatively to what I have heard previously from others. They did not get proper information and such sorts of things.
>
> Interviewer: So you got all the knowledge you needed?
>
> Worker: Simply, all the knowledge I needed.
>
> Interviewer: Have you yourself taken part in influencing the knowledge, have you yourself asked which sort of knowledge you needed?
>
> Worker: Yes, I think so. Also because I have taken a strong interest. I like new things. It may also influence (the project leader). She really takes interest in her work. I think this means a lot (D2).

Regarding the tests, she kept in touch with the technician responsible for this part of the development. During the production stage she taught her colleagues to carry out the work on the new product.

Generally the *electronics firm* was introducing organizational changes, which meant that the skilled workers would become involved in the development process at an earlier time than previously. Instead of production workers taking part only in the gate meeting held before the zero series, the management had realised that the workers ought to join the gate meeting held before or during the construction stage. In this way they could influence the tests for the control of the product and take part in updating test equipment. This would also increase their competence in relation to production and make it easier for them to give feedback to the engineers.

As already mentioned dissonance between development, production layout, and production sometimes stems from time pressure and traditional working methods, and now developers' failure to inform properly has also been mentioned. Another fact is the differencies in the ways that the construction staff and production staff have of defining what the necessary tasks are for making a new product. One was the logical relationships when drawing and designing a new product, another was the convenient steps to be followed to produce it. As mentioned above, this was touched upon in the interview with the machine technician who talked about the difference between her display and the welders point of view. The problem was spelt out much more clearly in another interview at the *metal firm* as seen from the following observation.

The same day as the researchers visited the *metal firm* for the second time the production technicians had been shown the documentation of the new Automatic Filling unit and had talked with the project leader about its production. One of the technicians explained that this conversation meant that he and the project leader had agreed upon how the work had to be carried out so production could produce the designed product without going back to the project leader to ask for changes. The task of the production technicians was to locate the work at the different work stations and prepare production drawings so the production flow became optimal. Due to this procedure production technicians looking at the requirements of the production workers, might arrange a work flow which differed from the flow expected by the product developers. The technicians and the production workers were interested in creating work tasks of some magnitude and representing an overall solution. Therefore, the technicians would combine a number of the developers' drawings and make one task out of them instead of several smaller ones. This gave the workers a more meaningful task and increased their understanding of quality as they would themselves control the task. Such a layout also decreased the movement of the product between work stations and thus reduced production costs according to what the technician explained. When the task was divided in smaller sub-tasks without control of these sub-tasks the result could be that problems were sent from one work station to the next. It was his opinion that time had run out for this sort of division of work. On the other hand, the technician was aware of the fact that combining the developers' drawings meant that some sub-products were missing which the development department reckoned existed. The technicians talked about phantom products' in such cases because they were found in the drawings but did not exist in production; they had to be produced if someone asked for them.

Another matter which could cause disagreement between the *metal firm's* production technicians and the developers was the use of components. The technicians wanted the developers to chose standard components that were quick and easy to get, so production was not delayed, whereas the developers thought more freely about the use of alternative materials and did not look into whether they were easy to get or not. Yet, an interview with the purchasing manager gave the impression that good communication between him and the developers in general solved the problem as people often were in mutual contact due to the relatively small size of this company.

7. CONCLUSIONS

This chapter has focused upon the firms' efforts to achieve a more satisfactory product innovation by integrated product development activities. We have explained their experiences concerning eight concrete product development projects and the new structures and processes related to the implementation of integrative product development. The aim has been to reach an understanding of the actors' attitudes and behaviour in connection with this integration and related changes of activities and structures. The presentation has been concentrated around

- aim and organization of the integration of business functions.
- experiences with the stage-gate procedure and the use of documentation.
- the role of employees without management responsibilities.

As a conclusion the results will be summarized in an organizational paradigm the elements of which comprise: (1) Actors, their qualifications and commitment; (2) Attitudes; (3) Processes; (4) Structure; (5) External relations; and (6) Renewal. Each of these elements is characterized by promoting and hampering traits of importance for the change towards an integrated product development. The comments to this paradigm will include some results known from the organizational literature on product development. Table 1 gives an overview of relevant traits.

The results have to be understood within the limitations which have characterized the selected cases, cf. section on the data. Important conditions comprised the size of the firms and their flat hierarchical organization which made it relatively easy to communicate across hierarchical levels and between employees in general. Yet, this general situation did not prohibit some barriers regarding communication.

7.1. Actors, Qualifications and Attitudes

The management of the visited firms had the experience that a more satisfactory product development process had to build upon priority to the market and its customers rather than technological fixation. In this matter, the management was in accordance with Cooper's (1993) recommendation that a strong market orientation was critical to success. In this connection, it was positive to product development along these lines that the top management saw to it that they acquired qualified managers of development, and those managers selected project leaders who had an understanding for the market orientation and an integrated product development. The central role of the project leaders during project development and their characteristics of power and vision are underlined by Brown and Eisenhardt (1995). It was also such characteristics which the interviewed managers of development expressed.

It was negative for the orientation towards the market and the customers, that some engineers lacked such an understanding and were more interested in technological questions. The management valued their ability for solving technical

Table 1. Overview of Promoting and Hampering Traits when Changing Towards an Integrated Product Development Process Oriented Towards the Market and a Focussed Development Organization.

Element	Promoting Traits	Hampering Traits
Actors, their qualifications and commitment	Qualified management (board, directors, managers of functions) Committee for product development Manager of development Product development leader Active technicians and production people Selected customers Other relevant external partners	Lack of qualifications regarding crossing understanding and group work
Attitudes	Market orientation Exploitation of knowledge Promoting and using human resources Balance between autonomy and control Climate of trust and openness	Keeping to a technological orientation Keeping to traditional work roles and methods Orientation towards one's own section
Processes	Communcation, cross-functional Knowledge diffusion Cooperation	Slow learning processes Planning failure
Structure	Procedures for integrated product development (stage-gate model)	Segmented organization
External relations	Fieldtest by customers Cooperation with suppliers and knowledge organizations	Delivery failures
Renewal	Strengthening of the actors' qualifications and other promoting traits	Reduction of hampering traits

Note: This overview presents a summary of the presentation in the previous sections of this chapter. Not all of the traits are discussed in this concluding section.

problems, but regretted their poor understanding regarding the learning about the market and their customers. As mentioned in the section on the role of the project leader, the management recognized the dilemma between the developers' wish for autonomy and the leaderships' wish for control with the product development activities. It will be remembered that this dilemma was one of the tensions Dougherty (1996) also found in research on large, complex organizations. The results from the four visited firms show that the management expressed an attitude similar to "subtle control" and acted according to this recommendation by balancing control and autonomy.

Another central group whose qualifications did not always meet to the standard of the integrative model were the sales people. It seems natural that the sales people could have difficulties understanding technical problems unless they had an education as engineer or technician. Similarly development people might lack an understanding for the sales and marketing function. The education of these occupations will not usually promote an understanding of the different functions and their interrelationships. Among the examples of lacking qualifications, were also seen poor behaviour in relation to effective group work and proactive participation in cross-functional meetings.

7.2. Structures and Processes

The development model of the stage-gate type meant that the firms in a far better way could utilize the knowledge which was distributed among the various business functions. This was made possible by the cross-functional communication processes. The project leaders have consciously promoted cooperation across jobs, divisions, and functions. This happened *inter alia* by the composition of work groups and by consulting technicians and workers instead of managing by directing people. These structures and processes have been to the advantage of a smooth product development process and a better working environment. A comparison with Jassawalla and Sashittal (2000) is relevant here. They declared that it was not enough to introduce cross-functional groups because the development of new products demanded a social climate of trust and openness and acceptance of risks. Therefore project leaders responsible for new product development should create commitment, rich information exchange and qualified interaction and learning. The conclusion with respect to the project leaders of the visited Danish firms is that these leaders worked along the lines suggested by Jassawalla and Sashittal.

The wish from the management concerning more cross-functional communication and a broader definition of the work role was met by resistance among some employees because they wanted to keep to their traditional role. With regard to the jobs of technicians and workers, the management's wish was based on the new possibilities of combining work tasks provided by new technology. But it was also connected to a change in the work role of the engineers giving them more creative tasks which implied that technicians and workers had to take over more responsibility. The resistance was partly motivated by the unknown risks connected to more responsibility and partly to lack of qualifications not only in a narrow occupational sense but also regarding broader social interaction.

Among the hampering traits concerning a more satisfactory product development process were found *slow learning processes* as seen for example in connection with gate meetings. The managers of product development worked hard on this problem but nevertheless the manager at the electronics firm reported that even after three years with integrated product development procedures they were not fully implemented. The direction of the development was correct with more integration, and deviations were followed up by reminders regarding the arrangement of gate meetings and the writing of satisfactory documentation about the product development activities. In this connection, be referred to O'Connor (1994) who estimated the time frame for full implementation of a stage-gate model to five years.

The integrative product development processes concerning the single product were dependent upon other new product development initiatives and the planning of the running production, marketing and sales. Here the PIE investigation showed a set of barriers related to *planning problems*. They comprised fast and unpredictable changes of resources attached to a given project. It meant that cross-functional communication was reduced due to lack of manpower and some tasks had to be changed in respect of less resources. The effectiveness of the new pattern depended upon the fulfilment of broader task responsibility among the actors staying with the task. In case of pressure from the next work stations or emergency situations, the product development process would be speeded up by omitting a gate meeting. The result could be poor coordination between construction and production. In this connection it is relevant to refer to Van de Ven and associates (1999). From their large investigation of innovation they pointed out that the people working on new products were "fluidly engaging and disengaging over time in a variety of roles." The planning problems of the four Danish firms gave similar examples although to a lesser degree. Another observation by Van de Ven and associates (1999) referred to the product development process where they had found processes which moved "from simple to many divergents, parallel and convergent paths; some related, others not." The PIE researchers did not get such an impression from their visits. But the managers and developers could tell about conditions similar to the American experiences prior to the change towards integrated product development. Those responsible for product development would keep the product development away from going off on a tangent by the help of the integrated procedure and a product development based on a relatively detailed business specification.

7.3. External Relations

The product development process was promoted by a number of external contacts. This issue is more thoroughly treated in Chapter 6 on "The organization of actors' learning in connection with new product development." Field tests were carried out by customers. In this way information was gathered which could be used for improvements of the new product before it was finally launched. Through suppliers, the firms received ideas for alternative ways of designing and producing the product. Consultants contributed to the organization of team work and design. Technological institutes and universities gave access to relevant test equipment. The various contacts showed some stability, but the four visited firms did not disclose a differentiation of roles concerning the external contacts, for example as gate keeper, as was found in other research (Brown & Eisenhardt, 1995). The reason is, at least partly, the smaller size of the investigated firms and less weight put on teams.

The product development was in some instances hampered by the behavior of suppliers due to unsatisfactory quality, or breaking of time limits. A part of these hampering traits can be explained by lack of knowledge among the developers concerning how to make agreements with suppliers.

7.4. Renewal

These documented hindrances for a successful change towards an integrated new product development process have to a certain extent been met by organizational *renewal measures* which were going on, or subject for, considerations during the PIE investigations. So, the firms did not stick to one model of integrated new product development. This observation underlines the finding by Davidson et al. (1999) which showed that success was dependent upon how the process was adapted to their companies. Their results demonstrated the importance of processes which provided clarity with regard to action, ownership across functions, top level responsibility, integration with other business processes and flexible adjustment to the firms needs. The work with renewal of the integrated product development procedures in the PIE firms showed top level responsibility for the procedures and pointed to similar processes as those favoured by Davidson and colleagues (1999).

Concerning some employees' preference for traditional roles and norms, they were counteracted by *training and organizational changes*. Regarding such training both developers and sales people were gathered for seminars. In the electronics firm the project leaders problem with traditional work habits in relation to the Dimmer project was met by more detailed production prescriptions and introducing a coordinator in a middle management position to observe the process. Concerning the gate meetings it has been mentioned how the project leaders made their own changes to the official procedures to achieve more interest and activity from the participants. The preparation for a more active work role among workers took the form of training in group work.

The changes mentioned above of renewal were not being seen by the management as the end of the renewal processes directed towards more efficient new product development. They had ideas for further improvements. For example when the PIE projects' interview phase stopped at the end of 2001 one of the machine factories' manager of development was just starting a new project for training of the developers in cooperation with some other firms. In the electronics firm some of the workers were expected to fill a more active role regarding new product development so far as testing was concerned. Regarding planning problems, the managers of development still worked on a reduction in ongoing projects. Also, new information and communication technology was getting a larger role even though one of the managers of development would not go so far as controlling the resource distribution between the projects by ICT as such a system would demand too much manpower to become of any help.

The experiences of the management and non-managing employees of the four firms have clearly shown how the competitive task of the firms has been met by a double set of changes to secure competitiveness. Both the development of new products *and* the creation of new structures, processes, and relationships in an interplay with new attitudes and norms have taken place.

REFERENCES

Brown, S. L., & Eisenhardt, K. M. (1995). Product development: Past research, present findings, and future directions. *The Academy of Management Review, 20*, 343–378.

Cooper, R. G. (1993). *Winning at new products*. Reading, MA: Addison-Wesley.

Cooper, R., & Kleinschmidt, E. (1986). An investigation into the new product process: Steps, deficiencies, and impact. *Journal of Product Innovation Management, 3*, 71–85.

Davidson, J. M., Clamen, A., Karol, R. A. (1999). Learning from the best new product developers. *Research – Technology Management* (July–August), 12–18.

Dougherty, D. (1996). Organizing for innovation. In: S. R. Clegg, C. Hardy & W. R. Nord (Eds), *Handbook of Organization Studies* (pp. 424–439). London: Sage.

Hein, L., & Andreasen, M. M. (1985). *Integreret produktudvikling*. København: Jernets Arbejdsgiverforening.

Jassawalla, A. R., & Sashittal, H. C. (2000). Strategies of effective new product team leaders. *California Management Review, 42*, 34–51.

Laursen, K., & Foss, N. J. (2000). *New HRM practices, complementarities, and the impact on innovation performance*. Copenhagen: Department of Industrial Economics and Strategy, Copenhagen Business School.

Lundvall, B. Å. (1999). Det danske innovationssystem. DISKO-projektet: Sammenfattende rapport. København: Erhvervsfremmestyrelsen, Erhvervsministeriet.

O'Connor, P. (1994). From experience. Implementing a Stage-Gate process: A multi-company perspective. *Journal of Product Innovation Management, 11*, 183–200.

Reichstein, T., & Vinding, A. L. (2002). Documentation of the IDA-DISKO database. Department of
    Business Studies – IKE Group, Aalborg University.
Van de Ven, A. H., Polley, D. E., Garud, R., & Venkataraman, S. (1999). *The innovation journey.*
    Oxford: Oxford University Press.
Vinding, A. L. (2002). *Interorganizational diffusion and transformation of knowledge in the process
    of product innovation.* Ph.D. Thesis. IKE Group/DRUID. Department of Business Studies,
    Aalborg University.

PART IV:
KNOWLEDGE INSTITUTIONS,
INTERACTIVE LEARNING AND
PRODUCT INNOVATION

INTERACTION BETWEEN FIRMS AND KNOWLEDGE INSTITUTIONS

Anker Lund Vinding

ABSTRACT

In this chapter it is argued that firms that interact with knowledge institutions increase their potential for exploiting knowledge. This is especially the case if the firms have employees with an academic degree employed. These employees will contribute to absorptive capacity in the traditional sense but also to the formation of social capital. Due to prior basic knowledge and understanding to researchers and scientist, the process of recognizing, assimilating and applying new knowledge from these institutions will become easier and hence increase the likelihood of producing more radical innovations. The estimation of an ordered probit model including 1983 firms from the Danish manufacturing and service industry supports the hypothesis.

1. INTRODUCTION

The work by Nelson and Winter (1982) was a breakthrough in many ways, e.g. in terms of understanding the importance of non-codified knowledge in the process of technological change. Since then, this argument has been further developed as concepts such as "the knowledge based economy" and "the learning economy" has gained influence in the economic literature. Shorter product cycles, more uncertain and fluctuating markets, more intense use of information technology and more

Product Innovation, Interactive Learning and Economic Performance
Research on Technological Innovation and Management Policy, Volume 8, 257–283
Copyright © 2004 by Elsevier Ltd.
ISSN: 0737-1071/doi:10.1016/S0737-1071(04)08011-4

intense competition characterize such economies. These circumstances enhance the demand for firms' ability to change rapidly.

As argued by Lundvall in Chapter 2, we are facing a change towards a more crucial role for the creation, distribution and use of knowledge and information (see also Lundvall & Johnson, 1994). Besides growth in the quantity and complexity of knowledge, processes such as learning, forgetting and diffusion of knowledge are of growing importance. Thus, the ability continuously to participate in learning processes and to develop and absorb new knowledge is a crucial element for firms' competitiveness. According to Foray and Lundvall (1996), society is moving towards a networked learning economy where the opportunity and capability to access and join knowledge – and learning-intensive networks determine the relative success of individuals and firms.

Interorganizational interaction in innovation processes are also considered a first-best option, instead of last resort because of firms potential access to information, resources, markets and technologies. Dodgson (1993) and Schill (1994) point out that external interaction is well established in innovation strategies of the firm. This is due to benefits such as increased scale and scope of activities (Gulati et al., 2000), shared costs and risks (Dickson et al., forthcoming; Teece, 1986), improved ability to deal with complexity, enhanced learning and welfare effects, flexibility and efficiency and increased speed in the innovation process (OECD, 2000).

Despite the large amount of literature on the benefits and the extent of interorganizational interaction, success cannot be taken for granted. The costs associated with realizing product development collaboration are less frequently examined. The costs may be quite considerable and not always matched by the benefits of the collaboration for the overall outcome of the product development process. One reason why interaction is required is that non-codified knowledge is an important component in the process of innovation (Dosi, 1988; Pavitt, 1987; Rosenberg, 1982; Senker, 1995).

In Chapter 7 by Vinding, it was shown that human resources and network postioning in complete networks are crucial factors for product innovation. In this chapter the focus is narrowed down to academic labor and to network relationships to knowledge institutions. We will argue that in order to acquire, transfer and utilize knowledge, especially non-codified knowledge, from knowledge institutions a combination of a high level of absorptive capacity (Cohen & Levinthal, 1990) and strong ties (Granovetter, 1973) are complementary and both factors are important in the innovation process in terms of innovative outcome since they improve the learning curve of the firm (Steenhuis & De Bruijn, 2002).

Empirically, this calls for new indicators. A suggestion for an indicator which incorporates both aspects, concerns a proxy which combines, first, if the firm has employed university graduates and secondly, if the firm has developed a closer relationship with knowledge institutions. In this context the employment of university graduates may be seen as affecting innovation through three different mechanisms. First, it may be taken as a measure of absorptive capacity since it is a proxy for the stock of the knowledge base of the firm. Second, university graduates have similar relational and cognitive dimensions as employees in knowledge institutions due reflecting prior basic knowledge and understanding. Finally, a university-graduated person may be used as a "gatekeeper" who translates and transmits the information to other individuals inside the organization.

The second variable, i.e. closer relationship to knowledge institutions, may be assumed to strengthen the relational and cognitive dimensions and hence increase the probability of successful absorption of non-codified knowledge.

The innovative performance of the firm is tested on the basis of survey data on organization, employee skills and development of new products, covering 2,007 private firms from the manufacturing, construction and service sector. The chapter is organized as follows. Section 2 presents the theoretical framework and hypothesis. Sections 3 and 4 explain the data material and model respectively where the results are shown in Section 5. Finally, conclusions and implications are put forward in Section 6.

2. NON-CODIFIED AND DEPENDENT KNOWLEDGE, TIE STRENGTH AND ABSORPTIVE CAPACITY

The theoretical model takes its departure in the framework by Hansen (1999) who uses respectively the search and the transfer mechanisms as the two focal points.[1] He argues that within organizations weak ties are most effective in research while strong ties are more effective when it comes to sharing codified and independent knowledge. Weak ties are assumed to be inefficient when it comes to the transfer of non-codified and dependent knowledge.

But Hansen does not take into account that innovation is a cumulative activity (Dosi, 1988; OECD, 1992). He does not include in his model how prior knowledge of the firm affects the absorption of new knowledge. This is especially important when the unit of analysis is changed from intra- to interorganizational relations since prior knowledge has an impact on the ability to assimilate and utilize external knowledge. Thus, the concept of absorptive capacity has to be taken into account. Incorporating absorptive capacity in the framework of knowledge complexity and tie strength affects both the search and the transfer benefits.

As can be seen from Fig. 1, we assume that the search benefits are basically affected by the strength of ties. As in Hansen, weak ties are assumed to favor search

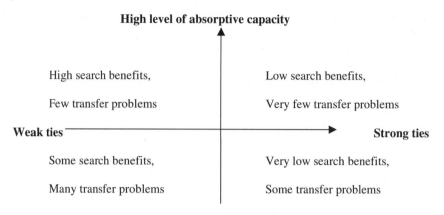

High search benefits,   Low search benefits,

Few transfer problems   Very few transfer problems

Weak ties   **Strong ties**

Some search benefits,   Very low search benefits,

Many transfer problems   Some transfer problems

Low level of absorptive capacity

Fig. 1. Search and Transfer Effects Associated with Four Combinations of Absorptive Capacity and Tie Strength in the Case of Noncodified and Dependent Knowledge.

compared to strong ties because they open up a wider span of opportunities. When the other dimension is taken into account, a high level of absorptive capacity favors search as compared to a low level of absorptive capacity. Organizations with a high level of prior knowledge know where to search.

In the transfer of noncodified and dependent knowledge absorptive capacity plays a central role since absorptive capacity facilitates the transfer of knowledge. A high level of absorptive capacity will make the transferring process easier to conduct. First, the organization is to a higher degree familiar with the type of knowledge exchanged, for instance in terms of a higher degree of prior basic knowledge. Second, the increasing familiarity makes it easier to choose the right means of exchanging the piece of knowledge and hence to select the most efficient way.

Organizations with a high level of absorptive capacity will later on be in a better position to absorb non-codified and dependent knowledge due to advances on the learning curve of the firm (Steenhuis & De Bruijn, 2002). This is especially the case if strong ties have been established where reciprocity, larger engagement from the source and establishment of specific heuristic have taken place. The second best solution is weak ties combined with a high level of absorptive capacity. The argument is that even though weak ties are characterized as being infrequent, distant, without reciprocity and specific heuristic a high level of absorptive capacity may compensate for the disadvantages. Organizations which for instance have invested in a high degree of research and development or high degree of highly educated employees, do not need the same degree of assistance in assimilating and interpreting and utilizing the knowledge being transferred compared to organizations, which have spent less money on R&D and hence having a low degree of absorptive capacity. This is in line with Carter (1989), Senker (1995) and Guellec (1996) who argue that educated people are aware of the tacit ability to acquire and use knowledge. Finally, a low degree of absorptive capacity presents the most severe transfer problems.[2] This is especially the case when dealing with weak ties where the disadvantages mentioned earlier cannot be compensated for, by the absorptive capacity. The disadvantages become less significant with a low degree of absorptive capacity and strong ties because strong ties are characterized by reciprocity, larger engagement from the source and establishment of specific heuristic, which will be helpful for an organization with a low level of absorptive capacity.

However, it has to be emphasized that it may be difficult to order the four combinations with respect to finding best practice of search and transfer effects in the case of non-codified and dependent knowledge. The purpose is only to illustrate that when dealing with noncodified and dependent knowledge a complementarity exists between absorptive capacity and strength of ties with respect to search and transfer mechanisms. Nevertheless, it may be argued that the two extremes will result in different innovative capabilities – strong ties and a high level of absorptive capacity should be to preferable to weak ties and low level of absorptive capacity. The impact on performance of the other two combinations: weak ties and high level of absorptive capacity and, respectively, strong ties and low level of absorptive capacity may be more difficult to predict.

In recent years, knowledge institutions have achieved much attention due to the large knowledge bases in these institutions. However, knowledge institutions cover a number of actors who play different roles in the innovation system. One way is to distinguish between basic, applied and strategic research where universities mainly carry out basic research. One of their purposes is to codify knowledge in terms of general theories and models that explain and predict reality. The aim of applied research is to develop knowledge for a specific purpose.

Sector research institutes, consultancy firms and technological institutes carry out mainly applied research. However, academic research may also be used as background knowledge in the sense that published papers are used to screen and identify new developments or identify researchers with specific expertise. The limitations of the codified knowledge may then be overcome by personal contact to the author(s) in order to acquaint oneself with the techniques used or interpretation of the material contained in the literature – hence access to knowledge of tacit and non-codified nature is opened up (Pavitt, 1998; Senker, 1995).[3] Schibany and Schartinger (2001) support this argument by emphasising firms' motives for establishing contacts with universities. In 73% of the cases universities capability to solve problems was rated as important or as very important. In 70% of the cases, they rated an expected learning process a crucial.

In addition, as argued in Granstrand et al. (1997), product innovations are increasingly based upon a number a scientific disciplines e.g. computing, materials and biotechnology. According to Granstrand the motives for the firms to interact with other firms and institutions are three-fold; "opportunities to introduce new technologies into products and systems for improved performance and new functionalities, the continuing relevance of old technologies, and the co-ordination of innovation and change in core products with complementary changes in the production system and supply chain" (Granstrand et al., 1997, p. 9). All three increase the inter-relatedness and the dependency of knowledge.

Following these arguments, knowledge institutions are important contributors of non-codified and dependent knowledge and non-codified knowledge is moreover an important component of innovation (Dosi, 1988; Pavitt, 1987; Rosenberg, 1982; Senker, 1995) and thus, for the performance of the firm (Barney, 1995; Barney & Link, 1991; Spender, 1996). On this basis I put forward a hypothesis arguing that.

Hypothesis 1. A high level of absorptive capacity and strong ties favor acquirement and transformation of noncodified and dependent knowledge from knowledge institutions, thus promoting the product innovative performance of firms.

The dependency on non codified and dependent knowledge is primarily related to high-tech industries (Cockburn & Henderson, 1997; Mansfield, 1995; Pavitt, 1984), and for that reason the use of knowledge from these institutions is more or less a precondition for survival. Low- and medium-tech industries have on the other hand less frequent interaction with knowledge institutions. However, the level of sophistication of innovations is increasing, due to a number of scientific disciplines e.g. computing, materials that are used across industries. This may also be the case for industries that are characterized as low- or medium-tech. Firms with the aim of combining existing technologies into new innovation may need information from external partners. In this respect knowledge institutions may be helpful by proving knowledge about how to combine existing technologies directly, or they may be used as marriage brokers to other partners. This leads to the second hypothesis.

Hypothesis 2. The importance of a high level of absorptive capacity and moving toward strong ties differs among industries with respect to how they influence innovative performance.

Moreover, it is also a well-known fact that small firms are more dependent on external resources e.g. lack of technological and related resources that limit the potential for finding synergies across technologies. This leads to the third hypothesis.

Hypothesis 3. The importance of a high level of absorptive capacity and moving toward strong ties are more important among small firms with respect to innovative performance.

3. DATA

The data for the analyses is described in Chapter 7, Section 2.

4. MODEL

On the basis of the theoretical and empirical discussion, a model is estimated in which a firm's innovation activities is used as a dependent variable, and the combination of tie strength and nature of knowledge as shown in Fig. 1 and traditional control variables as independent variables. The basic structure of the model may be specified as follows:

$$a = f(\beta_{1z} + \beta_{2q}) \tag{1}$$

a represents the innovative activity of the firm, where z and q are vectors concerning tie strength/nature of knowledge and other standardized variables used in the literature explaining the innovative activity of the firms. See Appendix A for descriptive statistics.

a expresses the innovativeness of the firm on an ordered scale from 0 to 3. 0 is equal to a non-innovator firm (1163), 1 indicates that the firm has introduced a product/service in the period of 1998–2000 that is new to the firm (673), 2 indicates that the firm has introduced an innovation that is new in the Danish context (117), and, finally, 3 indicates that the firm has introduced an innovation that is new to the world (54). Thus the dependent variable measures both innovativeness and the degree of non-imitative innovation.

z can be decomposed into two variables, where the first represents an indicator combining tie strength and absorptive capacity as shown in Fig. 1.

As argued earlier, one can assume that knowledge institutions (ACAKNOW), defined as consultants, technical support institutions, or universities, are important contributors of non-codified and dependent knowledge. At a first consideration it might be thought that universities are misplaced in this respect since the aim of universities is to codify knowledge. But the knowledge produced by the universities is complex and context dependent and firms need to get access to more than the codified part of this knowledge. This is why firms need to develop closer interaction, including personal contacts, in order to acquire the tacit skills and experiences that underlie published articles.[4]

In order to test the first hypothesis absorptive capacity is measured as having at least one employee with an academic degree while having no such employees is equal to a low level. As mentioned above, the presence of a university graduate employee plays three roles. First, it reflects the absorptive capacity since it is a proxy for the stock of the knowledge base of the firm. Second, university graduates operate and communicate on the basis of similar relational and cognitive dimensions as employees in knowledge institutions due to their academic training. Finally, university graduates may be used as a "gatekeeper" who translates the information to others inside the organization.

In order to measure the strength of ties, the question concerning to what degree firms have developed a closer relationship with knowledge institutions is applied. Moving toward strong ties is approximated as having developed a closer relationship, while firms that have not established a closer relationship with knowledge institutions are categorized as having weak ties. Thus, the two variables make it possible to locate each firm in one of the four quadrants in Fig. 1.

Table 1 shows the distribution for the four types of absorptive capacity and strength of ties presented in Fig. 1 for knowledge institutions and universities and

Table 1. Distribution of the Four Types of Absorptive Capacity and Strength of Ties with Knowledge Institutions, Weighted.

	Low/ Weak (%)	Low/ Strong (%)	High/ Weak (%)	High/ Strong (%)	N
Size					
less than 50	49	23	18	11	1330
50 and more	25	10	33	33	677
Sectors					
Supplier dominated	40	19	25	16	248
Scale intensive	30	24	22	23	256
Specialised suppliers	25	13	29	33	143
Science based	17	14	26	43	56
Crafts	63	22	11	5	317
Wholesale trade	39	17	27	16	349
Specialised services	58	21	12	8	330
Scale intensive services	54	22	20	4	87
ICT intensive services	6	5	44	45	197

Note: Absorptive capacity and strength of ties – Knowledge institutions.

technological institutes with respect to size and industry. For both firm size and industry large differences exist. It is not surprising that large firms and firms in the manufacturing industry and *ICT intensive* services have the highest percentage regarding high level of absorptive capacity and strong ties.

The second variable in z represents development of closer relationships to partners in the value chain LINK. Edquist (1997), Meeus et al. (2001) and (Tether, 2002) point out that knowledge institutions can be recognized as interfacing units that link innovating firms to external actors and facilitate information and technology transfer as well as technological collaboration. In addition, Kaufmann and Tödtling (2001) emphasize the importance of complete networks in developing radical innovations whereas customers in particular are involved in developing incremental improvements. LINK can take three forms: having established a closer relationship with none of the actors in the value chain (0); either one of the actors in the value chain (1); and finally established a closer relationship with both suppliers and customers (2).

q represents four control variables in the model. First, sectoral affiliation (*SECTOR*) where we apply Pavitt's taxonomy, with four sectors representing the manufacturing sector while five sectors represent the service firms.[5] Second, firm size is taken into account which according to the Schumpeterian hypothesis may be argued to be positively correlated with innovative activity due to the existence of R&D departments (Brouwer & Kleinknecht, 1996).[6]

The third control variable expresses competitive pressure of the firm. In the literature contradictory results exist concerning the level of competition e.g. Arvanitis and Hollenstein (1996) versus Geroski (1990). However, the variable is measured in a slightly different way. Instead of the level of competition, the firms are asked to rate the change in the level of competitive pressure within the period. Finally, the study controls for whether or not the firm is a subsidiary of a larger firm – *SUBSID*. Again, contradictory results exist. However the most recent studies tend to show a positive relationship due to arguments that subsidiary firms have access to the parent firm's larger resource base and thus benefits in terms of innovative activity.

5. RESULTS

5.1. All Firms

As mentioned previously, the dependent variable takes on four discrete ordered values. Hence, an ordered probit model is applied and maximum likelihood is the method used as the means of estimation.

Table 2. Ordered Probit Estimation of Innovative Performance, Absorptive Capacity and Strength of Ties with Knowledge Institutions, Weighted.

Variables	Model I						Model II					
				Marginal Effects						Marginal Effects		
	Coef.	Std. Err.	None	New to Firm	New in DK	New to World	Coef.	Std. Err.	None	New to Firm	New in DK	New to World
Intercept	−0.845	0.054	0.329	−0.218	−0.073	−0.039	−0.560	0.084	0.218	−0.149	−0.046	−0.023
ACAKNOW – relative absorptive capacity												
High absorptive capacity and strong ties	0.730**	0.072	−0.284	0.188	0.063	0.034	0.602**	0.077	−0.234	0.160	0.050	0.024
High absorptive capacity and weak ties	0.453**	0.062	−0.177	0.117	0.039	0.021	0.344**	0.070	−0.134	0.091	0.029	0.014
Low absorptive capacity and strong ties	0.209**	0.063	−0.082	0.054	0.018	0.010	0.166**	0.063	−0.065	0.044	0.014	0.007
Low absorptive capacity and weak ties	Benchmark						Benchmark					
LINK – closer relat. With vertical actors												
Both suppliers/customers	0.278**	0.064	−0.109	0.072	0.024	0.013	0.234**	0.065	−0.091	0.062	0.020	0.010
Either suppliers/customers	0.320**	0.056	−0.125	0.083	0.028	0.015	0.293**	0.056	−0.114	0.078	0.024	0.012
None	Benchmark						Benchmark					
SUBSID – belonging to a sub. firm, binary												
Yes	0.192**	0.049	−0.075	0.050	0.017	0.009	0.174**	0.049	−0.068	0.046	0.015	0.007
COMP – experi. Increased comp., binary												
Yes	0.109*	0.052	−0.0433	0.028	0.009	0.005	0.135*	0.054	−0.053	0.036	0.011	0.005

Table 2. (*Continued*)

Variables	Model I						Model II					
				Marginal Effects						Marginal Effects		
	Coef.	Std. Err.	None	New to Firm	New in DK	New to World	Coef.	Std. Err.	None	New to Firm	New in DK	New to World
SIZE – size of the firm												
>50	0.189**	0.067	-0.074	0.049	0.016	0.009						
25–50	0.020	0.055	-0.008	0.005	0.002	0.001						
<25	Benchmark											
SECTORS												
Supplier–dominated							0.086	0.094	-0.034	0.023	0.007	0.004
Scale intensive							0.030	0.088	-0.012	0.008	0.003	0.001
Specialised suppliers							0.335**	0.097	-0.130	0.089	0.028	0.014
Science based							0.185	0.171	-0.072	0.049	0.015	0.008
Crafts							-0.591**	0.109	0.230	-0.157	-0.049	-0.024
Wholesale trade							-0.083	0.092	0.032	-0.022	-0.007	-0.003
Specialised services							-0.421**	0.093	0.164	-0.112	-0.035	-0.017
Scale intensive services							-0.448**	0.155	0.174	-0.119	-0.037	-0.018
ICT intensive services							Benchmark					
N	1983						1983					
% of correct predictions	59						60					
Log likelihood	-1782						-1741					
Restricted log likelihood	-1943						-1943					
Likelihood ratio test	322.2						403.6					

Notes: There is no serious sign of multicollinearity between the independent variables. The multicollinearity is estimated by using the predicted probabilities of the dependent variable. These predicted values are then used to construct a weight variable which are applied in a weighted least squares regression.

A tolerance is computed by regressing each variable on all the other explanatory variables.

* significance at 5% level.
** significance at 1% level.

In Table 2 the estimations of Eq. (1) are reported for knowledge institutions. For both models the first hypothesis is supported. High level of absorptive capacity and moving toward strong ties seem to benefit acquirement and transformation of noncodified and dependent knowledge from knowledge institutions in the sense that these firms besides promoting the ability to innovate also reduces the degree of imitation, as illustrated by the marginal effects. However, the magnitude of the effect becomes smaller the less imitative the innovation is.

The LINK variable shows a significant relationship for both models and tells us that firms that have developed a closer relationship with suppliers and/or customers are better suited to deal with more complex and hence less imitative innovations.

Most of the four control variables in the two models are significant. The degree of increased competition (COMP) shows the right sign and is significant for both models in Table 2. Firms, who claims to be, exposed to increased competition are, ceteris paribus, more likely to innovate, which is in line with Geroski (1990).

Subsidiary firm (SUBSID) show significant results for both models. Subsidiary firms are hence more likely to increase innovative performance presumably due to access to the larger resource base of the parent firm.

The size variable is significant showing that firms with more than 50 employees are more likely to produce less imitative innovations compared to firms with less than 25 employees. A probable reason is that larger firms can more easily devote resources to the innovation process.

Finally, the sector variable shows that *crafts, specialized services* and *scale intensive services* innovate significantly less than the benchmark category *ICT intensive services*. On the other hand, firms characterized as *specialized suppliers* are more likely to develop "true" innovations.

5.2. Sectoral Estimations

Table 3 shows the estimations of Eq. (1) for each of the nine sectors in relation to knowledge institutions. In the sector estimations, the dependent variable takes on a binary value yes/no to the innovation question since some of the sectors have a limited number of observations.

As can be seen from the estimations in Table 3, the second hypothesis is supported in the sense that high levels of absorptive capacity and moving toward strong ties (ACAKNOW) differ among industries. The results for high-tech firms show insignificant estimates where-as for significant estimates are found for low- and medium-tech firms. Absorptive capacity and tie strength does to a varying degree have an influence on the more low-tech oriented sectors whereas *science-based* and *ICT intensive sectors* show insignificant results. A hypothesis might be

Table 3. Probit Model of the Ability to Innovate Yes/No, Absorptive Capacity and Strength of Ties with Knowledge Institutions, Weighted.

Variables	Supplier Dominated			Scale Intensive			Specialized Suppliers			Science Based		
	Coef.	Std. Err.	Mar. Eff.	Coef.	Std. Err.	Mar. Eff.	Coef.	Std. Err.	Mar. Eff.	Coef.	Std. Err.	Mar. Eff.
Intercept	−0.343	0.231	−0.135	−0.560	0.234	−0.223	−0.412	0.378	−0.155	−0.498	1.101	−0.221
ACAKNOW – relative absorptive capacity												
High absorptive capacity and strong ties	0.514*	0.268	0.203	0.553*	0.238	0.221	0.824**	0.305	0.311	−1.386	0.764	−0.564
High absorptive capaciy and weak ties	0.452*	0.226	0.178	0.266	0.236	0.106	1.079*	0.308	0.407	−1.309	0.911	−0.580
Low absorptive capacity and strong ties	0.182	0.232	0.072	0.219	0.228	0.087	0.122	0.369	0.046	−1.348	0.785	−0.597
Low absorptive capacity and weak ties	Benchmark			Benchmark			Benchmark			Benchmark		
LINK – closer relat. With vertical actors												
Both suppliers/customers	0.310	0.225	0.122	0.356	0.222	0.142	0.555	0.303	0.209	0.970*	0.499	0.430
Either suppliers/customers	0.128	0.196	0.051	0.398*	0.189	0.159	0.008	0.255	0.003	1.462*	0.589	0.648
None	Benchmark			Benchmark			Benchmark			Benchmark		
SUBSID – belonging to a sub. Firm, binary												
Yes	0.143	0.167	0.056	0.207	0.174	0.083	0.172	0.235	0.065	0.825	0.475	0.366
COMP – experi. Increased comp., binary												
Yes	−0.012	0.173	−0.005	0.280	0.180	0.112	0.243	0.253	0.091	−0.357	0.390	−0.158

Table 3. (*Continued*)

Variables	Supplier Dominated			Scale Intensive			Specialized Suppliers			Science Based		
	Coef.	Std. Err.	Mar. Eff.	Coef.	Std. Err.	Mar. Eff.	Coef.	Std. Err.	Mar. Eff.	Coef.	Std. Err.	Mar. Eff.
SIZE – size of the firm												
>50	0.263	0.245	0.104	−0.003	0.227	−0.001	−0.189	0.370	−0.071	0.972	1.141	0.431
25–50	−0.079	0.236	−0.031	−0.159	0.224	−0.064	−0.206	0.351	−0.078	0.015	1.087	0.007
<25	Benchmark			Benchmark			Benchmark			Benchmark		
N	241			255			157			73		
% of correct predictions	58			62			69			77		
Log likelihood	−157			−165			−90			−35		
Restricted log likelihood	−164			−177			−102			−48		
Likelihood ratio test	13.2			21.3			24.3			25.2		

Notes: There is no serious sign of multicollinearity between the independent variables. The multicollinearity is estimated by using the predicted probabilities of the dependent variable. These predicted values are then used to construct a weight variable which are applied in a weighted least squares regression. A tolerance is computed by regressing each variable on all the other explanatory variables.

*significance at 5% level.

**significance at 1% level.

that a high capacity of receiving knowledge was already reached for knowledge intensive firms. For these firms an improvement will only have marginal effect. They have learnt to become similar to knowledge institutions in cognitive and relational dimensions, since they have to work closely together with these partners just in order to survive.

Instead, these firms may experience other problems in terms of finding the right and qualified person for fulfilling the task of the firm. On the other hand, the results suggest that low- and medium-tech firms may achieve major innovative benefits if they have graduates employed while at the same time establish closer relationships with knowledge institutions. Hence, developing their social capital to knowledge institutions may become a competitive strength. Moreover, since the frequency of firms fulfilling these conditions is small, a large potential exists.

For developments of a closer relationship with actors in the value chain (LINK) significant estimates are found in the *scale intensive, craft* and *specialized services* for either suppliers/customers, whereas *science-based* sector experience significant estimates for both categories.

5.3. Size Estimations

Table 4 shows the estimations for two size categories, less than and more than 50 employees.[7] It is well-known that small firms are less likely to have employed graduates from universities and it is also less likely that they have developed close relationship with knowledge institutions. But for those who do move in these directions, the impact on performance is strong and clear. For knowledge institutions, large and small firms represented with a high level of absorptive capacity and strong ties have the same marginal effect for the ability of no innovation compared to the benchmark category. However, small firms with a high level of absorptive capacity and strong ties, show more than three times the likelihood to develop products, which are new in a Danish context and new to the world compared to large firms in the same situation.

This indicates that those small firms which are capable of fulfilling these requirements are in a better position not just to innovate, but also to produce less imitative product innovations. These results support the argument that academic research is a semi-public good, it is easy to transmit, but far from a free good. Firms have to invest in-house, both in human resources and in closer relationships, in order to search for and transfer research of this kind. However, since only 11% of these firms are categorized as having a high level of absorptive capacity and strong ties with knowledge institutions (see Table 1), there may be a large unexploited potential.

Table 4. Ordered Probit Estimation of Innovative Performance, Absorptive Capacity and Strength of Ties with Knowledge Institutions, Weighted.

Variabless	Less Than 50 Employees						More Than 50 Employees					
				Marginal Effects						Marginal Effects		
	Coef.	Std. Err.	None	New to Firm	New in DK	New to World	Coef.	Std. Err.	None	New to Firm	New in DK	New to World
Intercept	-0.409	0.157	0.163	-0.091	-0.046	-0.026	-0.571	0.112	0.210	-0.155	-0.038	-0.018
ACAKNOW – relative absorptive capacity												
High absorptive capaciy and strong ties	0.529**	0.107	-0.211	0.117	0.060	0.033	0.579**	0.118	-0.214	0.158	0.038	0.018
High absorptive capaciy and weak ties	0.252**	0.103	-0.100	0.056	0.029	0.016	0.358**	0.101	-0.132	0.098	0.024	0.011
Low absorptive capacity and strong ties	0.164	0.129	-0.065	0.036	0.019	0.010	0.177*	0.082	-0.065	0.048	0.012	0.005
Low absorptive capacity and weak ties	Benchmark						Benchmark					
LINK – closer relat. With vertical actors												
Both suppliers/customers	0.377**	0.103	-0.150	0.084	0.043	0.024	0.117	0.090	-0.043	0.032	0.008	0.004
Either suppliers/customers	0.118	0.087	-0.047	0.026	0.013	0.007	0.388**	0.077	-0.143	0.106	0.026	0.012
None	Benchmark						Benchmark					
SUBSID – belonging to a sub. firm, binary												
Yes	0.162*	0.080	-0.065	0.036	0.018	0.010	0.166*	0.067	-0.062	0.045	0.011	0.005
COMP – experi. Increased comp., binary												
Yes	-0.026	0.079	0.010	-0.006	-0.003	-0.002	0.246**	0.077	-0.091	0.067	0.016	0.008

SECTORS												
Supplier–dominated	0.318*	0.149	−0.127	0.071	0.036	0.020	−0.107	0.132	0.040	−0.029	−0.007	−0.003
Scale intensive	0.021	0.145	−0.008	0.005	0.002	0.001	0.003	0.122	−0.001	0.001	0.000	0.000
Specialised suppliers	0.397*	0.184	−0.158	0.088	0.045	0.025	0.283*	0.127	−0.104	0.077	0.019	0.009
Science based	0.346	0.194	−0.138	0.077	0.039	0.022	−0.075	0.340	0.028	−0.020	−0.005	−0.002
Crafts	−0.563**	0.196	0.224	−0.125	−0.064	−0.035	−0.624*	0.145	0.230	−0.170	−0.041	−0.019
Wholesale trade	−0.019	0.145	0.008	−0.004	−0.002	−0.001	−0.145	0.129	0.053	−0.039	−0.010	−0.004
Specialised services	−0.258	0.164	0.103	−0.057	−0.029	−0.016	−0.539*	0.126	0.199	−0.147	−0.035	−0.017
Scale intensive services	−0.175	0.204	0.069	−0.039	−0.020	−0.011	−0.682*	0.248	0.251	−0.186	−0.045	−0.021
ICT intensive services	Benchmark			Benchmark			Benchmark			Benchmark		
N				836					1171			
% of correct predictions				53					66			
Log likelihood				−823					−927			
Restricted log lokelihood				−887					−1024			
Likelihodd ratio test				127.4					195.2			

Notes: There is no serious sign of multicollinearity between the independent variables. The multicollinearity is estimated by using the predicted probabilities of the dependent variable. These predicted values are then used to contruct a weight variable which are applied in a weighted least squares regression. A tolerance is computed by regressing each variable on all the other explanatory variables.

* significance at 5% level.
** significance at 1% level.

The same kind of argument goes for firms that have developed a closer relationship to actors in the value chain. Small firms that have developed a closer relationship with actors in the value chain are more likely to develop products new in the Danish context and new to the world as compared to large firms in the same situation. The hypothesis that more radical innovations require interaction with suppliers, customers and knowledge institutions is especially supported for small firms. Moreover, the hypothesis that small firms to a higher degree are dependent on external interaction in development of product innovation is supported as well. On the other hand, large firms have significant estimates concerning closer relationships with either customers or suppliers and not both of them.

For both types of sizes belonging to a subsidiary firm is conducive for innovation whereas experienced competition only promotes the innovative performance for large firm.

6. CONCLUSIONS

In the knowledge-based economy knowledge is recognized as being the most important resource for the competitiveness of the firm. Some of the most important carriers of knowledge are consultants, universities and technical support institutions. Much of the knowledge in these institutions is noncodified and dependent – a type of knowledge that is of crucial importance for the development of product innovations. In order to capture this kind of knowledge the search and transfer mechanisms are essential for the firm. In this chapter, I have argued that the proposed definition of absorptive capacity, measured as having at least one graduated person employed as well as development of a closer relationship, has an influence on the search and transfer mechanisms. A theoretical model was developed where a high level of absorptive capacity and moving toward strong ties to knowledge institutions promote the search and transfer mechanisms which then will benefit the innovative performance of the firm, while a low level of absorptive capacity and moving toward weak ties were expected to be the least beneficial.

The estimation of an ordered probit model including 1983 firms from the Danish manufacturing and service industry support the hypothesis. Thus, moving towards strong ties to knowledge institutions and having a high level of absorptive capacity seems to benefit acquirement and transformation of noncodified and dependent knowledge from knowledge institutions. Firms that fulfil the two requirements increase not just the ability to innovate but reduce also the degree of innovative imitation.

Moreover, sectoral estimations do not support the hypothesis that high-tech firms are more dependent on noncodified and dependent knowledge than low- and medium-tech firms. On the contrary, absorptive capacity and the strength of ties seem more or less to have its major influence among the low-tech oriented sectors whereas *science-based* and *ICT intensive sectors* show insignificant results. Given the fact that the frequency of interaction with knowledge institutions and the degree of absorptive capacity is relatively low for the low- and medium- tech sectors, one could put forward the hypothesis that there is a large potential to be gained for firms that invest in absorptive capacity and develop stronger ties to knowledge institutions, in the sense that they will be capable of producing less imitative product innovations. This argument may be strengthened due to the recognition that some technologies seem to be used across industries e.g. computing, bio-technologies and materials which increases the level of sophistication in new products/services. In this respect, knowledge institutions may be helpful in guiding firms that want to combine existing technologies into new ones.

The same argument is valid for small firms.[8] It is a well-known fact that small firms rarely have employees with university degree nor have developed closer relationships with knowledge institutions in particular. But, those who are capable of fulfilling these requirements are in a better position not just to innovate, but also to produce less imitative product innovations.

The complementarity indicates that the argument that academic research is a public good in being a free good, easy to transmit is incorrect. Firms have to invest in-house, in human resources and in building closer relationships, in order to search and transfer research of this kind.

However, the measurement of absorptive capacity may to some extent be misplaced. The distinction between high and low is based on having at least one employee with an academic degree versus having none. Indicators which to a larger extent take into account the stock or change of knowledge base in the firm would be more appropriate. For instance the stock of employees having a university degree or R&D expenditure.

Despite problems of measuring absorptive capacity, the results bear evidence to support policies in promoting interaction between firms and knowledge institutions in general. To be more specific, policies supporting interaction like center contracts, innovation incubators and science parks, and at the individual level mobility programs, where the latter seem to be particular interesting.

Given the results in this chapter for small and low- and medium-tech sectors, public subsidies to those firms, which for the first time hire graduates, should be taken up for further discussion (isbryderordningen). Employing university graduates will besides upgrading the skills of the firm, and thus increase the absorptive capacity, also increase the likelihood that the firm will establish a closer relationship with knowledge institutions towards strong ties which might benefit the firm in the long run. In this case universities contribute to the process of product innovations in two ways. First, by conducting research which might lead to new techniques, instruments or knowledge which might be applied in the industry. Secondly, and probably even more important, to educate graduates and promote social interaction by establishing personal networks between the graduates which might increase the interaction between the industry and research institutions as shown in this chapter.[9]

NOTES

1. Schibany and Schartinger (2001) emphasise in a survey on interaction between the university and the business sector that 58% of Austrian firms perceive the lack of information on the content of university research as a serious barrier to interaction.

2. The argument can actually be traced back to Harary et al. (1965). They point out that it is only within a certain distance (length of path) that communication will be feasible. If the distance is too long the cost of transmission will be too high.

3. Based on three technological fields, Senker (1995) found that in biotechnology, literature was more important than personal contacts while the opposite was the case for ceramics and computing.

4. Moreover, as can be seen from Appendix A Danish firms are reluctant to interact with universities and technical support institutions. Only 19% have developed a closer relationship and we know from another survey carried out in the same period which distinguish between interaction with technical support institutions and universities that only 28% of the firms have collaborated with universities. Hence, universities play a minor role in the estimations. However, a possible explanation for this feature might be found in differences in institutional set-ups. One of the reasons why firms in Denmark might not use universities and public research institutions as frequently as collaborating partners compared to product innovating companies in other countries could be the broad range of technological services offered by intermediate technological service organizations which are part of the Danish GTS-system (Approved Technological Service System).

5. The categorization of the service firms is taken from Laursen (2000). For further details on the categorization, see Appendix B and C.

6. See Cohen (1995) for an empirical review.

7. Due to a larger share of observations in the two categories the dependent variable is divided in four categories as original, hence an ordered probit model is applied.

8. As mentioned earlier, the sectoral classification applied in this paper, are among other elements, based on size, so a coincidence will be natural.

9. The results are in line with Schibany and Schartinger (2001) who point out that 64% of Austrian firms indicate that highly skilled personnel is the most important output from universities. In addition, more than 50% of the contacts between the university and the firm were established by graduated students. The same study showed that establishment of joint research projects may trigger other joint activities between universities and firms, i.e.

training activities for business people, mobility of university researchers to industry and business financing of research assistants at university.

ACKNOWLEDGMENTS

I would like to thank Associated Professor Jesper Lindgaard Christensen, Professor Bengt-Åke Lundvall, Professor Emeritus Reinhard Lund, research fellow Toke Reichstein and Associated Professor Peter Nielsen, who are the persons behind the PIE (Product innovation and Economic performance) project for comments as well as giving me the opportunity to work on the data.

REFERENCES

Ahuja, G. (2000). The duality of collaboration: Inducements and opportunities in the formation of interfirm linkages. *Strategic Management Journal, 21*, 317–343.

Arvanitis, S., & Hollenstein, H. (1996). Industrial innovation in Switzerland: A model-based analysis with survey data. In: A. Kleinknecht (Ed.), *Determinants of Innovation* (pp. 13–62). London: Macmillan.

Barney, J. B. (1995). Looking inside for competitive advantage. *Academy of Management Ececutive, 9*, 48–61.

Barney, W. L., & Link, A. N. (1991). Firm resources and sustained competitive advantage. *Journal of Management, 17*, 99–120.

Brouwer, E., & Kleinknecht, A. (1996). Determinants of innovation: A microeconometric analysis of three alternative innovation output indicators. In: A. Kleinknecht (Ed.), *Determinants of Innovation* (pp. 99–125). London: Macmillan.

Carter, A. P. (1989). Knowhow trading as economic exchange. *Research Policy, 18*, 1–9.

Cockburn, I., & Henderson, R. (1997). Public-private interaction and the productivity of pharmaceutical research. NBER Working Paper 6018.

Cohen, W. (1995). Empirical studies of innovative activity. In: P. Stoneman (Ed.), *Handbook of Economics of Innovation and Technological Change* (pp. 182–265). London and Oxford: Basil Blackwell.

Cohen, W., & Levinthal, D. (1990). Absorptive capacity: A new perspective of learning and innovation. *Administrative Science Quarterly, 35*, 128–152.

Dickson, K., Coles, A. M., & Smith, H. L. (forthcoming). *Technological entrepreneurs: Developing succesful collaboration strategies*. San Francisco: Sage.

Dodgson, M. (1993). *Technological collaboration in industry*. London: Routledge.

Dosi, G. (1988). The nature of the innovative process. In: G. Dosi, C. Freeman, R. Nelson, G. Silverberg, L. Soete (Eds), *Technical Change and Economic Theory*. London: Pinter.

Edquist, C. (1997). Systems of innovation: Technology, institutions and organisation. London: Pinter.

Foray, D., & Lundvall, B. Å. (1996). The knowledge-based economy: From the economics of knowledge to the learning economy. In: *Employment and Growth in the Knowledge-based Economy*. Paris: OECD.

Geroski, P. A. (1990). Innovation, technological opportunity, and market structure. *Oxford Economic Papers, 42*, 586–602.

Granovetter, M. (1973). The strength of weak ties. *American Journal of Sociology, 78*, 1360–1380.

Granstrand, O., Patel, P., & Pavitt, P. (1997). Multi-technology corporations: Why they have "distributed" rather than "distinctive core" competencies. *California Management Review* (Vol. 39).

Guellec, D. (1996). Knowledge, skills and growth: Some economic issues. *STI Review, 18*, 17–38.

Gulati, R., Nohria, N., & Zaheer, A. (2000). Strategic networks. *Strategic Management Journal, 21*, 203–215.

Hansen, M. (1999). The search-transfer problem: The role of weak ties in sharing knowledge across organization subunits. *Administrative Science Quarterly, 44*, 82–111.

Harary, F., Norman, R., & Cartwright, D. (1965). *Structural models.* New York: Wiley.

Kaufmann, A., & Tödtling, F. (2001). Science-industry interaction in the process of innovation: The importance of boundary-crossing between systems. *Research Policy, 30*, 791–804.

Lundvall, B. r i n g A ., & Johnson, B. (1994). The learning economy. *Journal of Industry Studies, 1*, 23–42.

Mansfield, E. (1995). Academic research underlying industrial innovations: Sources, characteristics, and financing. *The Review of Economics and Statistics, 77*, 55–65.

Meeus, M., Oerlemans, A. G., & Hage, J. (2001). Patterns of interactive learning in a high-tech region. *Organization Studies, 22*, 145–172.

Nelson, R. R., & Winter, S. (1982). *An evolutionary theory of economic change.* Cambridge, MA: Harvard University Press.

OECD (1992). *Technology and the economy: The key relationships.* Paris.

OECD (2000). Working group on innovation and technology policy; Science, technology and industry. Outlook 2000 Chapter VII: Innovation Networks.

Pavitt, K. (1984). Sectoral patterns of technical change: Towards a taxonomy and a theory. *Research Policy, 13*, 343–373.

Pavitt, K. (1987). The objectives of technology policy. *Science and Public Policy, 14*, 182–188.

Pavitt, K. (1998). The social shaping of the national science base. *Research Policy, 27*, 793–805.

Rosenberg, N. (1982). Inside the black box: Technology and economics. Cambridge: Cambridge University Press.

Schibany, A., & Schartinger, D. (2001). Interactions between universities and enterprises in Austria: An empirical analysis on the micro and sector. In: *Innovative Networks*. Paris: OECD.

Senker, J. (1995). Tacit knowledge and models of innovation. *Industrial and Corporate Change* (Vol. 4).

Spender, J. C. (1996). Competitive advantage from tacit knowledge? Unpacking the concept and its strategic implications. In: B. A. Edmondson (Ed.), *Organizational Learning and Competitive Advantage.* Newbury Park, CA: Sage.

Steenhuis, H., & De Bruijn, E. J. (2002). Technology transfer and learning. *Technology Analysis, Strategic Management* (Vol. 14).

Teece, D. (1986). Profitting from technological innovation: Implications for integration collaboration, licencing and public policy. *Research Policy, 15*, 285–305.

Tether, B. (2002). Who co-operates for innovation, and why an empirical analysis. *Research Policy, 31*, 947–967.

APPENDIX A: VARIABLE DEFINITION AND DESCRIPTIVE STATISTICS, WEIGHTED

Variable	N	Percent
Innovative performance	2006	100
Non-innovator	1163	58
Product/service innovation new to the firm	673	34
Product/service innovation new in the Danish context	117	6
Product/service innovation new to the world	54	3
ACAKNOW – Absolute absorptive capacity and strength of ties with knowledge institutions:	2006	100
High absolute absorptive capacity and moving toward strong ties	366	18
High absolute absorptive capacity and moving toward weak ties	453	23
Low absolute absorptive capacity and moving toward strong ties	371	18
Low absolute absorptive capacity and weak ties	816	41
ACAUNI – Absolute absorptive capacity and strength of ties with universities and technical support institutions only:	2006	100
High absolute absorptive capacity and moving toward strong ties	206	10
High absolute absorptive capacity and moving toward weak ties	614	31
Low absolute absorptive capacity and moving toward strong ties	185	9
Low absolute absorptive capacity and moving toward weak ties	1002	50
LINK – Closer relationship with vertical actors	2006	100
Both suppliers/customers	359	18
Either suppliers/customers	578	29
None	1069	53
SUBSID – Belonging to a subsidiary firm, binary	2006	100
Yes	1069	53

APPENDIX A   (*Continued*)

Variable	N	Percent
COMP – Experienced increased competition, binary	2006	100
Yes	690	34
SIZE – Size of the firm	2006	100
<25	568	28
25–50	762	38
>50	677	34
SECTOR – See Appendix B for classification	1983	100
Supplier dominated firms	248	13
Scale intensive firms	256	13
Specialised suppliers	143	7
Science-based firms	56	3
Crafts	337	16
Wholesale trade	348	17
Specialised services	330	17
Scale intensive services	87	4
ICT intensive services	197	10

APPENDIX B: SECTORAL CLASSIFICATION

Making use of the SPRU database, Pavitt (1984) developed a taxonomy of sectoral patterns of innovation based primarily on information about main knowledge inputs into the innovation processes, requirements of users and means of appropriation. These characteristics and variations are classified according to four sectors: *Supplier dominated*, two kinds of production intensive (*scale-intensive* and *specialized suppliers*) and *science-based*. Firms in the *supplier dominated* sector are traditionally characterized as manufacturing firms that are small in size and have a low technology orientation. Technological progress is therefore dependent on external actors such as suppliers of equipment and materials and, in some cases, large customers and government-financed research and extension services. Firms in the *scale-intensive* sector are low-technology oriented as well, but they do have some in-house development capability. Besides being large in size, those firms interact primarily with firms in the second part of the production-intensive sector – *specialized suppliers* – where the level of technology is higher and the firm size is smaller. For specialized suppliers, the pattern of interaction is more based on the user-producer relationship. In the *science-based* sector, the main sources of technology (which is quite high) are in-house development together with the underlying science developed in universities.

Since the empirical material covers the whole economy, Pavitt's taxonomy has to be extended. For this purpose, the categorization in Laursen and Foss (Ahuja, 2000) is applied. In their categorization, five additional sectors were added to Pavitt's taxonomy – ICT– (Information and Communication Technology) intensive services, wholesale trade, scale intensive services, specialized services and crafts. See Appendix C for a detailed assignment of all industries into the nine sectors.

APPENDIX C

The assignment of industries into nine sectoral categories

No.	Industry	Sector
1	Production etc. of meat and meat products	SCAI
2	Manufacture of dairy products	SCAI
3	Manufacture of other food products	SCAI
4	Manufacture of beverages	SCAI
5	Manufacture of tobacco products	SCAI
6	Manufacture of textiles and textile products	SDOM
7	Mfr. of wearing apparel; dressing etc. of fur	SDOM
8	Mfr. of leather and leather products	SDOM
9	Mfr. of wood and wood products	SDOM
10	Mfr. of pulp, paper and paper products	SDOM
11	Publishing of newspapers	SDOM
12	Publishing activities, excl. newspapers	SDOM
13	Printing activities etc.	SDOM
14	Mfr. of refined petroleum products etc.	SCAI
15	Mfr. of chemical raw materials	SCIB
16	Mfr. of paints, soap, cosmetics, etc.	SCAI
17	Mfr. of pharmaceuticals etc.	SCIB
18	Mfr. of plastics and synthetic rubber	SCAI
19	Mfr. of glass and ceramic goods etc.	SDOM
20	Mfr. of cement, bricks, concrete ind. etc.	SCAI
21	Mfr. of basic metals	SCAI
22	Mfr. Construction materials of metal etc.	SCAI

APPENDIX C   *(Continued)*

No.	Industry	Sector
23	Mfr. of hand tools, metal packaging etc.	SDOM
24	Mfr. of marine engines, compressors etc.	SPEC
25	Mfr. of other general purpose machinery	SPEC
26	Mfr. of agricultural and forestry machinery	SPEC
27	Mfr. of machinery for industries etc.	SPEC
28	Mfr. of domestic appliances n.e.c.	SCAI
29	Mfr. of office machinery and computers	SCIB
30	Mfr. of radio and communication equipment etc.	SCIB
31	Mfr. of medical and optical instruments etc.	SPEC
32	Building and repairing of ships and boats	SCAI
33	Mfr. of transport equipment excl. ships, etc.	SCAI
34	Mfr. of furniture	SDOM
35	Mfr. of toys, gold and silver articles etc.	SDOM
36	General contractors	CRAF
37	Bricklaying	CRAF
38	Install. of electrical wiring and fittings	CRAF
39	Plumbing	CRAF
40	Joinery installation	CRAF
41	Painting and glazing	CRAF
42	Other construction works	CRAF
43	Sale of motor vehicles, motorcycles etc.	SSER
44	Maintenance and repair of motor vehicles	CRAF
45	Service stations	SSER
46	Ws. of agricul. Raw materials, live animals	WTRA
47	Ws. of food, beverages and tobacco	WTRA
48	Ws. of household goods	WTRA
49	Ws. of wood and construction materials	WTRA
50	Ws. of other raw mat. and semimanufactures	WTRA
51	Ws. of machinery, equipment and supplies	WTRA
52	Commission trade and other wholesale trade	WTRA
53	Re. Sale of food in non-specialised stores	SCIS
54	Re. Sale of food in specialised stores	SSER
55	Department stores	SCIS
56	Retail sale of phar. goods, cosmetic art. etc.	SSER
57	Re. Sale of clothing, footwear etc.	SSER

APPENDIX C *(Continued)*

No.	Industry	Sector
58	Re. Sale of furniture, household appliances	SSER
59	Re. Sale in other specialised stores	SSER
60	Repair of personal and household goods	SSER
61	Hotels etc.	SSER
62	Restaurants etc.	SSER
63	Transport via railways and buses	SCIS
64	Taxi operation and coach services	SSER
65	Freight transport by road and via pipelines	SSER
66	Water transport	SCIS
67	Air transport	SCIS
68	Cargo handling, harbours etc.; travel agencies	SCIS
69	Monetary intermediation	ITIS
70	Other financial intermediation	ITIS
71	Insurance and pension funding	ITIS
72	Activities auxiliary to financial intermediates	ITIS
73	Letting of own property	SSER
74	Real estate agents etc.	SSER
75	Renting of machinery and equipment etc.	SSER
76	Computer and related activity	ITIS
77	Research and development	ITIS
78	Legal activities	ITIS
79	Accounting, book-keeping and auditing activities	ITIS
80	Consulting engineers, architects etc.	ITIS
81	Advertising	ITIS
82	Building-cleaning activities	SCIS
83	Other business services	ITIS

Note: SCAI = Scale intensive firms; SDOM = Supplier dominated firms; SCIB = Science based firms; SPEC = Specialised suppliers; CRAF = Crafts; WTRA = Whole sale trade; SSER = Specialised services; SCIS = Scale intensive services; ITIS = ICT intensive services.

PUBLIC-PRIVATE COLLABORATION ON KNOWLEDGE GENERATION AND APPLICATION IN NEW PRODUCT DEVELOPMENT PROJECTS

Ina Drejer and Birte Holst Jørgensen

ABSTRACT

This chapter focuses on public research as one possible external source of knowledge available for private companies seeking scientific support in relation to product development projects, and analyses inter-organizational relations between public research institutions and innovative firms including enabling conditions for effective knowledge creation in such public-private interactions. Two case studies of product development projects based on sensor technology are used to illuminate how innovation is carried out in such interactions. The chapter concludes with extracting crucial features for successful public-private collaboration on knowledge creation and innovation.

1. INTRODUCTION

Economic growth is increasingly connected with the generation and application of knowledge. This is illustrated by the emergence of a tightly knit relationship between science, technology and economic performance (OECD, 2000). Efforts

Product Innovation, Interactive Learning and Economic Performance
Research on Technological Innovation and Management Policy, Volume 8, 285–308
Copyright © 2004 by Elsevier Ltd.
ISSN: 0737-1071/doi:10.1016/S0737-1071(04)08012-6

to promote innovation and knowledge creation have thus gained a central position at the national as well as the international policy level (OECD, EU) for the last 10–15 years.

The public R&D system is an important part of the framework conditions for carrying out innovation and creating commercially applicable knowledge. Mansfield (1998) estimates[1] that 15% of the new products developed in the period 1986–1994 could not have been developed (at least, without a substantial delay) in the absence of recent academic research. Moreover, 8% of the new products were developed with substantial aid from recent academic research. Howells (2000) argues that a major reason for firms being increasingly reliant on external knowledge is an increase in the complexity of production. Product-related scientific problems are becoming more intractable, as is illustrated by the fact that the number of technologies applied is increasing in many consumer and business products. Many companies find that they do not possess the necessary scientific resources to cope with additional burdens and seek external support to overcome their own technical limitations.

This chapter focuses on public research as one possible external source of knowledge available for private companies seeking scientific support in product development projects. But a company cannot simply purchase research results as an input to a commercial innovation in a linear process of innovation (Mowery & Ziedonis, 1998). As illustrated by Kline and Rosenberg (1986) through their chain-linked model of innovation, the involvement of science and research is necessary throughout the entire process of research-based innovation. This requirement points towards the importance of inter-organizational relations between public research institutions and innovative firms in general, and enabling conditions for effective knowledge creation in public-private collaborations in particular.

Below, the process of knowledge creation in public-private collaborations is analysed applying two case studies of innovative product applications of sensor technology. Applying Kline and Rosenberg's chain linked model of innovation as the analytical framework the paper focuses particularly on the interplay between public research institutions and private firms in the process of transforming science to practical innovation. The paper concludes with identifying a range of crucial factors for a successful outcome of public-private knowledge collaborations.

This chapter offers a more specific analysis of the interaction between firms and knowledge institutions as it was analysed in Chapter 11 by Anker Lund Vinding – here we try to find out what kind of interaction that is characterising different stages of the innovation process. Compared to most of the other chapters in this volume, including Chapter 11, the cases refer to collaboration established from scratch while most of the cases in this book are about interactive learning within relationships that have been there for some time.

2. PUBLIC RESEARCH AND PRIVATE FIRM INNOVATION

Nelson and Winter (1982) discuss why public research exists as opposed to all R&D activities being carried out on market conditions by private firms. The heart of the R&D innovation problem is framed by the fact that "reasonable people will disagree about what technologies will be best when" (Nelson & Winter, 1982, p. 186). Therefore they argue for R&D primarily being conducted by competitive business firms who make "their own bets" rather than placing R&D under centralised, public control. But basic research is often taken out of the market system and conducted at universities, largely funded by government rather than profit-seeking firms. A major reason for this is that the information needed to guide basic research decision-making is not located in the operating parts of organizations that produce goods and services, but rather in the minds and experience of scientists doing basic research. Opposed to this is the large bulk of R&D directed at advancing industrial technology, which is dependent on information located in the production enterprises, and where good R&D decision making involves attending directly to economic benefits and costs (Nelson & Winter, 1982, pp. 391–392).

The boundaries between basic and applied research are not clear-cut though. Activities carried out at universities and public research institutes can be highly relevant for commercially oriented activities in private firms and vice versa. But knowledge production in universities and public research institutions does not automatically benefit industry. There will always be a knowledge "spill-over" from universities to industry through the research-based teaching of students who, after acquiring their degree, find employment in industry. But disregarding this and other indirect links between public research and industry, certain constraints may hamper private access to public research.

Cohen and Levinthal (1990) point to the importance of absorptive capacity for acquiring external knowledge, i.e. the ability of private firms to utilise public research results is dependent on the level of prior related knowledge in the firm. Prior related knowledge builds up the ability to recognise the value of new information, assimilate it, and apply it for commercial ends (Cohen & Levinthal, 1990, p. 128). This implies that if there is a large gap between the knowledge level in industry and the public research community, then the possibilities of a knowledge transfer from the public research community to private firms are limited.

But even if the necessary absorptive capacity exists in industry, other barriers may hamper the transfer of knowledge between public research and industry. Among such barriers are considerable differences in organizational set-up in public research institutions and private firms. In the traditional, linear description of the innovation process science and research appear only at the beginning of the process.

In reality matters are more complex, since it is often necessary to draw on research and the science base, and thus learn and create new knowledge, throughout all phases of the innovation process. Therefore formal collaboration between public research units and private firms may turn out to be a precondition for applying effectively public knowledge in industry-based innovation projects.

As argued by Lundvall (1992a), most forms of learning may be regarded as interactive processes. The economic structure and the institutional set-up form the framework for processes of interactive learning, which sometimes result in innovation. Cultural distance plays an important role, especially for learning and communication processes involving complex and ever-changing messages. Whereas Lundvall (1992b) discusses cultural space in relation to nations (as an argument for the importance of national systems of innovation), we argue here that cultural distances are also important in relation to different types of organizations. Public research institutions and private companies function under very different conditions and with different aims, which result in quite different cultures in the two types of organizations. Public researchers are primarily driven by an urge to expand knowledge, as well as an urge to make this knowledge expansion publicly known through scientific publications. Private companies on the other hand are driven by the urge to make a profit, which means that any new, commercially applicable knowledge that the firm develops or acquires should be kept within the company and far away from competitors. This can result in a clash between two cultures, which are guided by openness and closeness respectively. As an illustration of this Hendry et al. (2000) point to problems with confidentiality as well as a perceived lack of "business-like" approach from academics in firms' collaboration with universities.[2]

The nature and extent of a clash between public research and industry cultures may vary, as the institutional character of universities and the national research culture varies considerably between nations. Hendry et al. find that the "purist" view of the academic role is more outspoken in the U.K. than in the U.S. In a comparison with the U.K. and U.S. systems respectively, the Danish public research system, which is in focus here, may be characterised as being closest to the U.K. purist view on the role of academics. In Denmark, however, there are a number of intermediate institutions that facilitate the knowledge transfer from public research to industry, as for example the Authorised Technological Service Institutes. Recently, a strong policy focus on supporting an increased knowledge exchange between public research and industry has emerged. Universities with specific research aims are co-funded and co-chaired by industry. Industry engages in research training by employing industrial Ph.D. students, and public research institutes and industry engage in joint research projects. In a system of this type, knowledge institutions considering engaging in research projects with private companies are likely to be guided by the possibilities of achieving an academically relevant outcome from such an engagement. i.e. rather than settling with a pure knowledge transfer from the research institution to the firm, learning is sought on both sides.

The dynamics of public-private collaborations on knowledge creation and innovation are analysed within a Kline-Rosenberg setting below, as Kline and Rosenberg's chain-linked model of the innovation process stresses that links to knowledge and research are necessary throughout the entire innovation process. Furthermore, the model provides a framework for analysing the character of the links to knowledge and research in different stages of the innovation process.

3. PUBLIC-PRIVATE COLLABORATION IN A KLINE-ROSENBERG SETTING

Kline and Rosenberg (1986) presented their chain-linked model of the innovation process as a reaction to the linear model's description of the innovation process as smooth and well-behaved. The chain-linked model builds on a perception of the innovation process as complex, variegated and hard to measure. Whereas the linear model short-changes the importance of the process of learning through cumulated experience, the chain-linked model allows for learning through feedback processes as well as through links between the central innovation process and knowledge/research.

The chain-linked model describes the innovation process as a series of paths. The *first path* is the so-called central chain of innovation, which goes from design through development and production to marketing, but science is not part of this path. The *second path* consists of a series of feedback links, which iterate steps and send signals back from perceived market needs and users. The *third path* is the reason for the name "chain-linked model," as it links the central chain of innovation to science. The link to science lies alongside the development process rather than as an input in the beginning of the process. Further, the use of science occurs in several stages: when a problem is confronted in technical innovation, attention is first turned towards known science[3] and stored knowledge in serial stages. Only when all stages fail to supply the needed information is attention turned towards research. The *fourth path* consists of the rare direct link from research to innovation, which makes possible radical innovation (e.g. semiconductors, lasers etc.). The *fifth path* consists of a feedback from innovation to science (Kline & Rosenberg, 1986, pp. 289–293). Kline and Rosenberg limit these feedbacks to products of innovation, but in the present context we also include feedbacks related to testing of technologies, training of junior researchers and, not least, interactive learning that benefits not only the participating firm but also the research institution.

Kline and Rosenberg's model does not explicitly include the importance of the financial aspect of innovation. Kline and Rosenberg do however point to the rising development costs of new products, which involve an escalation of the financial risks associated with innovation and thus pose a threat to an organization's capacity to undertake innovation. The aspect of financing innovation cannot be ignored in an analysis of the process of innovation. We therefore add a *sixth and final path*, the financial one, which is crucial to the survival of the innovation process from the early stages right to the commercialisation of the product. Prior to the financial input to the project, a process of justification determines the extent to which the knowledge created is worthwhile for the organization and society (Nonaka, 1994, p. 26). The justification generally includes cost, profit, and the degree to which the knowledge/product can contribute to the development of the firm. Two perspectives may be highlighted: a short-term economic survival or a long-term, strategic relevance to the firm.

Figure 1 illustrates the flow paths of information and cooperation in the chain-linked model.

Kline and Rosenberg's model does not make any assumptions regarding whether knowledge and research inputs to the innovation process come from within or from outside the innovating organization. But the model illustrates that a close relation between the knowledge dimension and the central chain of innovation is necessary. Thus if the innovation project is carried out in a collaboration between a firm and an external knowledge institution, then the model underlines that the higher the degree of learning required for carrying out an innovation project, the higher is the need for a committed collaboration between the involved partners.

According to Kline and Rosenberg, the need to learn is by definition necessary in major innovation projects (*ibid.*, p. 297). This learning is associated with the unknown number of problems associated with product innovation projects, where each problem is only a step towards the final workable design. Kline and Rosenberg suggest that preplanning must be focused on goals, rough overall time schedules and budgets in more radical innovation projects. Further, care must be taken to reduce uncertainty throughout the innovation process, in particular in the early stages where the key problem is to stabilise product design and to organise a stable production and marketing around it. We argue, based on the two cases analysed below, that this does not only apply to radical innovation projects, but also to projects aimed at creating product innovations at a less radical scale, at least when these projects involve collaboration between public and private entities in a process of adjusting scientific research results to practical product applications. The challenge is thus to manage the uncertainty of the innovation process across institutional boundaries without losing the focus on the commercial and economic interests of the firm.

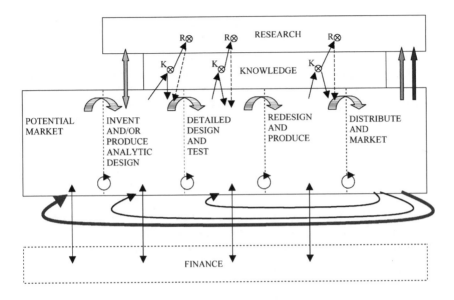

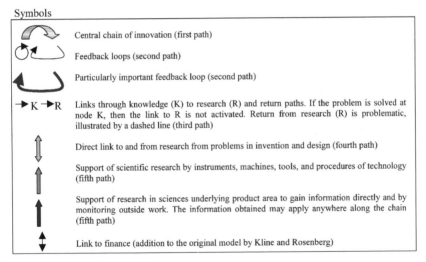

Fig. 1. Kline and Rosenberg's Chain-Linked Model. *Source:* Adapted from Kline and Rosenberg 1986 – the link to finance is an addition to the original model.

4. INTERACTIVE GENERATION AND APPLICATION OF KNOWLEDGE

Knowledge generation and application in a public-private interplay is a relatively unexplored phenomenon at the micro level. We have therefore selected two case studies (Yin, 1984, 1988) to investigate how product innovation is carried out in such interactions.

The selection of cases is guided by a technology foresight project focusing on sensor technologies conducted by Risø National Laboratory in collaboration with the Sensor Technology Centre A/S (Andersen et al., 2004). The cases represent two opposing perspectives on the knowledge creation process: a market-pull perspective and a technology-push perspective. The cases illustrate the creation and application of knowledge through direct public-private interaction. The discussion of whether the development of knowledge is technology driven or market driven can be dated back to such works as Schmookler (1962, 1966) and Schumpeter (1934), but was also taken up by Kline and Rosenberg who focused on the interaction between the market forces and the forces of progress at the technological and scientific frontiers. In the following we present two extreme cases where the market forces respectively the technology forces initiated the product development projects. These cases are as follows.

(1) A market-pull case: the development of a computer input device.
(2) A technology-push case: the development of a silicon microphone.

The first case concerns a product for the personal computer (PC) consumer market. The second concerns a device designed for the industrial market of hearing instruments and telecommunication. The cases thus represent different stages of the value chain.

5. THE MARKET-PULL CASE: THE DEVELOPMENT OF A COMPUTER DEVICE

5.1. Visions of a Potential Market

The idea behind the so-called "Free Pen" – a replacement of the traditional computer mouse – was contrived by an economist and marketing employee in the IT sector. The idea-owner envisaged a potential market for a device, which would reduce the physical problems experienced by many computer operators, such as shoulder, elbow, wrist and finger pains related to the design and the usage of the computer mouse. In 1997 the idea-owner concretised his idea in a research and development project and became a full-time entrepreneur. The ability of the idea-owner not only to realise the market need but also to give direction to the technological solution based on common sense or tacit knowledge was an important carrier of the process.

5.2. Invention and Design

The cordless pen was the guiding idea in the search for an appropriate technology for the new computer input device. The cordless feature was inspired by optics and laser elements in CD players. The search for relevant knowledge and the right technology was indeed a process of muddling through. A Danish firm producing CDs was contacted, as was a professor in Paris with expertise within the field. References from the University of Copenhagen finally led to the establishment of contacts with a national research laboratory and, in particular, a scientist working on optical lasers and speckles for measuring the rotation of ship propeller shafts. The technology had previously been patented, but had not been applied in a commercial product. Now the opportunity arose to apply the technology on a miniaturised scale in the computer input device.

5.3. Production and Marketing

The pen was released onto the market in 1999. The previous year was devoted to the development of the optical part, the laser detector and the processor (the ASIC).[4] Financial constraints, and pressure from public and private venture capitalists to present commercial results within the agreed project timeframe and budget, made market introduction urgent. It was the first time that miniaturised optical sensors were commercialised in a product, and minor technical problems continued to hamper market introduction. With 40,000 pens sold, repetitive complaints and lack of resources, the firm suspended its payments in the summer of 1999. Later the firm was reorganised with additional venture capital. The original firm fulfilled its royalty obligations, whereas the development of the second generation of the pen was carried out in a new firm. The justification used by the firm vis-à-vis external venture capitalists was based on two changes. First, with the development of the second-generation cordless, programmable and web-optimised computer pen the market potential was no longer restricted to the narrow, ergonomic-demanding welfare markets, but included new lifestyle customer segments on the global PC market comprising more than 300 million potential customers.

Secondly, the production was totally re-organised in order to reduce costs. An ambitious outsourcing strategy was made in which part of the R&D and the whole production was outsourced so that the core competencies of the firm was confined to the overall management process of the innovation and production, leaving room for marketing.

5.4. The Paths of the Chain-Linked Process

The *first path* of the process, the central chain of innovation from realisation of idea to market introduction, initially took two years. This was not the end of the process though, as feedbacks (*second path*) from the users after the first market introduction illustrated that the product was still suffering from serious problems. After the re-organization of the firm, feed-backs from each step of the innovation process were assured by a thorough monitoring of activities and products provided by subsidiaries and collaborating partners.

Long before the first market introduction was possible, the importance of the *third path* to knowledge and research had shown its importance though. As mentioned above, the link to knowledge and research was established through several channels, including relations with a national research laboratory. This collaboration was formalised through a research and development contract between the firm and the research laboratory. This contract was based on commercial conditions and reflected the necessary adjustment of the technology. It also covered such matters as assistance with additional patent applications related to the product, the identification of production companies with expertise within VCSEL lasers, and the specification of the requirements of a production contract with a large international firm. The effective public-private cooperation between the research laboratory and the firm was founded on trust, enthusiasm, and openness, and this persisted also during difficult stages of suspended payment. Three things contributed to this: first, patent regulation meant that the ownership of knowledge was never an area of dispute. On the contrary, the patent owner assisted the firm in applying for product-specific patents. Secondly, the formal contract of research was fulfilled, and royalty obligations were included in the reorganization of the firm. Thirdly, the outsourcing strategy and the ability of the firm to manage divergent economic institutions across cultural and national boundaries were imperative in gaining economies of scope in the project.

The result of the firm's interaction with the public research laboratory was first and foremost the development of a second-generation computer input device in which technological problems were solved. Three firm-owned patents within optics, magnetic and analog-2-digital conversion protected the knowledge created. Moreover, preparation of two patents relating to the second-generation pen is underway. Furthermore, on the basis of the previous results of the public/private collaboration, the firm succeeded in convincing a private venture capitalist co-funding the project that it was worthwhile to remain involved right through to the manufacture of a commercial and reliable product – that is, not to withdraw during the demanding final stage of this complex R&D project.

The *fourth path* in Kline and Rosenberg's model, i.e. the direct links from research to (radical) innovation was not activated, while the *fifth path* consisting of the support of scientific research by the outcome of the innovation process was represented by the further applications of the technological developments. From the perspective of the national research laboratory, the interaction with the firm was an opportunity both to test new technology and develop it into a commercial product. The challenge to adjust the technology to a much smaller scale than first imagined created new knowledge and competence within miniaturised optical sensors, an area that is expected to have further applications in, for example, energy flow meters and medical devices. This made the laboratory an attractive partner in other research and development projects.

We have added an additional link or path to the original model, namely the financial *sixth path*. In the case of the computer device the necessary financial backing for implementing the project was provided by private funds together with public venture capital (Vækstfonden), and at a later stage by private venture capital as well. In the Danish system it is fairly easy to get access to venture capital in the initial, developmental stage of a project, but much more difficult to raise additional capital to meet delays and problems. This illustrates the importance of an effective venture capital market – a market, that is to say, within which both the technological and commercial opportunities and risks of research-based projects can be appraised, despite the considerable uncertainty of such projects.

To summarise, the paths of the chain-linked innovation process of the cordless computer device illustrate the management challenge to bring a new product to the market within tight financial and time constraints. This task did not succeed in the first round due to a premature market introduction and the lack of a stable and cost-competitive production. However, justification of the re-organization of the firm, or in other words the quality of the product, was based on another and much larger market perspective together with an ambitious outsourcing strategy of production and part of the R&D activities based on commercial contracts. This justification was presented to and accepted by private venture capitalists, who financed the market introduction of the second-generation computer pen.

6. THE TECHNOLOGY-PUSH CASE: THE DEVELOPMENT OF A SILICON MICROPHONE

6.1. Visions of a Potential Market

The development of a silicon microphone for hearing instruments is the story of a technology searching for real-life problems/applications and a private firm looking to gear up its R&D activities. Silicon microphone technology has been known in academic circles for more than 20 years, but the development of a miniature silicon microphone for use in hearing instruments was an academic as well as a practical challenge. The innovation process was not initiated by a firm-based entrepreneur, as it is implicitly assumed in Kline and Rosenberg's model, rather the idea was conceived in the science community. The firm, which would house the innovation, thus became involved in the project through the request of the national research centre where the idea was founded.

The research centre was established in 1990 as an affiliation to the national technical university. It is a national research and development centre for advanced micro-technology in semiconductor materials. Within this field it is committed to educating scientists and engineers, conducting research on an internationally competitive level, and transferring new technologies to Danish industry through joint programmes.

The private firm engaged in the project is a medium-sized Danish-based international manufacturing firm. Based on the strength of highly specialised production of transducers and electromechanical components for hearing instruments, the firm has established a leading global position as a component supplier to the hearing aids industry.

A state Authorised Technological Service Institute with core competencies in the fields of electronics, software technology, optics, light acoustics, vibration and noise control was involved as an institutional bridge between science and industry. The Authorised Technological Service Institute viewed the joint project as a useful kick-starter of its competence-building within silicon technology.

6.2. Invention and Design

The preparation of a demonstration model of a silicon microphone began with an industrial Ph.D. project involving the private firm and the national research centre mentioned above. The Danish industrial Ph.D. scheme aims at supporting technological and economic development with public means by creating networks between industry and public research institutions. The industrial Ph.D. student is enrolled at a public research institution, while at the same time being employed in a firm, attached to a specific research project.

The development process was much more complicated and time consuming than had been foreseen. It was a challenge to identify a foundry to produce the wafers. Therefore, an additional research project on "High-Performance Interconnect and Stacking" (HISTACK) was initiated together with (among others) a Swiss firm/foundry.

During the project period necessary adjustments were made and ambitions were calibrated to the reality of the problem-solving process. The firm realised that it was involved in a long-term strategic development process driven by competitive pressures for innovation, but also by the innovation itself.

In 1999 a demonstration model of the world's smallest silicon microphone had been developed. Apart from preparing the demonstration model, the firm had improved its image as an innovative and strategic firm. Two product-specific patents were approved (involving the membrane and stacking), and together with the Authorised Technological Service Institute a patent was granted within packaging. The primary goal of the firm was now to make a detailed design and test and subsequently produce a silicon microphone in collaboration with wafer foundries. The justification, or the quality of the demonstration model, was based on its strategic relevance to the firm in terms of a new, promising technology for its conventional microphones. In addition, potential market volumes within the telecommunication sector and related economies of scale justified the costly and time-consuming research process. This was presented and accepted by the top management and board.

6.3. The Paths of the Chain-Linked Process

The *first path*, the central chain of innovation, consisted of a range of intertwined sub-paths, as the involved partners focused on different areas of the project. This implied that almost from the very beginning of the project a certain division of labour developed between the collaborating partners. The primary concern of the firm was to apply the technology in a commercial product. Packaging and testing was the focus of the Authorised Technological Service Institute, whereas the ASIC component was developed jointly by the firm and the Authorised Technological Service Institute. Wafer (chip) production and application was concentrated in the clean lab facilities at the research centre in joint collaboration with the firm.

During the period 1995–1999 a demonstration model of the world's smallest silicon microphone was developed. There was still a long way to go to finalise a prototype, not to mention to starting up the production of a silicon microphone though. Feedbacks from the market (*second path*) illustrated that the cost price in small quantities was still not competitive compared with that of the traditional microphone. This induced the firm to look for applications other than hearing instruments within telecommunications. But also earlier in the project it was evident that adjustments of expectations were inevitable. During the process it became clear that more attention should be directed towards the appraisal of technological and commercial opportunities and risks relating to the firm-specific part of the project.

The *third path*, the link from the central chain of innovation to knowledge and research was a formalised part of the project from the very beginning, as the research centre presented the project to the firm as a favourable way to explore the potential of alternative technologies in conventional miniature microphones. A major driving motive of the research centre was the opportunity to gain new knowledge through the process of putting the technology into a new use. These complementary interests contributed to laying the first bricks of a stable and strategic exchange of knowledge between the research centre and the firm. A governmental support scheme for strategic R&D collaborations, the Centre Contract Scheme,[5] was applied as the set-up for the collaboration. The Centre Contract Scheme co-funds strategic, commercially oriented R&D collaborations between (one or more) firms, (one or more) university departments and at least one Authorised Technological Service Institute with public means. The Authorised Technological Service Institute would act as an institutional bridge between science and industry.

In 1995 the Centre Contract was signed between the national research centre, the firm and the Authorised Technological Service Institute. As the contract in question was one of the first Centre Contracts to be drawn up, there was little guidance on the right form of cooperation and on how to manage intellectual property rights, on the publication and secrecy of knowledge, and on how to solve disputes. Smooth interaction among the three partners – the firm, the research laboratory and the Authorised Technological Service Institute – required clarification of divergent interests and goals from the very beginning. The negotiation process and the drawing up of a legal document in collaboration with lawyers were thus cumbersome but necessary processes. These initial efforts resulted in a model contract for subsequent Centre Contracts. The national research centre had an interest in engaging in applied research together with the front-runners of Danish industry. It was also focused on scientific publication of research results and educating people at the level of M.Sc. and Ph.D. The firm was interested in focusing its R&D activities and developing a new, cheap and reliable component using new technology for hearing instruments. The Authorised Technological Service

Institute wished to adopt the technological knowledge. More specifically, it wanted to develop test and packaging services to industry.

The Centre Contract Scheme, which was introduced at precisely the right time for the project, played an important role in facilitating the collaboration. The financial eligibility rules, which excluded direct support to firms, induced the partners to constantly focus on the firm's interests in the project. On the other hand it remains a constant dilemma how to balance the striving for long-term competence building against short-term commercial output.

Despite the importance of the Centre Contract Scheme as a formal coordination device, partners also felt that they needed informal coordination. In the initial phase individual "fireballs" and personal relations were central drivers of cooperation. In the subsequent phases, with new participants, the cooperation was sustained by team-building. In the clean room laboratory cooperation-related resources were allocated to project management and team-building. It was acknowledged that the challenge in joint collaboration projects is to create a common platform and shared values, and that this is particularly so in projects where people answer to various environments, the joint project and their hinterland.

Regarding the *fourth path*, the direct link from research to innovation, one could argue that this exists in the present case, as a research laboratory initiated the process. The link from research to innovation observed in the present case is not of the type envisaged by Kline and Rosenberg though, as this link involves a radical innovation. As was the case with the development of the computer devise, the fourth path is thus not active.

The *fifth path*, the support of scientific research by the outcome of the innovation process, resulted in physical as well as academic outcomes. The physical outcome consisted of an establishment of joint clean-lab facilities at the research centre, which had the opportunity of providing, with other industrial partners, a critical mass of research activity related to this technology. Silicon technology is a mass production technology with high start-up investment costs. New organizational forms, such as joint private-public project groups or firm consortia, are feasible ways to share the investment costs of laboratory facilities and to create the necessary critical mass of people engaged in pre-competitive R&D activities.

One academic outcome was the research centre's presentation of results at academic conferences as well as publications in international scientific journals. The collaboration with the firm and the problem-orientated research contributed to position the research centre at the forefront of international research in silicon technology and the centre filed a patent application based on the technology. More important, the research centre trained a number of M.Sc.s and Ph.D.s working with the development and application of the technology. Front-runners of domestic and international industry subsequently employed some of these graduates and researchers.

The *final path* consists of the financing of the project. Public financial support to the cooperative endeavour amounted to 20 million DKr for four years. This was distributed as co-financing for activities undertaken by the Authorised Technological Service Institute and the research centre. In addition the firm was guaranteed 35% risk coverage of its project investment through a loan of approximately four million DKr from the public venture capital fund (Vækstfonden). The additional research project on "High-Performance Interconnect and Stacking" (HISTACK) was co-funded by the EU programme ESPRIT. The 50% co-financing of costs in the EU-project were highly welcome to the firm because the project turned out to be more strategic than initially envisaged.

To summarise, the paths of the silicon microphone innovation demonstrate the uncertainty and complexity of the innovation process. The conceptual stage is organised in a committed collaboration between three different actors with each their interests and stakes in the project. This assures maximum openness to new sources of information and creates a critical mass of knowledge around a new technology. On the other hand, the organizational arrangement constantly faces the dilemma to balance the short-term economic interests and the long-term competence building, in particular in a situation where the financing guidelines of the Centre Contract prevent firms to get direct access to public research funds.

7. COMPARING THE TWO CASES

Table 1 extracts the characteristics of the individual phases of the innovation process in the two cases.

As mentioned earlier, the two cases represent extremes with regards to the dominance of market-pull and technology-push respectively especially in the initiation phase. The inherently close contact with the perceived market need in the market-pull case is illustrated by the fact that the process from initial idea and vision of a market, through the design and production phases to the marketing phase, was covered in a two-year period. The project did not end here though, as feedbacks from the market revealed crucial problems with the functionality of the product.

The technology-push case, which was driven by a technological curiosity first and the vision of a potential market second, had a longer duration, and the four-year period analyzed only resulted in a demonstration model of a possible final product. Both projects serve to illustrate some important features of the innovation process though, in particular in relation to the third path of the innovation process,

Table 1. Main Features of the Innovation Path.

	Market-Pull Case	Technology-Push Case
1st path: Central chain of innovation comprising 5 steps: potential market, analytic design, detailed design and test, redesign and produce, and distribute and market	The case covers all steps of the innovation process. 2 years of duration. After re-organisation, an ambitious outsourcing strategy aiming at economies of scope.	The case only covers the early stages of the innovation process until detailed design and testing. 4 years of duration.
2nd path: Feedback links between steps, in particular from market	Premature market introduction and critical feedback from consumers.	Indirect feedback from market – new technology not yet cost competitive.
3rd path: Linkage between innovation process and science	Commercial R&D contract between laboratory and firm, but collaboration also based on trust. Analytical design founded on the combination of existing technology and the accumulated knowledge of a national laboratory. Extended in a joint research process adjusting knowledge to application whereby new knowledge of both partners was created.	Centre Contract between firm, university and Approved Technological Service Institute. Analytical design founded on the accumulated knowledge of the university and extended in a joint research process adding to the knowledge of all partners.
4th path: Radical innovation from science	Not activated.	Not activated.
5th path: Feedback from innovation to science	Test of technology in a commercial product, totally different in size from the original one.	Joint research laboratory facilities with industrial and university partners. Problem-oriented research at the forefront of international research. Training of M.Sc. and Ph.D.s in silicon technology.
6th path: Financial input and justification	Public and private venture funds in the first phase. Justification of project based on immediate potential market volume and outsourcing strategy reducing production cost attracted further private venture funds.	Public venture funds and private co-financing to match the public research funds channelled through the Centre Contract. EU research funds for both private and public partners. Justification of project based on its strategic relevance to the firm assured continued financial support from top management.
Output	Commercial product to the consumer market	Demonstrator of a microphone for the hearing aids and telecommunication market.

the linkage between practical innovative activities and science, which is here exemplified by linkages between two types of organizations representing each of the two spheres: innovative firms and public research institutions respectively. In the following section we will discuss the important features of this path further.

8. IMPORTANT FEATURES OF PUBLIC-PRIVATE COLLABORATION ON KNOWLEDGE CREATION

Public-private research collaboration on product development builds on accumulated knowledge and adds to that knowledge in joint research processes. A successful project relies on more than a one-way transfer of knowledge from the research institution to the firm. It is a dynamic creation and application of knowledge in interplay between research and practical design. The two cases analysed serve to illustrate the point, raised by Kline and Rosenberg, that a close connection to science throughout the entire innovation process is a precondition for research-based innovation: research cannot be "delivered" as a simple input in the initial phase.

The following lessons can be drawn about the governance of public-private collaborations.

- *Room for flexibility and adaptation in research projects.* Kline and Rosenberg characterise the process of innovation as an exercise in the management and reduction of uncertainty. Owing to the associated uncertainty, a research-based innovation process is characterised throughout by a considerable degree of muddling through where the solving of technological problems is concerned. Thus there is a need for patience and flexibility in the collaboration as well as access to other knowledge sources where necessary. This is illustrated by the case of the silicon microphone. There, technical problems called for the formulation of an additional project capable of contributing – technologically as well as financially – to the original project; and thus expectations had to be adjusted along the way. In the case of the cordless pen, better opportunities for prolongation and additional funds would probably have prevented premature market release.
- *Dynamic creation and application of knowledge.* Public-private research collaboration builds on accumulated knowledge and adds to that knowledge in joint research processes, also in less radical innovation processes. A successful project relies on more than a one-way transfer of knowledge from the research institution to the firm. Such a project will also include competence-enhancing

elements for the research institution. These elements provide an intellectual incentive for the researcher's engagement and justify the involvement of publicly funded bodies in commercially orientated collaborative projects. In both case studies the public research institutions benefited from a scientifically relevant outcome of the project – for example, from the adjustment of technology to real-life problems, from competence building in testing and technological services, or from the training of graduate students and junior researchers. For the Kline and Rosenberg chain linked model this implies that paths three to five tend to merge in public-private research collaborations.

- *The management of divergent interests and perspectives*. The firm and the research institution will in most cases have opposing priorities regarding the outcomes of the project. The research institutions will often have the building of long-term competencies and the testing of theoretical findings as their first priority, while the firms' primary interest is the creation of a marketable, and economically viable, product (long-term competence building being a second priority). These differences should be made clear from the beginning, and the contract between the firm and the research institution should take the range of desired outcomes into account in order to minimise the risk of unmet expectations. This calls for both formal agreements and committed project management to make sure that potential conflicts over outcome are dealt with throughout the project.
- *Drawing up formal agreements and contracts*. In view of the economic interests of the firm and public research institution, a clear contract covering the obligations of each project partner, intellectual property rights, royalties and so on has to be drawn up. Also the project leadership must be clear, and the firm as well as the research institution must have the proper institutional set-up, i.e. one allowing a certain degree of autonomy for the project group. In both cases studied, the initial efforts to draw up formal agreements regarding the collaboration turned out to be a worthwhile investment. The contracts set out in clear terms the aims of the projects, property rights, royalties etc. However, since there is fundamental uncertainty regarding technology and future markets contracts will always be incomplete. This is why informal institutions and activities, such as team-building, project management, trust and openness in the collaboration are fundamental for the success of the collaboration.
- *Justification of the project/product* vis-à-vis the economic stakeholders is an absolutely necessary task throughout the innovation process as a successful innovation requires the coupling of the technical and economic challenges. The two cases illustrate different products, one ready brought to the market and another still in the design and test stage. The second generation of the cordless computer device is justified vis-à-vis private venture capitalists that there is

market volume and that the outsourcing strategy will reduce production costs. For the silicon microphone the justification vis-à-vis the top management and the board is based on the strategic interests of the firm to move to a radically improved product design combined with new markets.

- *Institutional transformations.* Public-private collaborations are embedded in the dynamics and complexities of the innovation system, and in this system the participating institutions constitute new roles and thereby transcend their traditional boundaries as knowledge user or knowledge producer. Apart from introducing graduates to the industry, the university research centre in the case of the silicon microphone was actively building a technological interface between research and industry. The research centre's constant search for technical solutions to real-life problems also benefited its own research. The Authorised Technological Service Institute built competencies in technological services and conducted leading-edge research within important areas of the technology. It also took out patents. The national research laboratory provided its research knowledge, but it also went a step further in the technological service. As happened in the case of the university research centre, the application of technology to real-life problems contributed to the excellence of the research. Likewise the Authorised Technological Service Institute sold its knowledge and acted as a technological service intermediary between research and industry. The involvement of firms in public-private collaboration also gives direction to the problem-solving process. The project management of the silicon microphone project was shared between the firm and the Authorised Technological Service Institute, while in the case of the cordless pen project it was the firm that remained in charge of the coordination. Both cases gave rise to new organizational forms and processes. In the microphone case joint clean room facilities were shared with other firms, all of which had an interest in building a critical mass in the pre-competitive stages of the silicon technology. An outsourcing strategy was employed in the cordless pen case, and as a result all processes except the core competencies of the firm were externalised.
- *Public support schemes and interventions.* The mechanisms created by the government to facilitate public-private collaborations on knowledge creation are important both in terms of the funding possibilities they offer, and in terms of the organizational framework they provide. Public venture capital played an important role in the realisation of both projects. It was not strictly dependent on the firms' collaboration with public research institutions, although the participation of the research institutions might have made it easier for the firms to document the high-tech innovative potential in the projects to the satisfaction of the relevant venture capitalists. In the case of the cordless pen, governmental facilitation of the public-private collaboration played a minor

role. The silicon microphone, on the other hand, relied heavily on government programmes.

Through his own efforts, the individual who had the original idea for the cordless pen eventually found a suitable research group. Several factors were then required to make the project a success. It was necessary to build on the enthusiasm of the entrepreneur. Also necessary were: clear agreements on such matters as property rights; the openness of the research institution, including a willingness to engage in a de facto integrated R&D department with the firm; and the availability of the proper funding mechanisms.[6]

With the silicon microphone, the market opportunity was not as clearly envisaged at the outset of the project as it was in the case of the cordless pen. In this case the initiative came from the public research institution, and a longer trial-and-error period, during which the possibility of applying a known technology in a new context was scrutinised, was inevitable. Therefore a supporting institutional set-up for carrying out the development project was necessary. Here the governmental Centre Contract Scheme, combined with the activities of an industrial Ph.D. acting as the initiator of the project, provided the necessary framework. Apart from making sure that the necessary formal agreements were drawn up, the Centre Contract guaranteed the inclusion of a privately orientated, but publicly research-based Authorised Technological Service Institute. The Centre Contract also co-funded the engagement of the Authorised Technological Service Institute and the research institution with public money. The technological complexity and the search for a proper market for the technology meant that much more support for the ongoing project was required than was the case with the cordless pen.

The two cases highlight the fact that the need for governmental facilitation of public-private research collaborations depends on the type of project at issue. We have presented two extreme cases, one driven by market-pull and the other driven by technology-push. Our conclusions therefore pertain to extremes. It goes without saying that in-between these extremes suitably modified conclusions can and should be drawn.

9. CONCLUSIONS

The present paper has analysed public-private research collaborations in product development projects. It has examined, in particular, certain mechanisms, within these collaborations, that facilitate the exchange and application of knowledge.

Innovation was conceived of here as a complex process of the kind presented by Kline and Rosenberg in their chain-linked model. Kline and Rosenberg's model of the innovation process illustrates the importance of a linkage between the central chain of innovation and the science and research dimension. In the present context we have studied this linkage in two cases of formal collaboration between the public science community and private firms hosting the innovation. This thus adds a further dimension to the model, in which not only radical innovations but also incremental ones are characterised by dynamic knowledge creation among the participating organizations. Formal collaboration on innovation between public research institutions and private firms also implies that the path from science to innovation and the path where the outcome of innovation supports science tend to merge as the interaction between science and innovation is two-way throughout the process – it is a process of interactive learning between the collaborating partners.

However, the cultural differences between public research institutions and private firms have to be taken into account. The confrontation of two very different types of organizations calls for mechanisms that help the parties overcome barriers posed by their different backgrounds. Such mechanisms are diverse but interrelated. They include: simple information channels that ensure firms know what they can gain from involvement with public research institutions and how these institutions can be approached; guidelines for organising collaborative projects; formal programmes containing supporting structures and public co-funding as a means to drive joint projects forward; programmes that aim to reduce barriers relating to the funding of projects with an uncertain outcome; and methods of overcoming barriers arising from the clash between public and private entities, with special regard for such matters as organization, motivation and so on.

The importance of guidelines for the organization of projects involving private firms and public research institutions cannot be ignored. A successful project requires differences in intended outcome to be dealt with from the outset and throughout the project. Conditions regarding issues such as project management, the division of labour and responsibilities and intellectual property rights must also be clarified in the collaboration agreement. The Danish Governmental Centre Contract Scheme, where a "model contract" was developed in relation to the silicon microphone project, is an example of a project giving high priority to formal agreements. To cope with the problem that such contracts never can cover all possible future events and outcomes, there is an important role to play for informal aspects of project management including trust and team-building.

Formal programmes supporting public-private research collaboration projects are primarily called for in cases in which there is a high degree of market uncertainty, where the technology is driving the projects. These projects will often be larger and more exploratory than those in which a perceived market need is the driving force and the technological search can, accordingly, be much more focused.[7]

The creation of knowledge across institutional boundaries changes the ways in which the involved parties interact. Traditional boundaries are transcended and new roles are constituted – to the point where it does not matter for the knowledge creation process whether the partner is a university, a national research laboratory, an Approved Technological Service Institute or a private firm. New institutional boundaries are drawn up, and in the long run these may challenge the way public funds are distributed among the collaborating institutions.

Both market-pull and technology-push projects depend on an effective venture-capital market, which might include both public and private inputs. In market-pull projects there is a need to develop the capital provider's competence to assess the technological and economic potential and risk. The same can be said for the technology-push projects, but in these cases it might also be appropriate to consider the interplay between the venture capital system and the public funds provided through the different collaboration support programmes.

To conclude, the analysis we have offered points towards a need for a range of mechanisms for promoting public-private collaboration on commercialising knowledge through new product development. Such mechanisms must take the differing needs of different types of development project into consideration. They must include basic guidelines and information channels as well as more formalised programme structures. The watchwords, where successful public-private research collaboration is concerned, are flexibility, openness and clarity about obligations and rights. Formal contracts may be crucial when it comes to starting up new relationships between parties with different backgrounds but a key to success is that they gradually find support in informal relationships of trust and mutual understanding.

NOTES

1. Based on a sample of 77 major firms.
2. Based on interviews with 59 manufacturing SMEs in the U.K. and USA concerned with bringing new products to the market. The observations mentioned here were more specifically related to firms' funding connections with universities.
3. According to Kline and Rosenberg science consists of two main components that affect innovation: (i) the current totality of stored human knowledge about nature; and (ii) the process by which that knowledge is corrected and added to. Research is described as the process that adds to and corrects science.
4. Applied Scientific Integrated Circuit.
5. The Centre Contract Scheme has later been replaced with the Innovation Consortium Scheme which shares the same basic aim of promoting collaboration between firms, the research community and technological service providers.

6. Eventually the success turned out to be short-lived: in early 2004 the firm behind the computer pen filed for bankruptcy because the pen never caught on with consumers.

7. The case of the computer pen illustrates that market driven product development projects are not guaranteed to become a market success – market as well as technological uncertainty is always prevalent to some degree.

REFERENCES

Andersen, P. D., Jørgensen, B. H., Lading, L., & Rasmussen, B. (2004). Sensor foresight – Technology and market. *Technovation, 24,* 311–320.

Cohen, W. M., & Levinthal, D. A. (1990). Absorptive capacity: A new perspective of learning and innovation. *Administrative Science Quarterly, 35,* 128–152.

Hendry, C., Brown, J., & Delfillippi, R. (2000). Understanding relationships between universities and SMEs in emerging high technology industries: The case of opto-electronics. *International Journal of Innovation Management, 4,* 51–75.

Howells, J. (2000). Research and technology outsourcing and systems of innovation. In: J. S. Metcalfe & I. Miles (Eds), *Innovation Systems in the Service Economy. Measurement and Case Study Analysis* (pp. 271–295). Dordrecht: Kluwer.

Kline, S. J., & Rosenberg, N. (1986). An overview of innovation. In: R. Landau & N. Rosenberg (Eds), *The Positive Sum Strategy* (pp. 275–305). Washington, DC: National Academy Press.

Lundvall, B. Å. (1992a). Introduction. In: B. Å. Lundvall (Ed.), *National Systems of Innovation: Towards a Theory of Innovation and Interactive Learning* (pp. 1–19). London: Pinter.

Lundvall, B. Å. (1992b). User-producer relationships, national systems of innovation and internationalisation. In: B. Å. Lundvall (Ed.), *National Systems of Innovation: Towards a Theory of Innovation and Interactive Learning* (pp. 45–67). London: Pinter.

Mansfield, E. (1998). Academic research and industrial innovation: An update of empirical findings. *Research Policy, 26,* 773–776.

Mowery, D. C., & Ziedonis, A. A. (1998). Market failure or market magic? Structural change in the U.S. national innovation system. *STI Review, 22,* 101–136.

Nelson, R., & Winter, S. (1982). *An evolutionary theory of economic change.* Cambridge, MA: Harvard University Press.

Nonaka, I. (1994). A dynamic theory of organizational knowledge creation. *Organization Science, 5,* 14–37.

OECD (2000). *A new economy? The changing role of innovation and information technology in growth.* Paris: OECD.

Schmookler, J. (1962). Economic sources of inventive activity. *Journal of Economic History* (March), 1–20.

Schmookler, J. (1966). *Invention and economic growth.* Cambridge, MA: Harvard University Press.

Schumpeter, J. A. (1934). *The theory of economic development: An inquiry into profits, capital, credit, interests and the business cycle.* Cambridge, MA: Harvard University Press.

Yin, R. K. (1984). *Case study research.* Beverly Hills, CA: Sage.

Yin, R. K. (1988). *Designing and doing case studies.* Beverly Hills, CA: Sage.

INTER- AND INTRAORGANIZATIONAL LEARNING PROCESSES IN THE INTERACTION BETWEEN FIRMS AND PATENT OFFICES

Jesper L. Christensen

ABSTRACT

This chapter focuses upon two types of interaction. One is the interaction between departments within the Danish Trademark and Patent Office (DKPTO). Additionally, the interaction between the DKPTO and firms is analysed. The chapter discusses in what ways an institution like a national patent office is important for product innovation, not just by providing an appropriability system for product innovations in firms, but additionally by improving the long-run capabilities of both firms and the DKPTO itself. The research builds upon interviews in the DKPTO, case stories from firms and of patent granting procedures.

With respect to internal competencies, it is found that no efforts were carried out to create environments for learning between the departments in line with the "learning organizations" described in earlier chapters. However, taking the tasks of the departments into account, the need for such efforts was not obvious. Links to external organizations are not only confined to industrial

Product Innovation, Interactive Learning and Economic Performance
Research on Technological Innovation and Management Policy, Volume 8, 309–340
Copyright © 2004 by Elsevier Ltd.
All rights of reproduction in any form reserved
ISSN: 0737-1071/doi:10.1016/S0737-1071(04)08013-8

firms. Many firms, especially the large firms, would not mind if the tasks of the national patent system were moved to the EPO-level. On the other hand, in particular, small, new firms may feel more confident with a national patent office.

1. INTRODUCTION

From previous chapters, in particular Chapter 5, it is clear that innovation studies have increasingly focused on the role of knowledge generation in the economy. Generally, the emphasis has been on the knowledge generated in the interaction between firms and various partners such as suppliers, customers, consultants, knowledge institutions, and universities typically both producing and diffusing knowledge. Other business services like institutes for test, control, certification etc. are mainly seen as producing standardised services without much interaction and learning taking place. Several of the chapters in this volume, in particular those in this section of the book, deal with interaction between firms and knowledge institutions. Likewise, this chapter discusses this type of interaction, but in addition the intra-organizational interaction between departments is in focus.

This chapter highlights an aspect of this interaction, which is often overlooked and scarcely researched. It sets out to investigate whether the presumption of little learning and competence build-up in what appears to be standardised services is actually true. It takes as point of departure the case of granting a patent, or providing services in relation to the patenting. It focuses upon two types of interaction. One is the interaction between departments within the Danish Trademark and Patent Office (DKPTO). Additionally, the interaction between the DKPTO and firms is analysed. The chapter discusses if the role of an institution such as the national patent office is important for product innovation, not just by providing an appropriability system for product innovations in firms, but also by improving the long-run capabilities of both firms and the DKPTO. The research builds upon interviews in the DKPTO, case stories from firms patent granting procedures. Thus, it is not examining the content of the patent, the knowledge dissemination stemming from disclosure of information from the patent descriptions, or the characteristics of the applicant firm (three issues often treated in studies on innovation and patents). Rather this study investigates the competence building and knowledge diffusion resulting from both the processing of the patent application and the provided services related to patenting.[1]

In line with several of the chapters in this volume, the chapter specifies the learning processes involved. The internal competencies resulting from processing applications are likely to affect other activities within the DKPTO such as business services, thus enhancing other departments' abilities to provide services. Thus, it may be assumed that even if the process of handling patent application does not directly influence innovation the competencies built may still benefit the overall innovation level in the economy.

Implications of the results are relevant for two different issues. It is assessed if the internal organization of the patenting processing is conducive for knowledge exchange and innovation. On a systemic level the results may have implications for the organization of the patent system, specifically whether a *national* patent office is necessary for national competence-building.

Section 2 discusses the theoretical basis for the research question. The section addresses the issue of the learning effects from the intra- and inter-organizational interaction much in line with the considerations in Chapter 2 by Lundvall. Subsequently, in Section 3, it is showed more specifically what may be learned in the interaction. This is done by way of explaining the procedures and interactions in connection with a patent application. The purpose of this section is to show at what stages learning and competence building may take place, while also exploring the intra-organizational learning processes that may produce learning effects from patent examiners to other departments of the DKPTO. Then, Section 4 continues on this track, showing not only where learning between the DKPTO and other organizations may take place, but also what is learnt in the interaction. This is done by way of seven illustrative case studies. The concluding section summarises the findings, and points to perspectives based on the research findings.[2]

2. LEARNING OUTCOMES FROM THE INTERACTION

2.1. How is Knowledge Transmitted?

With the case of the DKPTO in mind, this section highlights elements in the theory of innovation and knowledge diffusion, which may support the research in this chapter. The transmission and transformation of knowledge was already discussed thoroughly in previous chapters, especially Chapter 2. Here the intra-organizational aspects of knowledge are emphasized. As pointed out in Lundvall and Vinding's Chapter (5) on user-producer interaction in this volume, exchange of information and knowledge is an important feature of product innovation. Efficient information exchange often requires common channels and codes of information. Once established through interactive learning processes there is an incentive to keep relationships because of the costs involved in getting to know how to communicate. The establishment and maintenance of relationships between users of business services, like the process of producing the final patent application, and producers of these services is facilitated by common social and cultural background.

The media and the way knowledge is transferred may also differ according to the absorptive capacity of the recipient (Cohen & Levinthal, 1989). In the case of patents, there can be two kinds of the recipients. First, the patent examiner may need a broad and in some areas also a deep technological knowledge in order to undertake efficient screening of potential infringements of other patents. In this screening the examiner also needs knowledge on what are the most efficient search methods. Second, the other type can be other firms/entrepreneurs who are interested in the patent description. In order to use the knowledge from such descriptions the entrepreneur needs an absorptive capacity enabling him/her not only to understand the principles of the technology embodied in the patent and to find the relevant patent description in the first place. The entrepreneur also needs an element of creativity, as he must be able to apply this technology to other fields of use not covered by the patent or to see perspectives in the technology in terms of combining the technology with other existing technologies.

2.2. Storing and Transforming Knowledge – Organizational Learning and Cross-Departmental Knowledge Flows

When knowledge from the innovation process is transformed into codified knowledge, e.g. by way of a patent description, it becomes easier for the market to estimate the value of such intangible assets. The transformation of tacit knowledge to codified knowledge is, however, by no means a simple process, and is often not only difficult and costly but also possible only up to a limit.

The process involves for the transmitter to be conscious about the implicit habits, norms, routines rooted in the problem solving practises of the individual or team. The next step also involves describing that knowledge in a language, which is understandable to the recipient. The external recipient thus puts a constraint on the way the transmitter is to explain the tacit knowledge in a codified form. This constraint may be common terms of expression and ways of standardising certain explanations.

In recent years it has become common practise to organize work in a manner conducive for learning effects. This has been explicitly referred to in many books, articles and the business press as "the learning organization" (Argyris, 1992; Argyris & Schon, 1978). By gearing the organization to improve the accumulation of knowledge from daily activities, the learning effects are likely to increase. This is basically what Stiglitz (1987) defines as "learning-to-learn." Pedler et al. (1989)

define learning organizations as "an organization that facilitates the learning of all its members and continually transforms itself." Moreover, Pedler proposes that such an entity.

- Has a climate in which individual members are encouraged to learn and to develop their full potential.
- Extends this learning culture to include customers, suppliers and other significant stakeholders.
- Makes human resource development strategy central to business policy.
- Continually undergoes a process of organizational transformation.

Indeed, by way of evaluations, the members of the organization in question are also encouraged to reflect on the learning processes themselves. Within learning theories and in earlier chapters in this volume, this has been called "double-loop learning." This is a difficult task that requires agents to accurately identify what has been learnt and how. In case the knowledge accumulated could be characterised as tacit knowledge it becomes even more difficult to assess such learning processes effectively. This argument relates strongly to practically all evaluations as well as the issue for this current study: in virtually all evaluations the by-product, unintended learning effects are rarely valued often because there are no good measurements of them. The hypothesis developed in Section 1 on the possible knowledge generating/diffusion effects of daily activities of the DKPTO is similarly difficult to test as the effects are likely to be more or less hidden and implicit, even to the recipients. For example, the patent examiners may unintentionally transfer knowledge to other parts of the organization, not on the content of specific patents, but perhaps knowledge on general technological development. Likewise, they may be able to identify accurately what are the problems in the applications received. Where are the deficiencies in the ability of customers to put together an application? This knowledge may be transferred deliberately, but also informally through daily interaction, with the sales and marketing department, which may then try to educate customers on these points.

Intra-organizational learning may be spurred by procedural skills enabling members of the department/group to apply and use knowledge in different settings than where it was generated. Among several contributors to learning theories, it has been argued strongly that productive learning should basically be seen as situated learning, that is learning should be viewed as contextual and only useful if used in action and in a setting where the learning has been produced (Lave, 1991). We would argue that it is indeed a challenge for organizations to transform and diffuse knowledge produced within one unit to other units in a productive manner, but also that this is often an important part of organizational learning, and in this case, indirectly important for the product innovations of firms.

The other prerequisite for intra-organizational learning we would emphasize is co-ordination. The co-ordination issue is linked to the distinction between individual and collective learning. Even if organizational learning may go through individuals, the knowledge of an organization is more than the sum of the knowledge of its individuals. The organization may have shared norms and values, which preserve certain behaviours and routines. The routines, involving rules, procedures, conventions, cultures and strategies, make up the memory of the organization (Cohendet & Llerena, 2001).

The build up of routines is largely the outcome of a gradual learning process. This learning is based upon which solutions the organization successfully used for problem solving in the past. Identification of a problem and a strategy for its solution consequently involves remembering and retrieving solutions that previously were adequate for a problem resembling the one in question. A complementary aspect of this process is to remember solutions, which in the past failed to solve the problem. In other words, it is an important part of learning to forget unproductive routines and be able to rule out solutions likely to fail. In this way routines are important in the economising of information processing. Naturally it varies widely with the situation what should be left out and what deserves focussing. Therefore, routines are indeed context-dependent. Likewise, the relevant sum of capabilities is dependent upon the sum of knowledge of the members of the organization, but it varies what is relevant according to the situation, which points to the necessity of interaction between members of the organization. Only in this way is the individual knowledge of the members activated, as well as the shared meanings and languages developed in the organization.

The above discussion implies that firms may have unique ways of learning, which results in what is called "firm-specific capabilities" (Teece et al., 1990), "core competencies" (Prahalad & Hamel, 1990), and "firm specific competencies" (Pavitt, 1991).

Basically co-ordination and stimulation of intra-organizational knowledge flows may also be pursued differently according to what kind of knowledge is diffused. It follows from the discussion of routines and organizational learning being context dependent that the nexus of the learning processes is important, as also emphasized by Lund in this volume.

In many discussions, the creation of routines and learning has to do with the relation between the individual and the organization as such. However, we would argue that to a large extent the routines, capabilities as well as the shared languages and norms are created at an intermediate level of the organization. This may, of course, differ according to the size and structure of the organization. However, we would contend that in many organizations it is possible to identify the different types of groups.[3]

Difficulties arise when an organization is dependent upon the coordination of activities across different groups, be it e.g. two different functional groups or two different types of groups. In that case the codes of communication and intra-group objectives are not necessarily compatible. In the case of the DKPTO the patent examiners is one group and Sales & Marketing another. The activities of patent examiners are clearly guided by its' own (externally given) objectives. Likewise, the activities of the Sales & Marketing are determined by their main objective of selling various types of services and encouraging firms to apply for IPR. If the efficiency of knowledge diffusion activities of Sales & Marketing (S&M) is dependent upon diffusion of knowledge from patent examiners (as hypothesized in Section 1), it requires that extensive interdepartmental interaction be established with the objective of ensuring knowledge transfer. Two functionally separate departments (as is largely the case in the DKPTO) could, however, also handle respectively the sale and production of services. As mentioned, this is likely to require mechanisms of knowledge transfer, and with limited interaction between departments, this transfer is unlikely to take place. Alternatively, the Sales & Marketing department would need competencies from elsewhere.

2.3. Implications

In this final section we shall briefly state some of the most important implications, derived from the above theoretical development, for the further steps of the present study.

Even if the patent application process to a large extent is about handling codified knowledge, there is – as emphasised earlier – also tacit knowledge involved in relation to how to organize and undertake this application process. Some of the potential learning between the parties is no doubt possible to mediate by way of simple transfer of codified knowledge. However, we need to investigate whether the tacit element in the knowledge transfer is substantial. The transfer of this element, it was pointed to above, may be stimulated by proximity in various dimensions, geographical, cultural, languages.

Another implication of the theoretical discussion is that preparing the patent application involves transformation of tacit knowledge to codified knowledge in a language, understandable for the recipient. This is a difficult process, and for patent offices playing a role in building up the general innovative competencies of firms it may be essential that they are skilful in guiding firms on how to transform their tacit knowledge into codes that may be managed in a patent.

Moreover, the theory discussed the importance of the intensity and frequency of interaction between the parties in facilitating this mutual learning. The argument is that this interaction stimulates the build up of mutual trust and understanding, which in turn are very important to learning. This points to the need of further investigation of this aspect of the patent granting process. As was pointed out in Section 1, this involves several sub-issues. We may point to the interaction between patent examiners and other staff of the patent office, in particular the Sales & Marketing department. As was discussed here, the intra-organizational knowledge flows are important to take into account. In order to be efficient, it is most often required that such knowledge flows are deliberately stimulated by internal organization (tacit knowledge) or management/information systems (codified knowledge).

3. THE DKPTO IN THE INNOVATION PROCESS

After having established the theoretical background we proceed in this section with a description of how the DKPTO may have a role in innovation besides its' primary function as an important element in providing protection of intellectual property rights.

In many cases, it is important for the innovator to protect an invention and the protection of intangible assets is partly considered a motivating factor for their continuous involvement in innovation activities. It is also important that the society has rules for standardisation in order to protect the consumer and help companies prove that their products have a certain level of quality. So it becomes necessary to have certain regulation on such things as patents and standardisation to promote innovation. The Danish Patent and Trademark Office's primary task is to offer protection for inventions, which includes trademarks, design, and copyrights (Patent og Varemærkestyrelsen, 2000).

As a secondary function, the office offers consultancy services such as information services, guidance and training within the IPR-area. The patent office also offers courses on how to apply for patents for example at several of the regional Technological Information Centres and at universities. In addition, the office sells different services such as competitor analysis and market analysis. The most important services include novelty searches, infringement inquiries, state of the art inquiries, and analyses of competitors/profile analyses. See Appendix A for further specification. Educational activities, library and information services, info meetings, and courses are also part of activities (Patent og Varemærkestyrelsen, 2001a, b, c). The DKPTO also can help investigate whether a patent has been violated.

A wide array of different actors in the innovation system use these services. In addition to the direct use by firms, a number of intermediaries are using or buying the services from the DKPTO, thus enhancing their capabilities to assist firms in their innovation activities. An important group of intermediaries are the *patent agents*. The relationship to the patent agents is explained in more detail below as one example of external relations.

The patent agents compete with the patent office when it comes to selling patent-based services. While they do not have the right to issue patents and trademarks they operate within the same business service areas as the patent office. Thus, the patent agents often sell their services such as courses, market analysis, searches on prior art etc. in competition with the patent office. Even if the patent agents are competitors they are customers and collaborators. The patent agents' main job is to help companies write applications for a patent and establish a patent strategy.

The patent agents and the DKPTO have a common interest in increasing the knowledge on IPRs in general and of the products offered by the agents. The difference lies particularly with the fact that the DKPTO is not allowed to engage in the same type of close consultancy as the agent, first and foremost because the DKPTO only has a very limited right of guiding applicants on how to formulate the specific claims of the application. However, in the field of patent strategies and novelty searches the DKPTO does to a certain extent act as a competitor to the agents. Because of these built-in overlaps in the activities of both parties, a "common understanding on competition" has been made between these two parties. This leaves distinct areas of counselling to the patent agents. The common understanding on competition has made it possible to focus more on common interests in developing the IPR system and diffusing knowledge on the economic importance of protecting new products. Besides this, the agents constitute a major group of customers to the DKPTO. Around two-thirds of the applications filed at the DKPTO are filed via a patent agent. This normally means that most communication goes through the agents, who accordingly are the main customers to a range of the services offered by the DKPTO.

Courses and educational activities are also an important part of the external partnerships. The DKPTO often co-operates directly with patent agents when establishing different courses on technical and legal issues concerning patenting. Initiatives have also been taken to reinforce co-operation with universities in order to incorporate IPR education into existing curricula of especially technical and natural sciences education (Erhvervsfremme Styrelsen og Patent og Varemærkestyrelsen, 2001).

The activities of the DKPTO also influence the innovation system more indirectly as the DKPTO acts as a supplier to the industry of trained patent engineers. Because of a high mobility of people from the DKPTO this is an important channel of knowledge diffusion, which enable the industry and patent agents to enhance their capabilities within the field of IPR.

Other channels of knowledge diffusion includes that the DKPTO contributes to the technical/professional literature on IPR, prepare legislation and develop policies within the field of IPR.

In conclusion, patent institutions generally, are most often classified as regulatory institutions. They are of direct importance for firms who need to protect their product innovations through patenting, trademarks etc. However, the additional activities and the interactions with other institutions including the indirect function as educating staff indicates that important inter-organizational learning processes are taking place in addition to the intra-organizational learning described briefly above, and discussed in more detail below. Thus, it is an important question of this study whether some of these external linkages are related to business services, and whether these in turn depends on the competencies attained by the DKPTO staff through search and examination activities. This question is explored in the following section below concerning the internal relations and competencies of the DKPTO.

4. INTRA-ORGANIZATIONAL LEARNING AND WORK PROCESSES[4]

4.1. Introduction

Following the discussion of various external relationships we will now provide a general description of the main organizational routines and individual knowledge applied to the DKPTO's activities. The next step will be to link the knowledge and resources obtained by handling patent applications to some of the main business services, which have already been mentioned in the preceding sections. This is a question of what kinds of competencies are obtained through search and examination. In particular, the issue is how these competencies come into play through internal processes of knowledge diffusion. Thus, the competencies of the patent department may be said to benefit other activities of the DKPTO such as business services, if knowledge indeed is diffused across departments.

4.2. Knowledge and Resources of the DKPTO

In the "Knowledge Account 2000" (Patent og Varemærkestyrelsen, 2001a) (which is a supplement to the conventional account, but focused upon the knowledge base of the DKPTO), the internal resources of the DKPTO have been divided into "human" and "structural" capital. Generally speaking, human capital consists of the skills, knowledge, and competencies of individual employees. Structural capital on the other hand consists of the knowledge and experience embedded in the organizational structures, formalised processes, information technology, and formalised communication systems of the DKPTO. In other words, structural capital is the knowledge that stays with the DKPTO when individual employees leave.

The structural capital of the DKPTO consists of two main elements – structurally embedded knowledge and working processes. Working processes may be seen as a catalyst for knowledge diffusion as they may serve to diffuse both tacit and explicit knowledge. Furthermore, working processes themselves may be both codified and non-codified. Structurally embedded knowledge, on the other hand, is quite codified and directly accessible.[5]

The Intranet facilitates knowledge flows. It is the DKPTO's internal network for electronic communication. It is a very important medium for internal communication and it supports the internal knowledge flows between individual caseworkers and between different sections of the DKPTO.

Knowledge sharing by developing working culture and daily routines is a key to preserve and develop competencies, which support the diffusion of especially tacit (non-codified) knowledge. Regular section meetings and workshops support this type of knowledge sharing besides ordinary educational programmes. Statistics on the personnel may provide a general impression of the DKPTO's human capital (Table 1).

As mentioned, there is a high turnover of staff, rendering very high expenses for education and development of central competencies necessary for maintaining the core competencies of the organization. The educational activities of the DKPTO are also very important for the internal diffusion of knowledge, as teaching of new employees by experienced colleagues is an important part of the educational programme of patent examiners and engineers. Table 2 shows the resources (measured by working days) allocated to different types of educational activities.

The activities that are relevant to the primary functions of the DKPTO (patent casework) take up a large part of total educational and competence building activities. The activities basic training, training by colleagues, and advanced training of specialists, totalled a number of 1593 working days. These activities occur almost exclusively internally within the DKPTO. Generally, the education

Table 1. Number of Man-Years by Staff Category in 2000.

Executives and Heads of Section	Consultants	Engineers	Other Academic Staff	Office Workers and Other Staff
22.5	23.8	56.4	35.5	139.3
8.1%	8.5%	20.2%	12.7%	50.5%

Source: DKPTO Knowledge Account 2000.

Table 2. Competence Development and Educational Activities in 2000.

Activity	Number of Days	External/Internal
Basic training/patent course.	445	Internal
Training by experienced colleagues.	864	Internal
Advanced training of specialist incl. On-line search.	284	Internal/External
Basic juridical training and competencies.	210	Internal
Sales and marketing competencies.	35	Internal
Management training.	193	Internal/External
Networking competencies.	30	External
Professional and personal development.	495	Internal/External
Behavioural and attitudinal development.	396	Internal
Language proficiency.	230	Internal/External
Presentation and supervision techniques.	77	Internal
Presentation in writing.	28	Internal
Introductory meeting.	57	Internal
Total	3345	–

Source: DKPTO Knowledge Account 2000.

of individual staff members and the internal training processes by which human capital is developed and maintained are important prerequisites for maintaining and enhancing the ability of employees to carry out their tasks.

When the DKPTO takes on new employees (engineers and natural sciences candidates) a comprehensive educational programme is implemented in order to train new employees to become competent patent engineers. The training consists of a "two-step-training" programme. The first step is the basic training course, by which the employee obtains the so-called "announcement right." The second step by which the employee is appointed "patent engineer" requires additional training and experience (in particular training by experienced colleagues). The basic training programme consists of both theoretical and practical modules, which are necessary in order to obtain the basic competencies for handling patent applications. The duration of the course varies depending on the specific needs of the employees and developments in the field of patent technique. The training by experienced colleagues goes on for about 1 – 1 1/2 years. It has character of apprentice learning, and is combined with specialised competence building and training on specific technical issues. This additional training could, e.g. include international courses in patent technique under the Centre d'Etudes Internationales de la Propriété Industrielle (CEIPI). In addition to the specific technical skills, the apprentice learning also involves substantial transfer of tacit knowledge. In total it takes about three years of training before new employees can be appointed "patent engineers."

With this in mind, we proceed to discuss how the technical competencies might come into play in the production of business services.

4.3. Knowledge Transfer Involved in Business Services

Most of the business services require technical as well as knowledge on law on the part of the DKPTO's employees (and on the part of the customers in order to be able to utilise the information). The question is how, exactly, do the competencies within the DKPTO come into play in the "production processes" of the business services? What are the links to the competencies associated with (and acquired through) the handling of patent applications?

4.3.1. Organization and Production Processes

The production of technical business services is dependent on expertise on searching and assessing the international patent literature. In the DKPTO the business services are sold through the sales and marketing section, but they are produced in the patent section. Interviews with employees of the S&M and the Patent sections indicate a relatively clear division of labour between the two sections concerning the production of business services. Thus, the internal diffusion of knowledge that is required for the production of business services does not differ much from the codified processes as described in the internal handbooks and production guides. It should though be mentioned that there has been some people who shifted job from the patent sections to the S&M department, which implies a certain diffusion of knowledge across divisions.

The S&M section is the customer's gateway to business services and the S&M section is responsible for the initial communication to the Patent section of the customer's request. Thus the S&M prepares the case, which is thereafter taken over by the relevant employees in the Patent section. This is initially an employee who is assigned as responsible for the specific case. The case is then handed over to a technical expert/patent engineer. The responsible caseworker and the problem solver/patent engineer is often one and the same person. Alternatively, the job is handed over to the head of section who then hands over the job to a patent engineer of his/her choice.

Whether the service in question is a novelty search, infringement inquiry, or state-of-the-art-inquiry it requires more or less the same competencies and knowledge as required for search and examination of patent applications. The patent engineer also takes care of further communication with the customer, which is often of a technical nature.

4.4. Conclusions

The general conclusion concerning internal processes is that the interdependence between the competencies acquired through patent casework and those required for technical business services is not based on the formal (codified) or informal (non-codified) organization of production processes. It follows from the above that the S&M section could service industry with enhancing general awareness of IPR and sales of business services without having the technical expertise, as represented by the patent section, in-house. In principle, the technical search and examination processes could be bought from outside the organization (or even outside the nation) and re-sold through the S&M organization/department. However, a number of practical difficulties are associated with this idea. In particular, the possibility of communicating directly (in Danish) with the responsible patent examiner would most likely be limited or non-existent. This would reduce the potential value of the services in question. Moreover, the S&M section would need some security for supply of the search and examination that they sell. It is likely that flexibility in the production is greater if the production is done in-house.

Interviews in the S&M and Patent sections have indicated that the functionally separated working processes are characterised by codified, internal structures of knowledge diffusion while potential non-codified (informal) ones seem rather limited. Actual case-by-case co-operation between the sections is rather limited. Although most business services (in particular technical services) are produced with a quite clear division of labour, there is probably more room for non-codified co-operation internally within each section than between sections. One could therefore argue that the specific internal relations and the diffusion of knowledge between the S&M section and the Patent section is in fact not very developed, but perhaps that is not necessary. It may be argued that this streamlined organization of the work processes with limited cross-departmental knowledge flows is a rational way of organising activities. The community of practise-like organization discussed in the theoretical section only have its' merits in certain situations, it is not an universal best practise. In fact, the interviews within the DKPTO revealed that such an organization has been tried out in the DKPTO, but with poor results.

5. MUTUAL COMPETENCE BUILDING – CASES FROM DANISH ENTERPRISES[6]

5.1. Introduction

Section 2 pointed to some of the possible ways of competence building and knowledge transmission of relevance for innovation. Section 4 highlighted more precisely where in the patent granting process such learning processes are likely to take place. This section sets out to illustrate, via descriptions of real world cases, if some of the theoretical considerations are indeed also to be found in practise. Thus, the cases illustrate how patent offices may contribute to product innovation in firms by virtue of other activities than just filing a patent. As the primary purpose with the section is to explore in more detail the nature of the learning processes and learning effects of the interaction between the DKPTO and the firms, the cases are not chosen randomly. On the contrary they are picked under the presumption that they illustrate learning processes related to product innovation.

The section starts out with a short discussion on research strategy and methodology. The description of the cases are structured as a first presentation of the applicant firm, its industry and its technological competencies and patents. Secondly, we analyse the interaction between the firm and the DKPTO. Thirdly, learning effects are identified and possible implications for product innovation in the firm are discussed. Related, it is discussed if the cases give any evidence to the discussion on whether the firms benefit from the national location of the patent office.[7]

5.2. Case Studies as Research Strategy

The study includes case studies based first and foremost on interviews with an employee or manager engaged in the company's patent policy. The cases includes Rockwool, Østjysk Innovation, the Technological Institute, Pure Snack, Plougman & Vingtoft, Patentgruppen, and Kristoffer Larsen Innovation A/S. Østjysk Innovation, the Technological Institute and Pure Snack is reported one group and Plougman & Vingtoft and Patentgruppen as another group. The companies were selected in such a way that we can show different ways of using and interacting with the DKPTO.

To get a better understanding of the procedures of patent applications, the business services offered, and the patent examiners relations to customers, we used earlier reports (consumer analyses, descriptions of procedures for patent application and others), the DKPTO homepage and the DKPTO Intranet. Besides the material found we also held several informal meetings with employees of the marketing department of the DKPTO and patent examiners in order to get an understanding of the patent system and how it works. The informal talks with employees of the DKPTO were crucial for formulating the right questions for the case study.[8]

The interviews lasted between $1\frac{1}{2}$–2 hours and each interview was introduced with the respondent talking about his or her company. The questions were open-ended and a large part of questions requested the respondent to come up with example.[9]

5.3. Case: Kristoffer Larsen Innovation A/S

Kristoffer Larsen Innovation A/S is a one-man business. The company sells imported spare parts for trucks and has been the owners' main source of income the past 15 years. During the past 10 years the owner has also been busy inventing equipment for the production of pork. Today Kristoffer Larsen Innovation A/S has invented a house for free-range pigs and an advanced feeding robot that ensures that each pig automatically receives precise individual feeding. The robot thus identifies the pig, its weight and individual feeding need. By doing so it becomes possible to trace back in time what fodder each individual consumed. This allows you to investigate what are possible inexpedient effects of different types of fodder, medicines, environmental factors etc. Kristoffer Larsen Innovation A/S applied for patent on the ability of the robot to link each individual pig to the record of consumed fodder. Kristoffer Larsen Innovation A/S is constantly involved in new invention activities. Currently, the owner is for instance working on an outdoor pig toilet.

Generally most of the work with new inventions in equipment for outdoor pigs is informal and rarely patents are applied for. Today, Kristoffer Larsen Innovation A/S actually seems to be the only firm in Denmark who is applying for patents for equipment for outdoor pigs. Moreover, at the moment it makes no difference if you take out patents on your equipment for outdoor pigs or not. The chances of your idea being imitated seem to be small and the possibilities of exploiting the patents are limited as well. However, it is likely that the situation will change. First of all because outdoor pigs is a fairly new phenomenon but also due to changes in regulation and consumer preferences. Therefore, the respondent thought that taking out a patent would be the safe strategy.

5.3.1. Kristoffer Larsen Innovation A/S's contact to PVS

Kristoffer Larsen Innovation A/S has been busy inventing equipment for pigs since the mid-1990s and as the first inventions began to take form, he decided to apply for patents. Kristoffer Larsen Innovation A/S contacted the DKPTO in 1998 and set up a meeting. Among the participants at the meeting was the patent examiner Michael,[10] who at that time dealt with patents within the agriculture area. Later Michael became Kristoffer Larsen Innovation A/S's permanent case officer. Kristoffer Larsen Innovation A/S presented the feeding robot at the meeting and the participants from the DKPTO first impression was that the idea was promising. After the presentation, the meeting participants went to the library where a novelty search (a patent technical search) was conducted. No existing patents were found on the automatic feeding robot and the DKPTO requested Kristoffer Larsen Innovation A/S to go on with the patent, and to find a patent agent to help to formulate a patent application. Kristoffer Larsen Innovation A/S chose one of the larger patent agents in Denmark, who helped to select patent strategy, including the formulation of the patent claims. To ensure that the patent application was optimised Kristoffer Larsen Innovation A/S requested the DKPTO to make a patent family search. No infringements were found under the search and Kristoffer Larsen Innovation A/S became aware that the patent was too narrow. It was then decided to broaden the patent and so maximise the possibilities to exclude others. The patent application was reformulated, a new test was conducted and the application was finally accepted.

Kristoffer Larsen Innovation A/S has as part of the patent application bought the services novelty search and patent family search in order to set up the right claims. The patent on automatically linking individual pigs to its past consumption of fodder is technically advanced, and according to the respondent, it is highly uncertain if the patenting process could have been carried through without the assistance of the DKPTO. Kristoffer Larsen Innovation A/S has during the last years learned much about the patent system and how it works. The interaction with the DKPTO has especially increased knowledge on how to apply for patents and Kristoffer Larsen Innovation A/S is today much better at making descriptions of the patent. Also, Kristoffer Larsen Innovation A/S has learned how to judge a patent and the patent claims.

> ... I have increased my knowledge of the patent application and gained a better insight in the patent system. Consequently, it has become easier for me to participate actively in the patent application process. My increased knowledge of patents in general has also increased my interest in applying for new patents.

Kristoffer Larsen Innovation A/S believes that the interaction he has had with the DKPTO and the knowledge he has gained from his experience from dealing with the patent system, has had an impact on his innovation activities and will continue to have so. In conclusion, Kristoffer Larsen Innovation A/S's interaction with the DKPTO has first and foremost been vital in connection with his specific applications, but has also increased his knowledge of the patent system as such and increased his skills in applying for patents and judging relevant claims for the patent. In turn, this is likely to positively influence innovation activities also in the future.

5.3.2. DKPTO's Benefits from the Interaction With Kristoffer Larsen Innovation A/S

Kristoffer Larsen Innovation A/S describes the relations to the case officer Michael as informal and personal. The level of interaction between the two parties has been fairly extensive. It is also Kristoffer Larsen Innovation A/S's belief that the

DKPTO and especially Michael have benefited from the collaboration. Michael became aware of which types of problems one faces, when applying for patents for the first time. The intense involvement enables case officers as Michael to answer questions in the future, which goes beyond questions on how the patent system works and formalities in the formulation of the patent application. The case officer gains insight in the types of questions you might ask as a first time applicant and the surprises customers get when the cost of an international patent is first revealed, the procedures and complications of sale of the inventions, license deals etc. The case officer also becomes aware of which supporting possibilities there might be such as network possibilities, where to get technical advices, or which funds you can apply for if needed. This type of information can then be passed on to new applicants and thus help them get through the system in the most efficient way.

5.3.3. The Benefits from Having a National Patent Office
Kristoffer Larsen Innovation A/S believes that the contact with the Danish patent office has been fruitful due to the way the communication has proceeded. The respondent doesn't think he could have communicated in the same manner if the patent system was centralised and all patent examination were e.g. placed with the EPO in Munich. He mentioned the foreign language as a major communication barrier. Also he mentioned that the personal relations to the DKPTO has meant much to him in his work with patents, and he doubts that this type of relationship could be maintained if the patent system was fully centralised and his case officer was in Munich.

5.4. Østjysk Innovation (Pre Seed Capital Provider), Pure Snack (A Company Financed Partly by Østjysk Innovation) and the Technological Institute (A Government Approved Technological Institute)

In this case the two innovation supporting institutes Østjysk Innovation (a pre-seed capital provider) and the Technological Institute (an Approved Technology Institute – GTS) are used to illustrate how these types of organizations work with patents and interact with the DKPTO. In order to illustrate the interaction between the institutions and their portfolio companies, a one-man company Pure Snack is included. Pure Snack is supported financially by Østjysk Innovation and seeks to commercialise low fat snacks. The case study is based on interviews with Gyda Bay from Østjysk Innovation, Peter Lauridsen (the Technological Institute, Invention department) and Ole Knudsen (Pure Snack).

The most important function of Østjysk Innovation and the Technological Institute is to support entrepreneurs and researchers commercialising inventions.

The institutes help inventors with guidance in such questions as licensing, marketing and sales related questions. Both institutes also support the companies financially and in creating networks, the two types of support that they provide in the area of technical guidance. The GTS institutes have in-house engineers and consultants with expertise within several technical areas.

These institutes see patents as very important elements in the innovation process. They spend many of their resources supporting companies in their work with patents. Even though it is costly, both institutes encourage the inventors to apply for patents. Both Institutes use in-house expertise to screen for novelty and then buy novelty searches (patent technical searches) from the DKPTO or from the patent bureaus. The in-house novelty screenings are carried out in free databases available on the Internet and in databases that the institutes have paid access to. In addition to using the DKPTO to carry out novelty searches, Technological Institute also uses the DKPTO to acquire new information in the patent area, and send participants to many of the seminars provided by the DKPTO.

Like the Technological Institute, Østjysk Innovation only buys novelty searches. Gyda Bay mentions that they buy a limited number of novelty searches from the DKPTO since patent bureaus can provide more information in the novelty search in certain subjects. Østjysk Innovation uses the novelty searches as one of many factors to make final decisions on whether to support a project or not. Ole Knudsen of Pure Snack recognises this situation. Luckily, the novelty search for his invention had a positive outcome leading stjysk Innovation to support his business financially and to help him get a licensing deal. The novelty search was also useful in the process of attracting investors, Ole Knudsen suggests.

Østjysk Innovation lets the patent agents carry out their search because they have experienced that some of the patent agents are doing a better job within some technical areas. Also Gyda Bay finds it convenient that the patent agents can pass remarks on the searches and make comments on the chances of getting the patents and chances of infringement of other patents. Due to legal concerns, DKPTO services are limited in this respect.

Even though the three respondents leave much of the patent work to patent agents, they still believe they have learned much from dealing with patent questions. In general it is difficult for the respondents to point out the origin of their knowledge. Some knowledge might have come directly from interaction with the DKPTO, seminars in Denmark, abroad, and some from the patent agents, according to the respondents.

Peter Lauridsen mentions that there are a large number of employees from the Technological Institute, who have learned much from joining DKPTO's introductory courses and seminars in intellectual property right issues. The courses have increased the qualifications among employees in the work with patents and contributed to a better awareness of intellectual property rights in the Technological Institute in general. This, in turn, benefits the innovation activities in the customer firms buying consultancy services from the Technological institutes because of more qualified guidance of these firms.

5.4.1. The Benefits of a National Patent Office

None of the questioned institutes believe their portfolio companies would have applied for fewer patents, if the DKPTO had not existed. However, all three respondents find it convenient to have a national patent office due to shared language and culture, and the close localisation. Peter Lauridsen says,

> ... It is always nice to have the help on one's doorstep and not externally placed in Stockholm or Munich. Unfortunately, I think there is a tendency towards further centralisation of the patent system and it might very well lead to the EPO running the whole thing (Peter Lauridsen).

Besides the advantages of close geographic localisation, the shared language and the shared culture, the respondents also mention good personal relationships with the staff in the DKPTO as an essential reason to preserve a structure with a national patent office.

5.5. The Patent Agents: Plougman & Vingtoft and Patentgruppen

Patent agents complete around 80% of the patent applications the DKPTO receives. This makes the patent agents a very important customer group and makes it necessary to evaluate the patent agents' relationships with the DKPTO, their attitudes and their view of the DKPTO, as well as their expectations in future collaborations with the DKPTO. In order to answer these and other questions we have interviewed Peter Jensen[11] from Plougman & Vingtoft and JØrgen MØller from the Patentgruppen. The two bureaus differ in size and also to some extend in the provided services. Plougman & Vingtoft is the largest patent agent bureau in Denmark and they support their customers technically in further development of inventions if necessary. Patentgruppen consists of five patent agents and a number of other staff. The bureau is the fifth in size in Denmark measured by international patent applications in 2000. The Patentgruppen also differs from Plougman & Vingtoft in its service offerings. In comparison to most bureaus the Patentgruppen is highly involved in their customers' innovation process. While most bureaus evaluate the final innovation output, the Patentgruppen evaluate the patent possibilities of inventions early in the innovation process and continuously throughout the whole innovation process.

Both Plougman & Vingtoft and the Patentgruppen consider the DKPTO to be more of an authority and a sub-supplier than an actual collaborator. The bureaus consider also their role in the system to be rather different from that of the DKPTO. The patent agents can be considered as an intermediary between the companies and the DKPTO and it is the patent agents who help the companies with the patent applications. The patent agents' most important job is to work out the patent strategy, which involves drawing up the patent claims. Due to regulations, the DKPTO is not allowed to handle this function. The DKPTO is also limited in the guidance that they can provide when selling business services. When the patent agents sell a business service to their customers, they are allowed to comment on the company's chances of getting the patent. Peter Jensen sees this division of labour as a necessity because it gives room for both actors. Peter Jensen also mentions that their customers never address the DKPTO directly. According to the two bureaus, the division of labour is clear, the DKPTO is a sub-supplier of business services and the issuer of intellectual property rights.

5.5.1. The Bureaus' Use of the DKPTO

Plougman & Vingtoft often buy business services from the DKPTO. They buy various services like novelty search, patent family searches, and various surveillance searches (patent family surveillance, competitor surveillance, or technical surveillance). Before they buy the searches, they usually make their own introductory searches. Unlike Plougman & Vingtoft, the Patentgruppen sometimes make their own final novelty searches before they determine whether to apply for the patent or not. Jørgen Møller says, that it is possible to make good online searches within some technical areas if the technical area is new, such as for the mobile phone industry. For such a case, all the relevant material is available on line, which makes it unnecessary to scan the DKPTO's patent literature.

The Patentgruppen submits around 15% of all patent applications for trial in the DKPTO. This is because some of the Patentgruppen's customers want to apply for patent in Denmark first in order to save time. Some companies are not sure of the market possibilities of the patent and some companies' want to reduce the costs involved with gaining the patent. Unlike the Patentgruppen, Plougman & Vingtoft has never filed a patent application at the DKPTO, but they hand in patent applications in Denmark for registration. According to Peter Jensen, their customers are not interested in a patent that is only effective in Denmark. "... *Our customers are thinking internationally and there is a good reason to think that this tendency will continue in line with the increase in internationalisation.*"

In the Patentgruppen they also believe that fewer of their customers will want a patent, which only is valid in Denmark, and thus fewer are likely to have their patent application tried at the DKPTO. Jørgen Møller also mentions that the DKPTO probably will receive even fewer applications when the cheaper Community patent is introduced.

According to Peter Jensen there is no knowledge diffusion from the DKPTO to Plougman & Vingtoft when they interact. Actually the work with patent application does not give rise to much interaction with the DKPTO or any other patent offices. The only thing that is likely to give rise to exchange of knowledge is their employees' attendance at DKPTO's held courses in intellectual property rights. Plougman & Vingtoft's new employees often attend the introductory courses.

Both Plougman & Vingtoft and the Patentgruppen are aware that many of the employees that the DKPTO train end up in private patent bureaus and four out of five of the consultants in the Patentgruppen are from the DKPTO. Jørgen Møller mentions that it is an advantage to hire someone who has worked for the DKPTO because they know how the system works. The patent agents job is of course very different from the work in the DKPTO. The patent agents' job is to formulate a description of an invention in a legal-technical way and to make the patent application as broad as possible by formulating the right claims. The staffs in the DKPTO dealing with the applications on the other hand read and make a judgement of the application. Plougman & Vingtoft have only recruited few employees from the DKPTO. Instead they often recruit PhDs from the universities. They believe these are able to help customers with inventions, as well as to recognise the opportunities in inventions,[12] Peter Jensen says.

5.5.2. DKPTO's New Role

The DKPTO can, because of it status as an authority, stimulate and contribute to networking among the actors in the industry. This fact both respondents agree upon. The DKPTO's status as an authority allows the organization to fulfil a number of coordinating functions and to implement initiatives useful to society. Some of the initiatives that the DKPTO has implemented are listed below.

- *Education/courses:* the DKPTO is together with Patentagentforeningen and DIP (Dansk Industris Patentagenter) coordinator of the Intellectual Property Right education in Denmark. Courses are held in intellectual property rights, consequences of changes in the international patent system, etc.
- *Conference organiser:* the DKPTO continuously arranges conferences. The purpose of a conference could e.g. be to increase managers' awareness and knowledge of intellectual property rights at a strategic level.
- *The spring meeting:* the DKPTO hosts a spring meeting once a year. The participants at the meeting are usually 200 employees from the DKPTO, patent agents and industry associations. The purpose of the meeting is to have the players in the industry inform each another of their activities and to network.

- *Innovation forum:* Once a year the DKPTO and the patent agents hosts an event, where the invention of the year is elected.
- *Sparring partner:* the DKPTO to a large extent uses people from the industry as sparring partners in product development. The DKPTO has for example invented the program Ipscore and several publications at the request of the industry.
- *Information campaigns:* the DKPTO works with private patent bureaus on joint information campaigns, which seek to increase awareness of intellectual property rights.
- *Joint mouthpiece of the industry:* In many ways the DKPTO works as a mouthpiece of the industry and especially in international questions. The DKPTO discusses political and international questions with the industry at meetings.

Peter Jensen says, that the DKPTO has done a good job gathering the industry during the last four to five years and it has been fruitful in terms of networking. Plougman & Vingtoft also participates in several of DKPTO's activities listed above.

> ... We always participate in the popular spring meetings. It is an event, which offers possibilities of creating networks. I think it is of high value that a public institute is able to gather the industry and create events where networks are established. In Denmark, the DKPTO is the catalyst for organising industry events and meetings because they are neutral.

Both Plougman & Vingtoft and the Patentgruppen are aware that the DKPTO's role has changed, and they expect further changes during the next couple of years. The DKPTO thus is more than just an authority, granting intellectual property rights and a sub-supplier of business services. The DKPTO is also an organization, which brings the industry together, while stimulating the networking within the industry.

5.6. Case: Rockwool International A/S

The Rockwool Group is the world's leading manufacturer of stone wool. With more than 20 factories in Europe, North America, and East Asia, and a global network of sales companies and trade offices, the Rockwool Group covers all parts of the globe. The Group has more than 7,000 employees. The sale of traditional thermal insulation makes up 5/6 of Rockwool's revenue.

In Rockwool we interviewed Arne Kraglund, who is responsible for the patent department, Technology Search. The department is responsible for patenting and technology, as well as competition surveillance based on review of patent literature. The patent department consists of five employees.

The large players in the industry are all very conscious about using patenting. Rockwool's products have a long lifetime and the products can be easily imitated, so gaining a patent is an important way of protecting their inventions and market share. Rockwool would never run the risk of not applying for patents on new important inventions, because they realize that their competitors are just behind them with their own inventive activities. Additionally, there have been incidents where the large mineral wool producers have handed in almost identical patent applications, according to the company. Arne Kraglund believes that if Rockwool in such environment had chosen a secrecy strategy, waiting until the market for the products has been investigated and sale prognoses had been made, it would have failed.

5.7. Rockwool's Way of Using the DKPTO

Each year Rockwool hands in a large number of patent applications to both the DKPTO and to PCT authorities and today Rockwool's portfolio consists of more than 1000 patents or patent applications. Rockwool's patents are first and foremost product patents, but they also have patents on processes. Almost one-fourth of all Rockwool's patents are examined in the DKPTO and three-fourths are examined at a PCT authority. Arne Kraglund says that if they are convinced an invention will become a success in a number of countries the patent application will normally be handed in directly to the EPO.

Rockwool buys two types of business service from the DKPTO, novelty searches and state of art searches. Rockwool does not buy novelty searches from patent agents. This is due in part to their confidence in the patent authorities and also because they know the authorities have substantial and current holdings of patent literature, Arne Kraglund claims. The state of art searches are not used directly in the patenting process, but more as information material used for R&D. The state of art searches has for example been used to give a better insight in a certain technical area and as a tool for generating ideas. The state of art-searches are mostly useful if they address R&D outside Rockwool's key competencies. There is not much knowledge to gain from the patent literature of Rockwool's key product, stone wool.

5.7.1. Rockwool's Relationship to the DKPTO
Rockwool has a contact person in the DKPTO and it works out well. It is nice to always know which person to contact, Arne Kraglund says. The person who ends up getting the task will often call Rockwool and make sure that the description is properly understood. Arne Kraglund finds it convenient to have such good relations to the DKPTO:

... I don't just call the EPO and they do not call me to ensure they have understood a description correctly. I can definitely feel that the geographic distance to the EPO is long. Besides I like the idea of knowing the person I am calling and that is the case when I am calling the DKPTO. It gives one some sort of security that you know the people who are dealing with your patent applications and searches and also much can be unsaid if it is always the same person who is dealing with your company (Arne Kraglund).

According to Arne Kraglund, it is important that there is a good understanding between the DKPTO and Rockwool and he likes that the two parties are close geographically. Because the geographic distance is short, we can easily meet if it is necessary, noting that they actually meet once a year to discuss their collaborations, Arne Kraglund says. At these meetings, Arne Kraglund is asked to come up with ideas to improve the effectiveness of the DKPTO and assess their customer-client relationship. This implies that it is likely that the DKPTO has learned from its collaboration with Rockwool.

5.7.2. The Advantages of Having a National Patent Office
Rockwool supports the national patent office. However, Arne Kraglund thinks that Rockwool would do just as well without a national patent office amongst other because Rockwool has many years of experience with the patent work. But for the sake of small companies and newly established companies that might be low on cash, Rockwool supports the national patent office. From a society point of view Arne Kraglund believes that there is a necessity for a national patent office, adding that it is also convenient.

5.8. Conclusions from Case Stories

5.8.1. The Contribution of Patent Literature and Information to Technology Spillover in the Innovation System
None of the respondents believe that they have increased their specific technological knowledge through their interaction with the DKPTO. The patent literature and information (on which business services are based) likewise have only to a limited extent contributed as inspiration to new inventions. Two of the respondents (Arne Kraglund, Rockwool and Peter Lauridsen, Technological Institute) mention that they have used the state of art-searches as inspiration for new inventions, but, not very often. At the Technological Institute, these types of searches have also been used for adjustment of the direction of future inventions.

In general, it is believed that the technological knowledge that might be gained from patent literature is indirect. This result is no surprise and it is widely supported by research concerning the general importance of patent literature to the innovation process.

5.8.2. The DKPTO's Contribution to Increasing Knowledge and Awareness of IPR and to Facilitating Access to IPR Protection

The case stories show that the patent applicants learn a lot from working with patent questions on their own. Also, all the respondents clearly have gained a higher ability to see the IPR-angle of their innovations from dealing with patent questions; they are all able to read and understand the patent literature and the inventors are today better at giving full descriptions of their inventions or to codify the knowledge behind an invention.

With respect to learning effects of interacting with the DKPTO, the size of the firms may have a bearing on learning effects, as one should expect learning to be most intense during the first occasions of interaction. Thus, a large firm with it's own patent engineers, or even patent department, like Rockwool, may have learned much in connection with their first patent application. However, after having developed internal competences at a high level, it is likely that learning effects diminish. Vice versa, small firms may experience disproportionally higher learning effects.

5.8.3. The Importance of a National Patent Office

None of the respondents believe it would affect their patent activities negatively if the patent system were fully centralised in Munich and several of the respondents mention that they are indifferent to from where they buy their business services. The business services can be bought from the DKPTO, other patent authorities or patent agents. Several of the respondents also claim that it is just as easy to hand in a patent application to the EPO as to the DKPTO.

Even though the respondents do not think that they would apply for fewer patents if the DKPTO had not existed, they all mention advantages with having a national patent office. The respondents all agree that it is convenient to have a patent office in Denmark because of the shared language and culture, it is easy to meet and communicate, also because the respondents have good personal contacts in the DKPTO. Some of the respondents also mention that the DKPTO organise courses in IPR thus stimulating general awareness of IPR. Furthermore, the patent agents interviewed believe it is useful to have a national patent office to bring together the patent industry and to promote networking in the industry. So all the respondents could point out advantages of the national patent office. Some of the respondents point to additional benefits of a national patent office for small firms.

6. CONCLUSIONS – THE ROLE OF THE DKPTO IN KNOWLEDGE TRANSFER AND COMPETENCE BUILDING RELEVANT TO PRODUCT INNOVATIONS

Two types of learning processes have been investigated in this chapter. First, it was contended in Section 1 that the interaction between on the one hand firms, intermediaries or individuals applying for patents and on the other hand the patent office would add to the competencies with both parties. In the end, this may have positive effects on the innovative abilities of the firms and their awareness on and actual use of the IPR-system. Moreover, the competencies in the patent office may increase as a result of this interplay. Second, internal competencies resulting from processing applications may then be transmitted to other parts of the organization thus enhancing these other parts' ability to provide services, not only to firms directly, but also indirectly through various types of intermediaries.

In the theoretical framework, and in other chapters, notably Chapter 2 by Lundvall, we pointed to different ways of transmitting different kinds of knowledge such as codified and tacit knowledge. We thus pointed to the need to study the nature of knowledge to be exchanged between Sales & Marketing department and patent examiners as well as to which extent such knowledge transfer is actually taking place. If the efficiency of activities of Sales & Marketing is dependent upon diffusion of knowledge from patent examiners it requires that mechanisms of knowledge transfer be established with the objective of ensuring knowledge transfer. With limited interaction between departments, this transfer is unlikely to take place. In a dynamic setting, the establishment of such an appropriate level of learning processes may be part of an overall strategy for organizational development.[13]

With respect to the *internal* competencies, we found that it is crucial for the production (and supply) of technical business services that the technical expertise is readily available. In the DKPTO these services are supplied without any intensive cross-departmental knowledge flows or close cooperation between patent examiners and the Sales & Marketing section. The knowledge involved furthermore primarily is of a codified nature. The division of labour and procedures are strictly defined and the need for increasing knowledge flows was felt greater within departments than between departments. Consequently, there were no efforts to create environments for learning between the departments. However, taking the tasks of the departments into account, the need for such efforts was not obvious.[14] The accessibility of patent expertise was important, but we did not find arguments for having access to this expertise in-house. The separation of the two functional groups, and the codified nature of the knowledge needed, means that, in principle, it would be possible to buy the examination expertise elsewhere, if it were readily available. In practical terms, there are a number of objections to a separation of functions. For example, it is the responsibility of the government authorities to manage the application processing according to strict rules. This is due to considerations on equal process, secrecy, and the risk of disqualified processing.

We have shown in a discussion of the functions of the DKPTO what are its relationships to other organizations in the innovation system, including demonstrating that its associations with *external* organizations are not only confined to industrial firms. A wide array of other relations is important in the overall picture of the position of the DKPTO in the innovation system. This reveals that although the DKPTO has direct contact with many firms, its indirect role as a provider of information and knowledge to other organizations should not be underestimated.

The general impact of the DKPTO on transfer of knowledge conducive for product innovation in firms is, according to the case studies primarily in increasing the awareness of IPR. In addition, there is a flow of qualified patent caseworkers from the DKPTO to the patent agents (and to large industrial firms), which in itself means a transfer of knowledge relevant for the innovation process.

One may question if these functions could effectively be taken care of by the EPO, patent agents, or some other institution. Certainly many firms, especially the large firms, would not mind if the functions mentioned in Section 3 and Appendix A were fulfilled by the EPO. On the other hand, we saw in the case studies, that in particular, small, new firms may feel more confident with a national patent office in the proximity, with its familiar and national language.

NOTES

1. Appendix A explains in more detail what these services are.

2. The researcher was assisted by Research Assistant Mia B. Rasmussen, Department of Business Studies of Aalborg University. They undertook the field research in collaboration with the Danish Patent and Trademark Office. The author wish to thank colleagues in the Department of Business Studies, Aalborg University for comments. Also thanks to ESST-student Joseph Stewart, Texas for language editing. A special thanks to Ole Kirkelund and Steffen Rebien of the DKPTO for comments on preliminary findings and earlier drafts, as well as written notes on the content. Finally, I am grateful to all the people who helped with information and data during case studies, and internally in the DKPTO.

3. Typologies of such groups have been discussed in the literature on organizational learning. One of the best known such groups is a *functional group*. Another type of group is a *community of practice*, which is usually associated with Lave and Wenger (1991) and Wenger (1998). A third type of group is an *epistemic community*.

4. Substantial parts of this section have been written with the help of written inputs from Ph.D. Ole Kirkelund of the DKPTO. The author is grateful for these inputs as well as several discussions on the issue.

5. The most important resources include the following: Collections of handbooks containing technical and juridical literature as well as other relevant subjects. A collection of more than 30 mill patent documents. Internal handbooks on patents (and utility models, trademarks, design, and personnel). Internal checklists, guidelines, reports, and databases. Library resources including electronic journals and works of reference Intranet.

6. The work on the cases have been conducted jointly by the present author and research assistant Mia B. Rasmussen, who did the major part of the interviews.

7. This is a discussion that have been going on all through the 1990s, and is closely linked to what functions should be kept nationally and what could be centralised. This is discussed thoroughly in Christensen (2005) and is only a sub-issue here.

8. One of the researchers involved in the present casework had the daily work place physically at the DKPTO in about half of the research time (for 1/2 year). This greatly benefited the researchers assessments of the internal organization of the DKPTO and of the way the DKPTO operates in relation to external parties.

9. To avoid misunderstanding of the transcription of the interviews, the respondents afterwards passed remarks on the case stories. The stories are supported by quoted statements. Each case story is presented individually and subsequently the stories are linked together and the common denominators are emphasized.

10. The name of the patent examiner is fictitious but the author is aware of the real name.

11. The real name of the respondent has been changed.

12. Plougman & Vingtoft do not cover all technical areas. They have specialised within the areas bio technology, chemistry and software technology.

13. Note that learning is usually considered a positive thing. However, as learning processes may be costly there is a limit to how far it is rational to go in investing in the build-up of organizational structures conducive for learning processes. In fact, it may in some cases be rational to have less close interaction, as was discussed in Section 2, and as has been referred to in the litterature as "the strength of weak ties" (Granovetter, 1973; Hansen, 1998).

14. In fact, the studies within the DKPTO revealed that the DKPTO earlier worked a lot with organizational change and developed the organization into a community of practice-like set up. However, this showed to be inefficient and consequently it was changed to the functionally oriented structure.

REFERENCES

Argyris, C. (1992). *On organizational learning.* Cambridge, MA: Blackwell.

Argyris, C., & Schon, D. (1978). *Organizational learning: A theory of action perspective.* Reading: Addison-Wesley.

Christensen, J. L. (2005). Knowledge spill-overs from the patenting process. In: B. Andersen (Ed.), *Intellectual Property Rights: Innovations, Governance and the Institutional Environment.* Edward Elgar.

Cohen, W., & Levinthal, D. (1989). Innovation and learning: The two faces of R&D. *The Economic Journal, 99,* 569–596.

Cohendet, P., & Llerena, P. (2001, June 12–15). Routines and the theory of the firm: The role of communities. Paper for Nelson & Winther conference, Aalborg.

Erhvervsfremme Styrelsen and Patent og Varemærkestyrelsen (2001). Kompetenceudvikling og uddannelse på eneretsområdet, Cph.

Granovetter, M. (1973). The strength of weak ties. *American Journal of sociology*, *78*, 1360–1380.

Hansen, M. (1998). The search-transfer problem: The role of weak ties in sharing knowledge across organization subunits. *Administrative Science Quarterly*, *44*, 82–111.

Lave, W. (1991). *Situated learning: Legitimate peripheral participation*. New York: CUP.

Patent og Varemærkestyrelsen (2000, December). Management and evaluation of patents and trademarks. In: *Ernst & Young and Ementor Management Consulting*, Taastrup.

Patent og Varemærkestyrelsen (2001a). Videnregnskab 2000, Taastrup.

Patent og Varemærkestyrelsen (2001b). Virksomhedsregnskab 2000, Taastrup.

Patent og Varemærkestyrelsen (2001c). Partner i innovation – service til erhvervslivet. Taastrup.

Pavitt, K. (1991). Key characteristics of the large innovating firm. *British Journal of Management*, *2*(1), 41–50.

Pedler, M., Boydell, T., & Burgoyne, J. (1989). Towards the learning company. *Management Education and Development*, *20*(1), 1–8.

Prahalad, C., & Hamel, G. (1990). The core competence of the corporation. *Harvard Business Review*, 79–91.

Stiglitz, J. E. (1987). Learning to learn, localized learning and technological progress. In: Dasgupta & Stoneman (Eds), *Economic Policy and Technological Performance* (pp. 125–153).

Teece, D., Pisano, G., & Schuen, A. (1990). Firm capabilities, resources, and the concept of strategy. CCC Working Paper 90-8, Berkely.

Wenger, E. (1998). *Communities of practise: Learning, meaning, and identity*. Cambridge, MA: CUP.

APPENDIX A

Business Services

The descriptions provided here do not cover all kinds of business services. Only those that are seen as the most important to innovation activities of companies and inventors are included in the analysis. The review is based on the descriptions of individual services in the DKPTO's "Handbook of Products." The production processes connected to the services are also briefly described in the handbook and further information has been gathered through interviews with employees in S&M and in the patent section.

APPENDIX B: CENTRAL BUSINESS SERVICES

Novelty Searches

This service is intended to establish whether an invention is "new," which is important in terms of patentability. Novelty searches are, therefore, an important element of the casework involved in handling patent applications. However, novelty searches can also be delivered as a "stand-alone service" on different scales.

This service may quickly offer customers a preliminary indication concerning the possible patentability of an invention.

Infringement Inquiries

This service investigates whether a customer's product violates the IPRs of another company or person if marketed. The inquiry may be limited to material provided by the customer, but apart from this, infringement inquiries involves more or less the same search operations in patent literature and databases as is the case with novelty searches.

Besides offering a more thorough assessment of the technical properties of the customers' product, which is relevant for deciding to apply for a patent, infringement inquiries offer more or less the same advantages as novelty searches. Thus, it may guide decisions on further investments and development. In particular, it may guide decisions on whether or not to market a product.

State of the Art Technology Inquiries

Inquiries into state of the art within a specific technology area are equally based on searches in international patent literature both manually and in electronic databases. Searches into other relevant material are provided on the customer's request.

The purpose of this type of inquiry is to give inspiration to customers for further development of a product. It is somewhat broader in scope than a novelty search as the focus is on technology assessment of a technical area in general rather than on the customer's own product as in novelty searches and infringement inquiries.

Profile Analyses

The services mentioned above are quite technical in nature as they aimed at assessing technology, e.g. according to novelty or potential infringement of IPRs. Profile analyses can be both technical and non-technical depending on the type of profile in question. The DKPTO offers basically four different types of profiles, industry profiles, company profiles, product profiles, and technique profiles.

Monitoring

Monitoring consist of searches that are repeated periodically. This type of searches can be aimed at different types of information depending on the needs of the customer. The main types of monitoring include:

- Monitoring of a specific technical subject through patent literature or relevant technical literature.
- Monitoring of the activities of certain companies or inventors concerning patenting (or utility models, design, and trademarks).
- Monitoring of activities concerning a certain IPR identification number ("rettighedsnummer").
- Monitoring of changes in intellectual property law within a certain (e.g. technical) area specified by the customer.

PART V:
PRODUCT INNOVATION AND
ECONOMIC PERFORMANCE

DOES PRODUCT INNOVATION AND FIRM GROWTH GO HAND IN HAND?

Toke Reichstein

ABSTRACT

This chapter investigates the relationship between product innovation and firm performance. We apply a logistic regression to predict product innovation using a number of explanatory variables of which firm growth is of principal interest. We study the relationship at two different time periods using two comparable questionnaire surveys. These are combined with accounting statistics and labor market data. We find that firms which are experiencing high growth rates also are more likely to have been product innovating. We also find support for the user-producer theorem and that Schumpeter may have been right in his hypotheses concerning firm size and innovative activities.

1. INTRODUCTION

Long wave theory suggests that innovative behaviour plays a significant role in determining economic development and long term economic fluctuations (Freeman et al., 1982). Theoretically it has been suggested that a positive correlation between product innovation and macro economic growth depends on the substitutability between new and existing products (Katsoulacos, 1984). It has also been pointed out that product innovations are fundamental for escaping satiation (Andersen, 2001; Pasinetti, 1993). Contrary to the stochastic approach to

Product Innovation, Interactive Learning and Economic Performance
Research on Technological Innovation and Management Policy, Volume 8, 343–361
Copyright © 2004 by Elsevier Ltd.
All rights of reproduction in any form reserved
ISSN: 0737-1071/doi:10.1016/S0737-1071(04)08014-X

firm growth these statements suggest that product innovation may have a significant effect on growth rates at the micro and meso level.

With this background, the paper asks if product innovation and firm growth go hand in hand. Traditional micro economic theory of perfect competition neglects product innovation and hence indirectly suggests they do not. Goods are homogeneous and firms do not have control on prices. Technical change refers only to shifts in the production function and is mostly referred to as process innovation. Changes in factor productivity enable the firm either to produce the same quantity at a lower usage of production factors or to produce a higher quantity using the same amount of factors. In the traditional micro economic scheme technological change is limited to shifts in cost curves.

This chapter tries to link product innovation and firm growth empirically. We ask if firms that do well in a growth perspective are the same firms that engage successfully in product innovation activities. We apply a logistic regression in which product development is the binomial dependent variable. We search for a relationship using two separate growth rates. The first growth rate refers to employment and the other refers to sales. We include a number of control variables. This should increase the validity of the analysis by lowering the possibility that the correlation is due to omitted variables. Among the control variables are firm competence, organizational change, competition, customer relations, firm structure, firm size and sectoral association.

The outline of the chapter is as follows. Section 2 defines both firm performance and product innovation. The theoretical relationship between the two variables is discussed. Section 3 describes the datasets used and summarizes the descriptive statistics of the variables used. Section 4 develops the regression model and presents the results. Section 5 summarizes.

2. THEORETICAL AND EMPIRICAL BACKGROUND

To properly analyze the relationship between product innovation and firm growth it is necessary first to define what we mean by performance. Later we will also make clear how product innovation is defined in the data we use. This section discusses the theoretical arguments for a relationship between performance and product innovation. We will argue that many other variables may have a strong relationship with product innovation and that these should be controlled for in the analysis.

2.1. Measures of Performance

It is ambiguous to which measures of performance product innovation should be related. Different measures may be appropriate depending on the market structure, the strategy of the firm, which industry etc. It seems impossible to force all firms and industries into one template. We will nevertheless try to do just that.

Performance measures can be divided into three different categories (Hayes et al., 1988).[1]

- Process management measures.
- Business management measures.
- External reporting measures.

Process management measures mostly relate to issues internal to the firm. Among the measures are how long it takes to produce and deliver a specific good or service, the amount and types of materials used in the production process and the amount of factors used in the production process. These measures are fine-tuned continuously within the firm.

Business management measures may be argued to be directly linked to product innovation. In fact product innovation could be argued to be a business management measure of performance. Which products should the firm develop, what prices should the firm claim for its product(s) and when a specific product should be dropped from the product line are all questions that relates to business management.

The final type of performance measure is the external reporting measure. It holds variables like profits, capital values, revenues and values of partly finished goods. These are often seen as the traditional measures of performance as they also relates to market shares and growth in general. The aim is to test whether or not product innovation and firm growth are related. We therefore apply two external reporting measures to calculate the growth rates. This will give us a more detailed and complete story on the relationship in focus. More specifically we use firm employment and firm sales to calculate two types of growth measures.

2.2. Product Innovation and Firm Growth

Lundvall (2002) suggested that process and product innovation activities have an impact on the employment level over time. He argues that the development of new products and services tends to create more jobs in the innovating firm. This would suggest a significant positive correlation between the two main variables. Lundvall highlights that Danish firms that are involved in product innovation tend to create more jobs on aggregate than firms that do not engage in such activities. This pattern seems to be significant even at the sectoral level.

The rate of firms engaging in product innovation is fairly high. Gjerding (1997) showed that about 50% of Danish firms successfully engage in such activities over a three year period. But it was also noted that a considerable dispersion exists between sectors. The Construction sector seems to be less oriented towards innovation than other industries (Reichstein et al., 2004).

Despite innovation being highly risky and uncertain (Klein & Rosenberg, 1986), these findings suggest that Danish firms often submit to an innovation oriented strategy. It is also clear that it is economic motivations that drive firms to pursue innovation. Not only may it be costly to innovate but the outcome of the innovation may be very uncertain. Accordingly there must be some incentives in the form of economic gains from pursuing innovation.

The complexity of the innovation process, is described by the Chain-Linked model (Drejer & Jørgensen, Chap. 12, this volume; Klein & Rosenberg, 1986). Feedback loops, linkages and flow paths suggest product innovation to be a costly affair. Given product innovation is such a "problematic" and energy absorbing activity it is evident that only the firms with a certain level of surplus to release resources are able to participate in such activities. We would therefore expect that firms that do economically well are in a better position to follow an innovation strategy.

Kerin et al. (1978) argued that extra revenues attributed to product improvements or new products come from three sources: (i) New consumers who were not previously buyers of the product type; (ii) Consumers of competitive brands; or (iii) Consumers of a brand from the innovating company who switch to the new or reformulated brand or product (cannibalism). It is of course more efficient for firms to capture customers from the first and second sources. The third may not have a significant effect on the firm's general performance. It stands as a redistribution of income from one product to another. Even so, the third source may very well be coupled with a high performance. This argument points to a two way-causality between product innovation and firm performance.

But it is also possible to argue that we would not expect to find any positive correlation what so ever. Dosi (1984) argued that the effect of product innovation rests on the strategy of the firm regarding changes in prices and margins. Introducing a new product on a market may result in a temporary monopoly-like position. The demand function for the "new" product is defined by its technological features. How long the firm enjoys this monopoly-like position depends on the dynamics and characteristics of the specific industry to which the firm is associated as well as the appropriability of the product. When the firm introduces a "new" product on the market it faces three alternative strategies (Dosi, 1984).

- At the beginning charge a monopolistic price and later lower the price to a "limit-pricing."[2]
- Charge a "penetration price" below the entry deterring level in order to pre-empt the market, "go down the learning curve," and increase the margins only later when this strategy has built up additional entry barriers.
- Charge the "limit price" from the very start.

The strategy chosen shape how the firm performance changes after the introduction of a new product. The first strategy may increase revenues through a higher price while the second may increase the revenues as well as the level of employment through a higher demand and hence a higher production. Assuming that the last option will raise the demand it will have the same effects as the second but not to the same degree. By any standard there are several ways product innovation might influence firm growth rates in terms of employment and revenue. To what degree is more uncertain and may vary from case to case.

It may also be argued that product innovation does not influence growth rates significantly. The time when firms were small businesses with a single product on the market has past. Today many firms may be termed multi-product firms. These firms are large corporations that have a whole portfolio of products competing on the market. Consequently the product in which they have been innovating may be of small importance compared to the many activities of the firm. The effect of the product innovation may drown in the performance of one of the many other activities the firm has. Having noted this it should also be pointed out that the larger firm with a handful of products has spread its risk to a degree that enables it to find external funding for risky projects. Small single-product firms may have a disadvantage in this respect (Sutton, 1998). Hence larger firms with more than one product have a higher product innovation rate and hence do exhibit less volatile growth rate pattern.

There are also many other firm internal and firm external circumstances that may have a significant effect on its performance. As stated by Sutton:

> Two firms with rival products of equal clinical performance may achieve widely different results in terms of sales and profitability if they differ greatly in the size of their sales networks.
>
> John Sutton (1998)

Even though most scholars would argue that the correlation between firm growth and product innovation is evident, it seems that the relationship is quite complex. The last paragraphs question if we should expect to find an empirically based correlation. But we have also presented theoretical arguments for why we should expect to find a positive correlation.

2.3. Control Variables

It is evident that there is a long list of circumstances that influence the success of firm product innovation. This section discusses some of the many factors that influence the product innovation process. These will be included in the model to be tested in order to avoid the problem with multiple omitted variables. We discuss the competences embedded in the firm, the firm's general attitude toward change, firm structure, competition, customer relations, firm structure, firm size and sectoral issues.

The product innovation process is highly complex and product design calls for a certain level of competence in the development team. It therefore seems necessary to control for the composite of the firm in terms of worker skills. Also it has been argued that the employees with a high level of education learn more easily from past experience and hence adapt these for future innovation activities. The presence of a highly skilled work-force may ease and increase the pace of the development process (Carter, 1996). Statistics Canada (2001) also showed that innovating firms are more likely to have the employees engage in further training. This indicates that firms are very much aware of the importance of employing workers with a certain degree of skills. The Tomlinson Chapter in this volume addresses this issue further.

It is obvious that not all firms are oriented toward technological change in general. Dispersion in firm technological activity may be due to strategy considerations. Alternatively the firm may be part of a greater organization in which product innovation is performed by a specialized branch. The firm may hence look rather static with reference to product innovation activities. Both of these may prove important in explaining product innovation. Gjerding (1997) showed that firms that engage in product innovation are more likely to commit themselves to process innovations and organizational changes.

A firm facing a highly concentrated market would not have the same incentive as a firm operating in a market with a high degree of competition. The early Schumpeter (1934) argued that firms must innovate if they wish to survive in a competitive market. The later Schumpeter (1942) stated that the monopoly has accumulated resources which make it able to engage in innovative activities. It has been argued that monopolists innovate to raise entry barriers. As technological progress is cumulative the technological barrier becomes a weapon for market consolidation. Acs and Audretsch (1988) showed that innovative activity was promoted by large firms, but at the same time it was established that monopoly power undermines innovative activities of the entrepreneur. From this it is evident that it is necessary to control for both competition and firm size. Acs and Audretsch concluded that instead of a S-shaped relationship between firm size and innovative activity a U-shaped is more likely. Both small and large firms engage equally in innovative activity. This lends support to both the Schumpeterian hypotheses.

Customer needs are one of the key issues when discussing successful product innovations. Several contributions have emphasized and shown that it is important that firms have a feeling as to what the customers want (see e.g. Lundvall, 1988; Lundvall & Vinding, this volume; Teubal et al., 1976; Von Hippel, 1976). Lund reports in this volume that managers of product innovation activities strive to make actors in the product innovation process more market and customer oriented. The user-producer inter-action is by now considered a central issue in the product innovation literature. The SAPPHO project highlighted that technologies may be adjusted after they are introduced on the market (Rothwell, 1977).[3] Later Bacon et al. (1994) showed that a close contact between development engineers and customers tends to produce superior results in terms of product innovation. By carrying out several interviews Lund is also able to show in this volume that customer relations are important when engaging in product innovation. It is important to follow the development of the market in terms of customer wants and needs. At the same time it is evident that firms are aware of the need to create a close relationship to customers if they want successfully to engage in product innovation activities.

Finally, it seems important to control for sector differences. Technological opportunities are different across sectors as discussed briefly with reference to the construction sector. The Pavitt taxonomy is here used to distinguish between sectors. It groups firms in sectors according to how likely they are to engage in product innovation (Pavitt, 1984).

3. THE DATA

In the analysis we will use two survey datasets. To be consistent throughout the chapter we use the definitions of product innovation as they are presented in the surveys. The surveys built upon the Oslo manual (OECD, 1997) when defining different types of innovation. Product innovation is hence defined as "the introduction of a new product/service when excluding minor improvements of existing products/services." Four datasets have been combined to conduct the analysis. Accounting Statistics provided by the Danish Statistical Bureau, two datasets based on two questionnaires sent out to a number of firms as part of the DISKO and PIE projects, and the IDA labour market database. The two questionnaires are comparable and overlapping.

3.1. Accounting Statistics Data

Accounting statistics was used to acquire information on firm size, industry codes and the firm performance variables. Full time employees are used as the measure of firm size. Size measure of the DISKO data refers to 1994 while 1998 is the year of reference of the PIE data. Industry codes was used to control for differences across the sectors of the Pavitt-taxonomy. We have expanded it to include services sector. The same classification may be found in Laursen and Foss, 2003; Laursen and Mahnke, 2001, and Reichstein and Dahl, 2004.

In dealing with the performance measure we look at two different growth rates. These are.

- Annual average growth in firm sales.
- Annual average growth in number of employees (full time equivalents).

Each of them contains different aspects of the growth path of the firm. The years 1994–1995 are used with reference to the DISKO survey while 1998 and 1999 are used with reference to the PIE data.

3.2. The DISKO and PIE Databases

The DISKO survey was carried out in 1995 and got 1900 responses. The PIE survey holds 2,007 responses and was carried out in 2001. Weights based on size and industrial structures have been applied. In that way the results should depict characteristics of the total Danish private economy. Five hundred and thirty nine of the firms appear in both the datasets.[4] Given that the reader may find it difficult to remember that DISKO refers to mid-1990s and PIE refers to late 1990s, we will use the terms Period I and Period II throughout the rest of the chapter.

Product innovation is the dependent variable in the analysis. Respondents were asked whether or not the firm has introduced new products or services while disregarding small improvements of the existing products. By leaving such improvements out of the equation insignificant changes are avoided. But such small changes may be a booster for future major improvements or innovations and may hence distort the results.

The survey questionnaires are also used to measure general attitude toward change, change in competition, customer relations and the firm structure. A question whether or not the firm has introduced organizational change is used as an indicator of attitude to change. The firms were also asked if they had experienced a change in the competition from other firms. The firms were grouped into three categories (competition has become milder or is unchanged; competition has increased somewhat; competition is much stronger). Customer relations or user producer interactions have been controlled for by using survey questions that ask to what extent the firm has developed a closer relationship with customers. Finally the surveys provide questions on firm structure by asking if the firm is part of a greater organization or may be categorized as a subcontractor.

3.3. The IDA Database

The IDA database located at Statistics Denmark is an Integrated Labour market database. It covers a range of detailed data on all workers in Denmark. It holds information on educational level, age, wages etc. By sorting out the workers that are working in the firms analyzed in this paper it has been possible to control for relative competences in the firms. This has been done by counting the number of high-skilled workers in the firms and then dividing by the total number of employees. High skilled workers are defined as employees with at least a medium long education.

3.4. Structure of Categorical Variables

Table 1 summarize the distributions of the weighted observations between the categories of the categorical variables for both Period I and Period II. Period I holds 943.0 observations while Period II holds 1694.5. The share of product innovators has dropped from the mid-1990s to the late 1990s survey from 56% to 46%. The logistic regressions will show that a large part of this change in product innovation activities to some extent may be attributed to a change in the ICT intensive sector.

In terms of organizational change and customer relations the patterns are more or less the same. Around 50% of the firms acknowledge that they have carried out organizational changes during both periods. About 88% of the firms say that they have either to some or to a high extent developed a closer relationship with customers. The most significant change relates to firm structure. Period I data suggest 23% of the firms were either a part of a greater organisation or could be labelled a subcontractor. Period II data shows that about 54% of the Danish firms may be categorized in either of these groups. This is an increase of about 30 percentage points and may suggest that the weighting only redistributes according to the variables used in the weighting procedure. Finally the distribution of observations across firm size shows a rather right skewed pattern while the distribution of firms between the Pavitt sectors seems to be more stationary.

3.5. Structure of Continuous Variables

Three continuous variables are considered for each of the two datasets. Besides employment growth and sales growth a competence variable is calculated. It measures the relative share of employees with a medium education level or higher.

Table 1. Frequency Tables on Categorical Variables Across the Two Periods (Weighted).

Variable	Period I		Period II	
	Frequency	Percentage	Frequency	Percentage
Product development				
Not innovative	416.1	44.13	917.1	54.12
Innovative	526.9	5.87	777.4	45.88
Organizational change				
Not carried out	472.1	50.06	834.8	49.27
Carried out	470.9	49.94	859.7	50.73
Competition				
Milder/unchanged	34.6	3.67	244.0	14.14
A bit sharper	428.3	45.42	860.1	50.76
Much sharper	480.1	50.91	590.4	34.84
Customer relations				
Not/Small extent	114.0	12.09	205.6	12.13
Some extent	448.7	47.58	823.1	48.57
High extent	380.3	40.33	665.8	39.29
Concern				
Not part of	724.5	76.83	782.9	46.20
Part of	218.5	23.17	911.6	53.80
Firm size				
Employees = 25	439.7	46.63	436.1	25.74
25 < Employees = 50	260.9	27.67	649.2	38.31
50 < Employees = 100	130.0	13.79	335.3	19.79
100 = Employees	112.4	11.92	273.9	16.16
Pavitt sectors				
Supplier dominated	124.8	13.23	225.0	13.28
Scale intensive	105.1	11.15	234.9	13.86
Specialised suppliers	53.9	5.72	124.6	7.35
Science based	25.7	2.73	50.1	2.96
Construction	145.3	15.41	261.1	15.41
Whole sale trade	179.9	19.08	299.0	17.65
Specialised services	195.0	20.68	274.5	16.20
Scale intensive services	41.7	4.42	70.9	4.18
ICT intensive services	71.6	7.59	154.4	9.11

Source: The DISKO and PIE Questionnaire survey database.

Table 2. Moments of Continuous Variables (Weighted).

Variable/Moment	Period I	Period II
Employment growth		
Mean	0.0531	0.0389
Median	0.0500	0.0204
Variance	0.0294	0.0270
Skewness	0.4843	0.7627
Kurtosis	5.6105	5.3090
Revenue growth		
Mean	0.0768	0.0510
Median	0.0614	0.0346
Variance	0.0424	0.0471
Skewness	0.2177	0.2440
Kurtosis	3.5518	4.4916
Competence variable		
Mean	0.0491	0.0908
Median	0.0283	0.0577
Variance	0.0043	0.0126
Skewness	3.0662	2.5066
Kurtosis	13.8420	8.1136

Source: The DISKO and PIE databases.

Table 2 summarises the descriptive statistics of the continuous variables. On average, Danish firms experienced an employment growth of 5.3% and a sales growth of 7.7% from 1994 to 1995. The corresponding numbers for 1998–1999 are 3.9% and 5.1%. The higher mean growth rates in the mid-1990s is also reflected in aggregate growth rates for Denmark, which show that the growth of the economy slowed down during the late 1990s. Another feature of the growth rate distributions is that the level of variance is noticeably lower in the case of employment than in sales. This may be seen as suggesting that firms are aware of the value of the skills embedded in employees. Such competitive factors are often tacit or routinised capabilities that cause the firms to be reluctant to let employees leave the firm. This is also expressed by the fact that the mean employment growth rate decreases by 1.5 percentage points while sales decreases with 2.5 percentage points from Period I to Period II.

The descriptive statistics of the competence variable suggest that the firms on average had a bigger share of employees with a medium or higher level of education in the second period compared to the first period. In the mid-1990s the share of medium and highly educated employees in the Danish firms was 4.9% while the corresponding number in the late 1990s was 9%. This may indicate that low skilled workers are more likely to be fired during recessions compared to high-skilled workers.

4. THE MODEL AND RESULTS

This section builds up a model in which product innovation is the dependent variable. We hence model the probability of whether firms are product innovative. We use two different growth rates expressed by sales and employment. And we carry out the regression on two different periods. That amounts to four different regressions. The results of the model are reviewed and discussed.

4.1. The Model

We argue that if we want to understand the correlation between product innovation and firm growth, we need to control for different things with reference to product innovation. Innovation literature suggests various circumstances that shape and influence the probability of becoming a successful innovator. A vast amount of contributions on firm growth have argued that growth follows a stochastic pattern. It is hence important to control for different factors with reference to product innovation while it is less important to control for firm specific issues when studying firm growth. Taking into account that our dependent variable is binomial, we consequently use a logistic regression model explaining product innovation. Firm growth together with a number of firm specific variables is used to explain product innovation. The model may be described as;

$$\log\left(\frac{PD_i}{1 - PD_i}\right) = \beta_0 + \bar{\beta}\bar{X}_i + \varepsilon_i$$

Or written in a different way;

$$PD_i = \frac{1}{1 + e^{-(\beta_0 + \bar{\beta}\bar{X}_i + \varepsilon_i)}}$$

β and X signifies vectors of estimated parameters and the explanatory variables. Besides the two continuous variables six categorical variables are included. We have set the logistic regression to benchmark each of the outcomes of the categorical variables against one base level. Seventeen parameter estimates are calculated for the categorical variables while two are calculated for the continuous variables. Finally an intercept denoted β_0 is included.

We reduce the chance of finding implicit correlations by including the control variables. We have a lower risk for multiple omitted variables. Hence we increase the probability that the regression statistics of the main variables are valid.

The regressions are set to test against the event of the observation being a product innovator. This means that we would expect the signs of the parameter estimates with respect to the continuous variables to be positive. The binary variables are also expected to have positive parameter estimates. Only the binary variable indicating whether the firm is independent or a sub-contractor/part of a greater organization could be expected to send mixed signals. It is difficult to say if this increases the probability of the firm being an innovator. It depends on the position the firm is in with reference to its "mother" firm. The remaining categorical variables are expected to be negative. The logistic regressions have been set to test against the highest value of the variables. That implies that the benchmarks are "much sharper competition," "using customer relations to a high extent," "firms with more than 100 employees" and "the ICT sector."

4.2. Results

The results of the logistic regressions are reported in Tables 3 and 4 using the Period I and Period II data respectively. The left sides of the tables refer to the regressions in which employment is used as the growth variable. It is sales growth that is used in the regression results summarised on the right hand side of the tables. Parameter estimates, standard errors, odds ratios and global statistics are reported.

The global statistics of the regressions express support for the model specification. The likelihood ratios express a small chance of all estimated parameters being zero. The higher Hosmer-Lemeshow goodness-of-fit values in the Period II regressions suggest a better fit in the Period I regressions. This may be due to the disturbances in terms of the business cycle in Period II. The concordant estimates are between 74% and 75% signifying a high predictive power of the model. It is able correctly to predict if a firm is product innovative three out of four times.

The parameters of the growth rates depict a positive correlation. Both employment and sales growth has a positive parameter estimate which is significant at the 5% level. The odds ratio of the two is at about 2.2 indicating firms with a one percentage point higher growth has a 1.022 time higher chance of being a successful product innovator. The two Period I regressions show similar estimates. The reason is that the two growth rates are correlated. The Pearson correlation estimate for the two mid-1990s growth variables is at 0.46 and has a *p*-value under 0.01.

Table 3.   Logistic Regression Against Product Innovation Using Period I Data (Weighted).

Variable/Categories	Estimates	Std. Err.	Odds Ratio	Estimate	Std. Err.	Odds Ratio
Continuous variables						
Employment growth	0.8509**	0.421	2.342			
Revenue growth				0.7875**	0.3508	2.198
Comptetence	2.5025*	1.5202	12.213	2.5480*	1.5407	12.782
Binary variables						
Organizational change	0.7849***	0.1512	2.192	0.7765***	0.1514	2.174
Concern	−0.2426	0.177	0.785	−0.2715	0.1769	0.762
Competition						
Milder/unchanged	0.0670	0.3936	1.069	0.0661	0.3900	1.068
A bit sharper	−0.2542*	0.1517	0.776	−0.2572	0.1518	0.773
Much sharper		Benchmark			Benchmark	
Customer relation						
Not/small extent	−1.0745***	0.2482	0.341	−1.1173***	0.2483	0.327
Some extent	−0.6325***	0.16	0.531	−0.6858***	0.1611	0.504
High extent		Benchmark			Benchmark	
Size						
Employees = 25	−0.1200	0.2949	0.887	−0.112	0.2949	0.894
25 < Employees = 50	−0.4499	0.2739	0.638	−0.4537*	0.2743	0.635
50 < Employees = 100	−0.0445	0.3107	0.956	−0.0425	0.3109	0.958
100 = Employees		Benchmark			Benchmark	
Pavitt sectors						
Supplier dominated	−0.6011	0.4374	0.548	−0.5525	0.4384	0.575
Scale intensive	−0.524	0.4483	0.592	−0.5022	0.4502	0.605
Specialised suppliers	−0.3625	0.4844	0.696	−0.3521	0.4852	0.703
Science based	−0.2621	0.6199	0.769	−0.3175	0.6153	0.728
Construction	−1.5355***	0.4143	0.215	−1.5711***	0.4162	0.208
Whole sale trade	−0.5228	0.3888	0.593	−0.5321	0.3912	0.587
Specialised services	−1.2444***	0.4182	0.288	−1.2213***	0.4208	0.295
Scale intensive services	−1.2252**	0.503	0.294	−1.1630**	0.5048	0.131
ICT intensive services		Benchmark			Benchmark	
Intercept	0.7870	0.5952		0.8376	0.5984	
Global statistics						
Number of observations		943.0			943.0	
Likelihood ratio		175.3161***			176.2722***	
Goodness of fit		6.0153			2.875	
Somers' D		0.4890			0.4930	
Concordant		74.30%			74.50%	

Note: Stars indicate level of significance.
Source: The DISKO Questionnaire survey database.
*p-Value < 0.1.
**p-Value < 0.05.
***p-Value < 0.001.

Table 4. Logistic Regression Against Product Innovation Using Period II Data (Weighted).

Variable/Categories	Estimates	Std. Err.	Odds Ratio	Estimate	Std. Err.	Odds Ratio
Continuous variables						
Employment growth	1.0613***	0.3491	2.89			
Revenue growth				0.2345	0.2520	1.264
Comptetence	1.9038***	0.6531	6.711	1.6794***	0.6441	5.363
Binary variables						
Organizational change	0.8319***	0.1126	2.298	0.8515***	0.1121	2.343
Concern	0.1375	0.1140	1.147	0.1532	0.1136	1.166
Competition						
Milder/unchanged	−0.5996***	0.1795	0.549	−0.5875***	0.1792	0.556
A bit sharper	−0.3943***	0.1198	0.674	−0.3923***	0.1161	0.676
Much sharper		Benchmark			Benchmark	
Customer relation						
Not/small extent	−0.6716***	0.1917	0.511	−0.6690***	0.1911	0.512
Some extent	−0.4016***	0.1163	0.669	−0.3987***	0.1161	0.671
High extent		Benchmark			Benchmark	
Size						
Employees = 25	−0.6109***	0.1893	0.543	−0.5261***	0.1864	0.591
25 < Employees = 50	−0.6881***	0.1699	0.503	−0.6587***	0.1695	0.518
50 < Employees = 100	−0.5247***	0.1834	0.592	−0.5059***	0.1834	0.603
100 = Employees		Benchmark			Benchmark	
Pavitt sectors						
Supplier dominated	0.3484	0.2803	1.417	0.2161	0.2748	1.241
Scale intensive	0.3053	0.2764	1.357	0.1814	0.2715	1.199
Specialised suppliers	0.4696	0.2997	1.599	0.3403	0.2946	1.405
Science based	0.4177	0.3891	1.518	0.3014	0.3858	1.352
Construction	−0.8764***	0.2872	0.416	−0.9825***	0.2831	0.374
Whole sale trade	0.1118	0.2586	1.118	0.0010	0.2541	1.001
Specialised services	−0.4087	0.2838	0.665	−0.5238*	0.2793	0.592
Scale intensive services	−0.7061*	0.3663	0.494	−0.8000**	0.3623	0.449
ICT intensive services		Benchmark			Benchmark	
Intercept	−0.7277*	0.4133		−0.6653	0.4113	
Global statistics						
Number of observations		1694.5			1694.5	
Likelihood ratio		331.7015***			323.1493***	
Goodness of fit		9.8655			8.9062	
Somers' D		0.4970			0.4920	
Concordant		74.80%			74.50%	

Note: Stars indicate level of significance.
Source: The PIE Questionnaire survey database.
*p-Value < 0.1.
**p-Value < 0.05.
***p-Value < 0.001.

Growth rate parameter estimates have changed from Period I to Period II. While the employment growth regression appears to be more significant the opposite is the case for the sales growth rates now appearing to be non-significant. The employment growth parameter estimate has increased while the sales growth parameter estimate has decreased. The standard errors of the parameter estimates are more or less unchanged.

Considering the control variables a number of interesting patterns emerges. The customer relations variable exhibits a significant correlation with product innovation giving support to the user-producer hypothesis. The probability of being a successful product innovator increases with the level of customer contact. The organizational change variable suggests that the attitude of the firm towards change is relevant to consider if wanting to predict whether or not a firm engage in product innovation activities, which was also suggested in Chapter 6. Even though the statistical significance is somewhat lower, the competence variable exhibits a positive correlation as well. This suggests that the the the relative number of employees with a medium or higher level of education has a significant effect on the probability of the firm being a successful innovator.

The firm size estimates supports the hypothesis of the U-shaped relationship proposed by Acs and Audretsch (1988). Odds ratios indicate that firms with more than 100 employees are approximately 1.6 times the odds of being product innovative compared to firms with between 25 and 50 employees. The other size groupings are insignificant and with a higher odds ratio indicating that the likelihood of being product innovative more or less corresponds with that of the firms with more than 100 employees. The competition variable suggests a similar correlation. Firms that have responded by saying they have experienced that competition has become "a bit sharper" seem to be less likely to be product innovative compared to firms that respond by saying that they have experienced "a much sharper" competition.

The Pavitt taxonomy sectors indicate that the ICT sector is the most product innovation oriented sector in Period I. In Period II the ICT sector has dropped from being the sector with the highest density of product innovative firms. The construction sector exhibits the lowest density of product innovative firms giving support to the findings of Reichstein et al. (2004) and Dahl and Dalum (2001).

5. SUMMARY AND CONCLUSION

We conducted a logistic regression analysis using two separate but comparable questionnaire survey datasets. Product innovation was put in focus and specifically we studied its relationship to firm growth. We raised the statistical bar by carrying out the study on two separate data sets with a number of years in between. We find the analysis to be robust with a high level of validity.

The statistical evidence using the two questionnaire survey datasets suggests that product innovative firms are those with high growth rates. The two variables tend to go hand in hand. The theoretical considerations in the paper suggested that the correlation may reflect complex mechanisms. We did not test for causality. We can only say that it may be the case that product innovation leads to growth or that growth leads to product innovation. To test the direction of the causality we would need data covering a longer time period.

Other interesting results came from the analysis. We found support for the user-producer hypothesis as well as for the hypothesis that it matters whether the firm has a positive attitude towards change in general. Less statistically robust results are the positive correlation with the competence embedded in the firm and the support for a U-shaped relationship between innovation firm size and the competitive element.

NOTES

1. For a detailed discussion on the different types of performance measures see Chapter 10 by Lund in this volume.
2. The limit price is the price just below the cost plus a minimum profit for the potential entrant.
3. We refer to literature that deals with users while the survey asks about customers. Also the word consumer has been referred to in the cited literature. While users is a more widely used term than consumers we will in the present context nevertheless use all three of them interchangeably.
4. Reichstein and Vinding (2003), describes the data extensively.

ACKNOWLEDGMENTS

The author would like to thank the PIE researchers at the IKE Group who provided substantial support and comments throughout the writing of the paper. Also thanks to Henrik Sohrn-Frise for valuable comments.

REFERENCES

Acs, Z. J., & Audretsch, D. B. (1988). Testing the Schumpeterian Hypothesis. *Eastern Economic Journal, 14*, 129–140.
Andersen, E. S. (2001). Satiation in an evolutionary model of structural economic dynamics. *Journal of Evolutionary Economics, 11*, 143–164.

Bacon, G., Beckman, S., Mowery, D., & Wilson, E. (1994). Managing product definition in high-technology industries: A pilot study. *California Management Review*, *2*, 32–56.

Carter, A. P. (1996). In: E. Helmstadter & M. Perlman (Eds), *Behavioral Norms, Technological Progress and Economic Dynamics* (pp. 183–198). Ann Arbour: University of Michigan Press.

Dahl, M. S., & Dalum, B. (2001). In: OECD (Eds), *Innovative Clusters: Drivers of National Innovation Systems*. Paris: OECD.

Dosi, G. (1984). *Technical change and industrial transformation: The theory and an application to the semiconductor industry*. London and Basingstoke: Macmillan.

Freeman, C., Clark, J., & Soete, L. (1982). *Unemployment and technical innovation: A study of long waves and economic development*. London: Pinter.

Gjerding, A. N. (1997). *Den flexible virksomhed*. København: ERhvervsudviklingsrådet.

Hayes, R. H., Wheelwright, S. C., & Clark, K. B. (1988). *Dynamic manufacturing*. New York: Free Press.

Katsoulacos, Y. (1984). Product innovation and employment. *European Economic Review*, *26*, 83–108.

Kerin, R. A., Harvey, M. G., & Rothe, J. T. (1978). Cannibalism and new product development. *Business Horizon* (October), 25–31.

Klein, S., & Rosenberg, N. (1986). In: R. Landau & N. Rosenberg (Eds), *The Positive Sum Strategy: Harnessing Technology for Economic Growth*. Washington: National Academy Press.

Laursen, K., & Foss, N. J. (2003). New HRM practices, complementarities and the impact on innovative performance. *Cambridge Journal of Economics*, *27*, 243–263.

Laursen, K., & Mahnke, V. (2001). Knowledge strategies, firm types, and complementarity in human-resource practices. *Journal of Management and Governance*, *5*, 1–27.

Lundvall, B. Å. (1988). In: G. Dosi et al. (Eds), *Technical Change and Economic Theory*. London: Pinter Publishers.

Lundvall, B. Å. (2002). *Innovation, growth and social cohesion – The Danish model*. Cheltenham, UK: Edward Elgar.

OECD (1997). *Proposed guidelines for collecting and interpreting technological innovation data: The Oslo Manual*. Paris: OECD.

Pasinetti, L. L. (1993). *Structural economic dynamics: A theory of the economic consequences of human learning*. Cambridge: Cambridge University Press.

Pavitt, K. (1984). Sectoral patterns of technical change: Towards a taxonomy and a theory. *Research Policy*, *13*, 343–373.

Reichstein, T., & Dahl, M. S. (2004). Are firm growth rates random – Analyzing patterns and dependencies. *International Review of Applied Economics*, *18*, 225–246.

Reichstein, T., Salter, A., & Gann, D. (2004). *Last among equals: A comparison of innovation in construction, services and manufacturing in the UK*. Mimeo.

Reichstein, T., & Vinding, A. L. (2003). Documentation of the IDA-DISKO-PIE Datasets.

Rothwell, R. (1977). The characteristics of successful innovators and technical progressive firms. *R&D Management*, *7*, 191–206.

Schumpeter, J. A. (1934). *The theory of economic development*. Cambridge, MA: Harvard University Press.

Schumpeter, J. A. (1942). *Capitalism, socialism and democracy*. London: Unwin.

Statistics Canada (2001). Employer and employee persepctives on human ressource practices. The Evolving Workplace Series Catalogue no. 71-584-MPE, no. 1.

Sutton, J. (1998). *Technology and market structure*. Cambridge, MA: MIT Press.

Teubal, M., Amon, N., & Trachtenberg, M. (1976). Performance in innovation in the Israeli electronic industry. *Research Policy*, 5, 354–379.
Von Hippel, E. (1976). The dominant role of users in the scientific instrument innovations process. *Research Policy*, 5, 212–239.

APPENDIX

See Table 5.

Table 5. Tolerance Values and Variance Inflation Factors of Explanatory Variables.

Variable	Employment Growth		Revenue Growth	
	TOL	VIF	TOL	VIF
Period I				
Growth	0.97655	1.02401	0.98435	1.01590
Competence	0.90179	1.10891	0.90174	1.10897
Organizational change	0.89053	1.12293	0.88878	1.12514
Firm structure	0.95441	1.04776	0.96007	1.04159
Customer relations	0.91902	1.08812	0.92063	1.05825
Competition	0.94642	1.05661	0.94495	1.05825
Firm size	0.70849	1.41145	0.70863	1.41117
Pavitt sectors	0.69354	1.44187	0.69786	1.43296
Period II				
Growth	0.93978	1.06408	0.98418	1.01608
Competence	0.86953	1.15001	0.86950	1.15009
Organizational change	0.87768	1.13937	0.88316	1.13230
Firm structure	0.90494	1.10505	0.90656	1.10308
Customer relations	0.92195	1.08465	0.92186	1.08476
Competition	0.94790	1.05496	0.94773	1.05515
Firm size	0.82624	1.21031	0.48778	1.17955
Pavitt sectors	0.86654	1.15401	0.87712	1.14010

Source: The DISKO & PIE Questionnaire survey database.